Enterprising Women and Shipping in the Nineteenth Century

Far from the genteel notion of Victorian women as milliners and haberdashers, this book shows that women could and did manage male businesses and manage men. Women invested in the expanding shipping industry throughout the late eighteenth and the nineteenth century and actively ran non-feminine businesses such as ship-building. By setting the businesswomen firmly in the context of the industry, *Enterprising Women* examines the business challenges from the woman's perspective. It demonstrates how a woman needed to understand the business requirements while in some cases also being a single parent. As business managers, they had to manage a male workforce, deal with large and important customers and ensure they maintained their firm's reputation and continued to win orders. Nor were these women mere caretakers for the next generation, in many cases continuing to run the business in an active manner after their son or sons were of age. *Enterprising Women* reveals communities of independent women in England who were active entrepreneurs and investors, in a period when women were increasingly supposed to be relegated to a more domestic role. It includes brief biographies of many of these women entrepreneurs who were also conventional mothers, wives and daughters.

HELEN DOE is an Honorary Fellow of the Centre for Maritime Historical Studies, University of Exeter.

D1426570

Enterprising Women and Shipping in the Nineteenth Century

Helen Doe

THE BOYDELL PRESS

First published 2009
The Boydell Press, Woodbridge

ISBN 978–1–84383–472–4

The Boydell Press is an imprint of Boydell & Brewer Ltd
PO Box 9, Woodbridge, Suffolk IP12 3DF, UK
and of Boydell & Brewer Inc.
668 Mt Hope Avenue, Rochester, NY 14620, USA
website: www.boydellandbrewer.com

The publisher has no responsibility for the continued existence
or accuracy of URLs for external or third-party internet websites
referred to in this book, and does not guarantee that any content
on such websites is, or will remain, accurate or appropriate.

A CIP record for this book is available
from the British Library

This publication is printed on acid-free paper

Printed in Great Britain by
CPI Antony Rowe, Chippenham and Eastbourne

Contents

Tables and Figures

Figures

Illustrations

For my parents, Bob and Gee
who inspired and encouraged

Acknowledgements

This has been a long research journey which began with the discovery of a woman shipbuilder, Jane Slade, and which led to the search for others like her. As I soon found out, these maritime women challenged many cosy assumptions, including several of mine, and each new finding uncovered new thoughts about what a nineteenth-century woman could do.

There have been many people who have assisted me in my research. These include in Whitby, Christiane Kroebel, Rosalin Barker and the members of the Whitby Literary & Philosophical Society; in King's Lynn, Bob and Linda Cook who provided accommodation and friendly help and introduced me to Pat Midgeley and Dr Paul Richards of True's Yard Museum. In Cornwall Rosie and John Smith have frequently provided accommodation and great company. Local record office staff in a variety of places have been very helpful: Bristol, Dorchester, Exeter, Hull, Northallerton, Norwich, Strood, Truro and Whitehaven. The staff in the National Archives at Kew make it a pleasure to visit, as is the National Maritime Museum at Greenwich. Additional thanks go to the Merseyside Maritime Museum, the United Kingdom Hydrographic Office and the National Maritime Museum Cornwall. The late Robin Craig was an early enthusiastic supporter as has been Dr Graeme Milne and the many delegates and fellow speakers at various conferences.

Special thanks go to Professor John Armstrong and his wife Pam for their support, friendship and hospitality; to Dr Alston Kennerley who generously shared sources and documents and to Professor Roger Knight for his comments on the naval supplier section. Other researchers have been more than generous in their sharing of information; Dr Gareth Cole found ordnance ship suppliers; Gareth Hicks supplied information on the Plymouth Shipping Registers; Dr David Foster shared his data from the trade directories; Doug Ford in Jersey provided some additional material on Isabella Sanderson, and Dr Adrian Osler provided data on Jane B. Avery's ships; Sue Shapcott provided documents on Mrs Moon; Ron Pett in Hull provided information on Mrs Aaron Ross and pointed me in the direction of the Rose Downs Archive; transcripts of census data came from David Carter, Roy Dunnicliff and Don Dickson.

A 'thank you' goes to the staff at the University of Exeter including Dr Richard Crangle who patiently answered my many queries on relational database design. Professor Mark Overton was my mentor and he kindly read and commented on some of the economic aspects of my work. In the final leg of the journey, Dr Maria Fusaro generously took time from her busy schedule to read the whole work.

I have been fortunate indeed in Dr Michael Duffy who supervised the thesis upon which this book is based. It has been a very real pleasure and a privilege to work with him.

Friends and family take much of the strain and they have all been under-standing and supportive. My husband, Michael, has been constant in his support, and his practical assistance in so many different ways has been the major factor in the completion of this book.

Abbreviations

BPO	Bodmin Probate Office, Cornwall
BPP	British Parliamentary Papers
BRO	Bristol Record Office
CRO	Cornwall Record Office
DLSL	Devon Local Studies Library
DRO	Devon Record Office
DSRO	Dorset Record Office
HCA	Hull City Archives
MMM	Merseyside Maritime Museum, Liverpool
MRO	Medway Record Office, Strood
NMM	National Maritime Museum Greenwich
NRO	Norfolk Record Office
NYRO	North Yorkshire Record Office, Northallerton
TNA	The National Archives, PRO, Kew
UKHO	United Kingdom Hydrographic Office, Taunton
WLPS	Whitby Literary and Philosophical Society
WRO	Cumbria Record Office, Whitehaven

Introduction

Fanny Stephens was already a widow by the time of the 1881 census and at the age of forty-two she was the head and main breadwinner in a household that contained her four children and her mother. Fanny gave her occupation as the postmistress of Polruan, Cornwall. Just around the corner from her was the home of Thomas Werry Tadd, a master mariner, who was a forty-nine-year-old bachelor.[1] When Thomas died unmarried in 1884, he left his whole estate to Fanny, 'my intended wife' and named her as his executor. This was no short engagement as the couple had been engaged for three years. His bequest included his house and thirty-nine shares in the 60-ton Dartmouth-built schooner *Isabella*.[2] This could be the plot of a Victorian tragedy about the plight of widows where the despairing Fanny sees her second chance of happiness snatched from her.

Fanny, however, does not conform to the profile of a dependent victim of circumstance. She speedily achieved probate within three weeks and within another two weeks she had sold all the shares in the ship.[3] This is impressive speed but as the postmistress she had an occupation that required a fair knowledge of administration. Her swift sale of the shares, however, was not the act of a woman who sought to rid herself of an unaccustomed burden as Fanny was no innocent in share dealings in ships. She had been an initial shareholder in the schooners *Jane Slade* in 1870 and the *Undine* in 1875 and so understood the significance and value of shares in shipping.[4] By the time of the 1891 census Fanny had moved her home and the post office to her late fiancé's house.[5] She never did marry. Fanny was a woman who, from inclination or necessity, understood money management and the independence it could give her.

This book is about Fanny and her contemporaries who lived and worked within the maritime industry in nineteenth-century Britain. Around the coast there were mariner and merchant communities based in over eighty ports, from the large ports such as London and Liverpool to the smaller ones such as Fowey, Whitby, Whitehaven and King's Lynn. In these ports there were wives who brought up their children, balanced the household budgets and made decisions in the absence of their husbands at sea. There were widows, spinsters and wives who held shares in ships and widows who ran maritime businesses. This is a picture that runs counter to previous views of women in the nineteenth century.

---

[1] Cornwall Record Office (CRO): 1881 Census Lanteglos by Fowey.
[2] Bodmin Probate Office (BPO): Will of Thomas Werry Tadd 1884; CRO: MSR Merchant Shipping Registers Fowey 3/1865.
[3] CRO: MSR Merchant Shipping Registers Fowey 3/1865.
[4] *Ibid.*, 5/1870 and 4/1875.
[5] CRO: 1891 Census Lanteglos by Fowey.

Women as Economic Actors in the Nineteenth Century

Studies of the early feminist movement and the legal changes affecting women and their property have made broad assumptions about the way nineteenth-century women lived.[6] The supporters of the separate spheres argument view women as increasingly restricted by society and, in the case of married women, unable to control property or income in their own name or make contracts. Coverture, the change in legal status when on marriage a woman became part of her husband's identity, is often blamed for this curtailment of women's economic activity. The period from 1780 to 1850 is seen as the critical period when women became increasingly constrained, as shown in the classic study of both men and women of the middle classes in Birmingham and Essex in this period, *Family Fortunes*. Here women are seen as the 'hidden investment' in any family-run enterprise, supporting the business through their 'identification with the domestic and moral sphere' and only becoming 'active economic agents when forced by necessity'.[7] The majority of the research relates to women in employment and in respect to women and enterprise it is concluded that 'for a middle class woman of the early nineteenth century, gentility was coming to be defined by a special form of femininity which ran directly counter to acting as a visibly independent economic agent'.[8]

This model of the separate spheres, where men operated in a public business and work-based world outside the home and women operated within the home and confined themselves to matters relating to children and domesticity, is one that has been consistently challenged, although never completely dismissed. Amanda Vickery, in an important article, argued that there was no previous 'Golden Age' for independent women from which a decline could be traced. Additionally she traced the separate spheres theory back to the historians who had formed this view from didactic and complaint literature, and she questioned whether such literature truly reflected prevailing attitudes and behaviour.[9] Vickery believed a more sceptical view must be taken of the image of the Victorian woman as 'cramped by custom, corset and crinoline'.[10] Elsewhere it has been suggested that there was considerable overlap between the spheres and that it is more a matter of

---

[6] Lee Holcombe, *Wives and Property: Reform of the Married Women's Property Law in Nineteenth Century England* (Toronto: University of Toronto Press, 1983); Mary Lyndon Shanley, *Feminism, Marriage and the Law in Victorian England, 1850–1895* (London: Princeton University Press, 1989).

[7] Leonore Davidoff and Catherine Hall, *Family Fortunes: Men and Women of the English Middle Class, 1780–1850* (London: Hutchinson, 1987), p. 272.

[8] Davidoff and Hall, *Family Fortunes*, p. 315.

[9] Amanda Vickery, 'Golden Age to Separate Spheres? A Review of the Categories and Chronology of English Women's History', *The Historical Journal*, 36 (1993), 383–414.

[10] Vickery, 'Golden Age to Separate Spheres?', p. 297.

change and continuity for both sexes;[11] while others have suggested that married women acted simply as surrogates in the absence of their husbands.[12]

Nineteenth-century women investors are a growing area of research interest, with several articles examining women investing in the Bank of England and in joint stock companies. The work on joint stock investments has moved the debate from the evidence of women investing, to considering their actions in relation to their investments. Women appear as less passive and with a growing confidence, albeit this is mainly seen towards the end of the century as opportunities increased with the increase in limited liability companies and the Married Women's Property Acts.[13] The question is whether this increased investment from mid-century is a new development or a continuity of existing behaviour, and so this gap in our knowledge of the first half of the nineteenth century needs to be filled to add to the limited findings on women who invested in canals and railways.[14]

Businesswomen are also a focus of research and there is a view that widows faced a number of obstacles if they wished to carry on their husband's business. Their financial position might be weakened by common law which only entitled them to one-third of their husband's estate; bequests often prevented widows from selling property to raise capital; and debts might be called in. There is also an assumption that women lacked skill and knowledge. 'Widows often did not have the necessary skills to carry on their husband's business, particularly if his work had taken place outside the home and she had not had the opportunity to become acquainted with the business (as was the case with mercantile trades, seafaring occupations and the building trades).'[15] Such assumptions misunderstand the role of the business manager which was a different role from that of the hands-on craftsman.

Women, especially married women in business, are too often invisible. Trade directories and newspapers are used extensively in a study of businesswomen in

[11] Robert B. Shoemaker, *Gender in English Society 1650–1850: The Emergence of Separate Spheres?* (London: Longman, 1998), p. 318.

[12] Lisa Norling, *Captain Ahab Had a Wife: New England Women and the Whale Fishery, 1720–1870* (Chapel Hill: University of North Carolina Press, 2000), pp. 36–50.

[13] David R. Green and Alastair Owens, 'Gentlewomanly Capitalism? Spinsters, Widows, and Wealth Holding in England and Wales, c. 1800–1860', *Economic History Review*, 56 (2003), 510–36; Josephine Maltby and Janette Rutterford, 'She Possessed Her Own Fortune: Women Investors from the Late Nineteenth Century to the Early Twentieth Century', *Business History*, 48 (2006), 220–53; Alastair Owens, '"Making Some Provision for the Contingencies to Which Their Sex Is Particularly Liable": Women and Investment in Early Nineteenth Century England', in *Women, Business and Finance in Nineteenth-Century Europe: Rethinking Separate Spheres*, ed. Robert Beachy, Beatrice Craig and Alastair Owens (Oxford: Berg, 2006); Janette Rutterford and Josephine Maltby, '"The Widow, the Clergyman and the Reckless": Women Investors in England, 1830–1914', *Feminist Economics*, 12 (2006), 111–38. Josephine Maltby and Janette Rutterford, 'Editorial: Women, Accounting and Investment', *Accounting, Business and Financial History*, 16 (2006), 133–42

[14] Sarah J. Hudson, 'Attitudes to Investment Risk amongst West Midland Canal and Railway Company Investors, 1700–1850' (unpublished doctoral thesis, University of Warwick, 2001).

[15] Shoemaker, *Gender in English Society*, p. 139.

Leeds, Sheffield and Manchester in the late Georgian period where the women were central to urban society, were largely engaged in feminine trades and there was a broad continuity in their commercial activity.[16] Most of the cases were widows or spinsters, but in London until the mid-nineteenth century married women had a unique advantage through a legal status known as *feme sole*. The custom of *feme sole* trader was known to exist in thirteen English boroughs in the medieval or early modern period, but had gradually disappeared and only survived in the City of London until 1852. London offered not just a legal status for married businesswomen but greater market opportunities for many female milliners and women in the luxury goods trade.[17] However, the importance of the evidence from the London cases is that both men and women used any part of the law that gave them protection, especially if it was from creditors, thus confounding notions of a nineteenth-century patriarchal conspiracy.

Such research challenges assumptions about women's increasing retreat into gentility and the small (and therefore unimportant) size of women's business. Women used business networks, handed complex business, had financial accounting ability and were in partnerships with others both male and female, relations and friends. Phillips criticises the arguments on capitalism and patriarchy as too narrow and encouraging the widespread assumption that there are only two ways to discuss women's economic opportunities: 'that is that they were always limited, or that they became more so after the industrial revolution.'[18] In just one residential area of Glasgow (a rapidly expanding port city during the nineteenth century) there were 'considerable numbers of widowed and single women with occupations, running businesses and engaging directly with the market'. Women were financially supporting family firms and were major investors in railways.[19]

Much of the evidence garnered to date relates to women in the feminine trades, such as millinery and the hospitality trades. Although there were significant numbers of women retailers and manufacturers in the metal trades in Birmingham,[20] businesswomen in non-feminine industries are often seen as historical oddities or aberrations and their brief tenure is rarely examined in any critical way. Lady Charlotte ran her late husband's foundry from 1852 to 1855, but the main evidence about her role comes from her diary, and Isabella Elder's brief nine-month period as head of her late husband's shipbuilding firm gets attention without any questioning of what she may or may not have done in that

---

[16] Hannah Barker, *The Business of Women: Female Enterprise and Urban Development in Northern England 1760–1830* (Oxford: Oxford University Press, 2006).

[17] Nicola Phillips, *Women in Business, 1700–1850* (Woodbridge: Boydell & Brewer, 2006), pp. 49–53, 142.

[18] Phillips, *Women in Business*, pp. 3–14.

[19] Eleanor Gordon and Gwyneth Nair, 'The Economic Role of Middle-Class Women in Victorian Glasgow', *Women's History Review*, 9 (2000), 791–814.

[20] Maxine Berg, 'Women's Work; Mechanisation and the Early Phases of Industrialisation in England', in *The Historical Meanings of Work*, ed. Patrick Joyce (Cambridge: Cambridge University Press, 1987), pp. 64–98, (pp. 97–8); Katherine R. P. Jenns, 'Female Business Enterprise in and around Birmingham' (unpublished doctoral thesis, University of Birmingham, 1997).

time.[21] Such uncritical acceptance does little to further a real understanding of the businesswoman's role. In order to achieve this, some knowledge of the industrial sector in question is needed, and this background to the study of businesswomen has frequently been lacking. To appreciate the real challenges such women faced in a man's world the role of the businessman must be examined. For example, in the United States Rebecca Lukens apparently ran an ironworks in the early nineteenth century and led the business from serious debt to financial success over twenty-two years despite a severe recession in 1837.[22] It would be instructive to understand how her competitors also fared. Only then can historians get a better understanding of the nature of the achievement of these businesswomen in overcoming business, financial and personal hurdles.

Women in the Maritime World

Women in maritime history have had uneven coverage in published literature and fall into two categories, those who went to sea and those who remained dependent on the shore. The woman at sea has been a popular image and she can be seen as the heroic figure challenging men on their own territory, such as those who disguised themselves as men, or as the determined wife accompanying her husband. [23] As for the wife left on shore, the Victorian painters featured bereft and weeping women in fishing communities. The titles of paintings such as 'Men must work and women must weep', which is based on a poem of the same name by Charles Kingsley, portray a sense of dependence, loss and fatalism.[24] While tragedies happened and, in a life lived on and by the sea such things were almost inevitable, they were by no means the overwhelming feature of community life. This image of the dependent wife on shore has been strengthened by the study of the correspondence of Nantucket whaling wives.[25]

In those environments where men were frequently absent for long periods there has been a tendency to view the wife's partnership role as merely that of deputy husband. The use of this phrase indicates a reluctance to view women

---

[21] Revel Guest and Angela V. John, *Lady Charlotte: A Biography of the Nineteenth Century* (London: Weidenfeld & Nicolson, 1989); Joan McAlpine, *The Lady of Claremont House: Isabella Elder, Pioneer and Philanthropist* (Argyll: Argyll Publishing, 1997).

[22] Angel Kwolek-Folland, *Incorporating Women: A History of Women and Business in the United States* (New York: Palgrave, 1998), pp. 46–7.

[23] Joan Druett, *Hen Frigates: Wives of Merchant Captains under Sail* (New York: Simon & Schuster, 1998); Jo Stanley, ed., *Bold in Her Breeches: Women Pirates across the Ages* (London: HarperCollins, 1995); Suzanne J. Stark, *Female Tars: Women Aboard Ship in the Age of Sail* (London: Pimlico, 1996).

[24] Birmingham Museum and Art Gallery: http://www.bmagic.org.uk/people/Walter+Langley (accessed 28 August 2006).

[25] Norling, *Captain Ahab Had a Wife*; Lisa Norling, '"How Fraught with Sorrow and Heart-pangs": Mariners' Wives and the Ideology of Domesticity in New England, 1790–1880', *New England Quarterly*, 65 (1992), 442–6.

as acting independently and yet the studies of North American coastal towns in the eighteenth century have conflicting views.[26] In the whaling industry men might be absent for years, with the inevitable strain on the relationship between husband and wife. Based mainly on surviving letters between the couples, the findings reflected a shift in attitude from 'deputy husband roles' pre-1815 to a more distinctly gender-marked division between public and private spheres where the letters showed wives relying on 'male relatives to perform most functions not directly related to household maintenance'. From mid-century, due to industry changes, the whalers were absent for even longer periods – for four sometimes five years. This lengthy separation appears to have led to an increase in the number of wives accompanying their husbands and about one in six wives took this option. The rest remained on land, some taking on other work, sewing shirts or taking in lodgers. The network of family and neighbours was important both for material assistance and for emotional support. However, while the work of women is occasionally mentioned, this was not specifically researched and the conclusion from the letters was that 'acting as a stand in for an absent husband actually constituted a familial responsibility that may have inhibited rather than encouraged the wife to develop a sense of autonomy'.[27] This is not a view heavily endorsed by others. In New England in the eighteenth century seaport women had a 'degree of economic independence' and 'circumvented some of the worst aspects of patriarchal control'.[28] The difficulty of letters as a source is that the correspondence between a wife and her absent husband may express the woman's wishes, together with a concern to reassure the husband, while her solitary circumstances force her to act independently.

Patriarchal control features in research in Scottish fishing communities where there were many examples of the women running the finances and owning the enterprises. Women assumed special responsibilities because of the absence of men away at sea, but here there was an interesting contrast between those who worked for others and those who were in local small share consortiums. 'It seems that family relationships are likely to be much more seriously affected when working conditions are not only especially bitter and far distant from home, but the men sense the degree of their own exploitation by merchants or employers.'[29] In Shetland the women 'hold a social standing and confidence, which contrast markedly with the situation of women in Lewis (where the men were waged and were seen as the power in the household). And they have passed on to their

---

[26] Elaine Forman Crane, *Ebb Tide in New England: Women, Seaports and Social Change 1630–1800* (Boston: Northeastern University Press, 1998), p. 126; Norling, *Captain Ahab Had a Wife*, pp. 36–50; Daniel Vickers, *Young Men and the Sea: Yankee Seafarers in the Age of Sail* (New Haven and London: Yale University Press, 2005), p. 147.

[27] Norling, '"How Fraught with Sorrow and Heartpangs"', pp. 428–40.

[28] Vickers, *Young Men and the Sea*, pp. 46–7; Crane, *Ebb Tide in New England*, p. 243.

[29] Paul Thompson, 'Women in Fishing: The Roots of Power between the Sexes', *Comparative Studies in Society and History*, 27 (1985), 3–32 (p. 22).

children, too, an inner self-determination which has allowed them to make the most of their chances before them.'[30]

This book seeks to fill some of the gaps in the historiography by providing more information on women in business and women as active economic agents from 1780 to 1880. This is the period when many of them were assumed to be excluded by strengthening notions of a woman's place, and it was before the second Married Women's Property Act in 1882 which gave married women greater independence. The female investors in shipping are examined not just at one fixed point but over time as they bought and sold their shares. Additionally the business context is shown together with an examination of what factors helped to determine the success or failure of an enterprise.

Case studies provide a more in-depth picture of the woman concerned and the commercial environment in which she operated. These examine whether shipping shares were purchased in a growing local economy, under what circumstances a woman owned shares, how they were acquired and how they were traded. Any investment involves risks and the shipping trade was not for the fainthearted. The challenges for the business owner in particular trades are considered. These questions affected how the women made their decisions, in relation to both their investment and their business. The effectiveness of businesswomen has rarely been considered. The biography of Lady Charlotte Guest is based on her diaries and reveals a woman who was committed to her husband's business and excited by it.[31] When he died she ran the foundries until her second marriage three years later and the biography portrays a woman of achievement. It took other historians and a more critical business analysis to discover that, in her time, the foundries were severely undercapitalised and the whole business was at risk. The root of these problems had probably started before her time, but she appears to have merely continued her husband's strategy and been unaware of the depth of the difficulties facing the business. Once Lady Charlotte had relinquished the reins of management, her successors had to inject a significant amount of investment to put the business back on its feet.[32] It is not sufficient just to note that a woman ran a business, as this does not give any view of the decisions she made and how successful her business was. The family had to be researched to understand to what extent family pressures were driving the decisions. For women the domestic pull was strong and many still had to continue running a household and bringing up children.

---

[30] Thompson, 'Women in Fishing', p. 26.
[31] Guest and John, *Lady Charlotte*.
[32] Trevor Boyns and John Richard Edwards, 'Cost and Management Accounting in Early Victorian Britain: A Chandleresque Analysis?' *Management Accounting Research*, 8 (1997), 19–46.

Sources for Businesswomen

Researching women's history is made more complex by the apparent lack of sources. For the nineteenth century the census is the obvious starting point. The first usable census dates from 1841, but while it gives detailed information on many aspects it has particular traps in relation to the study of women.[33] Women's work or forms of income were frequently omitted and, for coastal communities where seasonal and multi-occupation work was usual, the information given is one-dimensional, frequently listing one occupation which is not necessarily the most important one. The census is questionable due to the bias of the collectors of statistics, the reasons behind the collection of the information, and changes in both methodology and categorisation.[34] Trade directories, too, have their own built-in bias as some were subscription-led and omit many businesses. Their coverage in some parts of the country is limited, particularly in Cornwall which is one of the areas considered here. Both the census and the directories can prove the existence of a woman in a certain trade, but they are certainly not comprehensive.[35]

Coverture, where a married woman's identity becomes that of her husband on marriage, is another hurdle to overcome. Many couples worked together in the family trade or business, but only the man's name appears, until on his death his widow is revealed to be suddenly capable of running a complex business, employing men and working in a male-dominated marketplace.[36] Much of the information on businesswomen, therefore, tends to be biased towards widows and spinsters.

Wills are another source utilised, both those of men who were making bequests to women and a few from women. Wills are also problematic as they state what the testator intended at the time of writing the will. The reality of what was left after debts were paid did not always match the intention. As a way of establishing a woman's investments, wills are also limited, since details are not often given of individual shares, or of how they were acquired. However, women were holders of real property (46 per cent of female testators in Sheffield and Birmingham and in both towns women had cash and goods to bequeath).[37]

Business records are of real value, but survival is rare for the majority of businesses, especially small businesses. In the one or two cases where business letters

---

[33] Bridget Hill, 'Women, Work and the Census: A Problem for Historians of Women', *History Workshop Journal*, 35 (1993), 78–94.

[34] Hill, 'Women, Work and the Census', p. 92.

[35] Edward Higgs, 'Occupational Censuses and the Agricultural Workforce in Victorian England and Wales', *The Economic History Review*, 48 (1995), 700–16, Hill, 'Women, Work and the Census'; Jane E. Norton, *Guide to the National and Provincial Directories of England and Wales, Excluding London, Published before 1856* (London: Royal Historical Society, 1950).

[36] Margot Finn, 'Women, Consumption and Coverture in England, c. 1760–1860', *Historical Journal*, 39 (1996), 703–22 (pp. 717–18).

[37] Maxine Berg, 'Women's Property and the Industrial Revolution', *Journal of Interdisciplinary History*, XXIV (1993), 233–50 (p. 245).

from women survive they have been invaluable as a source in showing the extent of the decision making. All of these sources have been utilised in the search for businesswomen. For maritime businesswomen, in particular the managing owners of vessels, contemporary shipping directories are a useful source. *Clayton's Directory of Shipping* was published in 1865 by a shipbroker of Hull and provides a list of vessels registered in each port, with the exception of Liverpool and London, and the name of the managing owner and their residence. The use of other similar directories such as *Marwoods, Turnbull's Directory, Lloyd's Register* and the *Mercantile Navy List* enables a wider coverage across Britain and across time. Additional use was made of shipping accounts, insurance records and port bills of entry. The shipping sector's importance in the nineteenth century is reflected in the extensive amount of information provided within Parliamentary Papers and these include annual statements of shipping and parliamentary committees on a wide range of shipping matters.

One major source previously untapped in the context of women is the Customs House Shipping Registers. These registers are a list of all ships registered in Britain and show the owners of each vessel, up to sixty-four shares per ship, and, importantly in this context, how they were disposed of. The registers, which came into existence from 1786, provide such a wealth of information that at one time there was a plan to transcribe all the extant registers, a project which, if it had been fulfilled, would have provided a highly valuable tool for historians of economic, maritime, and social history. The transcription project ran into difficulty due to the sheer scale of the work involved and, although some extracts were published,[38] historians have to consult the originals, which is a time-consuming task. The registers used here are from Exeter, Fowey, King's Lynn, Whitby and Whitehaven, all of which are smaller ports and therefore it has been easier to extract data on women, not just as a sample but for the whole period. Customs House Shipping Registers provide details of the owners and how the share ownership changed over time. Previous use of these registers has focused either on the vessels themselves or on samples of investors. In the latter case, only the initial ownership of the vessel on launching or registration in the relevant port is usually considered.[39] The key information for this study however has been found in the transactions as shares changed hands. These show how, why and from whom the shares were transferred, plus other incidental data entered by the customs officers. The investment by individuals in various vessels can be tracked over time, giving a rich set of information on an individual's economic decisions. The information is extensive and rather than sample from one large port, the five smaller ports have

[38] G. Farr, *Chepstow Ships* (Chepstow, 1954); Graham E. Farr, *Records of Bristol Ships, 1800–1838: Vessels over 150 Tons* (Bristol: Bristol Records Society, 1950); C. H. Ward-Jackson, *Ships and Shipbuilders of a Westcountry Seaport: Fowey 1786–1939* (Truro: Twelveheads Press, 1986).

[39] Ward-Jackson, *Ships and Shipbuilders*; Robin Craig, *British Tramp Shipping: 1750–1914* (Newfoundland, 2003), pp. 41–58; Graeme J. Milne, *North East England, 1850–1914: The Dynamics of a Maritime-Industrial Region* (Woodbridge: Boydell Press, 2006); S. R. Palmer, 'Investors in London Shipping', *Maritime History*, 2 (1972), 46–68.

been extensively researched in order to give a longitudinal and more representative picture rather than a snapshot.

The information extracted from the registers provides a further opportunity for debate relating to women, by not just noting that they owned shares but by also examining their actions and attitudes in relation to investment. To what extent were they the passive acceptors of male wealth or instead actively pursuing and managing their investments? Why were they actively participating in the high risk and uncertain world of shipping, contrary to the suggestion that women preferred low risk options for their investments such as government securities?[40] Finally, how can these shareholdings be quantified and the significance to the industry of the women's investment be measured?

The Structure of the Book

To answer the various questions the book examines both shipowners and the business managers. Chapter 1 considers the legal and financial environment for nineteenth-century women, together with some of the contemporary literature. It examines the national picture and considers to what extent women were restricted by law. It also considers the financial environment for women investors. A contemporary comment was that women had to overcome negative social opinion in order to go into business, so examples of contemporary literature provide some views.[41] Opportunities rather than the apparent constraints are the focus of Chapter 2 which explores the maritime environment within which these women worked and the close nature of the coastal societies in which they lived. This national picture leads to a more detailed study in Chapter 3 of the five ports, Exeter, Fowey, King's Lynn, Whitby and Whitehaven, which were chosen as the basis for the detailed investigation of the shipping investors. This chapter includes the broad findings and regional differences. Chapters 4 and 5 then provide a picture of the investors from the perspective of their marital status and their activity in relation to their shipping shares.

Women running businesses and managing men are the subject of the next chapters and the evidence here comes from across England. Chapter 6 considers the role of the managing owner and what this involved for both men and women. Ports had many other businesses within the shipping industry which played a crucial part in keeping the ships profitably at sea, so Chapter 7 looks at the port businesswomen. The businesses ranged from small to large and the challenges for a woman owner are considered. Technology had a major impact on the shipping industry in the nineteenth century and the various trades in ports were affected. Chapters 8 and 9 both look at shipbuilding businesses, but with very different customers. Chapter 8 examines two case studies of women whose yards

---

[40] Green and Owens, 'Gentlewomanly Capitalism?', p. 530.
[41] Bessie R. Parkes, *Essays on Woman's Work* (London, 1865).

were building for the navy; these women were dealing with a large and powerful customer in a time of war. The next chapter covers the whole period and looks at merchant shipbuilding and has six case studies. It looks at the different requirements when building for commercial clients and the different opportunities for women and how they managed in changing economic situations.

Chapter 10 pulls together the various strands across the research and reaches conclusions about the strategies adopted by businesswomen. It also considers the question of success, and how that can be measured when most women are only seen as business owners when they are widowed. Were they accepted as part of the business community? Why did these women run the businesses and become shipowners? Was it an active choice or force of circumstance? The conclusion considers the overall question of women's independent economic activity.

The women described here were not mere bystanders on the fringes of the maritime world. In a century noted for the legal and social limitations of the woman's role, they invested in ships, and managed ships, shipyards and other businesses. They handled the good times and the bad times in business. In a century marked by the dominance of the patriarchal model, these businesswomen were encouraged by male mentors, persuaded men to do business with them, dealt with male suppliers, worked alongside men and employed men, while at the same time many also ran a household and brought up children. They deserve their place in history.

I

The Legal, Financial and Cultural Environment

The law relating to women and marriage became a subject of national debate in the nineteenth century, largely due to the concerns voiced by feminists in their pursuit of changes in the law, in particular as it affected divorce, rights over children and property. This brought the role of women sharply into focus, and government statistics, particularly the census, were used by proponents and opponents alike. The extent to which these changes helped or hindered the real position of women in society is a debatable topic amongst historians. Increasingly the view is that women and men used the law in any way they could to gain an advantage, and the maritime sector reflects this.[1] This chapter examines three aspects of the national environment as it affected women investors and women in business. First, the legal framework, which was to change considerably over the period in question, from the Registration Act for Shipping in 1786, which provided a legal document for all shareholders, to the Married Women's Property Act in 1882 which finally gave all wives independent access to their property. Second, the financial environment also changed, with increased opportunities for investors in new joint stock companies and in new enterprises such as the railways. Third, some of the contemporary writers of the period reveal the contradictions in attitudes towards women investors and women in business.

The Legal Background: Wills, Wives and Wrecks

In 1835 the customs official in charge of the shipping register for Exeter made a note in the ledger relating to ownership of the 88-ton schooner, *Dispatch*. Sarah Barrett, a widow, owned 50 per cent of the ship, but sold her thirty-two shares to John Bennett 'in trust for the benefit of the said Sarah Barrett and her children by her late husband, Thomas Barrett, the said Sarah Barrett being about to be married to James Hore of Topsham, mariner'.[2] Sarah was attempting to use the law to protect her property for herself and her children, as on her remarriage all her property automatically became her husband's. Her case involved in some way the variety of legal systems that pertained at the time.

---

[1]   Bridget Hill, *Women, Work, and Sexual Politics in Eighteenth-Century England* (New York: Blackwell, 1989), p. 196; Phillips, *Women in Business*, pp. 23–47; Vickery, 'Golden Age to Separate Spheres?'

[2]   Devon Record Office (DRO): MFC 44/18 Exeter Shipping Registers 21/1831.

"There they d'sit glazin' 'pon wan 'nother
like a couple o' tom cats" Chapter III

1. The unprepossessing but wealthy widow and her suitors
Source: Charles Lee, *The Widow Woman: A Cornish Tale* (London: Dent & Sons, 1896)

During the nineteenth century much hard work was done to simplify the legal system. Until the early nineteenth century there was no single system of English law; instead there were four bodies of law administered in different sets of courts, each with their separate groups of legal practitioners and judges, and each having its own avenue of appeals.[3] The branches of law were equity, common, church and maritime law. In some degree the first three impacted on all women, but the fourth had a particular impact on women in the maritime sector, and in the case of Sarah Barrett, all four had a part to play.

Common law had its origins in feudal law and local customs. It dealt largely with land and personal chattels and only gradually did it come to recognise other forms of property.[4] Appeal in common law cases was to the Court of Exchequer. It was under common law that married woman were most disadvantaged through coverture. Common law considered that a husband and wife were 'one body before God, they were one person in the law and that person was represented by the husband'.[5] The man assumed full rights over his wife's property on marriage and any income or inheritance that she subsequently earned.

It is common law that is usually cited in the case of married women's rights and which is described as causing women to exist 'in a state of suspended animation'.[6] In a study of marriage settlements in early modern England, common law was not the only law that applied to property; there was also equity, ecclesiastical and, yet another legal system, manorial law. All of these were used to separate a married woman's inheritance and management of her property from her husband.[7] As will be seen, maritime law provided yet another dimension. In the nineteenth century, despite laws that apparently stopped married women from acting independently, they were still able to run businesses, argue their case (or their husband's case) in court, and also be sued and hold property independently of their husband.[8]

This is not to deny the other factors that impeded women's economic activity, and the historians writing about the obstacles caused by common law have helped to identify 'powerful incentives that propelled Victorian activists towards female emancipation'. However, emphasis on the disabling aspects of common law over-looks the ways in which men and women managed to avoid various legal restrictions, as in more detailed examinations of women's business activity in Glasgow and in London.[9] It has rightly been suggested that more attention should be paid to the way in which the law was interpreted and changed by judge's rulings, and

---

3   Holcombe, *Wives and Property*, p. 9.
4   Holcombe, *Wives and Property*, p. 9.
5   William Blackstone, *Commentaries on the Laws of England*, as quoted in Shanley, *Feminism, Marriage and the Law*, p. 8.
6   Finn, 'Women, Consumption and Coverture', p. 707.
7   Amy Louise Erickson, 'Common Law versus Common Practice: The Use of Marriage Settlements in Early Modern England', *Economic History Review*, 43 (1990), pp. 21–39.
8   Finn, 'Women, Consumption and Coverture', p. 707.
9   Gordon and Nair, 'The Economic Role of Middle-Class Women in Victorian Glasgow'; Phillips, *Women in Business*. Note: Scotland had a different legal system but it still appeared to restrict married women.

not just the legal enactments. Many historians have merely accepted the limita-tions of common law, but further research shows that women and men were able to manipulate the complex legal system to their own advantage.[10]

In Exeter, in Sarah Barrett's case, remarriage meant that her second husband potentially became the owner of her thirty-two shares. What she was attempting to do was to use equity law to protect her assets and those of her children by her first marriage. Equity law involved the use of trusts and was administered by the Court of Chancery.[11] Also originating from medieval practice it derived from the crown's power to use its prerogative in certain cases and had become the route for cases that involved contracts or torts (breaches of duty). This branch of law expanded in the seventeenth and eighteenth centuries largely as a response to the significant changes affecting it economically and socially due to the growth in the economy. 'Intangible property, including property held in trust and money invested in public funds and company stocks and bonds', was inadequately protected or not covered by common law. It is within equity that 'English women, at times assisted by English men, succeeded in suppressing, subverting, eroding and evading the strictures of the common law'.[12] Fathers set up trusts for daughters, husbands left property in trust for their wives and young children, while Sarah Barrett was setting up a trust for herself and her children.

The third system of law to affect women was that administered by the eccle-siastical courts which had exclusive jurisdiction over matrimonial cases and all matters of probate. Specially trained lay members practised law under the jurisdic-tion of the established church and appeal was to the Archbishops of Canterbury and York. However, the ecclesiastical court's jurisdiction was only in those cases where there was a will. Cases of those dying intestate were administered under common law, and related only to personal property, therefore excluding land.[13] Women's property could be protected under ecclesiastical law. Probate accounts from the late sixteenth to the early eighteenth century showed frequent references to marriage settlements that protected the wife's property.[14]

Under English law there was considerable freedom to bequeath one's property. The text of wills 'makes it possible to watch individuals making choices guided only by opportunity, custom and practice'. From the widow's perspective wills can be separated into four types: those that gave the widow absolute access to the estate; those that gave her access only for her natural life; those that reduced her access should she remarry; and wills that only gave her access to funds so long as she did not remarry. In a sample 82 per cent used trusts as a way of exercising 'power beyond the grave'. Responsibilities to children vied with concern for and responsibilities to wives. It is notable that retailers were a distinct group who showed clear evidence of trust in the 'business and practical abilities of women'

10   Phillips, *Women in Business*, pp. 39, 67–68.
11   Holcombe, *Wives and Property*, pp. 10–11.
12   Finn, 'Women, Consumption and Coverture', p. 720.
13   Holcombe, *Wives and Property*, pp. 11–12.
14   Erickson, 'Common Law versus Common Practice', p. 31.

by making an absolute gift of the business to their widows.[15] Within the maritime sector it was not just retailing businesses where the wife was left the business outright; for example in 1795 William Barnard left his sizeable shipbuilding business to his wife.[16] In many cases these bequests were formal recognition of their ongoing activity in running the business with their husbands.

All these legal systems meant potential confusion with different forms of proceedings, different terminology, different processes for appeal, and conflicting and overlapping jurisdictions. In common law the proceedings were mainly oral with witnesses appearing before the court, while in equity all statements were made in written form by authorised lawyers.[17] The impact was that for the average provincial lawyer detailed knowledge of all the legal systems was impossible. Nor was it possible for the customs officials who noted the transfer of the ship shares to act in any way as trained lawyers. However, what they did know were the proper procedures for registering shares in ships, which leads to the fourth system of law in this case.

In relation to women, maritime law has previously been dismissed as irrelevant due to its narrow specialisation.[18] This is understandable in the context of the women's movement and legal reform, but maritime law had an important part to play for the majority of maritime women, in particular those with shares in ships or business interests in the shipping world. This explains why Sarah Barrett's shares were written into the ship registry. Under maritime law, which governed most aspects of shipping, vessels could be divided into multiple shares. The owners held these as tenants-in-common, allowing each person to dispose of their shares as they wished without requiring them to consult with fellow shareholders. Shares in ships could be bequeathed, sold or mortgaged. In 1872 Stephen Lee of Lynn left his ships and his shares in ships equally divided between his wife, Hannah, and daughter, Susan. He stipulated that they were to hold them as 'tenants-in-common and not as joint tenants'.[19] This meant that the shares could be disposed of by either Hannah or Susan without reference to the other.

In 1786 the Act of Registration was passed to ensure that all British ships were registered in their home ports.[20] The implementation of this act was administered by HM Customs; officials in each port had to note the name, residence and occupation of each shareholder and note all changes. However, these officials were not legal experts and especially in the earlier years anomalies occurred. In Sarah's case, as she was not mortgaging her shares, nor was it part of a legacy, the way in which the customs officials decided to note her transfer of the shares to John

[15] R. J. Morris, 'Men, Women and Property: The Reform of the Married Women's Property Act 1870', in *Landowners, Capitalists, and Entrepreneurs: Essays for Sir John Habakkuk*, ed. F. M. L. Thompson (Oxford: Clarendon Press, 1994), pp. 171–91. R. J. Morris, *Men, Women and Property in England, 1780–1870* (Cambridge: Cambridge University Press, 2005), pp. 88, 103–5.

[16] The National Archives (TNA): PRO 11/1257 Will of William Barnard 1795.

[17] Holcombe, *Wives and Property*, p. 13.

[18] Holcombe, *Wives and Property*, p. 12.

[19] Norfolk Record Office (NRO): MF 1313 203 Will of Stephen Lee, February 1872.

[20] 26 Geo III, c.60.

Bennett in trust was to call it a sale. Gradually, as the nineteenth century wore on, regular guidance letters came from London to the ports on various aspects of legal title to shareownership. Stephen Lee's wish that his wife and daughter should have equal shares as tenants-in-common was frustrated. All the sixty-four shares in his five ships were shown as being owned jointly by Hannah and Susan rather than being individually assigned.[21] The will writer's intentions could be frustrated by alternative advice to the legatees, a misunderstanding of the terms of the will, or simply by being ignored.

Legal Reform in the Nineteenth Century and the Impact on Women

By the early nineteenth century, it was evident that these conflicting legal systems were much in need of clarification and simplification, and a unified court system was proposed to eliminate jurisdictional conflicts, conflicts that had often been costly in more ways than one for the suitor if he began his action in the wrong court.[22] This reform during the nineteenth century is indeed a major legacy of the Victorian era. Yet well before the law permitted such action, from 1780 to 1870 married women were already registering ship shares in their own names.

By 1857 the jurisdiction of marital matters and wills was removed from the ecclesiastical courts and given to secular courts, paving the way for future legislation regarding wives.[23] The Supreme Court of Judicature Act, 1873 provided for a new High Court of Justice with five divisions: Queen's Bench, Common Pleas, Exchequer, Chancery and Probate, Divorce and Admiralty. By 1881 this had been further reduced to three divisions: Chancery, Queen's Bench and Probate, Divorce and Admiralty. The final division earned inevitably the soubriquet of 'wills, wives and wrecks'. The 1873 act also provided for a single route of appeal.[24]

These changes simplified and, in many cases, speeded up the legal process, as Chancery, in particular, had been notorious for its long drawn out cases.[25] For married businesswomen and investors, however, the greatest reforms were to the law as it affected property. The debates on the iniquities of the system as it applied to married women raised considerable awareness. While the case of Sarah Barrett and others like her show that many women and their male relatives were able to circumvent common law, the big battleground for the feminists was the reform of common law which led eventually to the Married Women's Property Act of 1870.[26] While described as a 'legislative abortion' due to the number of amend-

---

[21] NRO: P/SH/L 1–3, 4–7 Lynn Shipping Registers.
[22] F. L. Wiswall Jr, *The Development of Admiralty Jurisdiction and Practice since 1800* (Cambridge: Cambridge University Press, 1970), p. 101.
[23] Holcombe, *Wives and Property*, p. 15.
[24] Wiswall, *The Development of Admiralty Jurisdiction*, p. 102.
[25] Highlighted in the fictional case of Jarndyce v. Jarndyce in Dickens's *Bleak House* (1853).
[26] Morris, 'The Reform of the Married Women's Property Act 1870', p. 177.

ments and changes that had to be made in order for it to become law, it was a milestone:

> with all its defects the act of 1870, like the Divorce Act of 1857 before it, was important in its recognition of the principle that married women should in certain circumstances own and control their property. As the Annual Register of 1870 noted rather wistfully, the act was the first recognition of a 'new principle, another small sign of the times ... that the old creeds were passing away, and, whether for good or evil, all things becoming new.'[27]

The act of 1870 gave married women the right to their own earnings from employment, from trade 'which she carried on separate to her husband' and from 'the exercise of literary, artistic or scientific skill', thus recognising that women were indeed acting independently of their husbands. This often ensured the security of a marriage or of widowhood when the husband experienced business problems.[28] However, there was still a long way to go in gaining legal recognition for married women's independent estate and, despite some loss of momentum, the Married Women's Property Committee continued to push for further reform.

On 1 January 1883 the Married Women's Property Act 1882 came into force, achieving the result for which the committee had been fighting for so long: 'that married woman should have the same rights over property as unmarried women and that husbands and wives should have separate interests in their property'. Married women were also specifically empowered to carry on trades and businesses separately from their husbands using their separate property.[29] It was hailed as a major victory.

The national debate on married women's property was considerable and heated and raised the profile of this aspect of the law. Yet in 1836 the example of Mary Hoskins appears to be in contravention of the law. She inherited a portfolio of twenty shares in *Fleece, Thames, Fame* and *Devon* which were all regular traders from Exeter to London. Here is the entry for one of them, the *Thames*.

> Letter of admin dated 15 Mar 1836 by which it appears that Mary Hoskins, the wife of Samuel Hoskins of Stonehouse in County of Devon Captain in the Royal Navy, sister and one of the next of kin to Robert Folliat late of the Parish of Topsham Lieutenant in the Royal Navy is sole administrator.[30]

This is unusual not just because it is a brother's legacy, but also because there was no will in this case, so Mary gained the letters of administration. All the shares were transferred into Mary's name. The customs officials accepted the information supplied and the shares continued to be noted in her name. She retained them until 1856 when they were sold. At no stage were they transferred to her husband's

---

27 Holcombe, *Wives and Property*, p. 183.
28 Morris, 'The Reform of the Married Women's Property Act 1870', pp. 173–9.
29 Holcombe, *Wives and Property*, pp. 201–3.
30 DRO: 50/1826.

name which was the correct procedure under common law. As will be seen in more detail in Chapter 4, married women were not constrained from owning shares by the apparent limitations of the law.

Women, Trusts and Wills

As seen in the case of Sarah Barrett, trusts were important instruments in assisting women's separate property, but they had wider implications. There is a view that trusts were not always to the advantage of the women concerned since they could also limit their independence, as sons had direct access to capital, while daughters only had access to the interest. Thus two forms of capital were created. Male capital was free to seek the higher returns and higher risk of entrepreneurial activity, whilst female capital sought the lower gains and risk of rentier or debenture-style assets.[31] Female capital was retained within the family and could be used in some cases by executors to provide support for family business ventures.

It is suggested that the petite bourgeoisie and those of lower status in the middle class rarely used trusteeships as their capital was too slender to be tied up in a way which limited income. Their daughters and widows were more vulnerable to the perils of marriage and remarriage, but these women were free to use the capital they gained from legacies to set up in businesses such as lodging houses, millinery shops and the host of trades which the nineteenth-century trade directories show were 'especially receptive to female entrepreneurship'.[32] However, the example of Sarah Barrett and others like her, such as Ann Dingle who bought shares in several Fowey vessels in 1837 and 1838 'in trust for her son', show that the trust mechanism was well used by a wide range of the middle class and not just by men.[33]

It is also argued that the male trustee chosen by husbands or fathers was another type of control on female activity and it is also implied that the appointment was a permanent one.[34] As a source, however, the great advantage of the shipping registers over wills is that they give a view of what happened after probate was achieved. Acting as a trustee took up considerable time and effort and women were capable of handling their own interests. Most trustees and executors were male,[35] and, especially if they had no direct business interests in the estate, did not always wish to take on the role. Aaron Ross, a chandler of Hull, left his estate to his wife in trust to his friends and executors Thomas Booth and William Rowson.

---

[31] Morris, 'The Reform of the Married Women's Property Act 1870', p. 181.
[32] Morris, 'The Reform of the Married Women's Property Act 1870', p. 186.
[33] CRO: MSR/FOW/7 Fowey Shipping Registers.
[34] Morris, 'The Reform of the Married Women's Property Act 1870', pp. 186, 264.
[35] David R. Green, 'Independent Women, Wealth and Wills in Nineteenth-Century London', in *Urban Fortunes: Property and Inheritance in the Town, 1700–1900*, ed. Jon Stobart and Alastair Owens (Aldershot: Ashgate Press, 2000), pp. 195–222 (pp. 214–16).

Rowson renounced his role, leaving just Thomas Booth.[36] And Mary Murphy of Whitehaven was named as one of three executors of her husband's will, but one had predeceased her late husband and the other renounced probate.[37]

Women did not always conform and trustees and executors did not always choose to take up their responsibility. On the other hand a well selected trustee could be of real benefit to a businesswoman in providing advice and looking after her interests. Mr Glassler of Portsea, Hampshire was such a trustee and took his responsibilities seriously. He was the executor of the will of Mrs Sophia Robinson and was appointed guardian to her daughter Charlotte. Sophia owned a sloop which was hired to the Ordnance Board in Portsmouth and was employed in arming and disarming warships. In 1794 Glassler wrote with a simple request that in future payments should be made to Charlotte. The particular interest in the letter is the mention that Charlotte was now married, to Francis Flower, a silk mercer of St Paul's Churchyard. Despite the marriage it was Glassler and not her husband who confirmed that he was writing in his position as her guardian and that she was the 'sole proprietor' of the sloop.[38]

Fathers used standard phrases in their wills, such as 'to be free from any inter-ference', to ensure that a woman's inheritance was not taken over by her husband, but this was not used in all cases even within the same will. William Salt, a retired harbourmaster of Fowey, made a clear differentiation between his children in his will written in 1867. He had four daughters and one son. His son John inherited a house, his daughter Susan inherited a house and contents, while his daughter Elizabeth received £36 and two shares in the schooner *Alert*. Five pounds and an annual sum of two pounds went to his daughter Caroline, wife of Samuel Lang-maid, with the following conditions: 'To be free from the control or interference of her present or any husband and to be payable by Jane Symons Slade out of proceeds arising from Russell Inn.' Jane was his other daughter and her treatment was markedly different even from that of her brother. Jane was the sole executor and she inherited the Russell Inn, which she had been running for some years, two shares in the brigantine *Capella*, William's shipwrights yard in Polruan, which Jane's husband Christopher had been running, and, finally, William's desk and its contents plus any other remaining assets.[39] The will was written while Jane's husband was still alive, but in her case her father had presumably judged that Jane was unlikely to be concerned by any potential interference from her husband. While there is no knowing what earlier arrangement had been made with his son in the way of disposal of property, it is clear that William knew which of his children, especially his daughters, had the business acumen or needed protection.

---

36   TNA: PRO Prob 11/2167 will of Aaron Ross, shipchandler, Hull, 1852.
37   North Yorkshire Record Office (NYRO): YTSR 1/20.
38   TNA: PRO WO 52/83 Ordnance Office: Bill books (series III) 1794–1795.
39   BPO: Will of William Salt 1871.

Maritime Law

Women who ran maritime businesses, and, in particular, investors and managing owners, had to be aware of the law relating to ships which came under the jurisdiction of the Admiralty courts. A background in maritime law, at least in terms of the general differences from other types of law, could be gained by working in shipping, or from a family familiarity in the case of women. If common and equity law developed in response to national requirements within England and Wales, maritime law developed in response to international needs, and its antecedents are long and can be traced back to various codes that were developed to handle disputes which often involved more than one national jurisdiction and the peculiarities of the maritime trades. The Rolls of Oléron are the most well known in English history, although they may in part derive from the Consolato del mare which was a body of maritime rules used in the northern Mediterranean. The island of Oléron was part of the estate of Eleanor of Aquitaine, who married Henry II of England in 1152, and the Bordeaux wine trade was an important trade for many English south coast ports. It is in Henry's time that local maritime courts are first mentioned.[40]

Admiralty jurisdiction was not straightforward as there was a continuing debate among the relevant lawyers and courts as to when maritime law prevailed or when the matter should come under common law. Events at sea were certainly maritime, but what about incidents in rivers, on shores or in harbours?

> The Common Law courts succeeded in establishing the general rule that the jurisdiction of the admiralty was confined to the High seas, and entirely excluded from transactions arising on waters within the body of the country such as rivers, inlets and arms of the sea as far out as the naked eye could discern objects from shore to shore, as well as from transactions arising with land, though relating to marine affairs. In contract unless the contract was made at sea it came under common law.[41]

The general investor in shipping needed to be aware of some aspects of maritime law, particularly in relation to the registration of shareownership, but other than that they could reasonably leave most matters to the majority owner or managing owner. He or she did require a reasonable understanding and a working knowledge of the law, as it affected claims on the vessel, such as the detention of the vessel in a foreign port or the tricky question of when salvage applied or not. Salvage is a way in which the owner, or the insurers, can recompense another vessel for assistance in saving a ship and its cargo from danger, and it is usually based on a proportion of the value of the ship and/or cargo. However the conflicting interests of the ships, mariners, and their owners often led to court cases, as in the case taken to the Judicial Committee of the Privy Council in 1866.

---

40 William Senior, 'The History of Maritime Law', *Mariner's Mirror*, 38 (1952), 260–75 (p. 263).
41 Wiswall, *The Development of Admiralty Jurisdiction*, p. 22.

The *Martaban* of Greenock had several owners including Mary Hamilton, wife of James Hamilton. The ship was involved in the salvage of the *Sir Ralph Abercrombie* of Dundee. The ships met, not in Scottish waters, but near St Helena, and the original case was heard in the Vice Admiralty Court on the island in the mid-Atlantic.[42] Disputes over the salvage rights brought the case to England. Such long distances, the stresses of the moments at sea and the inability to confer with the owners all added to the difficulties of such cases.

Maritime law had its own very different situations from those based on land, and words and phrases such as bottomry, respondentia and charter party were confusing to the casual observer. Much of the strange language related to situations outside the experience of the usual business owner for the shipowner did not actually hold his or her property and for the majority of the time was out of contact with it. The difficulty of communicating speedily with owners meant that much responsibility was devolved to the master. Over time decisions relating to these situations had become part of maritime law.

For instance, bottomry was an emergency measure when a mortgage on a ship was executed by a master who was out of touch with his owners and needed to raise money for repairs or to complete a voyage. The money had to be used for the exact purpose stated and was always primarily for getting the ship back to her port of registry. A bottomry bond took precedence over all other mortgages, but if the ship was lost at sea before the voyage was completed the lender lost his bond.[43] This commercial practice was used widely in the greater Mediterranean world in the early modern period. Actions in bottomry went through the Admiralty courts and enriched the judges and practitioners of those courts. But, over the course of the seventeenth century, common lawyers and Parliament changed the rules of maritime law which sent this business to the common law courts (and lawyers) and led to a steep decline in bottomry.[44]

Respondentia was similar to bottomry but while the latter related to the vessel, respondentia related to the cargo. The cargo could be pledged in cases where the master 'is unable to obtain sufficient money for his purpose against the pledging of his owner's credit or vessel'. The holder of such bonds had a lien on the ship for settlement of his charges. It was the shipowner who had to settle since the lien was on the ship or cargo and not therefore the personal responsibility of the master, even though it was the master who signed the bond. Speedy communications via telegraphy eventually meant that there were few situations in which the master could not get proper advice from the owners.[45]

The charter party was the written contract between the commissioning freight owner and the ship's owners. This was signed either by the shipowners themselves

---

[42] TNA: PRO: PCAP 1/371 Records of Judicial Committee of the Privy Council.

[43] Wiswall, *The Development of Admiralty Jurisdiction*, p. 99.

[44] G. F. Steckley, 'Bottomry Bonds in the Seventeenth-Century Admiralty Court', *American Journal of Legal History*, 45 (2001), 256–77.

[45] E. F. Stevens, *Shipping Practice with a Consideration of the Law Relating Thereto* (London, 1935), p. 64.

or by their agents, who could be the master or an authorised agent in a distant port. The contract could either be on a time basis (where the vessel was hired for period of time and the crew and all other necessary requirements of operating a ship were provided), or for a specific voyage. It might be for a part cargo in a ship or the whole cargo. The charter party laid out the agreement regarding the movement of the freight, handling and all relevant charges, plus any other specific conditions.

Mary Hayes was the managing owner of the *Rippling Wave* which came before an Admiralty Court in Plymouth in 1882. No records of the case itself have been traced, but it was a serious one as the ship was confiscated by the court and subsequently sold.[46] Of the twenty-one ships in which Mary had shares (she was also the managing owner of three) only two had an uneventful demise. The rest were run down, sunk, wrecked, stranded or had simply gone missing.[47] Other shipowners had vessels involved in accidents in ports, damaged at sea and involved in countless other situations. The men and women who wrote to the Notes and Queries section of the *Shipping and Mercantile Gazette* for advice on maritime matters provide ample evidence of the wide range of problems that could beset the shipowner and master. This part of the daily newspaper became so important that the editor published a compilation of the main questions and answers in three volumes in 1874, 1875 and 1876. The publications were addressed to shipowners, shipbrokers, charterers, consignees and shipmasters, and promised:

> A Record of Shipping Law and Usage in Respect to Charter-Parties, Lay-Days and Demurrage, Bills of Lading, Delivery of Cargo, Afloat Clauses, Short Delivery, Stowage, Timber Trade, Pilotage, Wages, Co-Ownership, Brokerage and Commission, Masters and Mates, Marine Insurance, Admiralty Court Jurisdiction, &c., &c. L.[48]

Other sources of advice were local lawyers who specialised in maritime law, but this was an expensive option, or mutual insurance clubs. Maritime law and insurance involved complex matters and were quite foreign to those who were not intimately involved in the shipping business. Good knowledge and trust between owners and masters and their agents was essential, and if this relationship failed then there was recourse through the law. Women did not shy away from such action, and an early example in the seventeenth century was Elizabeth Page who took the master and fellow shareowner of her ship the *Content* to court over financial misdealings.[49] For those women who invested in ships or ran maritime businesses, it was a very different environment compared to that of the average business investor in such areas as railways or joint stock companies.

---

[46] CRO: MSR FOW 8.
[47] CRO: MSR FOW/5/6/8.
[48] W. Mitchell, ed., *Maritime Notes and Queries* (London, 1881).
[49] Bronwen Cook, '"A True, Faire and Just Account": Charles Huggett and the Content of Maldon in the English Shipping Trade, 1679–1684', *Journal of Transport History*, 26 (2005), 1–18.

The Financial Environment

There were, of course, other investment opportunities, although limited liability companies were not legally established until mid-century. In March 1801 the London Stock Exchange formally came into existence and the first industrial shares were quoted in 1811.[50] The investment market in the nineteenth century was not very efficient and research has shown that investors did not switch smoothly and easily from one type of investment to another in order to maximise their profits. The market 'remained strongly segmented, both geographically and functionally, down to the end of the nineteenth century and there was no easy route for such redirection of funds'.[51]

The opportunities for the investor with a small amount of capital were limited in the early part of the period. The Bubble Act of 1720 still prohibited the formation of joint stock companies except in a few cases approved by Parliament. Partnerships were the way in which ventures were financed and these meant unlimited liability for the partners involved. The canals and railways offered investment opportunities and women certainly were among the shareholders, but there were distinct differences between railway and canal investors. Investors in canal shares did not then proceed to invest in railway shares. Canal share buyers and sellers retained a 'strongly local investor base at the same time that railway companies were drawing investors from a wide geographical area'.[52] In the latter case, few investors can have had any intimate knowledge of the venture.

Pressure was brought to bear by speculation in mining ventures in the 1820s when 'peers, bankers, merchants and others with large investable funds' ignored the Bubble Act and invested in unincorporated joint stock ventures, and this led to the repeal of the Bubble Act in 1825. Gradual reforms improved the position of joint stock companies, but it was not until 1855 that limited liability was granted and the 1856 Joint Stock Companies Act laid the foundations for the joint stock boom.[53]

Women's economic influence and, in particular, their investment activities during the eighteenth and nineteenth centuries have increasingly been recognised by historians.[54] Women investors played an important part in companies that provided gasworks, waterworks, railways and tramways.[55] Similarly in Glasgow

---

[50] Mary Poovey, ed., *The Financial System in Nineteenth Century Britain* (Oxford: Oxford University Press, 2003), p. 14.

[51] Roger Burt, 'Segmented Capital Markets and Patterns of Investment in Late Victorian Britain: Evidence from the Non-Ferrous Mining Industry', *Economic History Review*, 51 (1998), 709–33 (p. 709).

[52] Sarah J. Hudson, 'Attitudes to Investment Risk Amongst West Midland Canal and Railway Company Investors, 1700–1850' (unpublished doctoral thesis, University of Warwick, 2001), p. 169.

[53] R. Burt, *The British Lead Mining Industry* (Redruth, 1984), pp. 84–5.

[54] Sharpe, 'Continuity and Change', p. 363.

[55] Morris, 'The Reform of the Married Women's Property Act 1870', p. 182.

women were major investors in railways and their funds supported family firms.[56] They invested in Bank of England stock and in other banks.[57] By the end of the century the percentage of women investors in a range of limited companies was increasing.[58]

While legislation to encourage company formation and increase joint stock companies and limited liability did not arrive until mid-century, there were two types of investment that already had some of the advantages of joint stock and limited liability and which pre-dated the Bubble Act and were unaffected by it. Mining and shipping investments were not part of the normal legislation since mining had its origins in the Stannary Laws and shipping had its origins in maritime law.

Mining, particularly Cornish mines, used what was known as the cost book system. Calls on capital potentially could be limitless and the shares could be transacted freely. The most productive mines tended to remain as cost book organisations and a significant number of shares were held by local wealthy families, many of whom were involved in banking. The capital was raised 'mainly from those with a direct involvement in mining – mineral owners, metal merchants, tradesmen, and mine supply merchants, as well as the occasional successful working miner'.[59] There were women investors in mining, but they, too, were members of the local and affluent upper middle class.[60] In mining, funds were put up by shareholders, known as Adventurers. A purser was appointed to keep an eye on the finances, and profits and losses were shared out quarterly. This system meant that little went to invest in the mine. As joint stock ventures took off, the local investors still kept the better productive deposits, these being reserved for local 'in adventurers' while 'out-adventurers' were encouraged to invest in the more speculative ventures.[61] Traditionally there were eight or sixteen shares in a mine, but by a process of subdivision the number gradually became larger, by the early nineteenth century reaching 1,024 shares. The expanding capital needs for mining, particularly deep mining, could increase share numbers up to 6,000 and above.[62]

In a business partnership each partner was fully liable for the actions of the rest, but the mining cost book companies operated a version of limited liability.

---

[56] Eleanor Gordon and Gwyneth Nair, *Public Lives: Women, Family, and Society in Victorian Britain* (New Haven and London: Yale University Press, 2004), p. 197.

[57] Green and Owens, 'Gentlewomanly Capitalism?'; Graeme G. Acheson and John D. Turner, 'The Impact of Limited Liability on Ownership and Control: Irish Banking, 1877–1914', *Economic History Review*, 59 (2006), 320–46 (p. 334).

[58] Maltby and Rutterford, 'She Possessed Her Own Fortune'.

[59] Burt, 'Segmented Capital Markets', pp. 712, 727.

[60] Information from a database on copper mine investors in 1799. I am grateful to Jim Lewis for this information. Jim Lewis, *A Richly Yielding Piece of Ground* (St Austell: Cornish Hillside Publications, 1997).

[61] Burt, 'Segmented Capital Markets', p. 720.

[62] Roger Burt and Norikazu Kudo, 'The Adaptability of the Cornish Cost Book System', *Business History*, 25 (1983), 30–41 (p. 32). See also A. K. Hamilton Jenkin, *The Cornish Miner: An Account of His Life Above and Underground from Early Times* (Launceston: Westcountry Books, 1927).

This 'gave the individual shareholder the opportunity to exercise an import level of control over the scale of liability that he personally committed himself. Some cost book company's rules included a nominal value of each share and limited the claims or calls that could be made up to that value.'[63] Above all, even with such limited protection within the cost book system, the advice to avoid expensive mistakes in this highly risky business was that 'a man must have experience, knowledge, skill and be a local resident or frequent visitor to a mine'.[64]

Investors in shipping had similar freedom to those in mining. An investor, male or female, acquired shares in a vessel through purchase or inheritance and these had to be entered in the registers held in the Customs House of the port to which the ship belonged. Registration in this way had become compulsory under the 1786 Shipping Registration Act.[65] Any subsequent changes of details in owners had to be noted, as some or all of the shares might be sold or further purchases made. While there was no upper limit to the number of investors in a mine, from 1824 the maximum number of shares in a ship was held at sixty-four with a maximum of thirty-two shareholders. Under maritime law shares could be bought, sold, bequeathed, gifted or mortgaged without reference to the other shareholders. Additionally shipowners had a type of limited liability, being only liable for the costs of the vessel, a freedom not available to other shareholders until the 1850s.[66]

Because shipping was limited to a maximum of thirty-two shipowners, increasing costs of new technology such as iron and steam had to be spread among a smaller number of investors. While for much of the nineteenth century the traditional 64th system was maintained, by mid-century the larger investment needs of some vessels were met by limited liability companies. In these cases, where the company owned the ship, the shipping registers simply listed the name of the company as the owner of sixty-four shares and not individual shareowners.

Trading in shares in ships was not via any type of stock exchange, as local owners sold among themselves, and sometimes shipbrokers, bankers, lawyers or accountants might act as intermediaries. While the market increasingly opened up for investors during the nineteenth century, mining, canals and shipping were all supported by local community investors and the experienced investor needed good knowledge to be able to assess the risk involved. Those in the maritime communities who invested in ships were successors to a long tradition. Because of the local nature of shipping investment and the smaller sums of money involved, shipping provided women with investment opportunities throughout the nineteenth century.

[63] Burt and Kudo, 'The Adaptability of the Cornish Cost Book System', p. 34.
[64] Burt, 'Segmented Capital Markets', p. 722.
[65] 26 Geo III, c.60.
[66] David J. Starkey, 'Ownership Structures in the British Shipping Industry: The Case of Hull, 1820–1916', *International Journal of Maritime History*, 8 (1996), 71–95 (pp. 78–79)

Attitudes to Women and Women in Business
from Contemporary Literature

For the historian, one method of assessing attitudes is to consider the views expressed by contemporary publications. The difficulty is that nineteenth-century readers could find a variety of possible models of gender roles in popular literature, and advice books gave a wide range of often bewildering advice to those contemplating investments. Women were particularly targeted during the Evangelical revival of the early nineteenth century.[67] Feminists used literature as a method of disseminating their views; the radical Unitarians agreed with both utilitarians and chartists that literature might perform both a social and a political function. In the early nineteenth century these feminists attempted to inspire their readership by highlighting their perspective of the position of contemporary women and showing modern images of female potential. In their view, literature and literary conventions were particular culprits in distorting the true image of women and their nature.[68] Alongside that came increasing emphasis on the 'moral importance of women's domestic role'.[69]

Fiction could be used effectively, but provided contrasting images. Mary Leman Grimstone wrote stories to show that women were 'either spoilt like children or required to respond with unquestioning submission'. She described one of her fictional heroines as 'of a class of woman who say little for themselves, and for whom little can be said'. All too often, it was argued, this was due to their lack of education.[70] Dickens's heroine, Dora, in *David Copperfield* (1850), is such an example, but in the same book is David's formidable aunt, Betsey Trotwood, a woman of strong views and independent mind. She had been married, but the marriage had not been a happy one and so she had separated from her husband and gone back to her maiden name. Yet she was not totally free of her husband who came back to demand more money from her. Aunt Betsey is also the cause of her own financial downfall. 'She thought she was wiser now than her man of business'[71] and put her money into mining and banking and lost it all, although she retained her house from which she was able to derive a rent. Similarly a key character in *Cranford*, published in 1853, loses all her money in a bank in which she had unlimited liability shares.[72] These fictional examples highlighted the dangers of investing without good knowledge or advice.

Many novelists, such as Dickens, Eliot and Collins, used the last will and testament, and financial crises, as important sources of tension in their tales, but, as

---

[67] Shoemaker, *Gender in English Society*, pp. 31, 38.
[68] Kathryn Gleadle, *The Early Feminists: Radical Unitarians and the Emergence of the Women's Rights Movement, 1831–51* (Basingstoke: Palgrave, 1995), p. 55.
[69] Shoemaker, *Gender in English Society*, p. 32.
[70] Gleadle, *The Early Feminists*, pp. 58–9.
[71] C. Dickens, *David Copperfield*, http://www.dickens-literature.com/David_Copperfield/35.html (accessed 12 August 2006), p. 512.
[72] Rutterford and Maltby, 'The Widow, the Clergyman and the Reckless', p. 120.

has been pointed out, these were not reflections of what was happening in the middle classes, 'in fact they were usually an account of how NOT to behave'.[73] Novels also provided role models, such as those of George Sand who provided new types of heroine. Edmée was the embodiment of intellect and sensibility and Marcelle Blanchemont was a woman with 'shrewd business acumen, great heroism and physical strength'.[74]

There is one contemporary novel that features a maritime woman of business, *The Widow Woman*, written by Charles Lee and published in 1896. Even at this late stage, after real emancipation in legal terms for married women and the opening up of the investment market in general, its view of a woman who held substantial property within a small fishing community is far from flattering. The widow is depicted as a woman living on her own, courted by three suitors who are mainly interested in her property. This is highlighted by the description of the widow, who is aged forty-three and, 'As for her appearance, she was large and very fat; and, to tell the truth and have done with it, her swarthy face was adorned with an emphatic moustache, and traces, less decided but still noticeable, of a beard'.[75] Her ownership of a fishing boat, a barking house and five cottages was what made her attractive to her suitors. She is shown as a woman of strong character who managed her interests effectively and in a markedly different way from other boat owners, as the description of the weekly payout to the shareholders in her venture displays.

> Elsewhere the shares were set out in heaps on the kitchen mantelpiece and those who want their money drop in when they like and help themselves. But Mrs Pollard had notions of order and regularity. She constituted the weekly paying off into a kind of Admiralty Court which all the crew were expected to attend. On these occasions a rough balance sheet was read out, repairs and provisioning were discussed, complaints made and all the affairs of the boat gone into generally. Much waste and grumbling and petty intrigue was hereby avoided; how much was only known to other boat owners, who looked on with envy, but never attempted imitation knowing it took a person of Mrs Pollard's rare determination to work successfully such a plan so foreign to Pendannack's dilatory, haphazard business methods.[76]

As a role model, Mrs Pollard may not have been physically attractive, but she reflects an independence of spirit and a management ability that was present in maritime communities.

There were plenty of books giving advice or indicating the right way to behave. William Cobbet's *Cottage Economy* (1822) was written for lower-class audiences and placed women firmly in the home, but nonetheless, in his expectation that

73 Morris, *Men, Women and Property*, pp. 88–90.
74 Gleadle, *The Early Feminists*, pp. 61–2.
75 Charles Lee, *The Widow Woman: A Cornish Tale* (London: Dent & Sons, 1896), p. 10.
76 Lee, *The Widow Woman*, p. 28.

the wife would manage all the details of running the household and its finances, Cobbet gave lower-class women somewhat more substantial responsibilities than their middle-class counterparts.[77] Earlier than Cobbet, Hudson wrote a school-book published in 1786 with the aim of introducing the 'Youth of both Sexes' to the types of business letters, receipts and invoices that they might encounter in business. It included promissory notes, salary and wages, dividends received from a bankrupt, money received in a partnership and bills of exchange, together with arithmetical tables of weights and measures and a glossary of business terms.[78] A young woman educated in this way was well prepared for the task of business management.

More specifically there was financial advice directed straight at women such as that written by 'A Banker's Daughter'. This was published in 1864 and its title was *A Guide to the Unprotected in Everyday Matters relating to Property and Income*.[79] The Banker's Daughter advised her readers on a wide range of matters from how to keep simple accounts to handling cheques, promissory notes, shares, loans and mortgages. There was general advice on investment, but shipping was not mentioned as a category, possibly because this did not attract the same type of widely speculative fever that mining, railways and banking did. Or more probably, it was seen as an essentially specialised type of investment. With regard to the purchase of Consuls via a broker the advice was that 'you must go with him (even though you are a lady) to the transfer office in the Bank of England'. And there were strong words on the protection afforded by marriage settlements: 'No prudent woman should marry without this provision.'[80]

On mortgages, the advice was again straightforward. The use of a lawyer was important to ensure that the applicant had proper title to the property in question. Some of the advice hinted that the author had witnessed some less than happy situations, personally or otherwise.

> Lending on mortgage requires great caution as to the character of the person borrowing. Unsuspecting persons have often been victimised when all has previously appeared properly done ... It may be suggested that a Lawyer should see to this. But, in practice, it often happens to Ladies to be quite indignant at the suggestion of their Lawyer, as to the substantial character of Mr B., who may be a personal friend or a connection of the deceased husband, and has attracted her partisanship by means of a persuasive tongue.[81]

---

77 Shoemaker, *Gender in English Society*, p. 36.

78 Peter Hudson, 'A New Introduction to Trade and Business: Very Useful for the Youth of Both Sexes' (London: Johnson, 1786), Eighteenth Century Collections Online, http://galenet. galegroup.com/servlet/ECCO?locID= exeter (accessed 12 June 2006).

79 A Banker's Daughter, 'Guide to the Unprotected in Everyday Matters Relating to Property and Income' (1864), www.indiana.edu/~letrs/vwwp/anon/unprotected.html (accessed 26 May 2004).

80 Banker's Daughter, 'Guide to the Unprotected', pp. 9–12, 74.

81 Banker's Daughter, 'Guide to the Unprotected', pp. 99–109.

The Banker's Daughter did not see any legal or social barrier to a woman becoming a director of a business, merely warning against their name being used unless 'you attend personally to it, or you may be liable, by the acts of others, to lose the whole of your property. You also mislead, by making the public fancy you attend to the concern.'[82]

The Banker's Daughter was writing advice for women who had access to ample funds. Bessie Rayner Parkes, a contemporary, saw lack of money as a major obstacle in the path of the middle-class woman who did not want to be a governess. Parkes criticised the fathers who left their daughters without independent means and called for them to settle more on their daughters as well as their sons.[83]

> If a girl were taught how to make capital reproductive, instead of merely how to live upon its *interest*, a much less sum would suffice her; and the father who gave or left her a thousand pounds would bestow upon her a benefit of which he could not calculate the result, instead of the miserable pittance of thirty or at most 50 pounds a year.[84]

The origin of the separate spheres theory has been traced back to the historians who had formed this view from didactic and complaint literature. It has been pointed out that there can be a difference between conventional lip service and unconventional behaviour, that there was no proof 'that the majority of women in comfortable households had no engagement with the world outside their front door' and that there was a difference between 'what a woman was told to do, what she thought she was doing and what she actually did'.[85] Maritime women may have officially espoused the middle-class concept of the woman's place at home, but their actions as shipowners and women managing 'male' businesses such as shipbuilding were direct contradictions.

Summary

Common law, with its apparent restrictions for married women, did not restrict those men or women who were capable of using other forms of law to suit their purpose. From 1786, when the Registration Act was introduced ensuring all share-owners in shipping had clear and legal title to their shares, to 1882, when married women finally were given full access to their independent estate, the legal environment changed considerably. Before the first Married Women's Property Act in 1870, married women were not held back from holding shares in ships despite the restrictions of the legal system. Trusts are often seen as tools used only by the more wealthy members of society and mainly by men who wished to control or

---

[82] Banker's Daughter, 'Guide to the Unprotected', p. 36.
[83] Parkes, *Essays on Woman's Work*, pp. 142–3.
[84] Parkes, *Essays on Woman's Work*, p. 146.
[85] Vickery, 'Golden Age to Separate Spheres?', pp. 301–2, 407.

protect their dependants. At all levels trusts were used by both men and women to achieve their aims. Neither were all trusts in place for ever; women were capable of dispensing with trustees and in turn trustees were able to be rid of an additional burden or simply to refuse to take it up. The best laid plans of testators were not always realised.

Not all situations went to court; cases could be settled out of court and legal cases are but a tiny fraction of the many transactions that were carried out without any reference to 'formal rules and common or statute law'.[86] Legal advice could be expensive and variable, and lawyers in small ports were likely to specialise in what brought them the greatest business: shipping, customs and excise and wills. So the niceties of some aspects of common, equity and ecclesiastical law are not likely to have been understood or adhered to.

The financial environment changed throughout the period and offered new opportunities for investors in a wide range of business ventures. However in the maritime world, over the centuries men and women invested directly in ships and trade, a situation permissible under maritime law and encouraged by the local nature of the investments. Shipping was a complex subject and good and trusted connections were essential. The industry had evolved over centuries to take into account the peculiar nature of maritime investments, shared property ownership of a moveable asset and trade that had to be managed at a distance with a variety of languages, customs and local laws. It was a very different investment world from that which featured in the advice from the Banker's Daughter.

The advice literature of the period was contradictory, attempting to protect on the one hand while educating on the other. The fictional images showed women of determination, but also as victims of financial disasters that were either self-inflicted from unwise investment or the result of fraud. These conflicting views of advisers and the fictional images of women seem to have had little impact on the actual conduct of the businesswomen and investors. If a woman was capable of selecting which legal system gave the best advantage in a given situation, then she could also decide whether to follow or ignore advisers and role models.

---

[86] Phillips, *Women in Business*, p. 50.

2

Maritime Communities

Nineteenth-century maritime Britain was an expanding sector of the economy. Ports around the coast handled an increasing amount of incoming and outgoing trade and port facilities were improved to attract more business. British ships sailed around the world linking countries and continents and remained dominant in international trade during the period. The coastal and short sea trades also employed large numbers of men and vessels plying shorter, less glamorous, but essential routes. As the gateway to Britain's industrial might the ports were required to handle ever greater volumes of goods, and intensive railway building between 1840 and 1860 transformed the distribution of raw materials and manufactured goods.[1] Shipbuilding activity increased and, while wooden sailing vessels were still built throughout the century, steam and iron gradually began to dominate the shipyards. By the end of the nineteenth century British ships carried half the world's trade and Britain built two-thirds of the world's ships.[2] Men and their families moved to those areas where work was available either in shore-based businesses or at sea.

Around the coast of England and Wales by 1871 there were eighty-four registry ports for shipping with a combined total of over twenty thousand ships and nearly four and a half million tons, of which two and a half million tons were registered in London and Liverpool. The other two million tons of shipping were spread around the rest of the ports. In all ports the sailing ship was still the largest category. Despite the advance of steam and iron, the locally owned wooden sailing vessel remained an important part of Britain's merchant fleet until the 1880s, as it could still compete effectively in many trades. Wooden vessels were relatively cheap to build and they continued to provide opportunities for local communities of investors and businesses. In 1879 sail still accounted for 63 per cent of the tonnage in the United Kingdom, 82 per cent of the number of ships registered and 60 per cent of the men employed in merchant shipping.[3]

[1]   T. R. Gourvish, 'Railways 1830–70: The Formative Years', in *Transport in Victorian Britain*, ed. Michael J. Freeman and Derek H. Aldcroft (Manchester: Manchester University Press, 1988), pp. 57–91 (p. 58).

[2]   David M. Williams, 'Introduction', in *The World of Shipping*, ed. David M. Williams (Aldershot: Ashgate, 1997).

[3]   British Parliamentary Papers (BPP) 1880 LXV: Tables of number of sailing and steam vessels belonging to United Kingdom and on register 1869–79.

2. Fowey Harbour in the 1860s

Source: Author

It is the speed of the investment in shipping in some of the smallest ports between 1829 and 1870 that is remarkable. Relative to steam and iron the wooden sailing ship was cheap to buy and the expansion of local investment in tonnage from the end of the Napoleonic wars was rapid. In England tonnage doubled in a generation; in Cornwall it expanded at a faster rate than its neighbour, Devon. The Isles of Scilly embraced the opportunity after the demise of their trade in kelp. Shipping registration went up by a factor of eight and most of it was in ships over fifty tons, suitable for foreign trade.[4]

These ports with their shipowning and mariner communities were lively and exciting places with the constant change of ships and men, the influx of foreign goods, the visitors and the contact with other countries. But from the 1870s steam and iron ships were increasing the pressure on the traditional sailing trade routes. The larger and more complex ships had greater needs for capital and in a world which was shrinking, through regular steam routes and the arrival of the telegraph, came new ways of doing business. Limited liability companies began to own ships and spread ownership in different ways to a wider range of people who were distanced from the everyday operation. A series of Merchant Shipping Acts and other legislative changes increased the regulatory pressure on shipowners and merchants. Throughout all of this, women invested in the sailing ships, female managing owners grappled with the changing legislation, and women running shipbuilding yards, ropewalks and sailmaking lofts experienced the changing competitive scene. Some smaller businesses survived, some disappeared and others gave way to large companies owning and running fleets of vessels, vast shipyards and factories.

The merchant and trading communities of large ports have been researched, notably Liverpool and the leading northeast ports and some shipping investors in London.[5] Small ports and small businesses are often overlooked, yet they played an important role in the logistics chain across the country, acting as feeders to the larger ports and suppliers to the bigger businesses. The research on Salem considered the community on shore as well as the men at sea and was welcomed as an important addition to the historiography.[6] One reviewer commented that 'the prevailing approach has usually been to isolate the professional lives of the men (or in one case, women) who went to sea'.[7] The result, he argued, has been

---

4   BPP 1830 XXVII: Return of Number of Ships belonging to Ports in United Kingdom, 1829; BPP 1871 LXI: Return of Number of Sailing and Steam vessels registered at each Port of Great Britain and Ireland, 1870.
5   Gordon Boyce, *Information, Mediation and Institutional Development: The Rise of Large-Scale Enterprise in British Shipping, 1870–1919* (Manchester: Manchester University Press, 1995); Graeme Milne, *Trade and Traders in Mid-Victorian Liverpool: Mercantile Business and the Making of a World Port* (Liverpool: Liverpool University Press, 2000); Palmer, 'Investors in London Shipping', *Maritime History*, 2 (1972), 46–68.
6   Vickers, *Young Men and the Sea*.
7   N. A. M. Rodger, 'Roundtable Discussion of Daniel Vickers and Vince Walsh "Young Men and the Sea"', *International Journal of Maritime History*, 17 (2005), 336–41 (p. 336).

to 'reinforce the invisibility of the female half of the maritime community'.[8] This artificial division between the ships and the shore not only isolates the women in the community, but also the shore-based functions, managed by men or women, without which no ship or seaman could remain afloat.

Maritime Communities

Communities can be complex to define and the term is used here in a mainly geographic context where there are shared customs, practices and institutions.[9] These were coastal communities with one dominant industry, shipping. London and Liverpool were also massive and fast growing urban cities with a wide range of industries. In these large ports the maritime communities, which included shipbuilding, warehousing, sailmaking, brokerage and other trades, were clustered around the dock areas. The merchants and shipowners were more dispersed and they tended to live more distant from the dock areas and be involved in other ventures. The type of sailor town depicted in eastern Canada in ports such as Halifax was more typical of large ports rather than the small seaports with family interconnections between shipbuilders, shipowners, merchants, masters and men.[10] In the smaller seaports the majority of people involved in the shipping industry in all its branches were living in the community within sight and sound of the sea and their ships. These were people involved in trade, both the very large and important coastal trade and foreign trade.

When such small coastal communities are considered in Britain, more often than not it is the fishing rather than the mariner community.[11] Fishing communities differed from mariner communities, as the absence of the fishermen, depending on the type of fishing, could be on a daily rather than a monthly basis and their vessels were much smaller. There have been no detailed studies of British mariner communities, although there have been some studies of the trade and shipping in Welsh communities and one book on the shipping of Fowey.[12]

---

8   Rodger, 'Roundtable Discussion of "Young Men and the Sea"' p. 337.
9   Dennis Mills, 'Defining Community: A Critical View of Community', *Family & Community History*, 7 (2004), 5–12; Bernard Deacon and Moira Donald, 'In Search of Community History', *Family & Community History*, 7 (2004), 13–18; Hanna Hagmark, 'Women in Maritime Communities: A Socio-Historical Study of Continuity and Change in the Domestic Lives of Seafarers' Wives in the Aland Islands, from 1930 into the New Millennium' (unpublished doctoral thesis, University of Hull, 2003); John K. Walton, 'Fishing Communities, 1850–1950', in *England's Sea Fisheries: The Commercial Fisheries of England and Wales since 1300*, ed. David J. Starkey, Chris Reid and Neil Ashcroft (London: Chatham Publishing, 2000), pp. 127–37.
10   Judith Fingard, *Jack in Port: Sailor Towns in Eastern Canada* (Toronto: University of Toronto Press, 1982).
11   Jane Nadel-Klein and Dona Lee Davis, eds, *To Work and to Weep: Women in Fishing Economies* (St John's, Newfoundland, 1988); Thompson, 'Women in Fishing'; Walton, 'Fishing Communities'.
12   R. Craig, *British Tramp Shipping, 1750–1914* (St.John's, Newfoundland, 2003). Aled Eames, *Ventures in Sail* (Denbigh, 1987); Ward-Jackson, *Ships and Shipbuilders*.

Livelihoods in the seaports depended on deep sea and coastal sailing trades. Ships traded out of Whitehaven on the northwest coast of Cumberland, Whitby on the edge of the Yorkshire moors in the northeast, Appledore in the north of Devon and, in Cornwall, Fowey in the south and Padstow on the north coast. Ships left these places to sail to many parts of the globe, carrying freight or passengers or both. Such places once inhabited by mariners, shipbuilders, sailmakers, block-makers and their families are now, in the twenty-first century, largely picturesque harbours concentrating on leisure and tourism. In the nineteenth century these seaport communities not only looked different from inland villages and market towns, but sounded and even smelt different, as has been evocatively described:

> The small sailing ship and industries required to support them, sail and spar making, ropewalks, repair grids below the tideline, shipchandlery and carpentry, gave the seaport towns their characteristic quality, for in those days the smells and feelings of a small seaport were quite different from those of the inland market towns. There were seasoned baulks of timber cut at the sawpits to give forth a rich, sweet scent, which mingled with the pervasive riggers tar at the quaysides, and salt, the salt wind that still blows around the empty quays today, tar from rigging and from the blackened wooden hulls, oil for the tanning of the brown sails, mud from a hundred harbours in the chain locker, all combining to make the smells of small seaport communities. And the sounds were those of the seaboard, the screaming of straining blocks, the chanting of yard crews and seamen about their work, and the musical clanking of mallets on caulking irons at the building slips and on the grids when the tide was low.[13]

The focus of the seaport community was literally the sea. All roads and lanes led to the quayside and, if inland the village green or town square was the place to gather, in these communities it was the town quay, where gossip and information were exchanged and vessels observed. Shipyards and associated businesses were right by the water's edge and in some places such as Polruan, Fowey and Apple-dore this was also where the ferry plied its trade. This made these areas natural gathering places for all members of the community.

This maritime dimension has defined the location and shape of the coastal communities. This was a world where in some respects the maritime-based community had more in common with a similar community across the sea than with their inland agricultural or mining neighbours. The technical vocabulary of the mariner's world and shipowner's world was totally foreign to the landsman. It might seem that these communities had a way of life, a language, a structure and a culture that set them apart. They were not wholly cut off from rural life, however, as many of these communities were also still rooted in the land. Farmers formed part of all the communities, if on the edge. Maritime families had links

---

[13] Basil Greenhill, *The Merchant Schooners* (London: Conway, 1988), p. 1.

with inland villages and in counties such as Norfolk the farmers were significant shareholders in the ships that carried their corn.[14]

Opportunities

Ports gained and lost trade and this variation over the period will be considered in more detail in a later chapter. Here, in relation to the communities, it is worth noting that overall the seaports for much of the nineteenth century were gaining from trade. Ports could increase their business by developing better facilities for the speedy handling of cargoes, and by developing good links with the hinterland for speedy redistribution of goods and carriage of goods or minerals for export. A thriving and busy port attracted men and women to share in its growth.

Men were attracted to these ports as they offered employment opportunities both on shore and at sea, and some small communities grew rapidly in size, attracting men and their families from other areas. When the new Warkworth harbour was created at the entrance to the Coquet River in Northumberland in the 1830s it heralded a boom time for the small communities of Amble and Alnmouth – over 170 sailing vessels were owned locally of an average size of 200 tons. Amble grew from a population of 247 in 1831 to well over 2,000 by 1891, all based on the coal exports. Ships were built there and the local community were regular investors.[15]

For the mariner, while it was a physically tough and demanding life, there was always the potential to become a master mariner and perhaps to become a master/owner or, for the very ambitious, to own a fleet of vessels. This was achievable and, in the expanding shipping industry, there were plenty of examples of those who had achieved such heights. The essential starting point was a basic education and a good knowledge of navigation.

A crew member learnt on the job from his colleagues, but he needed more than this if he had ambitions of becoming master of his own vessel. There is a difference between 'seamanship', the day-to-day activities of ship handling that were the critical skills for the seaman, and 'navigation', getting the vessel to a place. The former did not require reading or writing skills, but for the keen sailor education was needed on navigation. There were private teachers of navigation and sometimes public lectures. One woman who was much appreciated by her pupils was Mrs Mitchell. The *Royal Cornwall Gazette* of 1809 published the following notice:

> Died at Polruan, near Fowey, aged 83, Mrs. Mitchell, sixty years schoolmistress in
> that neighbourhood; having taught three generations reading, writing and arith-

---

[14] M. Stammers, 'Shipowners in Rural British Ports in the 19th Century: A Study of North Norfolk Ports' (n.d.), unpublished paper, cited with permission.
[15] Richard E. Keys, *The Sailing Ships of Aln and Coquet* (Newcastle: Author, 1993), pp. 2, 22, 91.

metic, among whom are many masters of vessels, who owe their nautical arithmetic to her.[16]

For mariners and their families there were many opportunities to progress. Before 1850 there were no formal qualifications; a master was appointed by the owner on the basis of his experience at sea. In 1845 the Board of Trade authorised a system of voluntary examinations of competency for men intending to become masters or mates of foreign-going British merchant ships, but it was not made compulsory until the Mercantile Marine Act of 1850. Four years later it was extended to masters and mates of home trade vessels (those in the coastal trades) by the Merchant Shipping Act of 1854. A master's or mate's certificate of competency was issued to each man who passed the examination. Men who were considered by the examiners to have sufficient experience as a master or mate were eligible, without formal examination, for certificates of service.[17] The certificates granted to a master mariner were highly prized. The status of Master Mariner together with a good reputation could take a man anywhere in the world and opened up new possibilities including the opportunity to create wealth.

Mariners were very well placed to benefit from a good career. A man could work his way up through the stages of seamanship until eventually he became the master. The next step was to gain a share in the vessel. Masters were very often also minor shareowners since the view was that the master who was not just a salaried employee, but was also a shareholder, had greater concern both for the vessel and cargo. The careful master could also do some trading on his own behalf in order to build up a retirement fund. Often they were given a percentage commission on the value of the homeward freight: 'this enabled them to make the progression from master to owner'.[18] In Appledore, Whitby, Polruan, Fowey and Robin Hood's Bay new and imposing houses were built by the retired master mariners to which they could retreat while still keeping an eye on their shipping investments. An observer of maritime communities in the early twentieth century, and who lived in both Fowey and Robin Hood's Bay, near Whitby, described this upward mobility in a fictional story of Bramblewick, which was based on Robin Hood's Bay. 'The families that made money in commercial shipping (into which they moved from the narrower horizons of the local fisheries) left the old village by the shore and moved "Up Bank" to new brick villas which became the badge of success and differentiation.'[19] For the prospective wives of ambitious mariners a cosy future beckoned.

---

[16] Isobel Pickering, *Some Goings On! A Selection of Newspaper Articles about Fowey, Polruan and Lanteglos Districts from 1800–1899* (Fowey: Author, 1985), p. 28.

[17] Alston Kennerley, 'Navigation Schools and Training Ships: Educational Provision in Plymouth for the Mercantile Marine in the Nineteenth Century', in *West Country Maritime and Social History: Some Essays*, ed. Stephen Fisher (Exeter: Exeter University 1980), pp. 53–78.

[18] Robin Craig, 'Printed Guides for Master Mariners as a Source of Productivity Change in Shipping, 1750–1914' in Craig, *British Tramp Shipping: 1750–1914*, pp. 121–36 (p. 123).

[19] Walton, 'Fishing Communities', p. 131.

Polruan in Cornwall and Appledore in Devon were typical mariner communities where almost every man was closely linked to the shipping industry. In Appledore in 1851, 46 per cent of the households were headed by a mariner, master mariner or a related category, and in Polruan, in the town itself, the figure was 55 per cent (Table 1).

Table 1. Maritime Occupations in 1851 (heads of household only)

Polruan	183 households	Appledore	483 households
Occupation	*Number*	*Occupation*	*Number*
Mariners	18	Mariners	34
Mariners' wives, widows, daughters	30	Mariners' wives, widows, daughters	99
Master mariners	7	Master mariners	12
MM's wives, widows	6	MM's wives, widows	24
Blacksmiths	9	Ship carpenters	9
Shipwrights	6	Shipwrights	7
Fishermen	5	Blacksmith	6
Ferrymen/boatmen	4	Fishermen	6
Shipbuilders	4	Ferrymen	6
Bargemen	3	Tidewaiters/Customs	5
Pilots	3	Blockmaker	4
Ship carpenters	3	Ropemakers	3
Sailmakers	2	Shipbuilders	3
Harbour master	1	Boat builder	1
		Sailmakers	2
		Shipowners	2
		Ship inspector	1
	101 (55%)		224 (46%)

Source: D. Carter: Transcript and Index for Census Enumerators' Books Appledore, Devon 1851; Cornwall Business Systems: The 1851 Census of Cornwall (CD-ROM 2000).

Port Businesses

There were many other job opportunities; as the ports grew so did the range of shore-based jobs among the myriad of other support functions. For every ship that put to sea there was a range of shore-based occupations from shipbuilders, sailmakers, blockmakers, ropemakers and chandlers to shipping agents, owners and insurance agents. For every ship that unloaded there was another range of occupations from brokers and merchants to dock labourers and warehousemen. Many men started their career at sea and then moved into shore-based jobs requiring good sea knowledge. For example, sailmakers were often ex-sailors. The mid-nineteenth-century trade directories listed a wide number of maritime occupations (see Appendix II). What are missing from these directories are the many labouring jobs and other specialist occupations such as sawyers and bargemen. Important parts of the local economy were grocers, butchers and inns which provided victualling for the ships. Additionally the inns also acted as places to find work, buy shares in ships and exchange information. Those in the shore-based businesses were well placed to use their knowledge to acquire shares in ships. These ancillary trades and the opportunities they offered for women will be considered in Chapter 7.

There were plenty of success stories and every local community could point to an example of a local man who had created an impressive business. The Holman family of shipbuilders, and subsequently a major insurance firm, started with two brothers, Thomas and John, who were master mariners and shipowners.[20] The Turnbulls, later to be Turnbull Scott and Company, a major shipping firm, began in Whitby with the purchase in 1817 of the 78-ton sloop *Yarm*. It was bought by Thomas Turnbull, a clockmaker, his brother John, a block and mast maker, and their partner William Hunton.[21] Both Holman and Turnbull later expanded to offices in London, but both kept a local base in their original communities. In Whitehaven, a local butcher, William Burnyeat, became a victualler to shipping and held a portfolio of shares in ships. The company he built up also became a major national company, eventually moving to Liverpool.[22] For every success story there was a wife and a family who shared in that success, but there were also disadvantages and significant risks.

Communities of Women

The most distinctive feature of these communities is demographic. With many men at sea for long periods, maritime communities had a higher number of women who were enumerated as the head of the household in the 1851 census. The smaller coastal communities were of two types, the fishing or the mariner community. The occupation of the men in fishing communities such as Polperro, Padstow, Looe and Mevagissey in Cornwall was largely as day fishermen, with a smaller number involved in long distance fishing. Mariner communities were those with high numbers of merchant mariners, such as Fowey and Polruan

---

[20] R. Craig, B. Greenhill, J. H. Porter and W. J. Slade, 'Some Aspects of the Business of Devon Shipping in the Nineteenth Century', in *A New Maritime History of Devon, Vol. II From the Late Eighteenth Century to the Present Day*, ed. M. Duffy et al. (London, 1994), pp. 99–107 (p. 100).

[21] Anne and Russell Long, *A Shipping Venture: Turnbull Scott and Company, 1872–1972* (London: Hutchinson Benham, 1974), p. 13.

[22] L. T. C. Rolt, *Mariners' Market: Burnyeat Limited, Growth over a Century* (Liverpool: Newman Neame, 1961).

in Cornwall, Appledore in Devon, Whitehaven in Cumberland and Whitby in North Yorkshire.

All the coastal communities in 1851 had a very high ratio of females to males heading households, as can be seen in Table 2, and Polruan and Appledore were significantly different. Women constituted one-third to one-half of the heads of household in maritime communities. These figures reflect the absence of men at sea. The communities of both Polruan and Appledore were dominated by mariners and master mariners, many of whom were in the trade to the West Indies and North America. The vessels on which they served may have been locally owned and manned, but the trades in which they were working took them to many other places across the world.

Table 2. Heads of household in selected villages, 1851 (ranked by % of women)

	Type	Male	Female	Total	% female
Padstow	Fishing	344	120	464	26%
Whitby	Mariner	1,755	727	2,482	29%
Looe	Fishing	155	68	223	30%
Mevagissey	Fishing	329	151	480	31%
Whitehaven	Mariner	1,941	924	2,865	32%
Fowey	Mariner	241	123	354	35%
Polperro	Fishing	96	57	153	37%
Polruan	Mariner	112	71	183	39%
Appledore	Mariner	239	244	483	51%

Source: R. Barker, Extract of Statistics Census Enumerators' Books from Whitby, Yorkshire 1851; D. Carter, Transcript and Index for Census Enumerators' Books Appledore, Devon 1851; Cornwall Business Systems, The 1851 Census of Cornwall (CD-ROM 2000); Cumbria Family History Society, Transcript and Index for Census Enumerators' Books Whitehaven, Cumbria 1851.

The marital status of the female heads of household is shown in Table 3. As expected, the maritime communities, on the whole, had a high percentage of married women whose husbands were at sea. Not surprisingly, Polruan and Appledore have the highest percentage of wives whose husbands are at sea. Padstow had a slightly lower percentage of married women as household heads, but the census data for Padstow also include several very small rural communities within its immediate hinterland. Here 17 per cent of the heads of household were in agriculture and 30 per cent were in occupations directly linked to maritime industry. Spinsters are more evident in maritime communities, again reflecting the fact that there were fewer young men at home in the community. A disadvantage for women of marriageable age in a coastal community was that the well travelled mariner had a wider pool of potential spouses to choose from.

It might be assumed that widowed households were a major feature of maritime communities. The loss of men in accidents at sea was a regular subject for some Victorian painters, such as Walter Langley's *Disaster Scene in a Cornish Fishing Village*, painted in 1889, and *Never Morning Wore to Evening but Some Heart Did Break*, painted in 1893.[23] Langley was a member of the famous Newlyn school of painters; he lived in Penzance where he had ample opportunity to paint the fishing scenes. Many of his paintings reflect loss at sea and the pain suffered by those who wait on shore. Certainly the figures support this higher number of widowed households in the maritime communities.

Table 3. Marital status of female heads of households

	Type	% widowed	% unmarried	% married
Padstow	Fishing	63%	23%	13%
Whitby	Mariner	65%	21%	14%
Polperro	Fishing	59%	18%	23%
Whitehaven	Mariner	55%	16%	30%
Mevagissey	Fishing	56%	11%	32%
Fowey	Mariner	44%	20%	37%
Looe	Fishing	47%	15%	38%
Polruan	Mariner	39%	11%	49%
Appledore	Mariner	38%	9%	53%

Source: As for Table 2.

Official statistics of the period show that being a mariner was indeed a high risk occupation. Lloyd's Marine Casualties were reported in the *Journal of the Statistical Society of London* from 1872. The report for 1878 showed the average per annum loss of life for the previous seven years as 1,850 men. In 1878 alone, 2,867 lives were lost from both steamers and sailing vessels.[24]

It is, however, too simplistic to consider that the risks at sea came from just collision and wreck; there were other causes of death. In the parliamentary report on mortality rates in 1858 the rate for seamen was 19.6 per thousand, causing a comment from George Graham, the Registrar General. 'The mortality among this important body of men is higher than it should be among men of their ages and physical advantage and it is evident that a proper standard of cleanliness, ventilation and good quality of food has not yet been attained.' The reported national mortality rate was 22.6 per thousand, which included people of all ages and deaths

[23] Birmingham Museum and Art Gallery, http://www.bmagic.org.uk/results?s=+langley (accessed 22 April 2006).
[24] 'Lloyds Statistics of Marine Casualties for the Year 1878', *Journal of Statistical Society of London*, 42 (1879), 505–21. This data also includes some foreign vessels insured with Lloyd's.

from infant mortality, disease, childbirth and old age.[25] Graham's concern is clear when the figure is compared with the national figures for men of a similar age (Table 4). The mortality rates for women show that once the child-bearing years were passed mortality rates were much lower than those of men. Late in the lifecycle women's health prospects were better; retired mariners suffered from ill health after a hard physical life with a poor diet often eaten in rough conditions at sea.[26]

Table 4. Mortality rates for men and women, 1858

Age	Males per 1,000	Females per 1,000
0	77.55	68.38
5	10.41	10.19
10	4.92	3.26
15	7.49	8.06
25	8.83	8.75
35	12.2	18.8
45	18.07	13.1
55	81.8	27.58
65	66.48	61.55

Source: British Parliamentary Papers (BPP) 1860 XXIX: Twenty-first Annual Report of the Registrar General of Births, Deaths and Marriages in England and Wales, p. 543.

In Salem, Massachusetts, there was a disproportionate rate of mariner's widows who were acutely impoverished because their households were 'terribly vulnerable to misfortune'.[27] Mortality rates for Salem in the late eighteenth century were very high, 35 to 40 per thousand, a rate that is partially explained by the strong focus of the Salem vessels on the tropical trades where men were more exposed to diseases such as yellow fever.[28]

Because of high mortality rates, it might be supposed that there was a higher number of younger widows in maritime communities, but this does not appear to be the case (see Table 5). While data such as the age of the women are not available for all of the datasets used, the evidence from those examined was inconclusive.

[25] BPP 1860 XXIX: *Twenty-first Annual Report of the Registrar General of Births, Deaths and Marriages in England and Wales*, p. 543.

[26] Conrad Dixon, 'Pound and Pint: Diet in the Merchant Service, 1750–1980', in *Charted and Uncharted Waters* ed. Sarah Palmer and Glyndwr Williams (London: National Maritime Museum, 1981), pp. 164–80.

[27] Vickers, *Young Men and the Sea*, pp. 146–9.

[28] Daniel Vickers, 'A Roundtable Response', *International Journal of Maritime History*, 17 (2005), p. 365.

There is no evidence to suggest that there was a higher number of young widows in maritime populations, either fishing or mariner communities.

Table 5. Average age of female heads of household in selected communities, 1851

	Type	Married	Unmarried	Widowed
Looe	Fishing	36	57	62
Fowey	Mariner	35	48	61
Polperro	Fishing	36	55	61
Padstow	Fishing	41	52	60
Appledore	Mariner	38	57	59
Polruan	Mariner	40	35	56

Source: As for Table 2.

In Salem, while women were considered as more independent, there seems to be limited evidence that wives were more than fleetingly involved in their husband's business affairs, although a high number of widows had to be self-supporting and many were very successful businesswomen.[29] However in England there is some evidence to support the link between demography and a higher number of women in business, though it is but a crude measure since it uses trade directories. A survey of the women in business in trade directories does give some support to a greater number of women running a business in maritime counties (see Appendix III). Caution needs to be exercised in making great claims as Yorkshire is a large county with a substantial agricultural and industrial hinterland while Cornwall, with its very long coastline, is at the bottom of the table. Trade directories are not fully representative of all businesses and remote counties like Cornwall were poorly covered.[30]

The Culture of Maritime Communities

These were communities in which the women had to be more self-reliant – it was part of the role of being married to a mariner. Absences were an accepted part of life in close-knit maritime communities where men were away for large parts of the year. Investigation of the maritime community of the Åland Islands in the Baltic in the twentieth century found a very different way of life for the families. Life was geared around departures and arrivals.

---

[29] Vickers, *Young Men and the Sea*, pp 146–56.
[30] Norton, *Guide to the National and Provincial Directories*.

For all seafarers' wives, however, the impact of the seafarer's work pattern on his family's life was absolute. Most aspects of her life were affected; her work, her social engagements, her ambitions and her opportunities. Her physical as well as emotional life rhythm was influenced by her husband's schedule of work.[31]

From the interviews with seafarers' wives it was concluded that 'they lived two separate lives; one when their partner was at home and one when he was at sea'. Worry was always a factor; despite improved communications in the twentieth century the wife's concern was 'to get her seafaring husband home alive and well'.[32]

Did this constant separation of families engender a sense of independence in seafarers' wives? This seems to be highly debatable and less simple than at first it might appear. In Nantucket there was no strong evidence of independent women in the research on the letters of whaling wives; their letters were full of a sense of longing for their husbands to be home.[33] In contrast, the study of Salem stressed 'an unusual potential for autonomy and dependency among maritime women' – although apparently contradictory these were 'flip sides of the same coin'.[34] In the Åland Islands the emotions for the women were complex. In most cases the women were more independent because they had to be. Even with the advantages of twentieth-century communications, everyday decisions had to be made in the absence of their partner. However, the women did not always see themselves as consciously independent, but merely doing what had to be done.[35]

For the majority of women in the nineteenth-century English seaports there are no extant letters or diaries and no indication of what their views might be. Conclusions must be drawn from the evidence of their actions and elsewhere. They were not apparently held back from running businesses; indeed the views of the men in their lives were supportive in their business enterprises. In the previously mentioned example of Jane Slade, the wills of both her father and her husband were positive indicators of their belief in both her business capability and her inclination to take on additional work.[36] Sarah Barrett's use of a trust to avoid her new husband acquiring her shares and Mary Hoskins handling the administration of her late brother's estate while, presumably, her husband was at sea, are just two examples of the many women who acted as independent economic agents.[37] It would appear that notice also needs to be taken of what the maritime women did, rather than what they said to reassure absent husbands.

---

[31] Hagmark, 'Women in Maritime Communities', p. 208.
[32] *Ibid.*
[33] Norling, *Captain Ahab Had a Wife.*
[34] Vickers, *Young Men and the Sea*, pp. 146–9.
[35] Interviewee G2005 in Hagmark, 'Women in Maritime Communities', p. 218.
[36] BPO: Will of Christopher Slade 1870; Will of William Salt 1871.
[37] Devon Record Office (DRO): MFC 44/18 Exeter Shipping Registers 21/1831 and 50/1826.

Foreign Connections

If all roads in a maritime community led to the sea this was also an important aspect of community life. The sea was not a barrier in the way in which a landsman or -woman might view it, but a broad highway to other places. For many it was the starting point for voyages to anywhere in the world. Vessels such as traders ran regular services to other maritime places along the coasts and further afield. Just as a market town had its links with the outside world via the regular coach services, so did the seaport with its advertised sailings to London, Bristol and New York. These seaports were linked by the mariners to almost every port in the world. From Whitehaven ships sailed to Ireland, Liverpool, Australia and the Far East.[38] From Whitby they sailed to France and the Baltic, as did the vessels from Lynn, which also travelled further south to Portugal.[39] The Fowey links were with the Mediterranean, the West Indies, the Azores, North America and Australia.[40]

This contact with foreign communities, through the men who sailed in the ships and through the foreign vessels that came into the ports, provided a cosmopolitan background to the seaports and the communities. Items that might in other circumstances be only for the specialist market could also appear in small coastal villages. At Bristol on New Year's Day 1874 the schooner *Jane Slade* unloaded a non-exotic consignment of linseed, brimstone and shumac from Sicily. Added to the bottom of the list were two boxes of oranges destined for J. Slade. Oranges in early January were a rare and valuable commodity and the consignee was Mrs Jane Slade of Polruan, majority owner of the ship and mother of the master, Thomas Slade.[41] Through these connections the women who lived in these communities were exposed to different cultures and languages even if they did not take the opportunity that was available on occasions to sail with their male relatives. Experience of a different way of life, a community of women inured to the absence of many of the men, and a shipping world with its own business language, all encouraged personal independence supported within a close-knit community.

Family, Friends and Business Contacts

An important aspect of these nineteenth-century communities must be recognised and that is the physical proximity of the extended family. The families in the maritime communities were closely linked and certain family names occur in a variety of the maritime spheres of influence within each community. Even a cursory examination of the shipping registers shows the same names repeated;

---

38 Cumbria Record Office, Whitehaven (WRO): YTSR 1/9–21 Shipping Registers.
39 North Yorkshire Record Office (NYRO): NG/RS/WH 2, 9,10 Whitby Shipping Registers; NRO: P/SH Shipping Registers: King's Lynn, Wells, Cley and Great Yarmouth 1825–1989.
40 CRO: MSR/FOW 1–9 Fowey Shipping Registers.
41 Bristol Reference Library: Bristol Presentment 1 January 1874.

published work on shipping registers for ports shows familiar family names reoccurring, and further investigation often reveals other connections by marriage.[42] The study of the complete shipping registers in Fowey from 1786 to 1939 gave some examples:

> The small village of Polruan alone can furnish several dynastic examples. Until the present century it was dominated by a few seafaring families, a village where perhaps every other habitation was the shore home of one and sometimes several mariners. Perhaps the most notable were the Tadds and the Hockens.[43]

Both of these families supplied generations of master mariners and shareholding links in a wide range of locally registered vessels. Through marriage links the families were connected with a number of other prominent families, such as the Slades, Butsons and Hicks. In Whitby the prominent names were the Turnbulls, Marwoods and Barnards. In Whitehaven it was the Brockbanks, Braggs and MacGowans, while in Lynn the Bagges and Hoggs appear, and Topsham was dominated by the Holman family. These extended families plus their local contacts forged significant links across both the business and social life of these communities.

The other aspect of the interconnectedness within the maritime communities was the interdependent links between the businesses. A consistent theme when writing on investors in maritime communities is to refer to the close connections within them. In Liverpool both family and close business connections were important for the shipowning and trading communities. The vessels belonging to Balfour, Williamson and Company were usually owned by one of the partners plus family and friends, and James Bibby and William Moss, who apparently ran separate competing firms, were found to have shared ownership together with other partners in each other's vessels.[44]

Neighbours, Friends and Business Contacts

On 11 November 1850, Janet Erskine of Kirkcudbright, Scotland wrote to Messrs Atkinson and Son of Whitehaven, regarding some confusion over her exact name in the share registers relating to the *Derwent*.

> Gentlemen
> I regret there should have been any detention to business on my account having put the same signature I always do, my name in full being Janet McMickan Erskine which Capt McMinn had most likely not been aware and I am quite sure no one

---

[42] Farr, *Records of Bristol Ships*; Keys, *The Sailing Ships of Aln and Coquet*; Ward-Jackson, *Ships and Shipbuilders*.

[43] Ward-Jackson, *Ships and Shipbuilders*, p. 36.

[44] Milne, *Trade and Traders*, pp. 136–9, 151.

made any enquiry regarding it which had caused the mistake I hope this statement will be quite satisfactory to the Customs House and perhaps Miss Steele may have some of my letters which would at once show my signature

    I remain Gentlemen

    Yours respectfully

    Janet M Erskine[45]

This simple letter is at the heart of some complex connections. 'Miss Steele' was Mary Steel, a fellow shareholder in the *Derwent*, and Atkinson and Son were attorneys in Whitehaven.[46] A look at the 1851 census reveals more. Mary Steel, a spinster aged forty-seven, lived with her sister, Elizabeth. Mary gave herself as head of the household and described herself as an annuitant, but she also took in lodgers. One of her two lodgers was John Sloan, aged sixty, who was the Controller of Customs, the man whose job it was to ensure that all share dealings were properly registered. His birthplace was Kirkcudbright, residence of Janet Erskine.[47] Living next door to Mary Steel were the Atkinson family, the solicitors, whose elder daughter, Mary Atkinson, was also a shareowner.

Public Houses and Inns

Inns or public houses performed a range of functions within the community. Well known as places for men to drink and eat, to socialise and to exchange information, they were often the meeting place for such societies and clubs as the Freemasons and Foresters. The Freemasons have been shown to be an important part of the extensive network used by men as they travelled abroad for work. While men in maritime communities might not seem to be home long enough to be members, this is not borne out by research on lodges in Cornwall. The strong networking systems within small communities and the need to have agents they could trust in trading communities across the world extended the networks across great distances.[48]

    Public houses were also important places for those seeking work. The publicans knew where the ships were being built or repaired and in whose yard.[49] Auctions of bankrupt stock, including ships' shares and sales of ships were held in public houses and, as shown, shareholders held their meetings there.[50] When Mary Ann Henwood sat in the Ship Inn with her fellow shipowners in 1873 it was just one of many similar meetings being held. The inn was run by Mrs Nurse who was in

---

[45] WRO: YTSR 1/11.

[46] WRO: YTSR 1/11; *Cumberland Directory 1847* Mannix & Whelan.

[47] TNA: HO 107/2436 1851.

[48] Roger Burt, 'Freemasonry and Business Networking During the Victorian Period', *Economic History Review*, 56 (2003), 657–88.

[49] Helen Doe, 'The Business of Shipbuilding: Dunn and Henna of Mevagissey, 1799–1806', *International Journal of Maritime History*, 18 (2006), 187–217 (p. 210).

[50] *Royal Cornwall Gazette*, 17 February 1837.

contact with a wide range of ship shareholders, master mariners and merchants.[51] Women who ran public houses or inns were in an advantageous position in relation to gaining information and many became shareholders.

Mary Ann Barnard of Lynn was the wife of Samuel Barnard, a publican. She owned two ships and was the managing owner, in charge of all the shore-based business and accounts. Also in Lynn was Harriet Enefer, the managing owner of one ship and the manager of the Maids Head, while Harriet Booth was a publican in Doncaster with shares in Lynn ships.[52] Jane Hayes of Bodinnick ran the Ferry Inn and she held a large number of shares, which is not surprising as her son James was a shipbroker.[53] In 1851 in Whitehaven the census listed fifty-four inns, public houses, taverns and a temperance house, almost half of which were managed by women: nineteen widows, three spinsters and four married women.[54]

Another occupation linked with shareholding was that of postmistress. Fanny Stephens of Polruan, Catherine Tregenna of Looe and Isabella Sanderson of Amble were all postmistresses and shipowners. All three held shares in a range of ships and bought and sold them.[55] Both innkeeping and running a post office provided contacts and information.

Summary

The life of the shore-based mariner's wife was one of leave taking and reunion. The husband's absence meant perforce that his wife had to take daily decisions that in other circumstances were shared. For the ambitious mariner and his wife there was the opportunity to make social progress, yet that opportunity was often hard won against a tough and risk-filled life at sea for the man and a life lived mainly alone and independent for his wife. In Salem the 'possibility' of an unusual degree of economic independence on the part of seaport wives is connected with the men's periodic absences and the complementarity of men's work and women's work.[56] In a community in which independent women were an accepted part of life, few might question the existence of women in business, even in normally 'male' roles.

It was an entrepreneurial and supportive environment that encouraged wide ownership of the merchant fleet. Examination largely among fishing communities found 'traditional shared values and wide diffusion of capital among the members' and a commitment to the industry, part of a network that had shared interests and concerns. Within the fishing communities, 'dialect, nicknames and the shared concerns for the fortunes of the fishing fleet, especially in bad weather' brought

---

[51] Greenhill, *Merchant Schooners*, p. 275.
[52] NRO: P/SHL 4–7.
[53] CRO: MSR/FOW/4, 5, 7.
[54] TNA: HO 107/2436.
[55] CRO: MSR/FOWY/5, 8, 9; *Clayton's Directory of Shipping 1865*.
[56] Lisa Norling, 'Roundtable Discussion of Young Men and the Sea', p. 328.

them together.[57] It was much the same in the mariner communities. The language of the ship was foreign to the landsmen, few of whom had regular exposure to the different cultures that linked the coastal communities. If inland the agricultural year was dominated by the weather and the seasons, on the coast foul weather brought concerns of a more emotional nature for those absent and unseen at sea. These close-knit communities were bound by their shared knowledge of the shipping industry and a maritime culture, all of which was strengthened and supported by family and business links, in particular 'the mothers, sisters and wives who did not go to sea, yet who brought up the future seafarers, cherished and supported them, and looked after their children and their businesses'.[58]

---

[57] Walton, 'Fishing Communities, 1850–1950', p. 128.
[58] Rodger, 'Roundtable Discussion of "Young Men and the Sea"', pp. 336–7.

3

Five Investor Ports

Much of the attention given to women investors has been in relation to investments in joint stock companies.[1] There were increasing opportunities to invest in joint stock companies and the arrival of limited liability in the 1850s reduced the risks for investors. What has not been considered is the evidence relating to the substantial number of women who invested in shipping particularly through the 64th system of shipownership.[2] This chapter provides the background to the shipowning system and to the five ports from which most of the investment data have been gathered.

Shipping had been an investment for centuries and women shipowners were a constant factor, long before the rush to invest in canals, railways, banks and limited companies.[3] As seen earlier the important distinction between investment in a company and shipping investment was the jurisdiction of maritime law, which provided wider opportunities and freedom for investors. It also gave them a direct relationship with their investment; they were not just investors but shipowners. The investor, male or female, acquired shares in a vessel through purchase or inheritance and some or all of the shares might be sold or further purchases made. Under maritime law, shares could be bought, sold, bequeathed, gifted or mortgaged without reference to the other shareholders.[4] In joint stock companies large numbers of investors diluted the power of the minority shareholder and the main decisions were made by the directors.[5] Shipownership was restricted to a maximum of thirty-two shareholders and few vessels had this many. In Whitehaven, where fractional shareholding was normal, the average number of shareholders across the registered ships in 1850 was ten, with a range from one to twenty-one.[6] There were no boards of directors; the shipowners formed

---

[1]   Maltby and Rutterford, 'She Possessed Her Own Fortune', pp. 220–1; Rutterford and Maltby, 'The Widow, the Clergyman and the Reckless', p. 112.
[2]   Maltby and Rutterford do include one shipping company, Orient Steam, but only from 1880. Orient Steam was a joint stock company and the female shareowners represented 12.5 per cent of the total shareowners and held 5.8 per cent of the shares. See Maltby and Rutterford, 'She Possessed Her Own Fortune', p. 228.
[3]   An early female Scottish shipowner is described in Florence E. Dyer, 'A Woman Shipowner', *Mariner's Mirror*, 36 (1950), 134–8.
[4]   David Starkey, 'Ownership Structures in the British Shipping Industry: The Case of Hull, 1820–1916', *International Journal of Maritime History*, 8 (1996), 71–95 (pp. 78–9).
[5]   Maltby and Rutterford, 'She Possessed Her Own Fortune', p. 228.
[6]   TNA: PRO BT 162/19 Account of vessels registered at Port of Whitehaven 31 Dec 1850.

the management committee, and delegation, if any, was usually to a shareholding managing owner or an agent. Even the master of the ship was often a shareholder, to encourage commitment.

With its strongly male traditions the world of ships and shipping does not at first glance appear to be an attractive environment for women investors. It also contradicts the view that female capital sought low risk options.[7] The ideal investment area for women has been described as one where 'investments were secure, and where returns might not be spectacular, but were nevertheless reliable'.[8] Ships were accident prone and were wrecked, lost and damaged. Between 1872 and 1878 the annual percentage of notifiable casualties to sea-going sailing vessels insured with Lloyd's remained around 20 per cent.[9] Insurance clubs were known to value ships lower (by as much as 50 per cent), to discourage fraud, and unknown numbers of ships were uninsured.[10] Trades were fickle and the shipowner had to be flexible and very well connected to ensure a steady trade. The masters they employed had great powers, able even to sell the vessel and the cargo in a distant port if circumstances required it. The investor in shipping literally waved goodbye to their investment, entrusting it to others' hands and to fate on a regular basis. However, women were very much a part of the industry and provided essential capital for the purchase of new vessels and the funds to keep them at sea. In this section on women shipowners questions of marital status, risk attitude and involvement will be considered in the light of the evidence from the Customs House shipping registers.

The Shipping Registers

The shipping registers are a valuable resource for those researching investors and, in particular, for research on women investors. There is a paucity of clear source material in relation to women's economic activity, especially when the activities of married and middle-class women are considered.[11] Census returns have proved problematic in identifying women's activity, and wills can only provide a one-dimensional perspective: a woman's holdings at the time of her death.[12] The lists of shares in wills, where they exist, provide little or no information on how, why, when or by whom these shares were acquired. Women who invested in companies can be identified in share registers, but these provide no clues as to how they were acquired or their method of disposal.

---

7   Morris, 'The Reform of the Married Women's Property Act 1870', p. 180.
8   Owens, 'Making Some Provision', pp. 26–7.
9   'Lloyd's statistics of marine casualties', p. 509.
10   Craig *et al.*, 'Some Aspects of Devon Shipping', p.101.
11   Beatrice Craig, Robert Beachy and Alastair Owens, 'Introduction', in *Women, Business and Finance in Nineteenth-Century Europe: Rethinking Separate Spheres*, ed. Robert Beachy, Beatrice Craig and Alastair Owens (Oxford: Berg, 2006), p. 8.
12   Hill, 'Women, Work and the Census', pp. 78–94.

Details of ships and ownership of ships have been of interest to government since 1181, when the sale of English vessels to aliens was prohibited. The Navigation Act of 1651 consolidated and strengthened the legislation from previous centuries into one act.[13] The next major change was the 1786 Act of Registration and it was this act which led to the formal identification of all British vessels over 15 tons and full details of the ownership of the vessel. From 1786 British-owned ships had to be registered in their home port and the details of the vessels and the owners, including name, number of shares, and occupation, had to be declared on oath at the local customs house. The great bonus of these registers is that they not only give the initial investors in a ship, but they also detail the changing ownership of the shares as owners purchased, sold, mortgaged or inherited their shares.[14] This enables the researcher to track the fortunes not just of the ship but also of the individual owners. These registers give information about the choices made by investors, such as when they purchased their shares, when and how they disposed of them, or when they purchased more. They can even hint at how the investors acquired the knowledge to take these decisions, although there are complexities in using these registers to achieve any quantification of capital formation.[15] The shipping registers were simply lists of ships and their owners and were not established for the same purpose as company registers which show the capital invested. The price at which the shipping shares were purchased was not recorded. That information has to be accessed from the rare survival of ship account books and share transfer forms. Shown below is a typical example of the shareholding in a Fowey-registered vessel, *Alert*. A 93-ton schooner, it was built locally and registered in 1842. The schooner remained on the registers until 1891 by which time the shares had changed hands many times. By the time Christopher Slade died in February 1870 he had acquired forty-six shares in the vessel and these were inherited by his widow who sold them a few months later in May.[16]

The registers show that during the nineteenth century sailing vessel ownership was broadly of three types: owner/master, fractional ownership and multiple vessel ownership, usually by companies. In the smaller ports the most frequent pattern of ownership was either owner/master or fractional shareholding. The owner/master was typically the owner of a smaller vessel employed in the coastal trade. For this owner the vessel was his living, usually a subsistence living, and the members of his small crew were often relatives. Many of the examples from Wales of women managing owners are cases where the husband was the master and the wife handled all the shore-based business aspects.[17] Fractional ownership arose as a method of spreading the initial capital cost of building and outfitting a vessel. These owners then continued to share both profit and loss. Owners came

13   Rupert Jarvis, 'Ship Registry – to 1707', *Maritime History*, 1 (1971), 29–45.
14   Palmer, 'Investors in London Shipping', pp. 46–7.
15   Craig, *British Tramp Shipping: 1750–1914*; R. Craig, 'Capital Formation in Shipping', *Research in Maritime History*, 24 (2003), pp. 41–58.
16   CRO: MSR/Fowey/5 Fowey Shipping Registers.
17   *Clayton's Directory of Shipping 1865*.

Table 6. Initial shareholders in *Alert*, 1842

Shares	Name	Occupation	Residence
9	J M Carnall	Sailmaker	Fowey
14	William Salt	Mariner	Polruan
2	Phillip Salt	Mariner	Polruan
5	James Bray	Blacksmith	Polruan
6	William Abbott	Baker	Polruan
5	Christopher Slade	Shipwright	Polruan
4	Nicholas Butson	Shipbuilder	Polruan
1	James Tippett	Mariner	Polruan
9	John Knight	Merchant	Lostwithiel
1	Charles Lacey	Blockmaker	Fowey
2	Sam Buller	Butcher	Fowey
2	Mary Whitford	Spinster	Fowey
2	Edward Thomas	Ropemaker	Fowey
2	Edward Strike	Shipbroker	Fowey

Source: Cornwall Record Office (CRO): MSR/Fow/5 Shipping Registers.

from a wide range of backgrounds, not just merchants and master mariners but also butchers, local trades people, innkeepers, and private individuals. While the involvement of the ship-related occupations such as ropemaker, sailmaker and blockmaker is understandable (there were occasions when shares were offered in lieu of payment) these vessels also offered an investment opportunity for some non-maritime-related businesses and private individuals. Each ship was a separate financial entity and was accounted separately by its owners, led by the managing owner or majority owner who accounted to their fellow shareholders for the year's performance and any loss or profit on their investment.

The survival of the ship registers varies in each of the five ports. Fowey, Exeter and Whitehaven have the most complete series from 1786, but all of the registers consulted cover the period from 1840 to 1880. Whitby is less fortunate as the surviving registers are not complete, but information was extracted from the registers that nominally cover 1849 to 1858; however, due to the survival of a transaction register, some transactions in vessels were noted up to 1889. The resultant database of transactional information covers the period from 1824 to 1889 in all five ports, with information from some ports covering the whole period.

The organisation of these registers changed slightly over time, but the requirements for details of both the vessel and the owners remained. The early registration requirements included notification of the subscribing and non-subscribing owners. Subscribers were those who appeared in person at the Customs to swear an oath and they had to represent at least two-thirds of the shares. Each registration was numbered within the relevant year, for example the *Gem* of Fowey

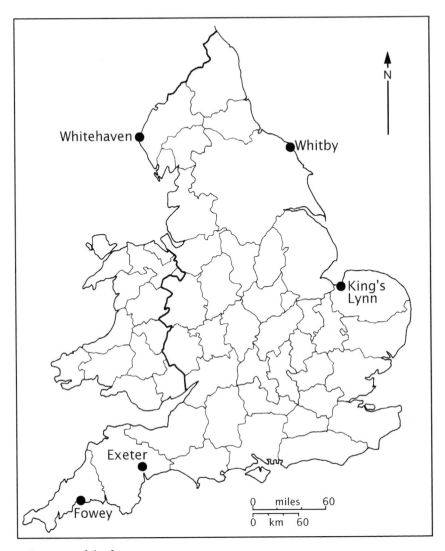

3. Location of the five ports

was 8/1871.[18] Subsequent changes of ownership, through death, sales of shares or mortgaging of shares, were all noted. In the early part of the century these changes frequently led to the vessels being registered *de novo*, as if new. This caused a confusing system of duplication in registration, made harder before the introduction of an official number for vessels. This constant need for re-entering the vessel's details when significant changes of ownership or rebuilding occurred led to separate transactions books being introduced from 1855, and these just recorded the changes in shareownership. Another problem with the earliest registers was the failure to remove vessels that were no longer active. Additionally, changes of ownership in shares were not always notified promptly. Where there was no will and administration was complex it could be some years before ownership was clarified. In other cases the owners simply omitted or forgot to mention the changes, especially if minor. Apart from local knowledge there was no way of auditing the ownership until proof of title was required, as in a sale of shares.

The Five Investor Ports

While ports moved up and down in significance over the nineteenth century, the two largest ports of London and Liverpool remained the leaders in both foreign and coastal trade and attracted huge investments to their infrastructure and a thriving maritime business community, among whom were many female investors. However, ascertaining the amount of shipping registered at these ports poses real difficulties, although some sampling techniques have previously been used.[19] It is technically possible to take a snapshot of London or Liverpool in a one-year sample. This would capture just the initial investors and miss the transactions over the years. Or a sample of vessels could be taken and then tracked through the voluminous registers, an almost impossible task given the absence of any master index. A smaller port, however, does allow this full tracking and enables longitudinal research on the registers. The major advantage is that the full extent of economic change over time can be considered, together with the many linkages between the vessels and their owners.

Port history is dominated by the large ports. By the end of the nineteenth century the leading ports of Britain were London, Liverpool, Cardiff, Newcastle and Hull for foreign trade, and London, Liverpool, Greenock, Newcastle and Glasgow for the coastal trade. These ports had become 'huge, wealthy and proud' and their business communities gained considerably from the commercial growth.[20] In any

[18] CRO: MSR/Fow/8.
[19] See R. Craig and R. C. Jarvis, *Liverpool Registry of Merchant Ships* (Manchester, 1967); Palmer, 'Investors in London Shipping'.
[20] Gordon Jackson, 'The Significance of Unimportant Ports', *International Journal of Maritime History*, 13 (2001), pp. 5–6; Gordon Jackson. 'The Ports', in *Transport in Victorian Britain*, ed. Michael J. Freeman and Derek H. Aldcroft (Manchester: Manchester University Press, 1988), pp. 218–52 (pp. 218, 246–9).

statistical analysis the major ports were in a wholly different league from the rest. While London and Liverpool measured their registered ships in thousands, the rest did so in hundreds. Seven ports had between 600 and 799 registered vessels in 1871, forty-eight ports had from 100 to 599, and the rest, twenty-nine ports, had fewer than 100 registered vessels.

These ports were critical to Britain's commercial and industrial expansion, providing the shipping and the mercantile services such as insurance, banking and broking that ensured the movement of goods and people in and out of the ports. However, it was not just these ports that scrambled to win their share of the import, export and re-export markets, which had grown rapidly through the eighteenth and into the nineteenth century. Five mid-sized ports across England were selected for detailed investigation. They are Exeter, Fowey, Lynn, Whitby and Whitehaven (see map). Four of the five examples come from the biggest grouping of mid-sized ports and one, Exeter, just fell by 1871 into the smallest group (see Appendix IV). The smaller ports played an important role in the overall transport system and yet they are frequently overlooked. One port historian has strongly argued that such ports cannot be measured in a purely statistical way. They were 'crucial to economic development *in the way that it occurred* in Britain' by providing services to the larger ports, such as shipping, carrying trade, additional repair facilities and harbour space, and they remained critical to the provision of vital supplies to their own smaller-scale hinterlands.[21]

> Ports are not to be measured only in terms of throughput, proportion of national customs duties or share of imports or exports of particular goods. Their significance lies on the one hand in their role within an integrated system in which their coastal exports are necessary for regional centres larger than their own; and on the other in the importance of their own hinterlands in the provision of necessary foodstuffs from home or abroad and the disposal of foodstuffs, manufactures and raw materials that could not otherwise be sold.[22]

Their assistance to the domestic economy should not obscure their role in Britain's foreign trade. Even if a smaller port had little direct foreign trade the shipowners of these smaller ports traded via larger ports either directly or through agents. A ship can and does follow trade and has no need to be limited to the imports or export requirements of its home port. The *Warlock* of Whitehaven spent much of its time trading between the Far East and Liverpool, and the *Jane Slade* of Fowey traded between the West Indies, the Mediterranean, London and Bristol.[23] The ships owned in the Isles of Scilly travelled far and wide, such as the 300-ton *Chieftain*, which won the tea race to London in 1847.[24] The *Ann Banfield*,

21 Jackson, 'The Significance of Unimportant Ports', pp. 5–9.
22 Jackson, 'The Significance of Unimportant Ports', p. 16.
23 WRO: D/BH/24/22/43 Records of *Warlock*, barque; Doe, *Jane Slade of Polruan*.
24 R. M. Barton, *Life in Cornwall in the Mid-Nineteenth Century* (Truro: D. Bradford Barton, 1971), p. 133.

in which Ann Banfield held twenty shares, set out in August 1864 with a prospective list of ports of call including Mauritius, Adelaide, Melbourne, Sydney, Hobart Town, Launceston, Auckland, Hong Kong, Shanghai and Singapore.[25]

Investors are attracted by good business prospects and the anticipation of a return on their investments. Knowledge is an important factor in reducing risk and investors preferred to deal with people they knew and industries they understood.[26] Local shipbuilding attracted investment, as did a busy port. Apparently thriving communities, in this case with plenty of shipping movements and busy shipyards, promoted a sense of confidence which encouraged business and investors. The health of the local economy was particularly important for female investors as they were less able to move away. Women, with the demands of family, were less flexible in their ability to physically move with the industry. The fortunes of the five selected ports changed over time and so, in order to understand the women investors, there is a need to examine the changing environments in which they lived.

Port Comparisons

Comparisons can become complex when debating the performance of ports. There are contemporary statistics available for the number and tonnage of ships, entries and clearances, and the cargoes shipped. For example, there is a difference in the value of cargoes handled: bulk cargoes like coal and grain or specialist high value cargoes such as those flooding into London via the East India Company. Different types of trade brought different pressures on ports; timber was more disruptive than coal, due to its space requirements.[27] However, by the end of the period, the main bulk cargo that dominated coastal trade and, increasingly, the export market was coal, driven by the needs of industrialisation. In 1790 UK coal production output was 7.6 million tons, by 1816 it had risen to 16 million, and by 1854 it was 54.7 million.[28] A further dimension is whether the shipping was coastal or foreign. For instance, due to the speedy turn-around of the regular coasters, the number of ships entering quite small ports could be large. Irrespective of types of traffic or cargo, the biggest challenge for ports in the nineteenth century was the efficient management of the flow of both goods and vessels.

Additionally there were other factors affecting a port's relative success, some over which the port in question had little or no control. These were the external factors, such as the wider economy, technological changes, the political environment and its geographical position. Acting together with these external factors were those internal factors where the port took responsibility, such as the provi-

---

[25] CRO: MSR/SCI Shipping Registers of the Isles of Scilly.
[26] Hudson, 'Attitudes to Investment Risk', p. 151.
[27] Jackson, 'The Ports', p. 222.
[28] Ronald Hope, *A New History of British Shipping* (London: John Murray, 1990), p. 267.

sion of facilities, dues, and navigation aids. The most critical factor was the business community: the merchants, shipowners and associated businesses.

'A port is not a place, but a community of merchants'[29] and it was the merchant who owned or chartered the ships, whose goods flowed into and out of the ports, who argued for better facilities, and then, of course, complained about the charges. These merchants required speedy access to internal markets and were prepared to move to other ports to get the best accommodation for their trade. Male and female investors played an important role in providing the finance necessary to drive both port improvements and also new shipping and business finance, some of which found its way to the larger ports. The big ports may have had the major shipowners, but neither they nor the medium-sized ports were self-sufficient, as 'small port people invested in major port ships and sent their locally registered ships to seek employment in major ports'.[30] As will be seen, this is supported by the research into these smaller ports, but first I will present an overview of the five selected ports and what can be deduced about their business communities. A thriving port was an attractive place for investors; a declining port was a greater problem for the female investors who were less able to move out of the area due to their family commitments. Therefore the port environment is of particular importance when considering the female investor community.

Exeter

In the nineteenth century the once busy port of Exeter was no longer a major player in national statistics, but it remained a place of constant activity mainly due to its coastal trade. The boundaries of the Customs port included the city of Exeter, Exmouth, Teignmouth, Topsham and other smaller creeks, until 1852 when Teignmouth became a separate port.[31] While the city was a regional centre, its geographic position so far up the river Exe was always a challenge for shipowners as it had excellent communications with the hinterland, but poor communications with the sea. It could claim to be the earliest canal port in Britain with a canal constructed in 1566 to enable goods to be brought into the city from Topsham. Initially a lighter transported goods to Exeter until the canal was enlarged to take ships in 1701, and then in 1827 it was fully extended to Topsham. Also in the early nineteenth century the canal was deepened, straightened and lengthened and a small basin at Exeter was added where ships could float and discharge cargoes into new warehouses.[32] The regular trade with London was in small coastal vessels which carried passengers, parcels and assorted merchandise. Ann Alice Morton

---

[29] Adrian Jarvis, 'Port History', in *Harbours and Havens*, ed. Lewis R. Fischer and Adrian Jarvis (St John's, Newfoundland: International Maritime Economic History Association, 1999), pp. 13–34 (p. 15).

[30] Jackson, 'The Significance of Unimportant Ports', pp. 8–9.

[31] David J. Starkey, 'The Ports, Seaborne Trade and Shipping Industry of South Devon, 1786–1914', in *A New Maritime History of Devon*, ed. M. Duffy *et al.* (London: Conway, 1994), pp. 32–47 (p. 33).

[32] Gordon Jackson, *The History and Archaeology of Ports* (Tadworth: World's Work, 1983), p. 34.

of Exeter lived close to the main quay and had the majority shareholding in four such vessels.[33]

The coal trade was a large import trade for Exeter, totalling 33,000 tons in 1843, but the arrival of the railways in 1844 and the larger ship sizes caused problems. The development of a national railway system gave merchants the opportunity to take their cargoes into other ports such as Southampton, Teignmouth and Bristol in order to achieve distribution inland rather than experience the difficulties posed by navigation up the Exe. The first shipping to be affected were the regular traders such as those belonging to Mrs Morton.[34] By 1869 Exeter was ranked thirty-seven among British ports as Plymouth took more of its trade.[35] Despite these limiting factors, Exeter maintained a steady business in the coastal trade throughout the period, carrying low value bulk items such as pig iron, building stone and materials for the Exeter paper mills. The opening of the Exmouth dock in 1868 affected shipping traffic as it gave an alternative unloading point. Topsham managed to survive the competition for some years but eventually lost out by the end of the century when reconstruction of Exmouth dock encouraged more ships to use its facilities. By this stage Exeter-registered ships were less closely linked with the trade of the Exe River and only called at their home port on 43 per cent of their voyages.

Exeter's shipowners invested in vessels that traded with Newfoundland, Labrador, the West Indies and the Mediterranean, in fish (notably dried cod) and fruit. In common with many of the southwest ports, dried cod was transported from Newfoundland to the Mediterranean and fruit was brought back.[36] Many of the women shipowners came from the areas close to the main shipbuilding site of Topsham, rather than Exeter.[37] Although the number of ships registered at Exeter had dropped from 181 in 1845 to 105 in 1869, part of the reduction can be explained by the designation of Teignmouth as a port in its own right.[38] Shareownership was widespread; in one case sixty-six local residents owned shares in one vessel, a situation that could occur in spite of the share limitation through joint ownership of shares. Owners of multiple vessels were the Row brothers and the Holman family of Topsham, who owned seven ships and thirty-two ships respectively.[39]

Exeter was a port limited by its geography. In the earlier part of the nineteenth century it was still a regional hub for shipping, but although it remained an important regional base, its shipping and investment suffered because of the problems of getting larger vessels into the city. The railway gradually took over as the main

---

[33] DRO: 3289s/10, 37/1837, 9/1832, 3/1852, 43/1837.

[34] E. A. G. Clark, 'The Ports of the Exe Estuary, 1701–1972', in *The New Maritime History of Devon, Vol. II*, ed. M. Duffy *et al.* (London: Conway, 1994), p. 73.

[35] Starkey, 'The Ports, Seaborne Trade and Shipping Industry', pp. 36–7.

[36] Starkey, 'The Ports, Seaborne Trade and Shipping Industry', pp. 36–44.

[37] DRO: 3289s Exeter Shipping Registers.

[38] Starkey, 'The Ports, Seaborne Trade and Shipping Industry', p. 42.

[39] Clark, 'Ports of the Exe Estuary', p. 74.

distribution method for goods into and out of Exeter and by the 1880s shipping had moved to more accessible ports such as Plymouth and Exmouth.

Fowey

On 29 December 1830, a poster was placed in the town of Fowey in Cornwall, advertising a meeting to consider changes to the port environment. It was addressed to the merchants, shipowners, pilots, mariners and others 'interested in the trade of the port'.[40] The inhabitants of Fowey were waking up to the realisation that facilities needed to be improved in order to encourage more trade. They had the advantage of a large and natural deep-water harbour, well placed between Plymouth and Falmouth, but they were somewhat late in their commercial awakening. Compared with the other ports considered here, Fowey's glorious past had been centuries ago when it could boast of being one of the country's most significant medieval ports. By 1830 many other ports had been expanding and reaping the benefits of the increase in trade and their visitors could see the investment in docks, piers and warehouses. Fowey had a natural advantage as a large deep-water river port, but was the newly awakened local will sufficient to make the port successful?

The town of Fowey had for many years been dominated by a battle for control fought with immense energy by two politically motivated parties. The town had the right to elect two Members of Parliament and votes were bought and sold. Most elections in the eighteenth century had been uncontested and the Rashleigh and Edgcumbe families had kept control, supported by the Fowey Corporation. This cosy system was shaken by J. T. Austen (he later changed his name to Treffry) who was determined to break their grip on the town. Austen was an entrepreneur and his primary interest was to increase trade, preferably his. In 1813 he published a chart of Fowey harbour, respectfully addressed to the 'Merchants of the United Kingdoms', and designed to attract their business by demonstrating the harbour's facilities. Watering points, slips, and four shipyards are all shown with great detail, together with two ropewalks.[41] Other attempts were made to attract new opportunities. There was a failed attempt by Austen to get the Packet vessels based there during a temporary strike at Falmouth, and Rashleigh, together with the Corporation, had tried, and failed, to establish Fowey as a bonded port.[42]

Lack of investment in facilities was a real problem. Austen put his money into wharves from which he could export the copper from his mines, but with problems in carrying the copper over Rashleigh's land Austen was forced to turn his attention away from Fowey to build a new port at Par.[43] Fowey's harbour was under the jurisdiction of an absentee authority, the Corporation of Lostwithiel, which was five miles up river. The Lostwithiel burgesses appointed the highest

---

40   CRO: R/5088 Notice of public meeting 1830.
41   United Kingdom Hydrographic Office (UKHO): A511 Austen 1813.
42   CRO: R/5083 6 August 1814.
43   John Keast, *The King of Mid Cornwall: The Life of Joseph Thomas Treffry, 1782–1850* (Truro: Dyllansow Truran, 1982), p. 60.

bidder to collect their dues and had little interest in enhancing the facilities down-river. Harbour dues of 1s 4d per vessel and 2s 8d for foreign vessels remained unchanged between 1799 and 1850.[44]

Shipbuilding had always been a part of Fowey business, but in the wider Port of Fowey, Mevagissey had been the dominant producer of tonnage, much of it for the smuggling trade.[45] By 1832, the end of open smuggling, the end of the political battles after the Reform Act, the growth of the exports of copper and the opening up of the Mediterranean all combined to improve trade for Fowey. The shipbuilders stood to gain from improved trade, not just from the investment in new building, but also from increased repair and maintenance business as more vessels traded to and from Fowey. Shipbuilding activity expanded, as larger ships were built and local investors in shipping increased, including many women. The port's investors were mainly local tradesmen, and shares were held in a wide range of vessels.[46]

In contrast to Exeter, in 1860 Fowey openly welcomed the arrival of the railway connection with the main network. 'The advantages', enthused a newspaper report, 'are scarcely capable of exaggeration.' China clay could now more easily be sent to the port for shipment and Fowey was convinced this would ensure its triumph over tidal harbours. Fowey had the specialist port's problem of an imbalance of imports and exports and was predicting an import tonnage of 29,000 and an export of 47,000 (mainly china clay).[47] As the trade flow increased so did the pressure to improve the harbour facilities, but matters did not improve signifi-cantly until the Harbour Commission was formed in 1869 by Act of Parliament. Conservatism or myopia by the port authority often stifled improvements in some ports, while the successful ports, driven by their merchants, took bold initiatives to capture trade.

From a low base at the beginning of the nineteenth century, a notable aspect of Fowey's business community was its investment in ships, not just for the local trades, but for trades that took Fowey vessels across the world and their cargoes to other ports. Between 1829 and 1870 the rate of Cornwall's expansion in sailing ships was rapid. In 1829 the number of vessels over 50 tons registered in the Cornish ports was 270 with a total tonnage of 22,291. By 1870 there were 535 ships with a total tonnage of 66,770. The number of ships nearly doubled and the tonnage trebled. This growth was at a faster rate than that seen in Devon, or the registration figures for England, as Cornish investors seized the opportunity with enthusiasm.[48] Women shipowners were particularly active in Fowey and there are several examples of significant shipowners, such as Ann Hicks, Mary Hicks

---

[44] CRO: B/Los 295 List of harbour dues of Corporation of Lostwithiel 1799–1800.
[45] Doe, 'The Business of Shipbuilding', pp. 190–1.
[46] Ward-Jackson, *Ships and Shipbuilders*.
[47] *West Briton*, 2 November 1860.
[48] *BPP* 1830 XXVII: Return of Number of Ships belonging to Ports in United Kingdom, 1829; *BPP* 1871 LXI: Return of Number of Sailing and Steam vessels registered at each Port of Great Britain and Ireland, 1870.

Hayes, Jane Slade, Jane Hicks and Mary Roberts, who will be discussed in more detail later.[49] The Newfoundland cod trade, emigrants and fruit were carried in Fowey-owned ships, a high proportion of which were owned by investors from Polruan.[50] Even shipbuilding was centred there from 1865, and from 1870 the busiest yard was run by Mrs Jane Slade.[51] By the 1880s, the port's dedication to wood and an inability to move into iron and steam meant that major shipbuilding was at an end. The related businesses declined, with the exception of shipbroking and insurance.[52]

Fowey had geographic advantages in its natural deep harbour, but this was not sufficient without trade to attract ships. Inbound cargoes of timber and coal were essential items for the mines and local building, both housing and ships. It was, however, the outbound trade of minerals that kept the port busy throughout the century. Because of the limitations of the inbound cargoes, the ships in which the people of the port invested extended beyond the mineral trade. The vessels of Fowey brought back cargoes from the Mediterranean, Newfoundland and the West Indies to larger ports such as Liverpool, Hull, London and Bristol.

Lynn

On the east coast of Norfolk is the port of Lynn, another river port.[53] It was thriving at the beginning of the nineteenth century and was among the top twenty ports in terms of shipping tonnage with more than ten thousand tons in 1800.[54] Its position close to the Baltic had made it one of the few English Hanseatic ports in the Middle Ages. Being situated at the mouth of the Ouse enabled the merchants of Lynn to supply seven counties up river, taking their goods into the heart of the Midlands. Coal, salt and wine and other goods such as hemp and Greenland whale oil were imported.[55] In 1818 Lynn was a bigger importer of seaborne coal than Yarmouth.

A trade directory in 1854 shows the population in 1851 as 19,355, having risen from 10,259 in 1811, and, as is the way with trade directories, it extols the virtues of the port. 'The port of Lynn, from its position in relation to the inland Navigation connected with it, on the one hand, and its free communication with the German Ocean, on the other, has been of considerable importance, especially in the corn and coal trade.'[56] The reference is in the past as the railway had arrived in 1846

---

49 CRO: MSR FOW.

50 Ward-Jackson, *Ships and Shipbuilders*; Doe, *Jane Slade of Polruan*.

51 Helen Doe, 'Politics, Property and Family Resources', *Family & Community History*, 4 (2001), 59–72 (p. 68).

52 Helen Doe, 'Blockmakers, Sailmakers, Ropemakers, Blacksmiths and Brokers in the Port of Fowey', *Journal of the South West Maritime History Society*, 16 (2003), 148–71.

53 The port was known as Lynn rather than King's Lynn.

54 H. J. Hillen, *History of the Borough of King's Lynn*. Originally published 1907 (Wakefield, 1978), p. 537.

55 Hillen, *History of the Borough of King's Lynn*, pp. 538–9.

56 *White's Gazetter and Directory of Norfolk 1854*, p. 572.

and by 1848 Lynn was connected to the main railway network. The railways now handled distribution, and a writer in 1907 described the impact in dramatic prose:

> And the packets too which once plied between Lynn and other ports, were now safely berthed in the desired haven, yet were the captains at their wits' ends, because an important carrying trade was deflected, and the sacks of corn, which were once poured into the holds of their vessels, were now placed upon trucks and whirled from one part of the kingdom to the other.[57]

The directory of 1854 describes the harbour as holding up to 300 ships. The registration of vessels had steadily increased since 1811, growing from 116 to 180 in 1850. The total tonnage quoted for 1850 was 19,673, so the average size of vessels at 109 tons had shown little increase on the average for 1800 of 106 tons. It gave the principal import still as coal, mainly from Durham and Northumberland, and spoke of the benefits to the navigation of two steam tugs for use during 'contrary winds and adverse tides'.[58]

Lynn suffered from heavy silting which obstructed navigation up river and John Rennie was employed to straighten part of the Ouse. The Eau Brink Cut was completed in 1821 at a cost of around half a million pounds. The sum reflects the determination of the commercial community and, perhaps more importantly, since Norfolk was predominantly an agricultural region, the benefit to local agriculture of better drainage. The Cut was successful and it was not until 1852/3 that the river below Lynn was straightened.[59]

Despite the lack of women listed among the forty-seven shipowners in the trade directories for Lynn,[60] there were many women shipowners, such as Mary Ann Barnard, Mary Jary and Hannah Lee.[61] Most of them lived in the south of the town which was a mariners' and merchants' area. The north of the town was the residence of the fishermen and their families.[62] Lynn was not as active as the other ports in terms of its number of registered ships (see Figure 1 later in this chapter), or its number of women investors. Mid-century Lynn had several local banks: Everards and Co, East of England Banking Co., Gurneys, Birkbeck and Creswell and Jarvis and Jarvis.[63] Although the Freemen of Lynn from 1790 to 1836 feature a high number of maritime trades, from mid-century Lynn was more of a strong regional market town and was the base for a large number of brewers and maltsters rather than a maritime base.[64]

---

57 Hillen, *History of the Borough of King's Lynn*, p. 600.
58 *White's Gazetter and Directory of Norfolk 1854*, p. 572.
59 Jackson, *The History and Archaeology of Ports*, p. 35.
60 *Kelly's Directory 1858*.
61 NRO: P/SH/L 1–7.
62 Pers. comm., Mrs Pat Midgely, Trues' Yard Museum, King's Lynn.
63 *White's Gazetter and Directory of Norfolk 1854*.
64 *Ibid.*; NRO: A Calendar of Freemen of Lynn.

Whitby

The mid-century trade directories of Whitby listed 141 shipowners of whom eight were women.[65] Whitby stands at the edge of the sea with the moors at its back and the River Esk divides the town to the east and the west. The importance of the alum industry had stimulated shipbuilding and demanded the importation of large quantities of coal. Whaling was another industry that had also required sturdy local vessels. Whitby ships were much sought after as their national reputation had been secured by Captain Cook's choice of Whitby-built ships for his explorations.[66] By the end of the eighteenth century, it is claimed that Whitby could rival London and Newcastle in its output and contributed over 10 per cent of the total tonnage built in England and Wales by the early 1790s.[67] By the early nineteenth century Whitby's alum and whaling industries had declined, but its shipbuilding and associated rope and canvas still made it a notable source of ships for other parts of Britain. A trade directory was able to boast in 1849 that the 'wealth of Whitby has been chiefly derived from shipbuilding, and chartering of its numerous vessels'.[68] Colliers, Baltic and other foreign-going vessels plus general coastwise traders were built in the various yards beside the Esk.[69]

Gideon Smales, a Whitby shipowner, in his evidence to the Select Committee on British Shipping in 1844 was asked, 'The prosperity of the port of Whitby greatly depends upon the prosperity of the shipping trade?' 'Yes', he replied, 'it is our staple trade.' Both shipbuilding and shipownership were to remain the main activities until the 1880s despite the lack of an export trade.[70] Shipowning was stimulated by the winter problems of the great coal fleets of the northeast. Colliers were built sturdily in order to cope with the constant groundings, but this still caused damage and so sheltered deep-water ports were sought for the winter. Whitby and Scarborough became considerable shipowning places as they were able to provide adequate shelter. This is a prime example of the valuable services rendered by smaller ports to their larger neighbours who were at times 'overwhelmed by traffic and eager to empty harbours'. Whitby together with Bridlington and Scarborough served the Tyne and Tees ports in this way.[71]

The port was not without its problems; the estuary had a tendency to silt up and there were severe navigational problems encountered in attempting to cross the bar and enter the harbour. One suggested explanation for the lack of investment and neglect of the harbour and pier was that so many vessels, while owned in Whitby, traded out of other ports. The swing bridge across the Esk caused difficulties for the shipbuilders as it limited the size of their vessels. The yards

[65] *Slaters Directory of Whitby 1849; White's Gazetter and Directory of Norfolk 1854.*

[66] Stephanie Jones, 'The Builders of Captain Cook's Ships', *Mariner's Mirror*, 70 (1984), 299–302.

[67] Stephanie A. Jones, 'Maritime History of the Port of Whitby, 1700–1914' (unpublished doctoral thesis, University of London, 1982), p. 23.

[68] *Slater's Directory of Whitby 1849.*

[69] NYRO: NG/RS/WH/Registers of Whitby ships.

[70] Jones, 'Maritime History of the Port of Whitby', p. 99.

[71] Jackson, *The History and Archaeology of Ports*, pp. 10, 43.

were sited up river from the bridge, and this, combined with the lack of nearby coal and iron resources and the absence of any local boiler-making or engineering industry, reduced their ability to compete as iron and steam became established technologies. Whitby vessels once known for their low prices were now considered expensive by comparison with other northeast ports.[72]

Due to its limited access to any substantial hinterland, Whitby never became a commercial or regional centre, and yet had more tonnage than Bristol in 1791 and 1841 and so is considered as of far greater consequence as a port of ownership.[73] The Port of Whitby was dominated by a small number of shipowning families who had originally owned tonnage at the port in the eighteenth and early nineteenth centuries and whose shipping interests had been passed to succeeding generations. Whitby has been described as 'an active shipowning community, rather than just a convenient port of registry for shipowners and companies based elsewhere'.[74]

One of the significant shipowning families was the Smales. Their business had started as mast makers and timber exporters. By 1855 Gideon Smale owned eighteen vessels ranging in size from 150 to 258 tons. Suddenly in 1861 the majority were sold and by 1865 the family owned just nine vessels. These included two very large vessels, the 444-ton *Merrie England* and the 655-ton *Canada Belle*, both built in 1862.[75] This presaged a change to larger vessels, but large vessels were comparatively rare in Whitby due to the port's limitations. In 1866 the Smales Brothers built the 476-ton barque, *Princess Elflaeda*, costing £6,600. The barque was owned by the third generation, four brothers: Gideon Junior, George W, Charles and Edward H. Smales. It sailed between the British ports of Sunderland, Cardiff, London, Newcastle and Glasgow to the ports of the Black Sea carrying a variety of cargoes including grain, timber and coal.[76]

Whitby had one of the highest percentages of women managing owners in *Clayton's Directory* of 1865. These included women such as Sarah Nesfield, Hannah Wood and Joanna Barnard, whose careers will be discussed in Chapter 6.[77] Banking was a particularly strong sector in Whitby; eight banks were based there and one had, in 1800, been founded by a woman, Margaret Campion, together with her son, Robert. They had interests in shipowning, sailcloth weaving, flax dressing, spinning and merchants, both general and wine.[78] Whitby also had a very high percentage of widows, as seen in Chapter 2, many of whom were living in the relatively wealthy areas of the town such as West Cliff and Fishburn Park, which were built after 1856.[79] Whitby seems to have been an attractive retirement place for widows.

---

72 Jones, 'Maritime History of the Port of Whitby', pp. 19, 119, 162.
73 Jackson, 'The Significance of Unimportant Ports', p. 10.
74 Jones, 'Maritime History of the Port of Whitby', p. 167.
75 NYRO: NG/RS/WH/Registers of Whitby ships.
76 Jones, 'Maritime History of the Port of Whitby', p. 119.
77 *Clayton's Directory*.
78 Jones, 'Maritime History of the Port of Whitby', pp. 478–81.
79 Pers. Corr., Rosalin Barker, Whitby Literary and Philosophical Society, 10 July 2006.

By 1876, where once investment in local shipping had prevailed there was now decline, and local ownership fell from 73.7 per cent in 1876 to 69.2 per cent in 1882 and then to 59.6 per cent in 1892. Steam took over from sail and although important steamship owners such as Turnbull, Robinson and Harrowing retained ties with Whitby, they established offices in London and Cardiff and declared these as their official residence.[80]

Whitby was the largest of the five ports in terms of registered shipping and was based close to the expanding shipbuilding centres of the northeast. The expansion was in steam and iron, however, and Whitby was not blessed with either close links with raw materials and labour or with the space in the port to accommodate the new breed of vessels. Inevitably, shipbuilding became a declining feature of the port.

Whitehaven

Rather than a background of moors, as in the case of Whitby, Whitehaven's backdrop is the fells and mountains of Cumberland. These were to become an increasing obstacle to good transport links with its hinterland and so the port had to look to its links outwards. At the end of the eighteenth century, Whitehaven, due to its trade in both imported tobacco and exported coal, could be reported as second to London as one of the top five ports in Britain.[81] The port area covered the coast from Ravenglass to Ellenfoot (later renamed Maryport) until 1838 when Maryport became a separate Customs port.[82] In 1847 Whitehaven was described as a 'large and opulent Sea Port and market town'.[83] It was not always so; it had been developed from a fishing village in the early eighteenth century by the Earl of Lonsdale, the local landowner, who had coal to export. The harbour was constantly improved from 1767; the new West Pier was finished in 1839 and a new north pier was finished in 1841 to become 'the country's most complicated system of pier harbours'.[84] Despite this there was still pressure on the existing facilities and the 1847 guide reported that 'of late years the demand for coals to Ireland has exceeded the existing means of supply, vessels having frequently to wait from four to six weeks for a turn to load'.[85]

Whitehaven had the benefits of access both to the Atlantic and to Ireland. The guide explains that 'although several large vessels are employed in the importation of West Indian, American, and Baltic produce still the principal part of the shipping is engaged in the coal trade with Ireland'. Additionally iron ore was shipped coastwise to Welsh furnaces, pig iron was shipped to Liverpool, London and other places, and lime was extensively shipped to Scotland. The Harbour trustees accounts quoted in the trade directory of 1847 show the significance of

---

[80]   Jones, 'Maritime History of the Port of Whitby', p. 168.
[81]   D. Hay, *A Short History of Whitehaven* (Whitehaven, 1966), p. 29.
[82]   Hay, *A Short History of Whitehaven*, p. 27.
[83]   *Mannix and Whellan, Directory of Cumberland 1847*, p. 374.
[84]   Jackson, *The History and Archaeology of Ports*, p. 107.
[85]   *Mannix and Whellan, Directory of Cumberland 1847*, p. 375.

the income from the coastal trade: £3,033 15s 1d, while foreign tonnage brought in £425 3s 11d and ballast tonnage £1,328 2s 9d. Whitehaven's once important foreign trade was now going to other ports such as Liverpool.[86]

This shift of foreign trade had an impact on the shipping in the port. While Liverpool's shipping jumped from a fleet that numbered 393 in 1775 to reach 796 in 1800, Whitehaven's fleet declined from 214 in 1790 to 181 in 1822.[87] Yet in the nineteenth century, despite the continuing dramatic growth of Liverpool, Whitehaven's fleet began to expand as investors continued to provide shipping for the coal industry. In 1846 there were 267 vessels with a total tonnage of 42,000 and a shipping industry that employed 2,252 men.[88] As the shipping numbers grew steadily so too did the population and the town was now said to number '18,000 souls'.[89] Coal, however, was a high volume, low value trade and the sturdy smaller coal ships required less capital.

The main competitor for Whitehaven's shipping trade still remained Liverpool, with its extensive industrial hinterland, access to the Midlands and vast investment in docks, and, despite Whitehaven's efforts, its shipping declined from 1865. It was a difficult port to enter and the problem was exacerbated as ships increased in size. Shipbuilding sites were squeezed as the Earl of Lonsdale sought to reclaim his land for railway and dock developments, even though the railways were prevented by the Cumberland fells from providing direct rail access and there was only a circuitous coastal route.

Shipbuilding had been an important business. Daniel Brocklebank had started his yard in 1775 and his sons continued it. They established connections with the growing port of Liverpool as early as 1819, but maintained their presence in Whitehaven until 1865 when their lease expired. They were not alone. Ancillary business, too, moved to Liverpool, such as William Burnyeat and Son who were major suppliers of victuals and chandlery.[90]

Whitehaven, despite its impressive past in the eighteenth century, struggled with the new demands of the nineteenth. Yet despite this it remained a sizeable port, continuing its strong trade with Ireland and exporting coal, while its ships worked in a wide range of trades in many parts of the world.

Shipbuilding, Insurance and Banking

The business communities in these small ports mirrored their metropolitan rivals in the services provided. A successful shipowning port required reputable shipbuilding yards and banking and insurance services. All of the five ports had a strong shipbuilding base and other specialist financial services.

86 *Mannix and Whellan, Directory of Cumberland 1847*, p. 376.
87 Hay, *A Short History of Whitehaven*, p. 30.
88 *Mannix and Whellan, Directory of Cumberland 1847*, p. 376.
89 *Mannix and Whellan, Directory of Cumberland 1847*, p. 379.
90 Rolt, *Mariners' Market*, pp. 11–13.

At the beginning of the nineteenth century shipbuilding yards could be found in almost every harbour around the coast, but even then there were noticeable differences in scale between them, and the northeast was already showing its strength. The 1805 parliamentary survey of shipbuilders and shipwrights in Great Britain noted 8,621 shipwrights working in 510 private yards, an average of sixteen men to a yard. The majority of yards had fewer than twenty shipwrights and the biggest yard in South Shields had 181 men. Whitby listed a total of eight yards with 265 men. Fowey had no separately listed yards, but a total of twenty-nine men. Exeter itself had none, but Topsham had fifty-five shipwrights working in three yards. This is similar to Lynn where there were three shipyards with fifty-one men employed. Apart from Liverpool the survey gives no information for the northwest, which is an odd omission.[91]

The shipbuilders of Whitby and Lynn had good reputations and were on the list of ports from which Henley and Son, coal merchants of London, solicited shipbuilding tenders.[92] Topsham and Lynn were two of the outports that were favoured by the Navy Board for building warships. The yard of J. and T. Brindley of Lynn built eight gun brigs for the navy between 1797 and 1812, and Davy of Topsham was another significant builder of warships.[93] Whitehaven had a strong shipbuilding presence, the firm of Brocklebank and Son being just one of several yards. Fowey-built ships occasionally attracted external investors, such as the *Twins* in 1803 built for London owners, and launched one navy warship, *HMS Primrose*, in 1807.[94]

Shipbuilders and shipowners were vital to one another, with the greater flexibility on the part of the shipowner. In 1840 the Comptroller of Customs of Whitehaven published a list of Whitehaven shipping and gave their place of build; just 42 per cent were built in Whitehaven.[95] In Fowey, between 1816 and 1840, 74 per cent of vessels were built within the port, but from 1841 to 1880 it was only 33 per cent.[96] While the local shipowners could and did buy vessels from elsewhere they still required local yards for the essential maintenance and repair work. The increasing numbers of North American vessels, particularly from Prince Edward Island, were sailed across under a basic rig (carrying a cargo of timber) then re-rigged and coppered in local yards.

Whitby and Exeter are notable for the strength of their ship insurance provision. Holman's of Topsham developed an expertise for which they are still known today. The family business began with shipowning, then added shipbuilding. John Holman became a surveyor for Lloyd's and from this developed an extensive

91 BPP 1805 VIII: An account showing the number of shipwrights and also of apprentices employed in the merchant yards of Great Britain according to the returns made to the Admiralty in April 1804, pp. 467–91.
92 Ville, *English Shipowning*, p. 45.
93 BPP 1813–14 VIII: An account of the number of ships of war of all sizes, built in the Private Yards at the outports since 1791, pp. 442–7; National Archives: PRO: ADM 49/102.
94 CRO: MSR/FOWEY Registers of Shipping.
95 W. Sawyer, *A List of Cumberland Shipping corrected to February 1840*.
96 Ward-Jackson, *Ships and Shipbuilders*, p. 103.

knowledge of shipping and most of all a 'shrewd evaluation of risk'.[97] He began by running insurance clubs. The West of England Insurance Association was formed in 1832 and he began to attract not just local shipowners, but shipowners from elsewhere. By 1855 he had established his own Protection and Indemnity Insurance business, a business that eventually moved to London by the end of the century.

Whitby also had strong insurance businesses. Both Turnbull and Marwood were well known families running insurance clubs and both published their own competitors to Lloyd's Register of Shipping.[98] These insurance clubs, like those run by Holman, attracted a wide range of members. The Whitby Marine, British, General, Sea & Neptune Insurance Association in 1850 had owners registered from Liverpool, Sunderland, Newcastle, Hartlepool, Belfast, London, Exmouth, Brixham and Padstow, to name just a few examples.[99]

Whitby also had a very strong banking tradition. Eight out of 96 banks in the northeast were based in Whitby and most of them had been founded and managed by local shipowners. The stability of the Whitby banks was of particular note.[100] Lynn, too, had plenty of banks, but these do not appear to have had shipowning links. There were, of course, banks in the other communities, but all of them were branches of larger concerns. There were, however, strong links with shipowning in Fowey where Henry Hocken of the shipowning family in Polruan was the manager of the local bank.[101]

Investment and Disinvestment

For much of the nineteenth century the number of vessels registered in a port generally reflected local ship investment. There were a few exceptions, such as those vessels registered there which in fact were based elsewhere. With overall movement of shipping and shipbuilding to the north it might be expected that the southern ports showed a gradual decline in ships registered, but the statistics do not show this. Investment in shipping in all the ports except Fowey was in decline. Fowey's export china clay trade and the investment in ships for the fruit trade were providing a steady increase in local vessels.

The vessels registered were all sailing vessels with the exception of one steam ship registered in Whitby. While the number of vessels is a useful indicator, it can hide a different picture when tonnage is considered. More vessels do not necessarily mean larger vessels. As can be seen from the tonnage figures in Appendix IV,

---

97 Craig *et al.*, 'Some Aspects of Devon Shipping', p. 100; Starkey, 'The Ports, Seaborne Trade and Shipping Industry'.
98 *Marwood's Directory of Shipping 1855*; *Turnbull's Annual Maritime Advertiser Directory & Shipping Register 1854–55*.
99 Whitby Literary and Philosophical Society (WLPS): 0102/2a List of ships insured.
100 Jones, 'Maritime History of the Port of Whitby', p. 478.
101 CRO: MSR/FOW/6 *Gallant* 1884.

Figure 1. Registered vessels in five ports, 1851–1871

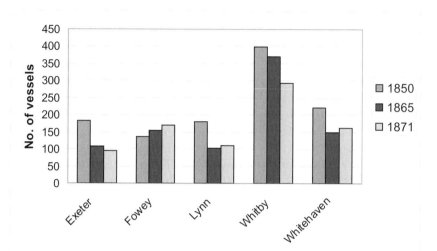

Sources: TNA: PRO: BT 162/19 Account of vessels registered at ports, 31 December 1850; *Clayton's Register of Shipping, 1865; Mercantile Navy List 1872*, xxii–xxvi.

the five ports were within the mid-range of ports in 1871, but their position relative to each other changed over time. However, while overall numbers on the registers at ports are useful when considering investment, another aspect is the willingness of the port's investors to buy new tonnage and dispose of old. So before moving on to a comparison of the female investors in the ports, it is worth considering the relative state of investment in the business communities.

The *Mercantile Navy List*, which published the official statistics on shipping, also lists the number and tonnage of vessels removed or deducted from the register, whether by purchase or sale, or broken up. It provides these figures split into the two categories of steam and sail. These figures show active investment or disinvestment by the local owners and give a measure of the strength of the local shipping industry. The list does not reveal the average age of the vessels on the register, which is another useful indicator. In England and Wales in 1871 there was an overall increase in shipping tonnage of 2 per cent from the previous year (see Appendix IV). In the five ports considered here (see Table 7), only Whitehaven shows an increase in tonnage, and Whitby, where the physical problems of the port were beginning to have a marked effect, shows a distinct drop in registered tonnage.

The figures were also given of the number of men, excluding masters, who were employed in the industry. This showed that owners were keeping a close watch on labour costs despite the increasing number of steam vessels (which had a tendency to require more men as specialist engineers because of the complexities

Table 7. Tonnage gained/lost from port registers, 1871

Port	Tonnage added	Tonnage lost	Net gain/loss
Exeter	806	879	-73
Fowey	314	515	-201
Lynn	0	680	-680
Whitby	2,234	5,786	-3,552
Whitehaven	682	579	103

Source: Mercantile Navy List 1872, xxii–xxvi.

involved). The ratio of men to ship remained between 8.4:1 in the 1850s and 9:1 in the 1860s, falling back to 8.8:1 in the last three years. At this stage the number of sailing vessels still numerically exceeded the number of steam vessels.[102] This was a point of importance to all of these smaller ports, none of which were to become centres of steam and iron ships.

For investors in shipping there were local investment opportunities throughout the period. Joint stock shipping companies were rare among these communities, all of whom preferred to stay with the 64th system of shareownership. It was this local investment and the 64th system that provided particular investment opportunities for women. The investors were important to the local economy, providing work ashore and at sea. Even a ship built elsewhere and registered locally provided income if it was manned, maintained and repaired locally. Steam vessels registered but not built locally were a less attractive proposition to those ports predominantly in sail. With no local facilities these did not bring income to the immediate community. If the ship was too large for the port and merely registered there as a matter of sentiment, as in the case of the later steam ships belonging to Holman's of Topsham, increasingly jobs on board were filled outside the community.

The shipping movements in a port were a visible sign to the investing community of the strength or otherwise of the industry. The vessels trading inwards and outwards from ports were not necessarily those belonging to the port. The charts below show where the strengths were for the different ports. Whitehaven's coal trade was a key element for the port, and in Fowey the china clay trade kept the port busy with foreign trade (see Figures 2 and 3).

Women Investors in the Five Ports

The women shareholders across the ports held between them 17,339 shares in 692 vessels of varying sizes, from 15 tons (the minimum size that could be registered) to 1,242 tons when substantial steam and iron vessels appeared in the registers. Some of these larger vessels were still owned under the 64th system despite the

---

[102]   Mercantile Navy List 1872, xxii–xxvi.

Figure 2. Coastwise tonnage mid-century in five ports

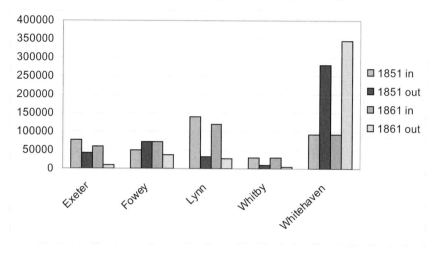

Source: BPP XLIX.1: Return of no & tonnage of vessels entered and cleared coastwise in 1851; BPP LIV.101: Return of no & tonnage of vessels entered and cleared coastwise in 1861.

Figure 3. Foreign trade tonnage mid-century

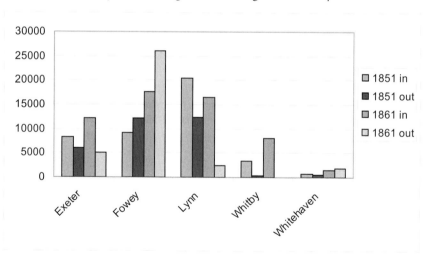

Source: BPP XLIX.1: Return of no & tonnage of vessels entered and cleared from and to Foreign Ports in 1851; BPP LIV.101: Return of no & tonnage of vessels entered and cleared from and to Foreign Ports in 1861.

increasing number of limited companies. The range of ownership by women was from a minority holding of one or two shares to a majority shareholding and even total ownership, as will be seen in later chapters. The local Customs officials noted the reason for the transfer of ownership of shares when registering the changes, such as the death of the owner and subsequent probate details, or purchase and by whom.

While there were ships that were solely owned by one individual, these were in the minority in all the ports as the 64th system of investment encouraged wide ownership of shares in ships. In the registers there are plenty of examples of investors of both sexes who had just one or two shares in a vessel, perhaps all they could afford or all they were prepared to risk. There are also many examples of multiple transactions, either buying or selling transactions within one vessel or transactions across several vessels, with some owners spreading the risk by owning small parcels of shares across many vessels. Among the female shareholders, the holder of the greatest number of shares in vessels was Elizabeth Luke of Charlestown near Fowey, whose husband died in 1871 leaving her with 696 shares spread across twenty-two ships.[103] Women are not found just as minor investors, holding the occasional share, but as examples of several different types of investor. Most of the share transactions investigated involved at least one further transaction from the initial acquisition. The greatest number of transactions on one set of shares were the tortuous dealings of Grace Tadd of Polruan, Fowey. Grace was involved in nine separate transactions over seven years relating to her inheritance from her husband of fifty-nine shares in the *Sabina*, as she sold, then repurchased and mortgaged as her circumstances changed.[104]

While all of the ports were among the mid-sized ports in England, there were differences between the activities of the shareholders within them. As seen, the activity in ports rose and fell over the period, with some going into decline, such as Exeter and Lynn, while others maintained steady progress, as was the case for Fowey. The reasons for the loss of port business were varied, but the movement of trade away from a port and the arrival of very large ships certainly caused problems. For example, Whitby and Exeter were unable to physically accommodate the larger vessels that were being built as iron and steam were increasingly used.

Across the period, there are distinct differences between the ports. Table 8 shows the data extracted from the registers by port. The actual number of vessels in which women invested is shown in the first line for comparison purposes, but the number of vessels in a port could vary significantly, as was shown in Figure 1. The next set of figures (line 2) show the total number of female shareholders found in each port. Then the total number of shares held by the women in that port (line 3). Line 4 shows the average size of the shareholding of the women in the ports, which could range from one share to all sixty-four shares. Finally, line 5 onwards shows the average number of vessels in which a female shareowner held

---

103   CRO: MSR/Fowey/5, 6 & 8.
104   CRO: MSR/FOW/7 & 8.

Table 8. Port comparison, female shareholder data

Port	Exeter	Fowey	Lynn	Whitby	Whitehaven
Period of registers consulted	1824–82	1834–99	1836–92	1848–92	1840–92
1. Female investor ships	118	211	70	144	149
2. Women shareholders	110	310	63	138	246
3. No. of shares	5,549	5,227	3,356	4,965	1,550
4. Median no. of shares held	21	4	32	21	4
5. No. of ships per shareholder					
17 to 22 ships	1	4			
6 to 11 ships		6	1		4
5 ships	1	6	2	3	4
4 ships	8	7			4
3 ships	8	20	1	4	8
2 ships	12	41	9	28	32
1 ships	81	226	50	103	194
Average	1.63	1.8	1.4	1.35	1.42

Source: Investor Database
Cornwall Record Office (CRO): MSR/FOW/ 3–9 Fowey Shipping Registers
North Yorkshire Record Office (NYRO): NG/RS/WH/2, 9 & 10 Whitby Registers
Whitehaven Record Office (WRO) YTSR 1/9–12 and YTSR 16–21 Register of shipping
Devon Record Office (DRO): 3289s/3–17, 10 Exeter shipping registers
Norfolk Record Office (NRO): P/SH Shipping Registers: King's Lynn, Wells, Cley and Great
Yarmouth 1825–1892

shares (this could range from one vessel to a maximum of twenty-two). The ratio of female shareholders to the number of ships with female shareowners (lines 1 and 2) was higher in Fowey and in Whitehaven and, as previously shown, these were not the two biggest ports for overall ship registration. These two ports also had the lowest average size of shareholding. It is probable that this is a reflection of the amount of capital available for investment in those ports. Whitby had the highest number of shares per transaction, while both Fowey and Whitehaven shares changed hands in smaller quantities. This pattern was consistent across all shareholders, male and female; for example in a sample year, 1850, the average number of shareholders per vessel in Whitby was two, while in Whitehaven the average was ten shareholders.[105] This suggests that the shareholders in Fowey and Whitehaven had access to less capital within these communities and needed more shareholding partners. Women typically had less access to capital than men; for example, the average sworn value on probate was less for women than for men, so this excluded large investments.[106] Where the net for more shareholders was

---

[105] TNA: PRO BT 107/332 1850 Transcripts of Port Registers, SU-Y.
[106] Morriss, *Men, Women and Property*, p. 234.

cast wider and shares were available in small numbers, the women in these ports had greater opportunity. Shares could also change hands between investors more easily when smaller sums were involved.

Summary

The five ports had active communities of women investors and the differences between the ports were more reflective of the overall economy in the locality than of attitudes to women. Women had less opportunity to access larger amounts of capital, which is why Fowey and Whitehaven with their widespread shipowner-ship feature such a high level of women investors. The economic fortunes of the ports affected men as well as women and when shipowning, with its connotations of support for both the family concerns and the local community, moved away, the alternatives were to invest in more remote joint stock companies. It remains to be seen from further research whether the women investors from the ports transferred their attention to such areas.

It is easy to dismiss these communities as insignificant beside the dominance of the large ports, but, as has been pointed out, they were not unimportant to the success of the overall shipping industry. The men and women who lived in these ports and contributed as investors to the ups and downs of the fortunes of these communities were no less entrepreneurial in their dealings than their counterparts in the major commercial centres. If their investments were smaller in financial terms, in real terms they still required considerable knowledge and a willingness to take real financial risks.

4

Shipowning Wives, Widows and Spinsters

On 13 May 1873 ten shareholders of the newly launched schooner, *Thetis*, sat down in the Ship Inn in Fowey to agree some important resolutions. The master, Captain Beale, was appointed at a salary of £6 per month plus gratuities and 10 per cent of the profits. Victualling was set at thirteen pence per day per man and 'it was resolved that Mr Thomas Pearce be appointed Agent of the Vessel at five pounds per year'. Every resolution agreed had an important consequence in terms of the future earning for the shareholders, who were paid annually after all receipts and disbursements had been made and in relation to their shareholdings. Those present represented twenty-eight of the sixty-four shares and acted in the same way as a board of directors, with the agent as chief executive. Sitting with the nine other shareholders was Miss Mary Ann Henwood, a farmer's daughter aged twenty-five. It appears that Mary Ann, who held one share, had no problems in sitting on equal terms with male shareholders, none of whom appear to be relations. She was present again when the shareholders next sat down in January 1874, again at the Ship Inn. The agent was able to report that the vessel had done well in the fruit trade and in the first year of operation the shareholders would receive £13 4s 7d per share. This was a promising start as a return on their initial investment of £57 19s 9d per share.[1]

Mary Ann was just one of the female shareholders whose names are listed in the shipping registers. The Customs House officers were required to note the name, residence and occupation of every shareholder. Male shareholders were noted by their economic status such as merchant, shipowner, sailmaker and, occasionally, gentleman. However, the main classification of the female shareholders in the shipping registers is a social classification, as almost all of them are noted as widows, spinsters or wives. In the last category in most cases the name of their husband is given. The occasional glimpse is afforded of women who had other roles, such as grocer, innkeeper, confectioner, shipowner and shipbuilder, but these are few. This chapter examines the women shareholders from the perspective of their marital status. It considers the importance of inheritance of shares, especially for widows, many of whom inherited from their husbands. Spinsters feature prominently, but inheritance of shares was for them a less important acquisition route. Wives represent 10 per cent of the shareholders, so how did they acquire shares before the Married Women's Property Acts of 1870 and 1882, and what

---

[1] Greenhill, *Merchant Schooners*, pp. 274–5.

4. Reception on board the *Eleanor Dixon* of Whitehaven
Source: The Beacon Museum, Whitehaven

happened after the acts came into effect? For all groups family links were important both as routes into the shipping market and reasons for remaining there.

The World of Women

Across the five ports shares were held by widows who had inherited from their
late husbands. Spinsters are also well represented and, despite the restrictions
of common law and coverture, wives held shares in their own name. Widows
account for just over half of the sample, spinsters for 36 per cent and wives feature
in 10 per cent of the transactions (see Table 9). These marital status percentages
for the female maritime investors show a different profile from previous findings.
Spinster investors in the Birmingham Canal Company between 1768 and 1840
outnumbered widows by a ratio of 47 to 14 per cent.[2] Women formed a significant and growing proportion of government fund holders from 1810 to 1840, but
here the ratio of spinsters to widows was a more balanced 47 per cent to 53. It
has been suggested that the high number of spinsters in the population of major
cities may be the reason for this high number.[3] Spinsters again feature as the
largest group of female investors in a sample of limited companies from 1880.[4]
In these same research findings, wives hardly feature as shareholders before 1882
when the second and more effective Married Women's Property Act was passed.
Just 1 per cent of investors in the Birmingham Canal Company were wives, with a
similar percentage in government stock. The average of 10 per cent of wives, with
a variation across the five ports from 4 to 14 per cent, who invested in shipping
merits further investigation in more ports. Table 9 shows the marital status, where
known, of the women investors in the database. Forty-six out of the total 866
female investors had no clear marital status. Both Whitehaven and Fowey show a
higher percentage of wives and spinsters.

Table 9. Shareholder marital status, 1824–1892

	Widows		Spinsters		Wives		Total
Exeter	70	64%	31	28%	8	7%	109
Fowey	140	50%	99	35%	40	14%	279
Lynn	38	68%	13	23%	5	9%	56
Whitby	104	76%	27	20%	5	4%	136
Whitehaven	88	37%	126	52%	27	11%	241
Total	440	54%	296	36%	85	10%	821

Source: Investor Database. See Appendix V for detailed sources. Note marital status could not
be identified for 46 women.

2   Hudson, 'Attitudes to Investment Risk', p. 204.
3   Green and Owens, 'Gentlewomanly Capitalism?', p. 513.
4   Maltby and Rutterford, 'She Possessed Her Own Fortune', p. 232.

Acquisition

With a high number of widows, inheritance was a significant factor, but a sizeable number of shares were purchased in share acquisition. Unlike the later limited companies which widely advertised share offers in newspapers, buying shares in ships was a very local process. The buyers and sellers knew each other and all that was required to make it legal was to register the initial ownership or change on the appropriate form at the Customs House. Ships were occasionally publicly auctioned, but this practice was not frequent. The close connections and information networks that assisted the sale and purchase of shares in the communities were shown earlier in Chapter 2. The shipping registers provide details in most cases of how the shares changed hands, particularly after *de novo* registration was changed. *De novo* meant registering as if new and occurred when there were big changes of owners. The ship was then re-entered as if a new entry into the registers, which causes difficulties in identifying in some cases how original shares were acquired. The ship simply reappeared on the registers with a different list of owners and information was not always given about the reason for the change. Where the vessel was clearly a new one then it is evident the investor was an initial purchaser of shares. Where it is clearly a *de novo* registration of an earlier registered ship, with no trace of how the female investor acquired the shares, then it is categorised as unknown, as detailed in Table 10. From 1855 the widespread adoption of separate transaction registers resolved this problem and from this time the full details of a ship were only given once and then subsequent changes of ownership were noted.

Of those where the source information is available, 430 of the transactions (which could involve any amount of shares from one to sixty-four) were acquired through inheritance and 344 of these were inherited from husbands. Fathers were clearly identified in 5 per cent of cases, but are likely to be underrepresented and could be hidden among the unknown category. When there was no evidence from wills or other sources as to the relationship between the woman and the deceased it was placed in the unknown category. Two per cent were other relatives, such as mothers, sisters, and brothers, and in one case a stepfather was identified and in another a fiancé. Thirteen per cent were unknown (Tables 10 and 11).

Widows

The largest group of women shipowners were widows – 54 per cent of the total database and the major group in almost all ports. It has been argued that widows, particularly those with dependants, were advised to be more risk averse, and widows were the least important class in number in the sample of joint stock companies from 1880, which included at least one shipping company. There is a different profile over time as more widows inherited ordinary and preference shares in the Tinsley Rolling Mills and shares in the Prudential Assurance Company

Table 10. Acquisition of shares

	Purchased	Inherited	Not known	Total
Exeter	42	71	82	195
Fowey	216	192	152	560
Lynn	16	47	24	87
Whitby	25	80	81	186
Whitehaven	81	40	228	349
Total	380	430	485	1,377

Note: This table shows the number of transactions, i.e. when a woman first appears as the owner, and not the number of shares acquired.
Source: Investor Database (see Table 8).

Table 11. Source of inheritance

	Husband	Father	Mother	Sister	Brother	Other	Unknown
Exeter	65				3	1	3
Fowey	157	11	3			1	21
Lynn	38	7					2
Whitby	57	3					20
Whitehaven	27			1			14
Total	344	21	3	1	3	2	60
% of total	79%	5%	1%	0%	1%	0%	14%

Note: As in Table 9, this shows the number of occasions on which a woman inherited and not the number of shares acquired.
Source: Investor Database (see Table 8).

Ltd. The marked increase in women shareholders was combined with a decline in the size of their shareholding. 'As husbands died so wives became widows and perhaps had to share the husband's holdings with children or other heirs.'[5] The comparatively short period from the beginnings of the limited liability companies compared to the longer existence of ship ownership supports the increased presence of widowed shipowners and is marked in Exeter and Whitby.

A widow was not automatically in a better position financially, just because of an inheritance. Her standard of living could be considerably worse and this 'depended on a number of factors, including her status and wealth, the occupation of her deceased husband and whether she was familiar with her husband's

---

[5]   Maltby and Rutterford, 'She Possessed Her Own Fortune', p. 239

occupation.'[6] Gentry and middle-class widows often invested their money in loans or property and lived off the proceeds; recent research suggests that widows 'owned a sizeable proportion of the London housing stock' and played a vital role in the provision of loan capital through the bond and mortgage market.[7]

The case of Grace Tadd of Polruan in Cornwall serves to illustrate the difficult situation in which a woman might find herself on widowhood and what part shares played. Grace was left a sizeable estate by her husband Peter Tadd. Peter was one of the mariners whose career had been successful. He became a master mariner and built up a portfolio of property and shares. When he died in 1868 he left Grace his shares in many local ships and a substantial bequest of fifteen houses.[8] She had two children, Peter, aged sixteen, and Mary, aged three. Despite this apparently wealthy inheritance, the reality shown in her share dealings gives a picture of precarious borrowing and repayment problems. She mortgaged all of the sixty-four shares in the *Ann Elizabeth* in 1871, paying off the mortgage two years later. In 1871 she mortgaged forty-six shares in the *Ossena*, repaying this loan in 1876.[9] She had fifty-nine of the sixty-four shares in the *Sabina*, which was lost at sea in 1876. Her marital home of Holly House in Fore Street, Polruan was sold in 1874 to pay off the Devon and Cornwall Banking Company.[10] By 1881 she had moved down the hill to East Street where she took in a boarder to help with the payments, William Boley, aged ninety-two.[11] The move down hill was significant. While the better off and rising master mariners and their families moved up the hill, Grace's move was a distinct change downwards, as was her letting of a room. 'In the gentility conscious nineteenth century it signified a loss of genteel status.'[12] Grace died in 1883 aged sixty-eight leaving no will and there is no sign of any administration of her estate.

Widows and Inheritance

Some husbands guarded against the type of situation in which Grace found herself by setting up trusts, handing all financial matters into the care of other men. In the maritime communities, several women inherited their shares jointly with trustees or another beneficiary. In these cases the number of shipowners could exceed the statute limit of thirty-two. Joint inheritance of a share was accepted and two names on a share and sometimes three names was not uncommon. Setting up trusts had a cost. There was significant management cost. This might have been

---

[6] Shoemaker, *Gender in English Society*, p. 138.
[7] *Ibid.*
[8] From 1837 all types of real estate could be disposed of by will – see Karen Grannum and Nigel Taylor, *Wills and Other Probate Records* (London: National Archives, 2004), p. 88.
[9] CRO: MSR Merchant Shipping Registers Fowey (1786–1890).
[10] Deeds of Holly House, Polruan, private collection.
[11] CRO: 1881 Census Lanteglos by Fowey.
[12] Hill, *Women Alone*, p. 47.

explicit in terms of lawyers' fees or implicit in terms of demands made upon family members and friends who were trustees of the will.'[13] Table 12 shows the spread of joint inheritance. It is not always possible to identify the relationship in every case; an avenue of further research would be to examine the details of the will in each case to establish the pattern of such trusts.

Table 12. Number of transactions left by husbands and fathers to joint beneficiaries

	Husband	*Father*	*Unknown*
Exeter	9		
Fowey	12	11	
Lynn	12	7	
Whitby	6	3	16
Whitehaven	1		7
Total	40	21	23

Source: Investor Database (see Table 8).

Trusts have been described as 'fragments of independence' and as

a result of the clash between one type of male power and another type of male power, between the identity, ambitions and responsibilities of the dead and those of the living which came to a focus on the fortunes of wives, widows, daughters, sisters and nieces.[14]

Edward Hawkins of Exeter died on 11 September 1859. His widow, Sarah, was left a wealthy woman. Edward's effects (non-real estate) were initially sworn on probate as being under £18,000, but two years later this was adjusted upwards at the Stamp Office as 'Effects under £30,000'.[15] Sarah inherited the full owner-ship of four vessels, a majority share interest in four others and eight shares in a schooner called *Fountain*. Edward had been a coal and guano merchant, both potentially lucrative trades at this time. Sarah was in her late forties with seven daughters to provide for, the youngest of whom was eleven. In his will, written two years before he died, Edward left all of his real and personal property to his brothers-in-law, Peter Varwell and Edward Fox, in trust. Sarah was to have the rents, dividends and income from the trust until she died or remarried, and her children were tenants-in-common of the estate. Monies could be released to help with their education or maintenance. Sarah could require the trustees to sell or dispose of his real or personal estate.

---

13 Morris, *Men, Women and Property*, p. 258.
14 Morris, *Men, Women and Property*, p. 263.
15 Bodmin Probate Office: Calendar of wills.

Peter Varwell was Sarah's older brother and Edward Fox was married to her older sister, Elizabeth. The trustees had wide powers to sell or buy property and shares at their discretion. They were not to be held answerable for 'any banker broker or other person in whose hands any of the trust premises or monies shall be placed nor for the insufficiency of any stocks funds or securities nor otherwise of any involuntary losses'.[16] They could reimburse themselves for all expenses that might be incurred from the trust. Sarah and her children were therefore heavily reliant on the expertise and honesty of the two trustees. It is noticeable that the will specifies that the trustees were to act at Sarah's request. Whatever the balance of the decision making between the trustees and Sarah, she had some critical decisions to make and her trustees, who were shipowners and who both held shares in the Hawkins ships, were in a good position to advise her.

Sarah's case looks like a classic example of paternalism in action: the grieving widow with a young family who is not to be overly worried with business matters, which can be safely left in the hands of trusted male advisers. Yet the earlier reference to a clash of male wills should be extended to a clash of female and male wills. A research benefit of the shipping registers over an examination of wills and probate is the ability to view what happened after some of these trusts were established. The maritime examples provide several cases where the trustees' role came to an early end. Not all trustees, it appears, remained in control for the lifetime of a widow, such as the thirty-year trusteeship in Jane Hey's case, highlighted in a study of legacies.[17] Mary Hicks Hayes and Ann Hicks both inherited from James Hayes, a shipbroker of Polruan who died in 1873. Mary was James's widow and Ann was his sister. Two trustees were appointed. They were respected professional men: Arthur Davies, the local doctor, and James Kendall, the local vicar. In his will, James Hayes left shares in several vessels and initially these were all reregistered in the name of Davies and Kendall as the trustees. Two years later both women 'bought' their shares from the trustees, taking into their own control all the shares left by James. They then went on to deal in shares, as will be seen in the next chapter.[18] Money is unlikely to have changed hands in this type of case. The Customs House official forms allowed for transfer by purchase, inheritance or marriage. The transfer from the trustees was not directly an inheritance nor was it truly a purchase, but purchase was how the officials decided to handle such a case.

Mary Dodgson of Whitehaven was another case of a widow dispensing with trustees. She had inherited twenty-six shares in five vessels from her husband Stanley Dodgson, a shipowner, who died in February 1870. Mary was appointed executor together with three others. The will was proved at Carlisle in April 1870 and six months later Mary bought out the other executors, taking all the shares into her sole name. At the same time she did this she also notified another bequest from Henry James Johnson, a grocer. Henry, perhaps her father, had died intestate

16 Exeter Probate Office: Will of Edward Harris 1859.
17 Morris, *Men, Women and Property*, p. 308.
18 CRO: MSR FOW 3–9.

in March 1864 with probate the same year. Mary now registered these extra shares in her name six years later.[19]

For many of the widows inheritance was straightforward and the shares were simply reregistered in their names, although a large inheritance such as a whole ship involved the widow in more decisions, as will be seen later. Georgina Playford of Lynn inherited the 156-ton brig *Caroline Lesure* and Mary Rounce of Rotherhithe also inherited a ship, the 198-ton *Champion*.[20] With clear title to all the shares in these ships, they could make their business decisions without consultation or delay.

Those whose husbands died intestate were in a more complex position. The widows had to apply for a grant to administer the estate and distribution was dictated by law. The personal estate, cash, credits, leases, goods and chattels were distributed one-third to the widow and the remainder to the deceased's children, shared equally. If there were no children then half went to the widow and half to the remaining next of kin. Real property such as freehold land went to the eldest son and if there was no son then to all the daughters equally.[21] The customs officials required proof of administration or probate before reregistering shares. In the shipping registers, administrations were less common than wills (see Table 13) and, in the case of the former, almost always the widow was registered as the new owner of the shares.

Table 13. Wills/administrations

	Wills		Admin.		Unknown	
Exeter	8	100%				
Fowey	76	62%	18	15%	28	23%
Lynn	37	80%	5	11%	4	9%
Whitby	47	69%	14	21%	7	10%
Whitehaven	21	62%	3	9%	12	35%
Total	189	68%	40	14%	51	18%

Source: Investor Database (see Table 8).

The *Fancy* was a small 62-ton sloop built in 1825. By 1857 she had been rebuilt and reregistered as a 47-ton smack. The majority owner was Richard Chappell, a carpenter of Polruan who had forty-four shares at the time of his death on 4 January 1860. He left no will and letters of administration were granted to his wife, Maria, in May of that year. However, there had been a previous transaction between husband and wife which was noted in the registers at the same time as Maria registered her ownership of the shares. On 13 December 1859, one month before his death, Richard Chappell had 'previously executed a deed of gift … in

19   WRO: YTSR 1/19 Shipping Registers.
20   NRO: P/SH/L 1–3 King's Lynn Shipping Registers.
21   Grannum and Taylor, *Wills and Other Probate Records*, pp. 5, 46–7.

favour of Maria Chappell his wife'. By doing this Maria had clear title to the shares and any income without having to go through probate. The ship was lost in August 1868 when she foundered off Rundlestone.[22]

Inheritance could be complicated and as ships were sometimes family-owned, internal divisions had to be resolved. Mary Pine inherited forty-eight shares from her husband in the *Dove*, a 39-ton sloop built in Topsham in 1824. This gave her majority control and her son, John Pine, was the master. The vessel was very much a family ship as her mother, Mary Smith, held the balance of the shares. In December 1845, on the death of her mother, Mary Pine bought eleven shares from 'Robert Bussell and Sally his wife, Charles Hutchins and Mary his wife, Sarah Smith spinster, Jabez Ireland and Eliza his wife'.[23] These were Mary's sisters and their husbands who inherited their shares from Mary Smith, but it leaves five shares unaccounted for. Two years later Mary became sole owner with the following entry on 29 December 1849 which hints at a resolution of family arguments and challenges:

> By last will and testament of Will Smith of Topsham Mason deceased dated 29 April 1813 and probate dated 1818 that his daughter Mary Pine is entitled under his will to five shares in the vessel *Dove* of Exeter.[24]

Women Bequeathing to Women

Shares were also passed down from other women. In the previous case of Mary Smith there were no sons so the shares had been passed equally to her other daughters. In another case, Jane Parker shared ownership of the 99-ton schooner, *Britannia*, with her son John Parker, a ropemaker. She held her thirty-two shares for six years, then on 30 June 1843 at the age of sixty-seven she transferred them by deed of gift to her five daughters, all of them spinsters, thus making provision for them.[25] Margaret Clarke of Whitby inherited the *Robert* on the death of her husband in 1852, when he died without leaving a will. When Margaret died eight years later she ensured there was a clear inheritance for her daughter, Elizabeth, by writing a will to that effect.[26] When inheriting shares from other women, most of the bequests were just as straightforward as in Elizabeth Clarke's case. Mary Ann Jamieson of Whitby and Mary Atkinson of Whitehaven inherited shares from women. Fowey had most examples: Jane Bowden, Mary Truscott and Ann Macdonald all received their shares via inheritance from other women. There is just one instance of a joint inheritance and this was the Ross sisters of Fowey who inherited four shares jointly in the *Jane and Jennifer* from their mother.[27] When

---

22 NYRO: NG/RS/WH/9.
23 DRO: 3289s/5, 51/1836.
24 Shoemaker, *Gender in English Society*, p. 139.
25 DRO: 3289s/5, 9/1837, DRO 3289s/6, 5/1842.
26 NYRO: NG/RS/WH/2.
27 CRO: MSR/Fow/5.

it came to bequeathing shares to other women, women did not see any need to leave complex trust situations for their heirs, even when the shares in question were numerous, as in the case of Sarah Ann Hewett, who inherited twenty-four shares in the *Honour* in 1877. Sarah was free to sell her shares, which she did one year later.

Spinsters

In 1851 there were 20 per cent more unmarried women than men over the age of forty in England and Wales and this was the cause for some concern at the time.[28] Single women are described as being doomed to a subservient role at home, often as an unpaid carer for a brother or elderly parents.[29] Beatrice Webb fought against the assumption that as 'an unmarried daughter she was endlessly at the beck and call of her family until (and if) she married'. It has been concluded that this was the case for the vast majority of single women whose families could afford to keep them at home.[30] Independence was not a goal it seems. But for a single woman, for whom many ways of earning income were unacceptable or unavailable, income had to come from elsewhere. Unless they were very wealthy, spinsters could not afford, any more than widows, to invest in risky ventures. It has been argued that this aversion to risk is why spinsters appear in such numbers in Bank of England stock.[31] However, spinsters were also present as shareholders in ships, not the safest of investments.

As Table 14 shows, inheritance was not a significant factor in their acquisition of shares: just 5 per cent of spinsters can be shown as inheriting shares. Most of those who inherited did so from their fathers, as might be expected. However, despite the guidance from contemporary writers, such as the stern words of caution about the risks inherent in investment from the Banker's Daughter, 49 per cent of the total database of spinsters purchased their shares in ships.[32]

Some spinsters who inherited were also subject to the benefits and limitations of trusts. Like widows, spinsters also were able to dispense with their trustees. John Hicks of Bodinnick left a large and very complex will. In it, his daughter, Rachel Hicks, inherited thirty-six shares, the majority share, in the 75-ton schooner, *Charlotte and Hannah*. John Hicks died in March 1855 and in the same year the shares were transferred from the trustees to Rachel and were noted as a purchase transaction. This left her free to sell or retain them as she wished.[33] Mary Dobson of Whitby was a spinster who inherited forty-eight shares in the *Gem* from John Schofield. These were held jointly with Francis Kildill Robinson and

28 Shoemaker, *Gender in English Society*, p. 140.
29 Geoff Best, *Mid-Victorian Britain, 1851–75* (London: Fontana Press, 1975), p. 304.
30 Hill, *Women Alone*, p. 80.
31 Green and Owens, 'Gentlewomanly Capitalism?', pp. 520–30.
32 A Banker's Daughter, 'Guide to the Unprotected'.
33 CRO: MSR/FOW/7.

two years later she bought him out.[34] In both cases the movement of the shares freed the women to make their own decisions. In Mary's case this meant selling the shares, an action she might well have been pleased with when the ship was wrecked two years later.

Table 14. Transactions by marital status

	Purchased		Inherited		Unknown		Total
Widows	211	26%	343	42%	263	32%	817
Spinsters	198	49%	23	5%	228	56%	406
Wives	47	46%	32	31%	23	23%	102
Total	456		398		514		1,325

Note: The total in this table is less than in Table 13 as the marital status was unknown for some investors.
Source: Investor Database (see Table 8).

Thirty-six per cent of the women in the database were spinsters and the majority had made an active decision to invest in the local shipping industry. Some of them had sizeable portfolios of shares. Sarah Isabella Bragg of White-haven held sixty-four shares in nine ships.[35] For the wealthy spinster, buying a few shares in ships was hardly a big risk and could be one way of exercising some independence. Zoe Treffry was the spinster daughter of a significant local family, the Treffrys of Place, Fowey. From the age of twenty-four Zoe dealt in shares, mainly in ships with strong family connections. By the time of her marriage in 1876 she had a personal portfolio of fourteen shares in five vessels.[36] Such portfolios spread risk. Anna Pyburn of Whitby was a spinster who clearly had access to ample funds. In 1849 she was major investor in two large ships, with forty-eight shares in the 574-ton *Evergreen* and thirty-two shares in the 323-ton *Renown*. She sold her interest in the *Renown* in 1857 and the same year provided a mortgage of £3,000 on all the shares in the same ship.[37] Her risk taking was of a greater magnitude than that of Zoe who was keeping her investment in small amounts in shares with family links.

Female Networks

Women, usually spinsters and often within the family, traded shares with each other. Catharine Tregenna was the spinster postmistress of East Looe and her brother Charles was a linen draper. Catherine held four shares in the *John Farley*

34 NYRO: NG/RS/WH/2.
35 WRO: YTSR 1/11, 12 & 19.
36 CRO: MSR/FOW/5, 6, 7 and 8.
37 CRO: MSR/FOW/5.

and the *Caradon*.[38] In 1868 Catharine sold two shares in each ship to her niece, Kate, who had reached the age of twenty-one. In Scotch Street, Whitehaven, lived two families named McGowan. James, aged fifty-three, was a timber merchant with a family of one son and two daughters, Elizabeth and Mary. Nearby lived Andrew McGowan, aged forty-four, and his wife Janet who had no children. Elizabeth McGowan bought shares from her aunt, Janet McGowan, in the newly built 222-ton barque, *Gleaner*.[39] Similarly, in 1853, Isabella Thompson bought two shares in the 176-ton brig *Wilson* from Jean Thompson; while Mary Nicholson sold four shares to Ann Smith and Sarah Smith of Waterloo Terrace near Whitehaven.[40]

Then there were ships with large numbers of female shareholders. Five spinsters held one share each in the Penzance-registered *Girl of the Period*; these were Elizabeth Mayne, and sisters Mary Ann, Emily and Susan Glasson, together with Charlotte Cudlip. Shareholder meetings for the *Pomona* must have been fashionable and colourful events as, on her initial registration in Whitehaven in 1843, forty-one out of the available sixty-four shares were held by fourteen women (see Table 15).

Table 15. Shareholders in the *Pomona*

Shareholder		Residence	Marital status	No.	Date
Hannah	Bateman	Calder	spinster	2	1843
Ann	Bell	Whitehaven	spinster	4	1843
Mary	Caddy	Beckermont	spinster	4	1843
Mary	Fisher	Whitehaven	spinster	4	1843
Bridget	Forrester	Whitehaven	spinster	2	1843
Rachel	Forrester	Whitehaven	spinster	2	1843
Mary	Robinson	Parton	spinster	8	1843
Mary	Pearson	Ulverston	widow	4	1843
Ann	Peel	Whitehaven	widow	2	1843
Ann	Reed	Workington	widow	2	1843
Elizabeth	Spedding	Whitehaven	widow	2	1843
Elizabeth	Hutton	Whitehaven	wife	1	1843
Margaret	Thompson	MuirKirk N Britain	wife	2	1843
Hannah	Whinnersh	St Bees	wife	2	1843

Source: WRO: YTSR 1/12.

Wives

For the widows and spinsters who were not constrained by trusts, they could control their own finances, and the majority of female shipowners had that freedom. Of the 1,377 initial transactions only seventy-four were held jointly with

38 CRO: MSR/FOW/8.
39 WRO: YTSR 1/18.
40 WRO: YTSR 1/12.

another beneficiary or trustee. Those shares retained in the name of the male trustee were simply transferred to him, so do not appear in the database. For the wife, unless her family had set up a premarital trust, her property became that of her husband. It was not until 1882 with the Married Women's Property Act that women gained the freedom to manage their own property. Here again shipownership differs markedly from previous research into women's investment. The percentage of married women who held shares in their own name was much higher than the 1 per cent or less who held railway shares or government stock.[41] In one port, Fowey, the wives formed 14 per cent of the female shareholders and half of these held their shares before the first Married Women's Property Act of 1870.

In some cases married women were inheriting from their fathers, who wrote protective legal phrases such as 'for her sole and separate use' into the wills to guard their daughters' personal estate from their husbands. 'Thus both men and women not only set up trusts, but went to considerable trouble to defeat coverture,'[42] which has clear echoes of similar findings in the eighteenth century.[43] So, Anna Browne, a wife of Tavistock, inherited eight shares in the *Robert Henry* in 1862 and subsequently sold them in her own name.[44] In Maria Pearson's case, she was the sole executor of Hugh Henwood Davey, a gentleman of Whitby (possibly her father), who died on 27 November 1858. Davey left her thirty-two shares in the Belfast-built 147-ton brig *John Cunningham*. Maria was the wife of Francis Pearson of Whitby, master mariner, and one year later she sold all the shares in her name to John Cummins, another master mariner.[45] Wives were clearly not constrained from acting in their own names.

While trusts and wills that protected the wife's inheritance can account for some of the situations, this does not apply in all cases, as in the previously quoted case of Mary Hoskins (Chapter 1). She inherited from her brother when he died intestate and the shares were registered in just her name and not her husband's.[46] In 1832 Martha Bell of Workington is listed as the owner of two shares in the 175-ton brig, *Bell*. She had been the executrix of the will of Jane Tiffin, who was possibly her mother.[47] This looks like a family ship, although Martha's husband William Bell, a shipowner, did not hold any shares in the ship. There seems to be no obvious explanation for joint ownership held between husband and wife such as that of the *Wannan*, a 196-ton brig in the coastal trade from Whitby. In the registration of the vessel in 1856 William Thomson and Mary Thomson, his wife, are subscribers and they are noted as having joint ownership of sixteen shares.[48]

---

[41] Green and Owens, 'Gentlewomanly Capitalism?'; Hudson, 'Attitudes to Investment Risk'.
[42] Morris, *Men, Women and Property*, p. 261.
[43] Erickson, 'Common Law versus Common Practice', pp. 21–39.
[44] NYRO: NG/RS/WH/10.
[45] NYRO: NG/RS/WH/2.
[46] DRO: 50/1826.
[47] WRO: YTSR 1/9.
[48] NYRO:NG/RS/WH/2.

All of these women were able to convince the customs officials that their name should be written in the register.

Marriage and Remarriage

When a widow remarried she became subject again to the rules of coverture and her shares were normally reregistered in her new husband's name, as in the *Lady Ridley*, a 46-ton schooner built in Sunderland in 1836. In 1852 Elizabeth MacNaught was the registered owner of the vessel with all sixty-four shares. On 24 June 1854 she married Matthew Gale Greenberry and the shares were registered in his name one year later when he sold half of the shares to John Scarth of Sandsend, shipowner. By January 1861 Greenberry had sold the other thirty-two shares to Scarth, ending Elizabeth's links with the vessel.[49]

The authorities in 1847 were taking no chances with regard to one remarried widow, Ann Snell of Menheniot, to ensure that she was in agreement with her new husband's actions relating to the sale of her four shares in the *Success*.

> 7th April 1847
> Richard Snell of Callington in county of Cornwall yeoman by his inter marriage with Ann Snell, widow of the late Edward Snell deceased the said Ann Snell also being a party hereto and signing and sealing has transferred by bill of sale dated 6th March 1847 four shares to Thomas Tadd of Lanteglos Master Mariner[50]

The authorities were also careful to note the changes of the remarriage of Jane Tadd, the widow of Samuel from Lanteglos. Jane had inherited four shares from him in 1854 in the *Ant*. When these shares were sold on 30 August 1867 the customs officers noted the changes in ownership and the time at which the transaction was noted in the register as the formalities were completed.

> 30 Aug 1867
> 11 am Jane Turvy formerly Jane Tadd of Lanteglos widow, now of Birkenhead in Chester
> 11.15 marriage of Jane Tadd to Thomas Turvy 24 July 1867 professor of music
> 11.20 Thomas Turvy of Birkenhead professor of music sells to Robert Stapleton of Bude master mariner[51]

Such retrospective changes also happened in Whitby, as when the ownership of sixteen shares in the 171-ton brig *Welthin* was changed when Elizabeth Granger married Matthew Coverdale. She inherited from her previous husband in November 1857, gaining administration of his estate in April 1858. She remarried on 25 October 1859 and the registry was changed a few months later when

---

49 CRO: MSR/FOW/7.
50 CRO: MSR/FOW/3.
51 CRO: MSR/FOW/7.

Coverdale sold the shares to William Granger of Robin Hood's Bay who was the majority shareholder.[52]

The customs officials were civil servants and not lawyers, yet they were careful to protect the proper transfer of shares from a single or widowed woman to her new husband, by insisting on proof and, in some cases, clearly noting the wife's agreement to the transfer. New husbands rarely lost much time in selling the shares they had acquired on marriage. Whether this was for cash reasons, a lack of knowledge or expertise in shipping or simply a disinclination to hold shipping shares is unknown. Not all husbands acted in this way. Two of Jane Parker's daughters who had received their shares as a gift, subsequently married and their husbands became the named shareholders.

Married Women and the Law

The previous cases of remarrying widows reflect how, before 1870, a woman's property became that of her husband on marriage and appear to support the view that in legal and practical terms a woman's position had deteriorated from the seventeenth century.[53] But marriage did not always mean that the wives became invisible. From a legal perspective all transactions should have been shown in the husband's name only or should have shown that the wife was acting with power of attorney. However, in the earlier cited case of Mary Pine, she purchased the shares not just from her brothers-in-law but their wives were named as well. The individuals who went to register the changes at the Customs House and the customs officials who wrote them down acted in the manner they believed was correct. A well informed lawyer might have had a different perspective.

Trusts set up before marriage could protect a woman's property. In the case of Emma Usherwood, no chances were being taken with her income. Her late father had been a wealthy man in Whitby with many shipping interests. When she was to marry the Reverend John Bolton a trust was set up. The trustees of the newly named Usherwood Trust Monies were Emma's mother, Mary, her brother William and her uncles, Thomas and William Marwood. Emma, at the age of twenty-two, signed the agreement by which her shares in her father's estate were passed to her trustees to hold for the duration of Emma's and John's lives. At the same time her fiancé also signed away his estate to the same trustees:

> [John Bolton] agrees that all real & personal property acquired by him, other than payment for services exceeding £150 in value shall be conveyed to [the trustees] – this property to form the 'Bolton Trust Monies'

52 NYRO: NG/RS/WH/10.
53 Davidoff and Hall, *Family Fortunes*, p. 276.

[the trustees] are to hold the 'Bolton Trust Monies' upon trust to pay the income from them to [John Bolton] during the joint life of [John and Emma] and after death of one of them to pay the income to the survivor.[54]

This is a useful reminder that it was not just women who were subject to trusts and that there were other reasons for such mechanisms to be used.

Some women gained protection within a marriage after marrying. The *Margaret* was a newly built schooner of 116 tons and was registered on 22 February 1827. Richard Henley held half of the shares and a few days later he transferred them.

> Richard Henly junior of Newton Abbot mariner has transferred by bill of sale date 3rd March 1827 32/64 shares to William Creed the ygr of Abbotts Carswell in County of Devon gentleman and George Davis of Newton Bushell wheelwright upon trust for Margaret Henly the wife of the said Richard Henly.[55]

Was Richard or his wife's family concerned that she should have some sort of security while he was away, or was this part of a separation agreement? Whatever the reason, Richard was acting in the same way as Sarah Barrett (see Chapter 1) who had sought to protect her and her children's shares. These transfers placed the shares and the income from them away from a possible threat and ensured the asset remained linked to the individual woman and not the marriage. Another case of shares being allocated to a married woman occurred in 1853. Jane Scott, the wife of John Scott, a shipowner of Liverpool, bought sixteen shares in the one-year-old Canadian-built brig, *Commodore*. She purchased them from her husband.[56] Whether through the use of third parties or not, shares were held independently by married women, at times with the full support of their husbands.

Impact of the Married Women's Property Acts 1870 and 1882

The registers show married women acting independently despite the apparent restrictions before 1870. The absence of husbands at sea, whether in the navy as in the case of Mary Hoskins or in merchant ships, meant that decisions that could not wait had to be made by the wives. The first Married Women's Property Act in 1870 was a very limited victory for the feminists. A woman could keep her earnings from any employment, occupation or trade and investments made with her earnings. She could retain property inherited during her marriage as long as it was not worth more than £200. She could also apply for stocks and shares to be placed in her own name, so long as they were not purchased with her husband's money without his consent. Despite this it was claimed that stock-

94

brokers objected to doing business with a married woman without her husband's consent and banks objected to taking deposits from married women and hesitated or refused to honour cheques.[57] The local customs officials do not seem to have had such reservations.

On 15 May 1879 John Holman had no problem in dealing with a married woman. He sold four shares to Elizabeth Lordan of Bayswater, 'married – no occupation'. The ship in question was the *Northcote*, a steam vessel. Elizabeth later sold the shares on 19 May 1887 to Eugene Collins of Hyde Park, just in time, as the ship foundered in the Bristol Channel one year later.[58] Elizabeth also bought two shares in another steam vessel, *Raleigh*, from Richard Holman. She was now listed as of Queenstown, Cork, and wife of John Lordan, gentleman. She subsequently exercised her independent powers to take a mortgage on the shares from Richard Holman at 5 per cent for sum due on account. Another shareholder in the *Raleigh* with four shares in 1881 was Henrietta Taylor of Horton Manor in Slough, listed as the wife of Charles Taylor, gentleman. Henrietta was a woman of wealth, as after the 1882 act her occupation was given as colliery owner when buying shares in another vessel, also called *Raleigh*, in 1884.[59] Similarly Mary Ann Barnard, a wife in Lynn, purchased two ships in her own name in 1880.[60]

A slightly odd transaction in 1880 is that of Robert Bovey junior, who had three shares in the *City of Exeter*. He is registered as selling one share to Mary Gorley Bovey, wife of Robert Bovey junior, shipbroker and shipowner of London. Is this Mary Bovey insisting on her right to have her share in her name?[61]

There is good evidence of wives purchasing shares in their own names before 1870. From 1835 to 1850 the shipping registers hold many examples of married women holding shares in their own right, even in cases where there seems to be no separate trust or other protection for the wife. However the 1870 and 1882 acts did have an effect, with a rise in married women shareholders post-1870 and an even greater rise post-1882. After 1882 the customs officials had no difficulty in registering the joint interests of a married couple. Mary Murphy of Fowey and her husband, Jeremiah, held a joint mortgage on sixty-four shares in the *Honour*.[62] However, the drop in the level of activity after 1860 is marked and is possibly due to the greater public debate over married women's property, with a resultant greater awareness of the legal position, which made some of the more unusual arrangements harder to achieve (see Figure 4). The numbers on which this finding is based are small and the impact of the acts on married women investors in shipping deserves more research than is shown here.

---

57 Holcombe, *Wives and Property*, p. 180, quoting Miss Lydia Becker in 1880 who was addressing the Social Science Association.

58 DRO: 3289s/10, 2/1878.

59 DRO: 3289s/10.

60 NRO: P/SH/L 4–7.

61 DRO: 3289s/10.

62 CRO: MSR/FOW/9.

Figure 4. Impact of Married Women's Property Acts

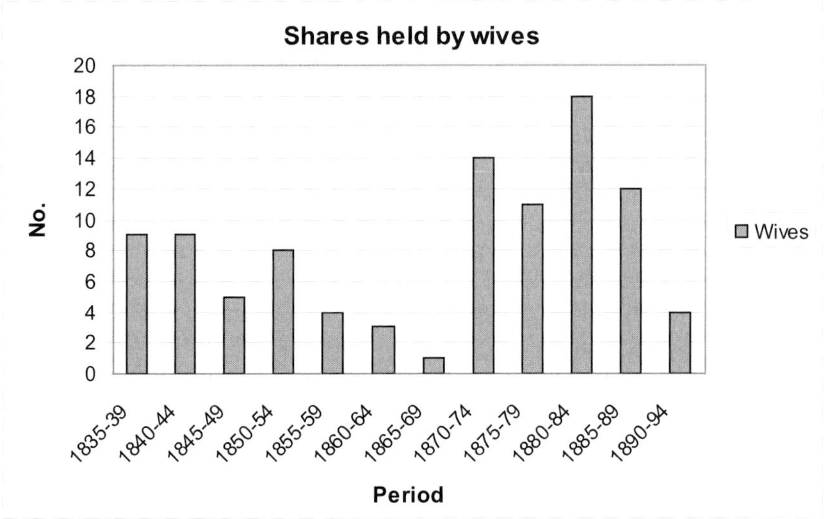

Shares held by wives

Source: Investor Database (see Table 8).

Family Finances

In 1898 in companies such as Prudential Assurance large numbers of women – sisters and unmarried daughters – were related to the directors, holding 23 per cent of the total share capital. 'Women as family members were significant investors, particularly for companies whose shares were not marketed to the outside world.'[63] It has been suggested that this was some form of financial provision for them, or a method of managing potential power clashes within the company. An additional reason was the preference for retaining shares and funds within the family. Holdings by female relations enabled the firm to remain a private firm without the need to go to the market for external investment. It also kept family funds out of the hands of future husbands.[64]

In all of the ports there were families who had significant investments in local shipping and, in each case, female relations held shares. This was the case in the Holman family of Topsham who were later to become a major national insurance company. Similarly, the Marwood and Turnbull families were big shipowners in Whitby, the latter also becoming a major company with offices in London.[65] In common with the findings in the limited companies, where the female share-

[63] Maltby and Rutterford, 'She Possessed Her Own Fortune', p. 230.
[64] Rutterford and Maltby, 'The Widow, the Clergyman and the Reckless', p. 131.
[65] Long, *A Shipping Venture*.

owners in the family firms often held shares of lower value than the males, the female relations of the maritime families also held smaller amounts of shares.[66] In both the Holman family of Exeter and the previously mentioned Marwoods of Whitby the female members held fewer shares than their male relatives.[67]

The transactions of shipping shares show how funds were moved within families, as in the case of Richard Carnall who owned the *Saint Catherine* and the *Touch Me Not*. In 1863 Richard mortgaged both ships: in April he secured a mortgage for £500 on the *Touch Me Not* and in November £280 on the *Saint Catherine* with John Harris of Lanreath at the standard 5 per cent. These were both discharged on 13 May 1864, but he still needed funds some months later. This time Richard sold his shares in both vessels to his mother, Honour Carnall, on 13 December 1864, and just one month later she sold them back to him. It was clear his financial difficulties were not over and by August of 1865 Richard had sold half his shares in the *Saint Catherine* to non-family members, and in March 1879 he sold the *Touch Me Not* to his sister Jane, who, at the same time, he appointed as the official managing owner.[68]

In all of these cases the female members of the family were useful sources of help in difficult times or extra protection from outside investors. Female money was being used within the family banking system. However, these cannot be assumed to be passive arrangements in every case since every request for help required some explanation or involved a negotiation between the parties. The balance of power could subtly change. One sister who was in an interesting working relationship within her family was Frances Jane Richardson of Exeter. Frances came from a large Exeter family and George Ball Richardson was her younger brother. In 1832 Jane, at the age of twenty-eight, acquired all sixty-four shares in the 44-ton *Liberty*, and the master was her brother George. The vessel was subsequently transferred to Poole in 1835, but George had served three years as the master of a vessel, an excellent start to his career.[69]

Share Intermediaries

The buying and selling of ship shares did not have a formal trading system and there were no share brokers as such in maritime communities. Family, friends and business contacts were all sources for the sale and purchase of shares. Shipbrokers did handle the purchase and sale of ships and shares in ships, but also organised freight and handled passenger bookings. As has been shown, the 64th system was one that encouraged close links between the owners and a primary link was the family. Martha Moon is a typical case. Martha's husband Richard was a master

---

[66] Maltby and Rutterford, 'She Possessed Her Own Fortune', p. 230.
[67] DRO: 3289s Exeter Shipping Registers; NYRO: NG/RS/WH Whitby Shipping Registers.
[68] CRO: MSR/FOW/5 & 7.
[69] DRO: 3289s/5, 23/1832.

mariner in Polruan. His vessel was the *Princess Alexandra*. He had been the initial registered owner of all the shares, but immediately resold most of them and was eventually left with four. This was common practice as the ship was commissioned from the shipbuilder or bought from another port by one individual who already had the co-owners lined up. Moon also had an interest in the *Kate and Ann*, built locally in 1858, which was a schooner of 124 tons.[70] Moon had purchased four shares in 1860 from Thomas Cobbledick, a Fowey butcher (who was not merely the Moon's next door neighbour, but Richard's father-in-law[71]), paying £120.[72] On 6 September 1864 Richard died leaving no will, and Martha, as his administrator, obtained probate in 1865. At that stage Martha took no action regarding the shares and it was not until 1867 that she sold two of the shares in the *Princess Alexandra*, receiving £55 from David Thomas, a master mariner of Cardiff. One year later she sold a further two shares to her father, Thomas Cobbledick.[73] Martha sold her four shares in the *Kate and Ann* in 1871. But she had not finished with share-holding. In 1880 she purchased two shares in the *Waterlily*, a 168-ton schooner built in Fife in 1866. She bought them from W. P. Hocken who was her brother-in-law and subsequently sold them again in May 1881 to John Edward Hocken.[74] Such inter- and intra-family trading was common. Shares moved not just between parents and adult children, but between siblings, cousins and in-laws.

Attorneys acted as connectors between lenders and borrowers and they have been shown to organise some loans from wealthy widows and spinsters to commercial firms. Most individuals preferred to invest in bank accounts or shares if they knew that the person or institution, 'like a local bank or London broker, belonged to a system that was both effective and trustworthy'.[75] The preference was to be able to see and speak to the individual with whom you were doing business, but if that was not possible, the agent or recommender needed to be able to vouch for their business reliability. As limited companies became more usual in shipping with the increased capital needs of new technology, some firms had to search more widely for investors. In Wales the Radcliffe company used as their agent the Reverend Cynddlan Jones who successfully recommended the shares to his extensive congregation.[76] But this was in the 1870s and these limited companies based just on one ship were operating alongside the traditional 64th system which many shareowners preferred. Turnbulls of Whitby and London retained the 64th system as late as 1906 before reluctantly following the trend and

[70]   CRO: MSR/FOW/8.
[71]   TNA: HO 107 1906 Fowey Census 1851.
[72]   CRO: MSR/FOW/8.
[73]   Bill of sale of shares in *Princess Alexandra*, private collection.
[74]   CRO: MSR/FOW/8.
[75]   Mary Poovey, ed., *The Financial System in Nineteenth Century Britain* (Oxford: Oxford University Press, 2003), p. 3.
[76]   Craig, 'Millionaires and Enterprising Nobodies', p. 11.

turning their vessels into single ship companies.[77] The 64th system had less need of extensive advertising to find investors.

Some master mariners were active share dealers, such as Nathaniel Hocken.[78] William Morgan, the Harbourmaster of Duddon in Cumberland, also dealt in shares.[79] All of these occupations handled shares and women had access to them. One individual who was very well placed to know of the reputation of both master mariners and ships was John Merrifield, who ran a navigation school in Plymouth.[80] His school taught many master mariners from Cornwall and Devon who came to Plymouth to gain their certificates of competency, the essential promotional step for an ambitious mariner.

There is one individual in Fowey who occurs with regularity in his dealings with women investors. J. H. Hocken was a shipowner who was also the local bank manager in Fowey and he sold shares to several single women, perhaps part of his investment advice as their banker. The list in Table 16 shows just those who purchased directly from him; he may also have acted as broker in other situations. His wife, Elizabeth, not only bought shares from her husband, but also from G. B. Bate of Fowey, a local shipbroker. Elizabeth bought two shares in the *Countess of Jersey* in 1881 and in the *Gallant* in 1884. These two vessels were steam tugs brought in to the port to aid sailing vessels.[81]

Table 16. Clients of J. H. Hocken, Fowey Bank Manager

Sold/Bought	Shareholder	Marital status	Vessel	No.	Date
Bought from	Grace Tadd	widow	*Sabina*	43	1871
Sold to	Jane Slade	widow	*Concord*	4	1872
Sold to	Mary Hicks Hayes	widow	*Ocean Traveller*	1	1873
Sold to	Ann Hicks	widow	*Ocean Traveller*	1	1873
Sold to	Jane Slade	widow	*Ocean Traveller*	1	1873
Sold to	Ellen Truscott	spinster	*Ocean Traveller*	1	1873
Bought from	Jane Carthew	spinster	*Silver Stream*	4	1874
Bought from	Emma Davies	spinster	*Concord*	2	1875
Sold to	Mary Hicks Hayes	widow	*Gudrun*	1	1882
Sold to	Mary Peters	spinster	*Capella*	2	1883
Sold to	Mary Peters	spinster	*Kingaloch*	2	1883
Bought from	Sophia Hocken	widow	*William Geake*	1	1889
Sold to	Elizabeth Hocken	wife	*Wild Wave*	12	1892

Source: CRO: MSR/Fow/7 and 8.

[77] Long, *A Shipping Venture*, pp. 138–9.
[78] CRO: MSR/FOW/6.
[79] WRO:YTSR 1/20.
[80] Kennerley, 'Navigation Schools and Training Ships', pp. 53–78.
[81] CRO: MSR/FOW/6.

Another intermediary was William Burnyeat, a Whitehaven butcher. He was a victualler to ships and was well known as a man who had shares in a very wide range of ships. He was an astute businessman who built up his business into a national company, later moving to Liverpool.[82] Two perhaps less obvious share dealers were Isaac Hodgson and Joseph Rothery. Isaac was a shoemaker whose other stated occupation was as a shipowner. He sold six shares to Jane Hodgson, presumably a relative. He also sold shares to Hannah Taylor Douglas, Mary Postlethwaite, Mary Newton and Marianne Pringle. The last named lived in Glasgow and all of them, with the exception of Mary Newton, were spinsters. Joseph Rothery was a farmer and his name appears as the joint holder of three shares in a large and newly launched vessel, the 785-ton barque *Parkinson*. His co-purchaser was Christina Murray of Dumphries, a spinster, and at the same time he jointly bought three more shares in the same vessel with Sara Ann Thompson of Carlisle, also a spinster. Shares in such a large vessel were correspondingly more expensive, so joint ownership was a way of spreading the cost, and yet there seems to be no connection between these two women and Joseph.[83] A family connection may well emerge on further investigation.

Neighbours could provide useful information in the context of share buying. Mother and daughter, Hannah and Harriet Jones of Whitby, owned sixteen shares in the *Ophelia*. Their next door neighbour was Isaac Bedlington, a shipowner, and another neighbour was Elizabeth MacNaught who owned the *Lady Ridley*.[84] Connections through family, friends, neighbours and lodgers were but one set of threads in the tapestry that made up the community connections.

Summary

Marital status was the major classification for a woman in the nineteenth century. Both men and women considered women first in relation to their family, and occupations, where they were recognised, came second. Widows, spinsters and wives owned shares in vessels of all sizes, from 34 tons to 1,200 tons, and some of these women owned whole vessels. Across the five ports over half of the shareowners were widows who had mainly inherited shares from their husbands. Wives appear as shipping investors and constitute 10 per cent of the shareholders in the data, and before 1870 most of the wives inherited from their fathers.

Women were not suddenly powerless or invisible because of the changing views in the nineteenth century. Greater public debate made people more aware, but did not prevent other arrangements being made. The attempt at control exerted from beyond the grave was not necessarily a lasting one. In the share registers it is clear that many widows and spinsters were able to dispense with the restrictions of working through trustees and with other joint beneficiaries in order to gain full

---

82 Rolt, *Mariners' Market*.
83 WRO: YTSR 1/20.
84 TNA: 1881 Census Whitby.

control of their financial situation. Those trustees who received little financial gain from their position were not unhappy to relinquish extra work.

Women have been known to hold influential positions within the family network; spinsters and childless widows became bankers and held positions of power.[85] This too is reflected in the activities of the female shareholders and mortgage providers. Many other transfers of funds within families simply went unnoticed by any formal arrangement.

The big debate for historians has been the impact of the legislation in 1870 and 1882, and further research on selected ports would reveal some valuable data on how married women reacted to the new freedom. It is, for instance, noticeable that before 1870 wives were active in many of the ports, especially in those places distant from London. Did their peripherality mean that women and men were more able to ignore the rigid application of the law? For widows and spinsters, who were without husbands, a major priority was the management of their finances. Inheritance was a significant route for acquiring shares, but the large numbers of wives, widows and spinsters who bought shares, often building on an inheritance, will now be examined further.

[85] Morris, *Men, Women and Property*, p. 245.

5

Active and Passive Female Shipowners

'Girls never have any capital, they hardly know what it means', wrote Bessie Parkes in 1865.[1] She was writing about the limited options for women to be financially independent, and might have been surprised at the extent to which her contemporaries in maritime communities used their financial muscle. In the previous chapter, the shipowners and their investment decisions were considered in the context of their marital status. In this chapter their actions in relation to the shares are considered, in particular the women's attitude to the shares. Were they caretaking an inheritance or actively pursuing and managing investments in the uncertain world of shipping? There were safer options for their investments, such as government securities.[2]

Debates about women investors have questioned whether they actively engaged with their investments. Within joint stock companies, where financial information on shares is also available, three types of women investors have been identified: speculators who bought and sold for gain, women in search of income, and women as family members. This last group held their shares by default, enabling the family to retain control of the firm or acting as caretakers for the next generation.[3] The categories of women ship shareholders do not fit neatly into these categories, although there is some limited evidence of each of these investor types, because the nature of the main source is different from company share registers. The biggest difference is the total absence of financial data in the registers, as the amount of capital in the ship was of no interest to the customs authorities. In addition, little has been found in the way of correspondence relating to the intentions of the shareholders with regard to their shares. What can be measured, however, is their activity in relation to the shares as shown in the transactions.

By examining how the women acquired their shares and their subsequent actions in retaining or disposing of them, four categories of female investors appear. First, there were women who were *active* investors, buying and selling shares in their own right. Second, the *financiers* provided capital in the form of mortgages. Third, there were women who were *passive* investors with shares gained through inheritance, but who simply left them as they were and took no further action. Finally, there were the *divestors*, the women who were temporary holders of shares through inheritance, but who sold the shares rapidly. The first three groupings

1   Parkes, *Essays on Woman's Work*, p. 143.
2   Green and Owens, 'Gentlewomanly Capitalism?'
3   Rutterford and Maltby, 'The Widow, the Clergyman and the Reckless', pp. 125–6.

5. Reception on board the *Thirlmere* of Whitehaven
Source: The Beacon Museum, Whitehaven

Figure 5. Women investor categories, 1824–1889

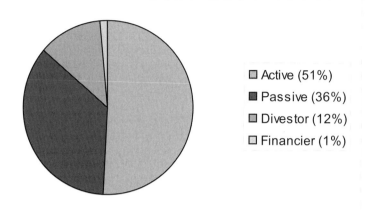

□ Active (51%)
■ Passive (36%)
▨ Divestor (12%)
□ Financier (1%)

Source: Cornwall Record Office(CRO): MSR/FOW/3–9 Fowey Shipping Registers; North Yorkshire Record Office (NYRO): NG/RS/WH/2, 9 & 10 Registers of Whitby ships; Whitehaven Record Office (WRO) YTSR 1/9–12 and YTSR 16–21 Register of shipping; Devon Record Office (DRO) 3289s/3–17, 10 Exeter shipping registers; Norfolk Record Office (NRO): P/SH Shipping Registers: King's Lynn, Wells, Cley and Great Yarmouth 1825–1892.

brought significant amounts of capital into the industry and enabled the local communities to remain self-sufficient in their funding. The active shareholders outnumbered the divestors and indeed the passive shareholders. It appears that when they acquired shares the majority of women were in no hurry to dispose of them, but as will be seen, these percentages must be considered as conservative, as each case hid a range of different strategies and attitudes to investment. The actions of the 867 women shareholders in the database in relation to their shares reveal the women as predominantly active: 437 (51 per cent) were active, 310 (36 per cent) were passive, 107 (12 per cent) were divestors and 12 (1 per cent) were financiers, as shown in Figure 5.

Differences appear between the selected ports in the actions of the women in respect of their shares (see Table 17). There were more women in Fowey and Whitehaven as shareholders than in the other ports, underlining the greater opportunities for the small investors, such as women. The smaller number of women in Lynn is in part a reflection of the smaller number of locally registered ships in that port. The overall percentage of active investors (those who were independent buyers and sellers of shares) is similar and the least active port is Whitby. This may be a data anomaly as it was not possible to view the transaction registers for Whitby and this would lead to a greater number being categorised as passive since no further evidence of share trading was identified. There was a similar gap in the data collection at Whitehaven but not as severe.

Four categories of female investors were defined in the introduction to this section: passive investors, divestors, active investors and financiers. The largest

Table 17. Port comparison, shareholder categories

	Active		Passive		Divestor		Financier		Total
Exeter (1824–82)	61	56%	31	28%	17	16%	0		109
Fowey (1834–99)	174	56%	90	29%	39	13%	7	2%	310
Lynn (1836–92)	32	51%	12	19%	16	25%	3	5%	63
Whitby (1848–92)	55	39%	59	43%	22	16%	2	1%	138
Whitehaven (1840–92)	115	46%	118	48%	13	5%	0		246
Total	437	51%	310	36%	107	12%	12	1%	866*

* One shareholder unclassified

Note: Active = women who bought and sold shares; Passive = women who inherited then took no further action; Divestors = women who sold their shares as soon as possible after probate; Financiers = women providers of mortgages.

Source: As for Table 8.

group, 50 per cent, were active shipowners. The smallest group were the financiers, just 1 per cent; only 12 per cent sold their shares on acquisition; and 36
per cent of the female shipowners in the database were categorised as passive.
Despite the advice to invest in safe shares, when they inherited shares in ships
many women held onto their shares and the majority continued to invest in more
ships. However, these percentages must be considered as conservative, as each case
hid a range of different strategies and attitudes to investment. Women were classified as active only if it was demonstrated that they were among initial investors in
a new ship or where they were identified as buyers of shares. The passive category
could hide women who were active in taking decisions as part of the shareholding
group, or who were initial subscribers, but were not identified as such in the earlier
registration system.

Active Investors

Half of the total number of women who had shares in vessels can be described
as active investors. These are the women who initiated transactions, buying shares
in their own name. In most cases these were widows or spinsters, but as already
shown there are also examples of married women purchasing in their own right
before the 1882 Married Women's Property Act. The range of activity of this group
of shareholders varied from the purchase of the occasional share to those who
were traders, buying and selling shares in more than one vessel, and it also includes
those who bought whole vessels. Some took an inheritance of shares and added

Table 18. Categories of investors and marital status

Active

	Exeter	Fowey	Lynn	Whitby	Wh'haven	Total	%
Widows	33	56	17	38	40	184	42%
Spinsters	24	82	9	16	63	194	44%
Wives	4	26	3	0	12	45	10%
NK*	0	10	3	1	0	14	3%
Total	61	174	32	55	115	437	

Passive

	Exeter	Fowey	Lynn	Whitby	Wh'haven	Total	%
Widows	21	55	8	46	40	170	55%
Spinsters	5	11	1	10	59	86	28%
Wives	3	9	1	3	15	31	10%
NK*	2	15	2	0	4	23	7%
Total	31	90	12	59	118	310	

Divestor

	Exeter	Fowey	Lynn	Whitby	Wh'haven	Total	%
Widows	18	25	12	18	9	80	75%
Spinsters	2	5	2	2	4	14	13%
Wives	2	5	1	2	0	8	7%
NK*	0	4	1	0	0	5	5%
Total	22	39	16	22	13	112	

Financier

	Exeter	Fowey	Lynn	Whitby	Wh'haven	Total	%
Widows	0	4	1	2	0	7	58%
Spinsters	0	1	1	0	0	2	17%
Wives	0	0	0	0	0		0
NK*	0	2	1	0	0	3	25%
Total		7	3	2		12	

* NK = Marital status unknown

Source: Investor Database.

to it, while others do not appear to have been previous investors, although this activity might have existed in the shadow of their husband's name.

Mary Murphy is an example of an active investor. Her husband, William Murphy of Whitehaven, died in May 1872 and left his forty shares in the *Elizabeth Conaway* to her. Mary was appointed as executrix together with John Ward and Joseph Alcock. Ward had predeceased Murphy and Alcock renounced probate. Mary proved the will herself at Carlisle and then, as the majority shareowner, appointed herself as the managing owner of the vessel, thus taking full control of the business affairs of the ship, which was involved in trade between Ireland, Whitehaven and Antwerp.[4]

Jane Ross of Summerland Place in Sidwell was one of three initial investors in a new sloop, the *Selina*, registered in 1841. She had twenty-one shares, one-third of the vessel. In Jane's case there is on the surface no connection between her and her fellow subscribers, who were William Gubb, a bootmaker of Exeter, and Thomas Herbert, a leather seller of Topsham. It is tempting to suggest that she was just being used as a money source by the other two shareholders, something that happened frequently when owners needed to raise capital to fund the building. However, in August 1842 Jane bought Gubb's shares and then in November 1846 she also bought out Thomas Herbert. She now had full control of the vessel. She eventually sold the ship to Samuel Lovering, an innkeeper of Exeter, in January 1847.[5] Jane, like many other female investors, was no sleeping partner.

Supporting a member of the family was often a reason for a woman's active involvement. At first sight Mercy Harrison of Robin Hood's Bay, near Whitby, appears as a typical divestor. Her husband Thomas left no will and so in 1861 she inherited sixteen shares each in the vessels *Claret* and *Arica*, and twenty-two shares in *Harrison* plus total ownership of *Fortitude*. Within the year Mercy had disposed of all of her shares in three of the vessels yet she kept the twenty-two shares in *Harrison*. This was not mere sentimental attachment to the name, but because her son was the master of the vessel and Mercy now became the managing owner. Additionally Mercy purchased eleven shares in the 197-ton brig *Mary Ann* to add to the ten she already held.[6] In this way Mercy managed the finances of her son's vessel and increased her holdings in what may have been a better investment. Ann Brokenshaw's husband, William, was a Fowey shipbuilder and, on his death in 1857, she inherited shares in three of the ships built by him: fifty in the brand new 155-ton schooner *Ann Beer*, launched one month before his death, eight in the 65-ton sloop *Lavinia* and twelve in the 49-ton sloop *Need*.[7] Their son George had not followed his father into shipbuilding; instead he was a farmer. Ann sold her eight shares in *Lavinia* to her son in 1859 and then disposed of her holding in the *Need* in 1860, but retained her majority shareholding in her namesake *Ann Beer*. She increased her shareholding by five shares, buying them from her son, when he was declared bankrupt in 1865.[8] She thus provided cash for her son in his time of need.

Not all mothers were driven by their sons' needs. Sarah Ash inherited sole ownership of a vessel, the 36-ton *Caroline & James*, in 1839. Her late husband had been a merchant of Starcross. Sarah retained the vessel for five years until she sold all the shares to her son, Henry Burden Ash, in June 1846.[9] An assump-

4 WRO: YTSR 1/20.
5 DRO: 3289s/6, 10/1841.
6 NYRO: NG/RS/WH/10.
7 CRO: MSR/FOW/5, 7.
8 CRO: MSR/FOW/5.
9 DRO: 3289s/5, 14/1839.

tion might be that she was managing the vessel for her son until he came of age; however Henry, a shipowner by occupation, was born in 1800 so he was thirty-nine when his father died.[10] While some mothers were the business managers for their mariner sons, Sarah had no such reason; her son was the owner and manager of several of his own vessels.

Investment decisions were made by women and not always for family reasons. Some of the cases highlight the pitfalls that arise when conclusions are drawn from just one entry in the registers, as in the case of Jane Hore. Richard Hore, master mariner, owned twenty-one shares in the 80-ton schooner, *Union*. In May 1848 his widow and sole surviving executor, Jane, sold the shares to the other shareholder, Thomas Paine the younger of Topsham. At first glance this appears to be a widow divesting herself of business interests on the death of her husband. This is, however, a case where the registers are missing some vital information. Richard Hore had died some years before, possibly as early as 1836, but the information of the transfer to his widow had not been noted. So Jane had held the shares for some years and she was not a newcomer to shipping. Jane and her son William had jointly bought thirty-two shares in the 76-ton *Perseverance* in 1836. William became master of the vessel in 1837. Jane subsequently purchased a further twenty-two shares in 1841, giving her majority ownership.[11] In 1848 she was an initial subscriber in the 110-ton schooner, *Elizabeth*. In all of these transactions only her joint purchase with William can be seen as a purely family decision.

While the activity of some women buyers can be seen in the context of family needs, Rebecca Martin's reasons were commercial. In 1854 Rebecca bought the 128-ton brigantine *Trio* from its place of build, Sunderland. It was fairly new, just three years old, and she kept the vessel for seven years before selling it back to the Sunderland owners. Rebecca is described in the shipping registers as a widow of St Austell, but this does not do her justice.[12] Rebecca was one of the influential pioneering china clay owners and merchants. She was an active businesswoman and the purchase of the vessel was part of her business strategy.[13]

It was not just widows who were active in purchasing shares. Zoe Treffry was mentioned earlier as an example of a spinster shipowner. The Treffrys were a significant local family; her great uncle, J.T. Treffry, had been a major entrepreneur in the earlier part of the century. Zoe's shares were mainly in ships with good Treffry connections. These included four shares in *Dorothy* in 1873 and in 1875 four shares in *Maria Stuart*, named after her younger sister. Then in 1876 she took two shares in *New Quay*, *Langurthowe* and *Elizabeth Davey*. All the ships except the last one had been owned either by her father or great uncle. She owned no shares in *Zoe Treffry*, the 79-ton Sunderland-built schooner registered at Fowey in 1857 by her father. By the time of her marriage in 1876 she had a personal

10 IGI website: www.familysearch.org/Eng/Search/igi (accessed 31 May 2004).
11 DRO: 3289s/10, 11/1841.
12 CRO: MSR/FOW/4.
13 Barton, *A History of the Cornish China Clay Industry*, p. 141.

portfolio of fourteen shares in five vessels.[14] She retained a separate personal estate on marriage, as her subsequent transactions when selling shares were also in her married name. Zoe was one of thirteen children. She had two sisters, Anne who was nine years older and Maria who was eleven years younger.[15] Few of her brothers and none of her sisters were investors so Zoe was the only female in her family to invest in this way.

Another active spinster shipowner of Fowey, Emma Davies, was aged twenty-nine in the 1851 census where she is shown as the daughter of William Davies 'Captain of Royal Marines on full pay and retired agent of mines.'[16] Emma bought and sold parcels of up to eight shares in five ships, *Concord*, *Thames*, *Chase*, *Maria Stuart* and *Zoe Treffry*, from 1857 to her death in 1877.[17] Her motivation does not seem to be linked to any particular family or business needs. The previously mentioned Whitehaven example of Sarah Isabella Bragg, who held sixty-four shares in nine ships, was very much the businesswoman. In the 1851 census she described herself as head of the household which she shared with her older sister. Sarah was one of the rare examples of a woman who listed her occupation, but she did not merely describe herself as a shipowner; she listed herself with the unusual combination of shipowner, ironmonger and midwife.[18] There seems little possibility that Sarah was suited to the traditional spinster governess role. A close relative, possibly her brother, and the potential source of her knowledge of ship-owning was John Bragg, a local shipbroker.[19] Wealthy spinsters like Zoe could be accused of spending their allowance, but Sarah's considerable investment and her other business interests suggest a more businesslike motivation, and she was not alone.

There were also those widows who inherited substantial numbers of shares in several ships, but in contrast to the divesting strategy, they built on their investment. Jane Slade was named sole executrix in her husband's will, and on his death in 1870 she inherited his shipbuilding business and sixty-four shares in seven vessels. Despite an adult family and several sons who were experienced shipwrights and businessmen, Jane took over the business and gradually built up the portfolio of shares to a total of ninety-four shares spread across twenty-three ships.[20] Mary Hicks Hayes inherited twenty shares in sixteen ships from her husband, a shipbroker, in 1873. The number of her shares had increased to forty-three across twenty-two ships by 1880 and she had become managing owner of three of them. By the time of her death in 1908 she had few ship shares (sailing

[14] CRO: MSR/FOW/5, 6, 7 & 8.
[15] Adelaide Rideout, *The Treffry Family* (Chichester: Phillimore, 1984), pp. 92–4.
[16] 1851 Fowey census.
[17] CRO: MSR/FOW/3–9.
[18] WRO: HO107/2436 Whitehaven 1851 census.
[19] WRO: YTSR 1/11, 12 & 19.
[20] NYRO: NG/RS/WH/2, 9 & 10.

ships by then were a very poor investment) and had placed her money in shares in the Capital and Counties Bank and a new hotel.[21]

In Whitby the number of active women investors who owned shares in multiple ships was lower. Hannah Wood owned shares in five vessels, all of which were around 200 to 250 tons in size.[22] In 1865, Suzanna Bell inherited two sets of sixteen shares in two ships from her husband Benjamin Wells, a saddler of Cley, Norfolk. From 1866 she proceeded to buy further shares in various ships from John Paul of King's Lynn. By 1882 she owned 106 shares in seven vessels. She was a fortunate owner as two of her investments were wrecked just two years after she sold her interest in them.[23] These investors were using their knowledge and their contacts to gain from their investments, buying and selling shares as conditions dictated.

One thing that was certain for every investor in ships was that as soon as it was launched, the vessel needed regular amounts of money spent on it for maintenance or repair. If trading was particularly bad or the vessel needed extra maintenance or serious repair, extra injections of cash could be required. Many coastal vessels were not insured and those that were in the mutual insurance clubs were not insured to their full value.[24] Hannah Barnard, a widow of Robin Hood's Bay, had forty-two shares in the *Jane* in 1849. She bought out the other shareholder, William Barnard, in 1857, giving herself total control of the vessel. But by June 1862 she needed funds and took out a mortgage for 'sum due on account with interest' from Henry and George Barrick of Whitby, shipowners. This was a type of overdraft arrangement which lasted until the vessel was lost in 1864.[25]

These active women investors used their knowledge and experience to buy and sell shares. It is not often that women can be seen taking such an active part, although it is known from correspondence that women were not mere bystanders when it came to their money. This is illustrated in the case of Jane Hey, a woman well aware of her financial situation and whose correspondence has survived. Although Jane did not have direct control of her inheritance, she made quite sure that the male relatives who were handling the trust were left in no doubt that she was keeping a close eye on their actions on her behalf. She corrected mistakes and was quite comfortable discussing the merits of railway share issues, coupons and debentures.[26] The example of Mary Ann Henwood in the previous chapter reveals how even young spinsters were able to participate fully with their fellow shareholders in the key decisions relating to their investment.

All of these female shipping investors needed knowledge to buy, sell and make decisions together with their fellow shareholders. As a witness to a parliamentary committee commented in 1833 in relation to London shipping investors, it

---

21   CRO: MSR/FOW/3–9, Will of Mary Hicks Hayes, Bodmin 1908.
22   NYRO: NG/RS/WH/2.
23   NRO: P/SH/L 1–7.
24   Craig *et al.*, 'Some Aspects of Devon Shipping', pp. 100–1.
25   CRO: MSR/FOW/4.
26   Morris, *Men, Women and Property* (Cambridge, 2005), pp. 307, 313–14.

required a 'thorough knowledge of the business to make money out of it'.[27] This knowledge needed to be good, but did not need to be perfect or even systematic to be successful, as at least one study of a major shipbroking firm has shown.[28]

Financiers

A small number of women were financiers, providing the capital for others, but securing their money by a mortgage on shares. The number of women providing mortgages was just 1 per cent, but this is likely to be an understatement of the true picture since some funds were reallocated within a family, such as from mother to son, without the requirement for a formal mortgage, as women often operated as the 'network banker' in extended families.[29] Women such as Ann Brokenshaw and Mercy Harrison were using their shares to support their sons, and other findings have shown the importance of shareholdings by female relations in maintaining control in a private company.[30]

The earlier example in Chapter 4 of Richard Carnall and his financial dealings with both his mother and his sister shows how the capital held by the female family members could be used. It was almost a 'form of exploitation for female capital with nowhere else to go'.[31] However those women who provided mortgages were hardly being exploited, as their capital was protected, as long as the ship was insured, and they had a return on their investment.

The rules on ship mortgages were clear:

> A common method of raising money to help meet the cost of a purchase of ship is by mortgage or bond, a bank or other party agreeing to advance a sum on the security of the vessel. The document embodying the agreement is on special form, and has to be registered at the Custom house where the ship is registered, and the Registrar enters the details in the register book, and records on the mortgage form the date and the time of the entry in his book. It is important to note that, if there is more than one mortgage on a ship, they take priority according to the date of registration, and not according to the dates on the mortgages themselves, therefore prompt registration of a mortgage is very important. The mortgagee has a preferential claim, as in the case of bond holders generally, and if interest is not paid regularly, he may apply for authority to take possession of his security.[32]

---

[27] Quoted in Palmer, 'Investors in London Shipping', p. 59.

[28] Lewis R. Fischer and Helge W. Nordvik, 'Economic Theory, Information and Management in Shipbroking: Fearnley and Eger as a Case Study, 1869–1972', *Research in Maritime History*, 6 (1994), 1–29 (p. 5).

[29] Morris, *Men, Women and Property*, p. 246.

[30] Rutterford, and Maltby, 'The Widow, the Clergyman and the Reckless', p. 131.

[31] Morris, *Men, Women and Property*, p. 245.

[32] C. D. Macmurray and M. Cree, *Shipping and Shipbroking: A Guide to All Branches of Shipbroking and Ship Management* (London: Pitman, 1934), pp. 346–7.

Family ties are obvious in the case of Jane Reynolds of Charlestown who came to the rescue of her son, Philip, master of the *Laurel*, a 69-ton sloop built in 1832. He had inherited the ship from his father in 1848, but ten years later sold the vessel to a Redruth wheelwright, then repurchased it in January 1862. In 1863 he took out a mortgage of £37 10s with Andrew Innes, solicitor, and James Hamilton, merchant, both of Kirkcaldy in Fife. This was on tough terms: from 22 April 1863 the interest rate was the usual 5 per cent and it rose to 7 per cent from 22 October. Philip stayed with this arrangement, repaying them in January 1864, but his financial struggle was not over as on 25 April 1865 his mother stepped in to provide a mortgage of £137 with the interest set at 5 per cent. By May the same year, Philip had finally sold the vessel and had cleared the debt with his mother.[33]

In all of these cases the female members of the family were useful sources of help in difficult times or extra protection from outside investors. Female money was being used within the family banking system. But these cannot be assumed to be passive arrangements in every case. Women who loaned money within the family are described as 'important locations of power within the wider family network'.[34] For every request for help from a family member some explanation was needed and details were negotiated, potentially putting the lender and the borrower in unequal positions of power.

Not all mortgages have an obvious family link, however, as is seen in the case of Elizabeth Andrews, a widow of Liskeard. In 1850 and again in 1852 she provided John Puckey with a mortgage arrangement on his four shares in *Unity* and *William West* and his seven shares in *John Wesley*.[35] Neither were women automatic providers of preferential rates. The usual rate of interest was 5 per cent, but in 1888 Grace Clark Dart of Appledore provided a mortgage of £200 at 7 per cent on forty-eight shares in the *Charlotte Ann* to Stephen Hare of Appledore.[36] In Penzance Elizabeth Carne, spinster, and Thomas Bodilly, merchant, jointly provided mortgages on all sixty-four shares in *Constant* (£645 at 6 per cent) and in *Nil Desperandum* (£1,000 also at 6 per cent).[37] Thomas Knight of Fowey, the managing owner of the 87-ton schooner *Rebecca*, rashly went to Jane Hodge in Plymouth for his mortgage in 1883. He must have been desperate as Jane and her business partner, Francis Hodge, were professional money lenders and lent Knight £50 at an extortionate rate of 45 per cent per annum. Knight paid off the mortgage speedily seven months later.[38]

Edward Arthur of St Columb, Cornwall was the owner of the Exeter-registered *Gliding Star*. He already had a mortgage on all sixty-four shares with the Exeter Bank. This was in the form of an overdraft, 'sum due on account current

---

33 CRO:MSR/FOW/9.
34 Morris, *Men, Women and Property*, p. 246.
35 CRO: MSR/FOW/7.
36 *Ibid.*
37 CRO: MSR/PENZ/2.
38 NYRO: NR/RS/WH/10.

with interest', up to November 1882.[39] On 7 December 1882, Jane Garland, spinster of Exeter, provided him with a £500 mortgage at 5 per cent. It is to be hoped the vessel was insured as it was abandoned at sea only five days later on 12 December. Elizabeth Harris of Exmouth provided a mortgage on sixty-four shares of the 168-ton *Anne* in November 1857 for £1,200 at 5 per cent. The vessel was trading to the West Indies and the mortgage was paid off in February 1860.[40] One year later Elizabeth was able to buy the *Rachel* from Sarah Hawkins which she then sold two years later.[41]

Emily Bryant was one of several mortgage providers to the owners of the 153-ton *John*. From 1855 to 1875 when the vessel was lost there were four different mortgages at various times on the shares, Emily providing the first mortgage of £220 at 6 per cent on thirty shares to Francis Daw. This was paid off when the shares were sold to the other part owner, Bastick, who then mortgaged all sixty-four shares to Emily for £420 at 6 per cent in 1861. The mortgage was cleared in 1865, but Bastick subsequently took out another mortgage with William Daw for £400 at 7 per cent.[42] The mortgages suggest that Bastick was experiencing tough trading conditions.

Some owners' financial difficulties led them into complex webs of borrowing. Hannah Trueman was a widow of Portsea in Hampshire who was of assistance to the heavily mortgaged Henry Dale, master mariner and sole owner of the *Amelia Hill* of Whitby. Together with other women, including a possible relative of Hannah's, Sarah Trueman of Whitby, they provided a total of £1,350 at various times to the hapless Henry. The registers show the confusion of the complex financial arrangements (see Table 19). Mortgages were noted in the order in which they were officially notified to the customs office and not from the date at which they were taken out, so Margaret Jackson's mortgage G was at a lower priority than the two later ones from Lampert and Holt. Margaret was also providing the largest amounts of money at the lowest rate of interest. The vessel was lost on 9 September 1860.[43]

Anna Pyburn of Whitby, who was referred to in the previous chapter, was a spinster with ample funds. She purchased the major part of the Liverpool-registered barque *Evergreen*, which was subsequently reregistered at Whitby. She owned half of the barque *Renown*, but sold her shares and then provided a mortgage on the same vessel for all the sixty-four shares at 5 per cent.[44] Some of these women, like Anna, who disposed of shares only to provide mortgages, were opting for the safer method of a regular fixed interest income to be derived from the mortgages rather than the irregular dividends that accrued from trade. Yet providing a mortgage on a ship was a risk in itself 'because of the uncertain value

39   DRO: 3289s/11, 1/1876.
40   DRO: 3289s/10, 1/1855.
41   DRO: 3289s/10, 81/1836.
42   DRO: 3289s/10, 8/1855.
43   NYRO: NR/RS/WH 9 & 10.
44   CRO: MSR/FOW/5.

Table 19. Mortgages on *Amelia Hill* of Whitby

	Date	Loan amount and interest p.a.	Lender
Mortgage A	15 July 1857	£100 @ 4%	Hannah Trueman
Mortgage B	1 February 1858	£100 @ 4%	Hannah Trueman
Mortgage C	22 February 1858	£200 @ 4%	Sarah Trueman
Mortgage D	22 February 1858	£400 @ 3%	Margaret Jackson
Mortgage E	24 February 1860	£126 17s 6d @ 5%	Lampert & Holt
Mortgage F	January 1860	£126 @ 5%	Lampert & Holt
Mortgage G	22 February 1860	£550 @ 3%	Margaret Jackson

Source: North Yorkshire Record Office: NG/RS/WH/10 Whitby Shipping Registers.

of the security'.[45] Knowing the credit worthiness of the borrower was also essential and more easily achieved in smaller locations.[46] Lending money in the form of a mortgage still required specialised knowledge of the business of shipping.

Passive Investors

On inheritance, the simplest option, especially in the case of fractional ownership, was to take the path of least resistance and do nothing with the shares. Thirty-six per cent of female shareholders were passive holders of shares they had inherited, but then appeared to take no further action. Involvement in decisions was not essential when there was a capable managing owner, and as long as dividends appeared or their absence was convincingly explained. The easiest option was to do nothing unless there was a need for the money. Some owners may have not known what to do with small shares, and simply filed them away, content just to receive the payments when they came and to let 'the experts' or those who 'knew best' make the decisions.

The vast majority of shareholders were locally based. However, those who were living at a distance when they inherited were at a distinct disadvantage as they were out of the local information networks. Alice Tratham of Teignmouth in Devon inherited sixteen shares in a Fowey vessel and held the largest number of shares, which usually meant that she took over responsibility as managing owner, but she passed the responsibility for the vessel over to Nicholas Lewarne, a fellow shareholder based in Fowey.[47]

Elizabeth Richardson of Whitby owned half of the 49-ton *Sophia*, having inherited on the death of her husband in 1867, but she did not apply to administer

---

[45] Palmer, 'Investors in London Shipping', p. 61.
[46] Hudson, 'Attitudes to Investment Risk', p. 78.
[47] CRO: MSR FOW/9.

his estate until 1869 when she was selling her shares.[48] The need for clear title to the shares when selling was often the catalyst for notification of inheritance to the customs officials. Ownership change was also slow to be registered, as in the case of Jane Pearce of Looe who registered her ownership four years after inheriting, when again she was selling the shares and proof of ownership was required.[49] Some small investors clearly felt no urgency to claim their ownership until the shares were sold, as in another Looe example, Caroline Skentlebury, who together with her sister Mary Parsons inherited eight shares jointly from their father in 1864. No action was taken until they were sold in 1868, although both women were married, and the shares were never transferred to their husbands' names.[50]

It has been suggested that widows tended to hold onto shares provided they gave a regular income from dividends. 'Spinsters, too as their parents died depended on investment income to keep them in the manner to which they had become accustomed, in other words to avoid having to work.'[51] Information on the amount of money involved in ship shares is limited, but some accounts have survived to give an idea of the cost of buying shares and the type of income earned. The best share payments were made in the first few years after the vessel's launch. The *Ocean Spray* of Fowey earned a profit of £608 in her first year of trading and gave her owners a 14 per cent return on their investment. The following year was one of the best trading years and gave a 23 per cent return. Among her owners was Miss Mary Salmon of St Columb, who had bought one share in the newly built 280-ton brigantine registered in December 1875. She had paid £67 for her share and the subsequent earnings were £9 10s in the first year, £15 5s in the second year, and the third payout in 1879 was £8. By 1883 the cumulative profits paid out to the owners came to a total of £71 10s per share and the vessel continued to earn money for its owners until 1900.[52] The owners of the 180-ton schooner *Thetis*, who included Miss Mary Henwood, paid an initial £57 17s 9d per share. The total they received in its short career (it was wrecked in 1876) was £34 6s 1d.[53]

Inheritance accounts for one-third of all of the first transactions in the database. Many of the passive investors had inherited and may not have had the same attitude to the shares as the initial purchaser, being content to accept whatever payment came in the way of dividends. Additionally they may have felt loyal to a late husband's decision, or simply were not under pressure to realise capital. Yet these investors, whether they chose not to take any action or whether it was inertia, were still performing an important role in the financing of ships.

[48] NYRO: NG/RS/WH/10.
[49] CRO: MSR/FOW/7.
[50] CRO: MSR/FOW/7.
[51] Maltby and Rutterford, 'She Possessed Her Own Fortune', p. 239.
[52] Account book of *Ocean Ranger*, by kind permission of Mr A. Samuels.
[53] Greenhill, *Merchant Schooners*, pp. 273–81.

Divestors

If the passive investors were content to let matters rest, the divestors moved speedily to dispose of their shares, ridding themselves of the responsibility. The 12 per cent who are described as divestors are those who inherited, mostly from their husbands, and then sold the shares rapidly as soon as the formalities of probate had been completed. These are almost always widows. This group includes all those who parted with their shares within one year, as it could take that amount of time to achieve probate in complex cases and, if there were many shares, to find a willing buyer. Because of the need for proof of title, the date of the grant of probate was entered in the shipping registers.

The reasons for divesting varied from an urgent requirement for cash in the event of the death, to a specific requirement under a will that liquidated the estate. Individual women may have been reluctant to have their funds tied up in a vessel with all the attendant risks of loss. In some instances fellow shareholders may have been keen to consolidate their holding in a vessel and so bought out the widow, as in the case of Elizabeth Cooper of Robin Hood's Bay. She inherited twenty-one shares in the twenty-year-old *George Andreas*, which was a 122-ton snow, which had been built in Germany. Her husband did not leave a will and as soon as she obtained probate she sold her shares to a fellow shareowner.[54] Grace Leaman of Par inherited sixteen shares in the *Tryphena* and also sold to a fellow shareholder. In some cases the fellow shareholders were family members, as in the case of the *Ariel*, a 189-ton snow that traded with the Baltic. This was owned by Thomas Pinkney, a whitesmith in Whitby, and his son David, a master mariner. On the death of Thomas in 1858, Elizabeth inherited his shares and mother and son sold the vessel the same year.[55] Selling to fellow shareholders was a simple and easy solution.

When disposing of a large number of shares, it was sometimes easier to sell them in small parcels, and this is what Amelia Brown did with hers. Her late husband William Brown was a shipowner and she inherited forty shares in *Billy* and fifty-eight in *Lady Normanby*. The shares in *Billy* were sold to two master mariners, Francis and Henry Roberts of Whitby, and the shares in *Lady Normanby* were sold to Brown and Harker, both master mariners, and a shipowner, Bovill.[56]

If the inheritance was a minority share, or a fractional shareholding in a ship, then disposal was simple and under maritime law there was no need to refer to the other shareholders. The transaction was notified to the customs officials when the necessary forms were signed by the seller and buyer. Inheriting a whole vessel, however, was more complex, as the widow, whether she wished it or not, now had full liability with the attendant costs and responsibilities. Ships were costly items: when working there were the insurance costs, maintenance and payment to

---

[54] NYRO: NG/RS/WH/1/10.
[55] NYRO: NG/RS/WH/2.
[56] NYRO: NG/RS/WH/2.

the master; when idle there were still potential port and storage costs. However, finding a buyer for a whole vessel, especially a large one, was a different proposition from the sale of a few shares. Sometimes there was a willing local buyer, as in the case of Elizabeth Westlake of Exeter who inherited the *Windsworth* from Henry Westlake of Plymouth, a master mariner. There was an existing mortgage on the shares and in the same transaction she was able to pay off the mortgage and sell the ship to Richard Penrose, a merchant of Plymouth, within one month in 1879. Such a speedy settlement suggests that Penrose was a keen and waiting buyer.[57] Also family members could come to the rescue. The Westgarths lived in Easington and on the death of George Westgarth in 1865, his widow Sarah inherited the 54-ton schooner *Dispatch*, which was by then fifty years old. She had a young family and the vessel was sold to another George Westgarth, perhaps her father-in-law. But she had also inherited forty shares in the 75-ton *Lindisfarne*; these she kept and she named herself as the managing owner. The vessel was lost one year later.[58]

Mary Ellery of Polruan inherited the *John and Jenefer* in 1873. Her husband, Elijah, had been the master of the vessel. He had over time been increasing his ownership of the vessel, buying shares in small quantities from the other owners. Mary was now faced with the ownership of a 91-ton schooner that was thirty-three years old and in need of regular maintenance. As the owner/master, all of Elijah's earnings came back into the family. Mary had the option of keeping the vessel and finding a suitable master. Apart from the question of finding and selecting a trustworthy master who was available, such an appointment added to the costs, and the profits in the smaller vessels simply did not allow for this. The *John and Jenefer* was sold within the year.[59] Similarly Eliza Flintoff of Thorpe sold her sixty-four shares in the 40-ton schooner *Duke of York*.[60] In this way the widows released themselves from unwelcome additional responsibilities and risks.

Some women inherited small fleets and these could combine fractional holdings in some vessels together with full ownership. Mary Roberts of Mevagissey was left several ship investments by her husband, Benjamin Roberts, a local builder and shipowner who died in 1885, and in the same year Mary also inherited shares from John Furse. This left her with good-sized holdings in three vessels, *Elizabeth Mary Ann*, *PM Willcock* and *Perseverance*, and the whole of the *Lizzie*. Within twelve months all were disposed of, mainly to local master mariners who were also fellow investors (see Table 20).[61]

Elizabeth Luke of Charlestown had a problem of much larger proportion. Her husband died in December 1871 without leaving a will and she was left with a fleet of ships and several related businesses. A rather paternalistic view of her circumstances was that:

57 CRO: MSR/FOW/8.
58 NYRO: NG/RS/WH/10.
59 CRO: MSR/FOW/8.
60 NYRO: NG/RS/WH/10.
61 CRO: MSR/FOW/5, 6, 8 & 9.

Table 20. Shareholding of Mary Roberts of Mevagissey

Ship	Tons	Built	No. of shares	Sold	Buyer
Elizabeth Mary Ann	121	1840	18	1885	James Gill Philp, Mevagissey M M
Lizzie	65	1864	64	1886	Buyer unknown
P. M. Willcock	73	1868	24	1886	P M Willcock, Pentewan, M M
Perseverance	51	1841	36	1885	Will Rosevear, Mevagissey, M M

Source: CRO: MSR/FOW/5, 6, 8 & 9 Shipping Registers.

William died, leaving a widow and infants, the eldest son of whom – Little Fred – was only 11 years old. There were other Lukes at Charlestown, but young and inexperienced in business. It must have been to Stephens that Elizabeth, the widow, turned for mature guidance.[62]

John Stephens may indeed have given advice as he was a local shipbroker, but there is no evidence to suggest that Elizabeth was not capable of making some of her own decisions. Her two sons were not the infants depicted. The 1851 census for Charlestown gives the age of William as three years old and that of Alfred as six months old, so by the time of their father's death in 1872 William was aged twenty-four and Alfred twenty-one, and in the subsequent share dealings they were described as merchants.[63] The business was an extensive one: while the late William Luke could be described as a shipbuilder, he was also a shipowner, china clay and stone merchant, rope manufacturer, smith and cooper. For the Luke family shipbuilding was an extension of their main business interests and the building of ships was for their own use in the china clay trade, the main export from Charlestown. Luke's shipbuilding yard was in a difficult space under the cliffs and high above the harbour, so launching was tricky and this limited the size of vessels that could be built.[64] Maintenance could only be performed in the harbour and space was at a premium there. William had also been a big investor in other Fowey-registered vessels and Elizabeth's total inheritance was nine ships and holdings in eleven other ships.

Such a large business inheritance needed some fast action and there was also a vessel under construction in the yard, *The Pride of the Channel*. Elizabeth embarked upon a policy of rationalisation. Two of the family vessels were retained but under the ownership of her sons; the rest were sold out of the family, with John Stephens buying one of the smaller ones, *Racer*. Disposing of so many vessels

[62] C. H. Ward-Jackson, *Stephens of Fowey: A Portrait of a Cornish Merchant Fleet 1867–1939* (Greenwich: National Maritime Museum, 1980), p. 13.

[63] Their ages taken from PRO: HO 107 1906 Census Charlestown 1851.

[64] Ward-Jackson, *Stephens of Fowey*, p. 11.

in a short time could have a negative impact on the local market and depress the value, so it appears that the vessels were sold to a range of places at a distance – London, Hull, Canterbury – to balance that effect. The shipowner could use the services of a shipbroker or authorise the master to proceed to a port and sell the ship at or above a certain sum.[65] Elizabeth sold (or merely transferred) the four shares in the *Gem* to her son and the rest were sold by 1873 to a variety of owners including Hannah Francis of Truro (see Table 21).[66]

Table 21. Elizabeth Luke of Charlestown, shareholding

Ship	Ton	Built	No.	Sold	Buyer
Challenge	78	1870	64	1872	W H and Alfred Luke, merchants
Jane	131	1867	64	1872	Alfred Luke, Charlestown, merchant
Little Fred	42	1870	64	1872	Thomas Hitchin of St Austell
Maria Louise	108	1866	64	1872	William West, St Blazey
Mary Lizzie	148	1868	64	1872	Thomas Row, London
Racer	68	1866	64	1872	John Stephens, Charlestown
Teaser	65	1868	64	1872	Thomas Abbott of Hull, MM
William & Anthony	200	1862	64	1872	Canterbury owners
Pride of the Channel	109	1873	64	1873	John Stephens, Charlestown
Engineer	118	1846	16	1875	Not known
John Clark	95	1863	16	1872	Not known
Rippling Wave	129	1869	16	1872	Not known
Sparkling Wave	154	1866	8	1873	Alfred Salvesta Lidgey
Thetis	172	1873	8	1873	Hannah Francis, Truro
Mersey	187	1839	8	1873	Will Smith of Polruan shipowner
Treffry ss			8	1872	Geo Petherick, St Austell gent
Juno	133	1864	8	1873	Not known
Jane Slade	159	1870	6	1873	Alfred Salvesta Lidgey, Truro, gent.
Gem	163	1871	4	1872	Alfred Luke merchant Charlestown

Source: Cornwall Record Office: MSR/FOW/5, 6, 8 & 9 Fowey Shipping Registers.

The Pride of the Channel was launched eventually in 1873 and Elizabeth registered the vessel. On the same day, 12 May 1873, ownership was passed to John Stephens who sold on to a parcel of mainly local owners including Elizabeth's sons William H. and Alfred Luke who had six and three shares respectively. Elizabeth did however have one venture into shipowning in 1871 when she purchased shares in the *Comet*, a 72-ton schooner built in Padstow in 1858, although this may have been the fulfilment of a promise already made by her late husband. Half of it was owned by Charles Warne, the master, and sixteen shares by John Stephens who was the managing owner, Elizabeth buying the other sixteen shares. It was not

[65] DRO: 3289s/10, 19 1848 Sale of *Susan*.
[66] CRO: MSR /FOW/5, 6, 8 & 9.

a long association – the vessel was totally lost at Antwerp in December 1874.[67] Elizabeth did not venture her money on ship shares again, leaving that to her sons.

The family strategy of slimming down their operations can be seen as the narrowing of a wide range of business interests. William and Alfred continued the family business as china clay merchants, and the census of 1881 shows Elizabeth as a widow living on dividends, William now a coal and manure merchant, and Alfred a shipowner and merchant.[68] Such a large inheritance as that of Elizabeth Luke was unusual, but whatever the number of shares, disposal was not always straightforward and was not necessarily the easy option.

Sarah Hawkins, mentioned in Chapter 4, was left an estate in trust and her trustees were both experienced shipowners holding shares in the Hawkins ships. The will stipulated that the trustees were to act at Sarah's request, and it should not be assumed that Sarah had no shipping knowledge. Indeed Sarah had been brought up in a family of shipowners and then married to one, so could not have been wholly unaware of the significance of decisions. The choices were to continue her husband's business or rationalise. She set out to sell the fleet and all the transactions were noted in her name, not those of her trustees.

So began the sell-off of the vessels. In December 1859 the *Maria Burriss* and the *New Margaret* were sold and in January the *Catherine*.[69] In February the *Marion* was lost at sea off Whitby.[70] In the same month Sarah bought sixteen shares in the *Cumberland Lass*, making her sole owner for two months until the vessel was sold to Hartlepool.[71] In August she sold her eight shares in the *Fountain* to her brother, Peter, and then also sold him the *Suffolk Trader* in October.[72] Finally, eighteen months after being widowed, she sold her last vessel, the *Rachel*, to another widow, Elizabeth Harris.[73]

Sarah was probably well out of the Exeter coal business as the arrival of the railway had impacted this once highly lucrative trade. A Topsham coal dealer, Richard Bussel, told the Tidal Harbour Commission that

> … before the Bristol and Exeter railway opened [in 1844] his sale of coals alone amounted to nearly six thousand tons per annum: it is now reduced to one thousand. Used to employ twenty sail of ships a year; navigated probably by 150 men. Now five ships, not employing more than 40 men, are sufficient for this trade. The trade of almost all the other coal dealers is reduced in the same scale.[74]

---

67 CRO: MSR/FOW/6.
68 PRO: RG 11 2302 Census 1881.
69 DRO: 3289s/10, 15/1840, 2/1852, 11/1849.
70 DRO: 3289s/10, 4/1852.
71 DRO: 3289s/10, 7/1856.
72 DRO: 3289s/10, 36/1854, 14/1854.
73 DRO: 3289s/10, 8/1836.
74 Starkey, 'The Ports, Seaborne Trade and Shipping Industry', p. 38, quoting from BPP 1846 XVIII 320–3 Second Report of the Tidal Harbours Commission.

These women were liquidating their inheritance, either to move their funds into more secure forms of investment as in the case of Elizabeth Luke, or to pay off debts. A widow was not automatically in a better position financially just because of an inheritance. Her standard of living could be considerably reduced and this 'depended on a number of factors, including her status and wealth, [and] the occupation of her deceased husband'.[75] This does not include her husband's financial ability or business skills. On death, the creditors appeared to ensure their share of the deceased's estate. The female divestors moved speedily to dispose of their shares, ridding themselves of the responsibility or liquidating the estate, but doing so was not without effort.

The maritime background against which these investors made their decisions was a world of risk assessment, capital investment, business connections and business judgement. The vessels in which these women invested ranged in size from 15 tons (the minimum size at which a ship was registered) to 1,242 tons. The vast majority were sailing vessels, with just a handful of steam vessels. The trades in which they were employed were both the coastal trade, carrying coal and other low value commodities around the coast, and foreign trade, carrying freight and passengers to Australia, the West Indies, North America, the Mediterranean and almost every point of the compass.

The Contribution of the Women Shipowners

The shipping registers with their transaction information show that a sizeable number of women were not just passive holders of inherited shares, but whether passive or active what did their combined investment mean to the shipping industry? The world of shipping and shipbuilding until the 1890s was 'substantially self-sufficient with regard to the accumulation of equity capital and, consequently, there would appear to have been little role for external finance'.[76] Even with the growth of ever larger and more complex ships by 1880 four-fifths of steam tonnage showed little difference in its financing from the shipowning partnerships of the 1820s.[77] This self-funding was relevant to the success of the shipping industry. By developing 'private links to attract funds from within their rich economy', British shipowners were able to establish a strong record of technological innovation and productivity growth, unlike many of the "old" industries'. The 64th system of shareownership was the starting point for many large shipping companies. Ten of the thirteen major shipping enterprises founded between 1839 and 1889, which includes many of the biggest names in British shipping, began their enterprises

---

75 Shoemaker, *Gender in English Society*, p. 138.
76 P. L. Cottrell, 'Britannia's Sovereign: Banks in the Finance of British Shipbuilding and Shipping, c. 1830–1894', in *Financing the Maritime Sector: Proceedings from the Fifth North Sea History Conference*, ed. Leo M. Akveld, Frits R. Loomeijer and Morten Hahn-Pedersen (Esbjerg: Fiskeri-og Sofartsmuseet, 2002), pp. 191–254 (p. 214).
77 Cottrell, 'Britannia's Sovereign', p. 195.

as 64th concerns.[78] Turnbulls of Whitby and London retained the 64th system as late as 1906 before reluctantly following the trend and turning their vessels into single ship companies.[79] Funding of sailing vessels throughout the century continued to be a local affair, utilising the available money in the community, even in the largest ports. In Liverpool, collaboration between local interests was essential to the growth of its shipping, while in London between 1820 and 1850 investment funds came from local sources within the shipping industry.[80] A significant factor that aided this process of local investment was the large number of women whose capital remained within the industry as shares or who provided mortgages on shares.

So what share of the investment in shipping did these women shipowners represent in the five ports? It is possible to make a snapshot comparison between the five ports in one year. In 1865 *Clayton's Directory of Shipping* was published and it listed the existing ships on the register for that year in ports across the country, with the exception of Liverpool and London.[81] The total percentage of shares owned by women in the five ports in 1865 is presented in Table 22. With the exception of Exeter, the numbers are surprisingly consistent, with an overall percentage of 13. The only available contrasting figures for women's investment are from Arendal in Norway where in 1874 women comprised just 4.2 per cent of the investors in shipping and supplied 1.7 per cent of the capital.[82] However, it seems that women had a tendency to hold on to their shares and were not as fast as their male counterparts in moving out of a declining market.

Table 22. Women's investment in vessels in 1865

	Women's shares	Total ships registered	Potential shares	% held by women
Exeter	1,929	109	6,976	28%
Fowey	996	155	9,920	10%
Lynn	1,137	104	6,656	17%
Whitby	2,736	371	23,744	12%
Whitehaven	844	150	9,600	11%
Total	7,642	889	56,896	13%

Source: Investor Database and *Clayton's Directory of Shipping*, 1865.

---

[78] Gordon Boyce, '64thers, Syndicates and Stock Promotions: Information Flows and Fund Raising Techniques of British Shipowners before 1914', *Journal of Economic History*, 52 (1992), 184–92.

[79] Long, *A Shipping Venture*, pp. 138–9.

[80] Milne, *Trade and Traders*. pp. 134–45; Palmer, 'Investors in London Shipping', pp. 61–2.

[81] *Clayton's Directory of Shipping*, 1865.

[82] Berit Eide Johnsen, 'From Integration to Segregation; Ship Ownership in Agder, Southern Norway, c 1860–1930', in *Financing the Maritime Sector: Proceedings from the Fifth North Sea History Conference*, ed. Leo M. Akveld, Frits R. Loomeijer and Morten Hahn-Pedersen (Esbjerg: Fiskeri-og Søfartsmuseet, 2002), pp. 71–114 (pp. 83–4).

Both Exeter and Lynn were ports in decline by 1865 and this is reflected in a drop in ship registration. This had declined in absolute numbers by 1865 below that of the other three ports. In Exeter the number of ships on the register declined by 40 per cent and yet the percentage of shares held by women was 28 per cent, much higher than elsewhere.

Another consideration is whether this shipping investment by women was confined mainly to these smaller ports. The scale of the task required to analyse the large ports puts a detailed investigation beyond the scope of this study. One source, *Marwood's North of England Maritime Directory, Shipping Register and Commercial Advertiser* for 1854, does provide the names of the shipowners in some of the largest shipping ports, which were situated in the northeast, and also includes Liverpool. Unlike *Clayton's Directory* produced ten years later, this is not a list of the managing owners. Marwood simply had a column headed owners. This means there are sometimes, one, two or three names or more listed. On occasions where there are clearly many owners the major owners are listed and the phrase 'and others' is used for the rest. This cannot therefore be a complete list of the women shareholders at the time, but it does at least give an indication (see Table 23).

Table 23. Women investors in 1854

Port	Ships registered	Ships with women investors	Percentage of ships
Berwick	60	0	0%
Hartlepool	133	20	15%
Liverpool	2,144	17	1%
Newcastle	900	27	3%
Scarboro	196	29	15%
Shields	862	80	9%
Stockton	183	9	5%
Sunderland	963	56	6%
Whitby	392	54	14%
Total	5,833	292	5%

Source: *Marwood's North of England Maritime Directory, Shipping Register and Commercial Advertiser 1854.*

This shows a wide range of participation by women, generally with higher percentages in the smaller ports, although Shields has 9 per cent. These data can only be a crude estimate of the women's investment since they do not give the size of the woman's shareholding and will certainly have underestimated the number of ships with women shareholders. The number of steam vessels was small, just 380 across all of these ports, of which 4 per cent had women investors. Women's participation, therefore, was not limited to the smaller ports, and the increased use of companies, which are more apparent in the larger ports, hides the names of investors. As local investment was important to women, those ports with high percentages of ships built locally and financed on the 64th principle would attract more female investors. The majority of Liverpool ships were not locally built: just 10 per cent of the total sail tonnage was locally built and 28 per cent of the steam tonnage.[83] Bigger ports were also more anonymous and the type of localised and family networking that favoured women's involvement was less prevalent.

A total summing up of the contribution of these women across the whole period is problematic, since the wealth of data available in the British shipping registers is also a limitation on analysis, as ships and shares were registered and reregistered across the century. Information is, however, available for Fowey, where it is possible to compare the number of women investors with the total investors for the port due to the heroic transcription of the whole of the Fowey registers by Ward-Jackson. For the period 1841 to1880 he gives the number of vessels registered as 319, a potential of 20,416 shares.[84] The number of shares held by women in the same period was 2,505, thus giving a percentage of 12 per cent of the available shares in the port being held by women over the period.

Summary

Nineteenth-century female investors are emerging as a rather more complex group than historians previously considered. They not only invested in safe places such as the Bank of England, a secure, if unspectacular place for their capital, but in shipping, where maritime losses, economic uncertainties, trade fluctuations and poor management were well known hazards. These shipowners were not the women speculators in limited liability companies who knowingly used their money and took risks to make gains, who were considered to be mostly rich women spending 'pin money'.[85] The shipowners in the smaller communities were hard-working and largely lower middle-class.

The shipping registers reveal a close-knit business world with commercial and family links between many of the shareholders. The same surnames appear and share dealing is mainly restricted to the local community until the 1870s. These local and family-related links were important reasons why women were able to invest to such an extent. When the industry changed to a world of big steam and iron ships, larger amounts of capital were raised through joint stock companies, so these local links were of less value. However, keeping the woman's capital within the family firm was still an aim. Meanwhile in the environment of the smaller wooden ships, the separate worlds of women and home, and men and business, are not only shown to co-exist, but frequently to overlap and interconnect, rather than collide. Men are seen as supporting and colluding with women in their share dealings.

---

83 *Marwood's Annual Directory.*
84 Ward-Jackson, *Ships and Shipbuilders*, p. 101.
85 Rutterford and Maltby, 'The Widow, the Clergyman and the Reckless', p. 127.

Women had opportunities through inheritance and purchase to acquire shares in ships. Many women actively traded in shares, both buying and selling, and some of the women became managing owners of vessels, a role that needed considerable industry knowledge. Because of the unique make-up of the communities, which tended to have greater numbers of independent women, and the peculiarities of the laws relating to shipping, women were able to hold shares and to make decisions as co-owners on the same basis as men. The membership of the group of owners of a ship was small when compared to other forms of shareholding and few female shareholders can have been totally unaware of the decisions that were regularly taken. When deciding in which ship to invest the shareholder needed to be aware of the potential for profit. Factors that affected the profitability of a ship included the type of trade, the competence of the master, and how well the ship had been maintained, together with knowledge of the attitude of fellow shareholders to matters such as insurance and maintenance, as well as the efficiency of the managing owner.

Making informed decisions was not that difficult for women in these communities. There were plenty of links and connections within the community, both informal and business-based. These close connections were typical of the fractional ownership system for sailing vessels and were not exclusive to Britain. In Arendal in Norway in 1874 there were 338 sailing ships and five steamships registered and almost 75 per cent of investors were linked to the shipping industry. These investors, who comprised business managers, 'captains and wealthy women', are described as 'members of a group – a closed unity – [who] through tight professional bonds and intermarriage, formed the upper classes of Arendal'.[86]

There were good business reasons for keeping these networks closed, as ownership of shares gave the owner access to the full financial and operational information on the vessel, and there were those who preferred to keep this information within a select group of associates, particularly if the vessel was part of a larger shipping company. Furness influenced the circulation of 64ths, so that he could ensure that the information was 'dispensed only to trusted allies', encouraging stronger ties with his suppliers and agents.[87] In Whitby, Whitehaven, King's Lynn and Fowey such matters were managed by keeping shares within the family or with close business partners. Women had multiple connections within such communities. There were, in effect, few real blockages to a determined woman who wanted good information, and the maritime communities appear to have had their fair share of both.

The nineteenth century was in many ways a special time for the ports, as never before 'had there been so much physical expansion, engineering splendour, capital investment or human endeavour'.[88] If the major ports were totally dominant during this time, the rest of the ports, while handling relatively small amounts of trade, had an important role in redistribution and some had very specific roles relevant

---

[86] Johnsen, ' Integration to Segregation', pp. 83–89.
[87] Boyce, '64thers, Syndicates and Stock Promotions', p. 190.
[88] Jackson, 'The Ports', pp. 218–19.

to local supply, such as the coal and mineral ports.[89] Another factor highly relevant to the men who served on board, and their families, was that a vessel's port of registry was not necessarily the same as its main place of trade – many entering London and Liverpool were registered in the smaller ports. Clearly vessels went where the trade took them, and women played a significant part in ensuring the supply of the ships that were so crucial to Britain's expansion. Women shipowners made deliberate and informed choices as active investors. While some may have been motivated more by direct family needs, such as supporting the family ship, others were investing as part of the close business community in ports. The contribution of these women to the health of the shipping economy deserves greater recognition.

---

[89] Jackson, 'The Significance of Unimportant Ports', pp. 1–17.

6

Managing Owners

On 6 November 1834 Stephen Quinn of Whitehaven signed his name to an apprenticeship document. He and his father, Daniel, agreed that Stephen would be apprenticed for three years to be taught the 'art, trade, mystery or occupation of a Mariner'. The curious aspect of this document is that the person to whom he was bound, and who was responsible for teaching him, was not a master mariner. Indeed the document had to have many changes made to suit the circumstances, as the named person was Hannah Wallace. In each instance where the pre-printed form used the words 'Master' or 'his' they were crossed out and the words 'Mistress' or 'hers' were substituted.[1] Hannah is described as 'acting and part owner of the brigantine *Cygnet*'; she was in effect the managing owner of the ship.

The managing owner was the business manager of the enterprise. Each ship was an individual business, capable of earning profits or, in poor trading conditions, making a loss. Good business management could minimise losses and maximise profits, but, with up to thirty-two co-owners, decision making needed to be simplified. The master was certainly important, as his was the critical hands-on role. He could, however, only act on the orders of the shipowners. Someone was needed to make decisions and sign forms on behalf of the owners since regular consultation even in a small community was not practical.

There were several names for the role: managing owner, managing agent, ship's husband, bookkeeper, ship's accountant. In the East India Company 'ship's husband' was the common term, although the official title was managing owner.[2] One early female ship's husband/managing owner was Christian Larkins, who took over responsibility for the *Warren Hastings* for two years after her husband's death in 1784.[3] The 'managing owner' is first mentioned in law in 1854,[4] but confusingly it is the ship's husband who is referred to in the Admiralty Court Act of 1861.[5] The managing owner is the term that was most used throughout the nineteenth century and this term is used here. This was the person who was appointed by the rest of the owners to act on their behalf, and they might also be paid a fee. Usually it was the majority shareholder, but not in all cases.

---

[1] WRO: Apprenticeship Indenture.
[2] Jean Sutton, *Lords of the East: The East India Company and Its Ships, 1600–1874* (London: Conway, 2000), p. 19.
[3] Jean Sutton, Personal correspondence, 5 September 2005.
[4] 1854 Merchant Shipping Act , 17 & 18 Victoria c.104.
[5] 1861 Admiralty Court Act, 24 & 25 Victoria c.10.

6. Mrs Mary Hicks Hayes, shipowner and managing owner
Source: Mrs Isabel Pickering

His, or her, decisions covered matters relating to the trade in which the ship was used, the appointment of the master, the management of accounts and matters relating to insurance and law. The managing owner dealt with the increasing bureaucracy and in some cases found cargoes. They were the main communicator with the other owners and had to answer to them for their decisions. They needed considerable knowledge of the trade in which the ship or ships were occupied, a working knowledge of maritime law and insurance and, critically, they had to have a good working relationship with the master. As will be seen, women appear as managing owners throughout the century.

By the mid-nineteenth century, the rapid increase in the number of limited companies owning ships and the expansion of the number of shareholders in the limited companies raised questions of ownership.[6] Additionally the different nature of the relationship between a shareowner in a limited company and the ship in comparison with the close relationship of the holder of 64ths with his or her ship led to concerns about who in maritime law was the managing owner. By 1876 this was clarified with the Merchant Shipping Act, which required that:

> The name and address of the managing owner for the time being of every British ship registered at any port shall be registered at the Customs House of the ship's port of entry.
> When this is not the managing owner then shall be so registered the name of the ship's husband or other person to whom the management of the ship is entrusted by or on behalf of the owner.[7]

This 'other person' referred to in the act was generally known as the managing agent. This was an individual who was employed by the owners, but had no shares in the vessel. A managing owner or agent might also employ a bookkeeper just to do the accounts, or some shipowners might prefer to do their own bookkeeping and used the agent for the variety of form filling and liaison with authorities. Jane Slade of Polruan owned shares in several ships and the majority in her namesake, the schooner *Jane Slade*. While initially she was named as the managing owner on the crew agreement she later handed this role to William Geake. Geake was an ex-schoolmaster who had become a professional managing agent/owner for several ships.[8] By the 1881 census, after retiring from running several businesses, Jane still described herself as 'ship's accountant'.[9]

Davis, writing about the seventeenth and eighteenth centuries, is one of the few historians to explore the complex relationship between the ship's husband or managing owner and the master of the ship. He describes the range of functions performed by the managing owner and suggests that there was no hard and fast dividing line between the managing owner and master roles. 'There was every

---

6   Robin Craig, 'Millionaires and Enterprising Nobodies', *International Journal of Maritime History*, 16 (2004), 1–15.
7   1876 Merchant Shipping Act, 39 & 40 Victoria c.80.
8   CRO: Crew Agreements *Jane Slade*.
9   CRO: Census 1881 Fowey.

gradation from the husband who did almost everything to the husband who did nothing' and yet even in the latter case 'approbation, advice and assistance [for the master] were expected'.[10] Certainly the rest of the owners had expectations that the managing owner was at least fully informed of the progress of the vessel and their investments.

There has been limited research published on the role of the managing owner and any mention is usually in passing and grouped with shipowners in general. Davis did treat them separately, but, as he wrote, 'Shipowning was no man's whole business and few men's main business.'[11] Greenhill, who wrote so eloquently about the many smaller ports, their trades, the schooners and masters, gives little detailed information on the owners and never mentions managing owners. He does however make a passing comment about the benefit of 'a good managing wife'.[12] Much of Greenhill's research related to the reminiscences of mariners and master mariners in the post-World War II era. Most of them were ex-coastal trade men who were sailing at the end of the nineteenth century and in the early twentieth, where the vessel was usually small and was most often wholly owned by the master. In 1888 Charity Ann Honey of Port Isaac was designated by her husband, Richard Honey, as 'the person to whom the management of the vessel is entrusted'. She owned no shares officially in the 75-ton schooner *P.M. Willcock*, which was wholly owned by Richard. Charity managed the books and other shore-based requirements while her husband was at sea.[13]

The Managing Women

Clayton's Directory of Shipping was published in 1865. This covered all ports across Great Britain with the exception of Liverpool and London. It appears to have been published just for one year. Its competitor was *Marwood's Annual Directory* which covered Liverpool and eight northeast ports. This had commenced publication in 1850 and continued annually until the 1860s. *Turnbull's Shipping Register* lasted longest, from 1849 to 1899, but this too covered a selection of ports.[14] Clayton specifically lists the managing owners of vessels, while the earlier *Marwood's* of 1854–5 listed the registered owners with no indication of any difference between them. *Clayton's* is therefore, despite the absence of the two largest ports, a very valuable source on ship management across Britain. The percentage of vessels managed by women in *Clayton's Directory* was 2 per cent. This is a very small proportion of all vessels, but it masks considerable variation. The top twenty ports are shown in Table 24.

10 Davis, *Rise of the English Shipping Industry*, pp. 160–1.
11 Davis, *Rise of the English Shipping Industry*, p. 160.
12 Greenhill, *Merchant Schooners*, p. 117.
13 CRO: MSR/FOW/5.
14 Stammers, ed., *Clayton's Directory*, 'Introduction'.

Table 24. Top twenty ports for women managing owners in *Clayton's Register*

Port	Ships reg. Steam	Sail	Port total	Female MO	% of ships reg.
Port Glasgow	5	11	16	1	6%
Arbroath		81	81	5	6%
Hayle		101	101	6	6%
Whitby	1	370	371	18	5%
Exeter		109	109	5	5%
Middlesborough	6	38	44	2	5%
Maryport		119	119	5	4%
Padstow		103	103	4	4%
Falmouth	1	98	99	4	4%
Ramsgate		31	31	1	3%
Aberystwyth	5	95	100	3	3%
King's Lynn		104	104	3	3%
Shields (N Shields)	3	642	645	18	3%
Grimsby	5	32	37	1	3%
Ayr	2	37	39	1	3%
Perth		39	39	1	3%
Weymouth	3	37	40	1	3%
Shields (S Shields)	1	299	300	7	2%
Sunderland	30	788	818	18	2%
Caernarvon		414	414	9	2%

Source: *Clayton's Directory of Shipping*, 1865.

This list does not reflect the managing wives referred to earlier. Working master mariners who wholly owned their vessels might have been named as the managing owner, but they still needed assistance with shore-side aspects of the business and someone to handle the correspondence and accounting. Using other professionals was costly, so the master mariner's wife, and in some cases his daughter, was the *de facto* managing owner.

In 1943 a guidance manual for shipbrokers and shipowners defined the role of the shipowner, a role that had hardly changed since the beginning of the nineteenth century, and explained the tasks faced by him, or in this case her:

> When a vessel is launched and handed over to the owner, his work and responsibility commences. He has to man his vessel, store and provision her, and to find cargoes for her. Incidentally he will doubtless insure his valuable property against the numerous risks to which it will be exposed.[15]

---

[15] Macmurray and Cree, *Shipping and Shipbroking*, p. 3.

Some owners, especially those men who were merchants or who had been master mariners, also found the cargoes, but for most shipowners it was often better to use a middle man with specific knowledge, the shipbroker. This was a particular need in foreign-going vessels.

> In the finding of freight the shipbroker appears, and anyone with experience of ship management will not deny the necessity for a shipbroker. The ramifications for the world's sea trade are so vast that it is quite impracticable for an owner himself to find the cargoes suitable for his vessel and her changing positions, and incidentally, negotiate and arrange the terms and conditions of the contracts of the carriage, or on the other hand for merchant or charterer to obtain the exact vessels required for his purpose.[16]

The real expertise of the managing owner came when there were problems to deal with. The managing owner had to have a working knowledge of the legal and insurance environment. During the nineteenth century the maritime sector was increasingly regulated and the owners and masters had to be aware of the changing requirements.

Manley Hopkins was an insurance expert who wrote several books aimed at shipowners and masters, endeavouring to assist them in their roles. In 1873 he explained that mariners were exposed to a 'class of casualties and perils from which the landsman is exempt',[17] and he listed a range of possible problems: 'There are troubles in port as well as at sea; monetary embarrassment, legal structures, opposed interests, conflicting authorities.' Foreign ports were a high risk and, although there were agents in many ports, he counselled the reader to be aware of the different categories.

> 'general agents' can handle the routine work in port such as entries and clearances at the customs, payments of dues etc. They can also supply money in the currency of the country, for payment of immediate outlays, or for the master's wants during his stay in port.[18]

However the main thrust of Hopkins's point was to ensure that the master never relinquished control to agents of any kind, for

> the master is at all times the agent for the shipowner; and he is, in a certain sense, when no supercargo is on board, agent to the proprietor of the cargo also; but when difficulty and accidents occur he assumes in a more distinct manner the character of agent for all parties concerned in the joint adventure. The consequences of his actions under such circumstances extend even beyond the ships and cargo-owners, and frequently affect another class of persons concerned in the safety of the property – namely the insurer or underwriter of the vessel, her freight and her cargo.[19]

---

[16] *Ibid.*

[17] Manley Hopkins, *The Port of Refuge: Advice and Instruction to the Master Mariner in Situations of Doubt, Difficulty and Danger* (London, 1873), p. 1.

[18] Hopkins, *Port of Refuge*, p. 14.

[19] Hopkins, *Port of Refuge*, p. 15.

Challenges for Women

A managing owner did not have to hold the majority shares as long as they had been appointed by the rest of the shareholders. However, there were specific challenges for a woman in working as a managing owner. She had to manage the master, who was a man well versed in the habit of command, and handle the variety of authorities, from customs officers to port officers, all of whom were male. She had to manage the rest of the shareowners, some of whom were experienced master mariners or shipowners. If the woman was the largest shareholder then this was less of a problem, but it did not necessarily mean that she was immune from unsolicited helpful advice and the views of the other shareholders.

Some women managing owners were minority shareholders. For example, Mary Edgar of Whitehaven only held eight shares in the *Cumberland* and four in *Elter Water*.[20] Mary Hicks Hayes of Polruan was appointed managing owner of the *Koh I Noor* in 1880 while only holding four shares (see Table 25). However, among the shareholders was William Smith, her father, who had been the previous managing owner, and the letter notifying the customs authorities of Mary's appointment was signed by Ann Hicks, her sister-in-law. Their shares, when added to those of Nicholas Dingle, her brother-in-law, should have given her a majority vote. As shown previously, these close family connections were far from unusual and helped men and women alike retain control within their close-knit world. Even with such connections, the list of fellow shareholders shows the wealth of experience that faced Mary and other managing owners in similar circumstances on the annual accounting days. A relative with considerable sea-going experience was not likely to be any less voluble in their views. There is no evidence that decisions were always taken on the basis of the shareholding, but rather on the basis of who was present at the time of the meeting.

There were some advantages. It was not a physically demanding role, travelling was not an essential element and much of the work was administrative, dealing with correspondence and keeping accounts. As for the accounting side, women had long had an accepted role in keeping the books. The 1786 schoolbook on trade for men and women (described in Chapter 1) included explanations and examples of promissory notes, bills of exchange, bills on booked debts and the correct form for receipts for bank stock. One example in the schoolbook was for money received for cordage for a ship, the ship in question being a private ship of war.[21]

---

[20] NYRO: YTSR 1/18 and 20.
[21] Hudson, 'A New Introduction to Trade and Business: Very Useful for the Youth of Both Sexes'.

Table 25. Shareholders in Koh I Noor in 1880

Name	Occupation	Residence	Shares
William Smith	Retd master mariner	Polruan	4
Richard H Williams	Civil engineer	St Austell	6
Nicholas Hicks Dingle	Master mariner	Polruan	5
Thomas Pearce	Merchant	St Blazey	4
Mary H Hayes	Widow	Polruan	4
John Olford	Gentleman	Lostwithiel	2
Jane S Slade	Shipbuilder	Polruan	2
John Slade	Innkeeper	Pelynt	2
John Palmer	Farmer	Duloe	2
Ann Hicks	Widow	Fowey	2
Alfred Luke	Merchant	Charlestown	3
Elizabeth Smith	Widow	Fowey	2
John E Hocken	Sailmaker	Polruan	1
W E Pearce	Yeoman	St Blazey	1
Richard Rundle	Auctioneer	Lostwithiel	1
Charles M Bradhurst	Accountant	St Austell	1
William Morcom	Innkeeper	Par	1
Catherine Harris	Spinster	Polruan	1
Richard Clogg	Butcher	Polruan	1
Edward C Osborne	JP	Edgbaston, B'ham	4
Thomas T S Carlyon	Gentleman	St Blazey	8
S Pascoe	Gentleman	Truro	3
R A Pearne	Master mariner	Polruan	1
W Hocken	Farmer	Tredinnick, Duloe	1
James Stephens	Merchant	Charlestown	1
Josiah Jenkin	Shipowner	Charlestown	1

Source: CRO: MSR/Fow/6.

The Shipowner's Paperwork

During the nineteenth century, as the management role was recognised and as trades became more regularised, came the increasing specialisation of the shipping agents. Large ports especially developed these new functions.[22] Milne describes some of the many bureaucratic demands on the masters and owners made by the customs and port authorities as 'a succession of certificates and signatures.'[23] Some owners used the specialised shipping agents who employed clerks to do the legwork. This was a boon for the overstretched managing owner or master, but it came at a cost and many preferred to keep it in-house.

While it is customary to consider the master as having responsibility for the

---

[22] Simon Ville, 'James Kirton, Shipping Agent', *Mariner's Mirror*, 67 (1981), 149–62.
[23] Milne, *Trade and Traders*, p. 106.

crew, recruiting them and managing them, the shipowners also had a role. The shipowners or their managing owner controlled wages, and an important aspect of ship costs was food. In 1887 at a meeting of the owners of the *Ocean Ranger*, it was proposed by Mr Stephens and seconded by Messrs Sherwell and Olford that 'due to the great depression in shipping and the cheapness of provisioning the said *Ocean Ranger* the future allowance for victualling be at the rate of 1s per day instead of 1s 2d per man'. In May next year the auditor noted that contrary to the proposal the managing owner had allowed the victualling at 1s 1d per man per day, a compromise he seems to have got away with.[24]

Even when the vessel sailed, the shipowner's involvement with the crew did not end. The seaman could leave provision for his relatives on shore. It was customary to issue an Advance Note, usually for one month's wages. These were drafts upon the owners or agents of the vessel, and were made payable three days after the vessel had sailed. There were also Allotment Notes where a dependant could draw weekly or at arranged intervals from the owners a specific sum of money which was later deducted from the seaman's wage at the end of the voyage.[25] When the crews for the local vessels came from within the very close-knit maritime communities, this was a role easily carried out by female managing owners.

Clearance

Once the vessel went to sea the managing owner then received correspondence from the agents in the various ports at which the vessel traded. This kept him or her fully informed of progress, cargoes agreed and other aspects of the trade. Together with regular letters from the master, the managing owner was kept well informed.

> The customs authorities at every port in the country demand that within 6 days of a vessel's departure, the owners will forward to them a detailed account of all the goods shipped. In the same way a manifest, which is the name given to this detailed list, must be included among the ship's papers as it is required for delivery to the Custom Authorities at the port of destination.[26]

The agents then sent the owners an account after the departure of each vessel, detailing in it all charges incurred and credits collected such as freight charges. These disbursements were compiled as soon as a vessel left port and sent to the shipowner.[27] As for any additional expenses,

---

[24] Ship account book *Ocean Ranger*, by kind permission of Mr A. Samuel.
[25] R. B. Paul, *Shipping Simplified, a Book for the Shipping Clerk* (Liverpool, 1918), p. 19.
[26] Paul, *Shipping Simplified*, p. 21.
[27] Paul, *Shipping Simplified*, p. 22.

The owner is liable for the various expenses in connection with any of the crew who are put into hospital abroad, and it may be some considerable time after the termination of the voyage before these expenses can be ascertained.[28]

It might be assumed that most of the female managing owners were in the less demanding, but prolific coastal trade. It was easier for these coastal vessels to remain in close contact with their home port and most of the time they were working in British ports with well known systems and processes. However, these managing owners were also well involved in the deep sea foreign trades, as can be seen in Appendix VI.

The Master and the Managing Owner

'The greatest problem of management, indeed, can be put in a nutshell; to find a paragon to be a master, and then devise means to assist him if he turned out a fool, and restrain him if he turned out a scoundrel.'[29] Davis summed up the crucial relationship and its pitfalls, while Holman in his guide to masters explained that 'The authority of a master is very large, and extends to all acts that are usual and necessary for the use and employment of a ship.'[30]

The master could authorise repairs, raise funds by pledging the ship or the cargo, and even sell the ship and/or cargo in some circumstances. Selecting the master was of even greater importance when, in a time before telegrams, he and his ship and cargo were out of sight and out of communication for months at a time (even years in the case of some trades). The master could be on a percentage or have a part share in the vessel, which motivated him to act in the best interests of the owners. Trust was essential, as were good and clear instructions, as, once the ship had left, the owners had to rely totally on the master. But in all trades the 'skill, honesty and business acumen of the master was crucial to profit and loss.'[31] Control over long-distance vessels 'could only be exercised retrospectively'.[32]

Notwithstanding the significant responsibility of the master, the final responsibility always came back to the owners, who were the employers, even if the master also owned a part of the ship. For the owners, 'The exercise of their functions was intermittent, and immense trust had to be placed in a single individual who was "primarily an employee" and was frequently out of communication.' This was often

---

[28] Macmurray and Cree, *Shipping and Shipbroking*, p. 322.

[29] Davis, *Rise of the English Shipping Industry*.

[30] H. Holman, *A Handy Book for Shipowners and Masters* (London: Maisey, 1915), p. 16.

[31] Simon Ville, 'The Deployment of English Merchant Shipping: Michael and Joseph Henley of Wapping, Ship Owners, 1775–1830', *Journal of Transport History*, 5 (1984), 16–33 (p. 22); Stammers, 'Shipowners in Rural British Ports in the 19th Century: A Study of North Norfolk Ports'.

[32] Yrjö Kaukiainen, 'Owners and Masters: Management and Managerial Skills in the Finnish Ocean-Going Merchant Fleet, c.1840–1889', *Research in Maritime History*, 6 (1994), 51–66 (p. 59).

the reason for the regular employment of relations as masters even if there were others more competent outside the family or business circle.[33]

Clayton was not able to list the names of all the masters of the vessels in his directory, but the majority are named. A comparison of the surnames of masters and the female managing owners gives 20 per cent with the same name. This is an overstatement in some cases, as it includes the many Williams and Davies in Wales who might not have any connection, while in other cases the names do not reflect a family relationship that existed, but was not obvious. Mary Hicks Hayes, for instance, managed three vessels. Her nephew, William Charles Smith, was master of the *Gem* and her brother-in-law, Nicholas Hicks Dingle, was master of the *Koh I Noor*.[34]

Among the 20 per cent with relatives as masters were those women, such as Joanna Barnard of Whitby, who were managing owners of more than one vessel, and not all her masters were relations. Joanna was the executor of her husband John's will together with her son, Matthew, and William Young, a farmer. Joanna became the managing owner of the 198-ton barquentine *Gratitude* of which Matthew was the master. She also became managing owner of the 217-ton *Emerald*, whose master was T. Feaster. Similarly Sarah Nesfield managed three vessels and only T. Nesfield, master of the 200-ton barquentine *Jane*, had the same surname.[35] Whether the master was a relation or not, the female managing owners still had the final responsibility on behalf of the rest of the owners.

Advice, Guidance and Knowledge

The shipping trade being, as indicated, a complicated business, and involving in some of its branches highly technical knowledge, it is impracticable for any one individual to undertake to become proficient in all branches. For instance, the designing and building of ships, marine insurance, and general average adjustments, the law both national and international, relating to shipping, call for specialists in these branches; all the shipbroker or a ship manager can aspire to is to have a knowledge of those aspects of shipping sufficient to enable him to apply the information given to him by the experts to his own particular requirements.[36]

If this was the general view, and it was one repeated in the many published guides, how did a woman, with no formal training, manage? There were specialists, such as maritime lawyers, agents and brokers, and owners based in larger ports had a wider range of experts to rely on. Women in the maritime sector were surrounded by useful sources of advice and information. Fellow shareholders and relatives who were experienced master mariners, shipowners and accountants

---

[33] Davis, *Rise of the English Shipping Industry*, p. 159.
[34] Isobel Pickering, *Pictures of a Parish* (Fowey: Author, 1993).
[35] NYRO: NG/RS/WH/1/10, NG/RS/WH/2.
[36] Macmurray and Cree, *Shipping and Shipbroking*, p. 5.

could provide advice. The mutual insurance clubs were an important good source of advice. As they were self-insuring each other, the clubs took a keen interest in the quality of the ships and the skills of the masters. When it came to claims they were able to call on expert advice from within the membership or pay for specialist advice if needed.

Attentive reading of the maritime press, such as the *Shipping and Mercantile Gazette*, with its Notes and Queries column, gave answers to a wide range of questions from masters, managing owners and shareholders regarding paperwork, insurance and maritime law. The answers given provided both reassurance and, on occasion, unwelcome reminders of the responsibility of the managing owner.

Question: Who is responsible for seaworthy ships?
Sir– being a small shareholder in different vessels, I shall be glad to know, for my guidance, whether the responsibility of sending vessels to sea in a seaworthy condition rests with the Managing Owners, or if every individual shareholder takes his proportion of the responsibility, even though he has no practical knowledge of a ship.
Southport April 12 1873 An Unpractical Shipowner

Answer: The Manager, Master, Agent, or other person who knowingly sends a ship to sea to the danger of the lives of those onboard is the person criminally liable; but in civil actions, the Co-Owners are all liable to the extent of the statutory enactment of £15 per ton for loss of life.[37]

Marine Insurance

On the envelope of a letter written by Miss Isabella Sanderson, managing owner of several ships, was a drawing of a ship and the motto 'Such is Luck'.[38] Appropriate words perhaps in the shipping industry, but some known risks could be mitigated by the use of insurance. Lack of insurance could be financially disastrous and yet many shipowners took this risk. John Long was a London shipowner who left behind some detailed accounts in the early part of the century. He insured directly through Lloyd's, but also carried the risk himself at times.[39] This may have had more to do with cash flow and in this regard local credit was essential. Understandings about credit for maintenance, sails or provisions with local suppliers helped the shipowner ride out cash-flow problems without recourse to expensive loans or mortgages.

Lloyd's of London were the premier insurers in the nineteenth century, but it must not be assumed that all ships were insured by them. This was most certainly not the case in the southwest or the northeast, where shipowners had an aversion to Lloyd's since they believed, in some cases rightly, that they were biased towards

---

[37] Mitchell, ed., *Maritime Notes and Queries* (p. 165).
[38] Letter from Isabella Sanderson to William Dixon 16 June 1857, courtesy of Doug Ford, curator Jersey Museum.
[39] Sarah Palmer, 'John Long: A London Shipowner', *Mariner's Mirror*, 72 (1968), 43–61 (p. 53).

London-built ships. Lloyd's were also seen as very expensive, and so many ship-owners formed local insurance clubs to mutually insure vessels, such as that run by John Holman of Topsham. He formed the Exeter Shipping Insurance Association in 1836 and a list of vessels insured by this mutual marine insurance society shows the insurance value of sixty-one vessels in 1844.[40] The insurance value was normally lower (by as much as 50 per cent) than the ship's value, to discourage fraud.[41] The list of vessels shows five managed/owned by women and two are in joint names, John and his mother, Jane Parker.

From this evidence, vessels owned by women constituted 11 per cent of the vessels insured by the Exeter Association. Their vessels tended to be lower in value, an average of £686 compared to the overall average of £1,058, and smaller, an average of 94 tons compared to 130 tons. The average age was also older at twenty years rather than sixteen (see Table 26). These statistics reflect the way in which some of the women became the visible owners, on the death of their husbands. Yet this does not infer that their involvement was less before their widowhood. Neither does it reflect all vessels since it excludes those not insured or covered by other insurance organisations. Yet despite owning 7 per cent of the insured value of the vessels there were no women on the Association's committee.

Table 26. Exeter Shipping Insurance Association, 1844

Total ships	61	Women's ships	7
Average ins. value	£1,058		£686
Range value	£200 to £4,000		£200 to £2,100
Average tonnage	130		94
Tonnage range	45 to 288		45 to 147
Average age	16		20
Age range	1 to 41		3 to 26

Source: R. Craig, B. Greenhill and W. J. Slade, 'Some Aspects of the Business of Devon Shipping in the Nineteenth Century', in M. Duffy *et al.* (eds), *The New Maritime History of Devon*, Vol. II (Exeter, 1994), p. 100 Table 9.2.

Whitby had several insurance companies and attracted shipowners from other parts of the country (see Table 27). Here, too, women managing owners were present. Of the Whitby vessels from 1851 to 1852 insured by women, the average insured value was £947. This is a higher average value than at Exeter, but on the whole Whitby ships were larger and more expensive. Sarah Nesfield managed two vessels, *Uhla* and *Star of Hope*, which were both in incidents requiring payment on 'general average' in 1866.[42] The names in Table 26 indicate that insurance was not

[40] Craig *et al.*, 'Some Aspects of Devon Shipping', p. 100, table 9.2.
[41] Craig *et al.*, 'Some Aspects of Devon Shipping', p. 101.
[42] Notice from Whitby Standard Insurance Association, 10 September 1866, personal collection.

constant and that some vessels were insured as and when the need arose rather than on an ongoing basis. Different policies meant that some vessels were insured with more than one class of insurance. These were decisions that required good knowledge of risk.

Table 27. Extract from Whitby Marine, British, General, Sea & Neptune Insurance Association, 1850–52

Ship name	Tons	Master	Owner	Residence	Sum insured (£)				
					Mar*	Brit*	Gen*	Sea	Nep*
a) 1850–51									
Elinor Russel	306	Robinson	Robinson, Ann	Whitby	1000				
Falcon	71	Bingham	Wellbank, Mary	Whitby					400
Lucerne	263	Page	Nesfield, Sarah	Whitby	1300				
Roseberry	208	Bowes	Wood, Hannah	Whitby	1200				
Waterwitch	223	Brown	Brown, Mary	Whitby		500			
William & Nancy	85	Farndale	Farndale, Ann	Whitby					500
b) 1851–52									
Aerial	256	Summerson	Robinson, Ann	Whitby	1400	300			
Aetna	259	Watson	Wilson, Jane	Whitby	600				
Cobourg	120	Cassap	Cassap, Eliz	Whitby		800			
Friendship	230	Wood	Wood, Hannah	Whitby	1500				
George	144	Stephenson	Wood, Hannah	Whitby	900				
Harlington	255	Hall	Penman, Isabella	Sund'ld		1000			
John	199	Davy	Davy, Elizabeth	London		1000	500		
William & Richard	175	Hodgson	Penman, Isabella	Sund'ld			500	500	

* Mar = Marine, Brit = British, Gen = General, Nep = Neptune

Source: Whitby Literary and Philosophical Society: 0102/2a & b 0102/2 List of ships insured 1851–52.

Problems of Management

As the concerned letters to the *Shipping and Mercantile Gazette* show, owning ships and managing their affairs was not without its problems. Joanna Barnard of Whitby was the managing owner of the *Emerald*. On 22 July 1862 the master, Thomas Teaster, made his protestation before Matthew Gray, a commissioner of oaths in Chancery.

On 10 June, the vessel had been leaving from the port of Duderham in the Gulf of Bothnia, bound for London laden with iron and deals. On 18 June the vessel met with stormy weather which damaged the main mast head, the main top, the foremast and head braces. The crew had to cut away immediately all the rigging, sails and gear attached to the main top mast, top gallant mast and main royal mast. They cleared away the wreckage as soon as possible and despite the ship labouring heavily and the pumps having to be attended to every two hours the ship arrived safely in Whitby Roads.[43]

The reason for notification of the protestation was to protect the master and owners in the case of claiming insurance. By swearing an oath before a Notary or Commissioner for Oaths they ensured that the facts were legally lodged in case of further ramifications, such as the involvement of another vessel. Some disputes ended up in Admiralty courts, with severe consequences. As mentioned in Chapter 1, the owners of the *Rippling Wave*, managing owner Mary Hayes, lost their ship in a case held in Plymouth under Admiralty jurisdiction.

> William Radford (High Bailiff of the County Court of Devon holden at East Stonehouse) transferred by bill of sale dated 30th July 1888 – by virtue of a warrant of Execution in an Admiralty Action dated 21st July 1888 – 64 shares to William Francis Hannan, shipbroker of Fowey.[44]

Ann Morton of Exeter had a different problem with the Superintendent of the Mercantile Marine office in London. She was the managing owner of the *Thames*, a regular trading vessel between London and Exeter. In 1869 the vessel sank off the coast of Devon and the crew agreement was duly completed, showing that the crew still remained. Crew agreements showed the names of all the crew and their dates of employment and discharge. The Superintendent, in a note to his colleague in Exeter, wrote 'The list is returned for date of discharge of crew to be inserted. The crew cannot remain as stated by you on the list after the vessel has sunk.' This clearly puzzled the Exeter officials and their brief reply the next day after consultation with the owner was: 'The men on board saved themselves when the vessel was sunk.'[45] This may seem a minor point upon which to spend postage, but such was the importance attached by the officials to the correct completion of the forms.

The Managing Owner and Other Shareowners

Regular communication with the other shareholders was expected. Meetings were usually held annually and the accounts were agreed and profits or losses accounted for. At these meetings, chaired by one of the shipowners present, the managing owner accounted for his or her decisions and the performance of the ships. Even when a vessel was majority-owned within the same family, as was the case with the *Ocean Ranger* where most of the shares were in the hands of the Hockens, the managing owner, also a Hocken, had to submit to being audited. In 1879 the shareholders voted to have Nathaniel Hocken, a shareholder, and Samuel Slade, a local

---

43 WLPS: 0116/11Protests Books.
44 CRO: MSR/FOW/8.
45 DRO: Crew Agreement *Thames* 11460.

businessman and non-shareholder, 'audit the accounts and pass them as correct before any subsequent meeting'.[46] After the accounts were agreed any payments were made, usually by cheque, to all the shareholders.

Not all shareholders felt the need to attend the meetings and if decisions were made then these were simply agreed by those present. Local shareholders were in a position to ensure they were kept well informed, but this was not always the case for those living at a distance, as shown in the following plaintive letter from a shareholder.

> One 64ths owner complained to Hall Bros., a Tyneside shipowning firm, that at 'one time you were good enough to let me hear occasionally of the movements of the ships in which I am interested, but I never hear a word now, which I much regret', Halls promised to rectify their omission.[47]

Multiple Vessels

As shown, women were not just occasional managing owners of one vessel. Some managed several vessels for a wide range of other owners and were able to derive more income from both the fees involved (a standard fee in Fowey was five guineas per annum[48]) and their own shares in the vessels. Appendix VI gives a full list of the managing owners with multiple vessels in 1865.

Jean Crawford of Greenock managed three of the largest vessels and these were trading in India, while Jane Avery and Mary Melmore had a small fleet of vessels to manage. How and why did these women become managing owners of several vessels? It was in some respects much the same as for a man: by being in the right place with the right connections and, importantly, the inclination or need to take on the responsibility. The following case studies illustrate some of the situations in which a woman became a managing owner of several ships.

Case Study 1: Mrs Ann Alice Morton, Exeter (four vessels)

Ann Alice Morton came from Saint Mary Steps in Exeter, close to the river. Born Ann Wellington, her father was a victualler and she had married John Morton, a cabinet maker. In 1861 Ann and John were living next door to Peter Palmer, widower and victualler of the Kings Head.[49] Palmer was not just her next door neighbour, he was also stepfather to Ann. He was a shipowner running four vessels occupied as regular traders between Exeter and London. When he died in 1863 he left his shares in his vessels jointly to Ann Morton and John Luce Ramson, a

---

[46] Account books of the *Ocean Ranger*, by kind permission of Mr A. J. Samuel.
[47] Milne, *North East England*, p 149.
[48] Account books of the *E S Hocken* and *Ocean Ranger*, by kind permission of Mr A. J. Samuel.
[49] 1851 British Census, Devon, Norfolk and Warwick (Church of Jesus Christ of the Latter Day Saints, 1997).

grocer. Ann was by now widowed with three children under the age of eleven. She already had twelve shares in two of the vessels and she proceeded to consolidate her holdings in all four. She bought John Holman's six shares in *Thames* after he died in 1863 and then bought John and Alfred Holman out of *Fame* in 1864. Her majority shareholdings enabled her to become managing owner of *Fame*, *Thames*, *Grocer* and *Devon*. This was in her own right and not held jointly with Ramson. She later sold her interest in *Fame* in 1865 to the master, Thomas Stockham.[50] The vessels were small and they shuttled backwards and forwards between London and Exeter carrying people, parcels and general merchandise. The days of such a service were numbered when the railway opened up from London to Exeter. Ann Morton disappears from view after the sinking of the *Thames* in 1869 and there is no sign of her in the 1871 census.

Case Study 2: Mrs Sarah Nesfield, Whitby (four vessels)

Sarah was married to Stephen Nesfield of Whitby. They had six children including twins, Ann and Dorothy. Stephen died sometime before 1850 and Sarah became the managing owner of three vessels, *Uhla*, *Star of Hope*, *Jane* and the 263-ton *Lucerne*. These were all substantial vessels for their time. Thomas Nesfield, her brother-in-law, was the master of the *Jane* and then in 1852 he had moved to the *Willey*, a vessel in which Sarah owed twenty-two shares. Sarah owned the *Lucerne* together with Dorothy Wilson, another family connection (one of Sarah's children was named after her). She also traded shares with another brother-in-law, William Falkenbridge, a builder, in the *Star of Hope* and *Isabella*.[51] By 1865, when she features in *Clayton's Directory*, Sarah was aged fifty-five and living with one daughter, thirty-year-old Mary. By 1871 she had moved to live in the household of William Falkenbridge. William was now trading as an architect and surveyor, but Sarah still gave her occupation as shipowner.[52]

Case Study 3: Mrs Jane B. Avery, North Shields (five vessels)

Jane's husband, George, was a shipowner with interests in over eighteen vessels.[53] He died in 1857 leaving Jane, aged forty-one, with eight children aged from one to eighteen. Jane began (or possibly continued) an active career as a shipowner and managing agent (see Table 28). At the time of George's death she inherited full ownership of three vessels, *Beecher Stowe*, *George Avery* and *British Lion*. Jane added to her fleet and, with sole ownership of most of the vessels, she was in complete control. Her ships travelled to India, Singapore and the Mediterranean.

---

50 DRO: 3289s/10, 37/1837, 9/1832, 3/1852, 43/1837.
51 NYRO: WH 2 & 9.
52 1871 Census Whitby RG10/4848.
53 Personal correspondence Adrian Osler, 18 June 2005.

From 1857 onwards she bought several additional vessels, wholly owning most of them and being named as their managing owner. Later she passed some shares to three of her children, but did not relinquish control. By 1881, after her death, her eldest son, Robert, is named as a shipowner of Newcastle.[54]

Table 28. Shares belonging to Jane Avery

	Built	Period	No.	MO	
Beecher Stowe	1853	1857–63	64		
George Avery	1853	1857–69		Yes	8/64 to M. L. Avery
British Lion	1856	1857–63	64	Yes	
Eddystone	1860	1861–9		Yes	Passed to R. B. Avery
Hesse Darmstadt	1863	1863–73		Yes	6/64 to R. B. then all shares
Blair Atholl	1864	1864–74	64	Yes	
Jane Avery	1865	1865–80	54/64		10/64 to R. B. Avery
Life Brigade	1866	1866–73	64		20/64 to E. H. Avery

Source: R. E. Keys, *Dictionary of Tyne Sailing Ships: A Record of Sailing Ships Owned, Registered and Built in the Port of Tyne from 1830–1930* (Newcastle: published by author, 1998).

Case Study 4: Mrs Mary Hicks Hayes, Polruan (four vessels)

Mary Hicks Smith was born in 1840 and when she was aged thirty-one she was still living at home with her parents.[55] It looked as if her fate was to be that of the typical Victorian spinster. An independent occupation was unlikely, and for most single women the prospect was 'lifelong dependent subservience to father and mother at home'.[56] Not far from Mary, lived Jane Hayes and her son James, aged thirty-nine, a shipbroker. They had just moved to Polruan from Bodinnick, a few miles upstream, where they had run the Ferry Inn. Did Mary see this as her last chance? By 19 June 1872 she and James were married. It did not last long – James died the following year in October. However, her prospects and status were now very different; she had moved from spinster to widow in eighteen months. As a widow she was independent and James had left her well provided for: shares in many ships, the house and furniture, land and another house, and a £175 policy of assurance in the Padstow Shipping Club on the late brig *Hannah Hicks*.[57]

By 1881 Mary was head of a household that included her sister, Elizabeth, and her nephew, William. She was not only buying and selling shares in ships in her own right, but was also now the managing owner of the *Perseverance*, the *Gem* and the *Koh I Noor*.[58] She later became managing owner of the *Rippling Wave*.

---

54 1881 British Census (Church of Jesus Christ of the Latter Day Saints, 1999).
55 CRO: 1871 Census Lanteglos by Fowey.
56 Best, *Mid-Victorian Britain*, pp. 93–168.
57 BPO: Will of James Hayes 1873.
58 *Lloyd's Register of British and Foreign Shipping* 1881.

Additionally she held shares in a further sixteen Polruan ships. James had left many of his shares equally divided between his sister, Ann Hicks, and Mary. Ann supported her sister-in-law and it was in Ann's name that the letter confirming Mary as the managing owner was sent to the customs officials. Mary remained a managing owner until the late 1880s, coming out of ship management when the decline in wooden schooners was most marked. She died in December 1907, her personal effects valued at £1,820. She left a few shares in ships together with her shares in the Capital and County Bank and the Fowey Hotel, reflecting her investment in the new business of tourism.[59]

Case Study 5: Miss Isabella Sanderson, Amble (three vessels)

Isabella was the postmistress of Amble in Northumberland and also a linen draper and grocer.[60] Clayton names her as the managing owner of three vessels, *Agenoria*, *Amble* and *Perseverance*. All the ships in which she held shares were built by her brother, James Sanderson, and his partner Thomas Leighton, who was Isabella's brother-in-law.[61] In 1851 Isabella is shown as the eldest unmarried daughter, aged fifty, living with her father John, a retired farmer. Her widowed brother James is also living there with his children. Ten years later, both her father and her brother had died and Isabella was head of a large household. This included her forty-five-year-old sister, Jane, and seventeen-year-old Ann, who was her late brother's daughter. Isabella and Anne Gibson, aged sixteen and twenty-three, are described as nieces. Finally she now also had her brother-in-law, Thomas, aged forty-one, and his wife and one child living with her.[62] The firm of Leighton and Sanderson had by now ceased building ships. The only two recorded income generators of this household are Isabella, postmistress and grocer, and Thomas, builder. It is clear from a letter written by Isabella in 1857 that she was the main driver of business.

> Amble, 16th June 1857
>
> To Mr William Dixon, Esq,
>
> Sir
>
> I intend to be at Alnwick this morning but being prevented I beg to say I will be at Alnwick on Thursday or Friday to give you a statement. My brother will not sell any of his property. I had the same thought. We are now in [a] way to get it cleared but up to this time I have been trying all I could to get that £300 but I will not get that until the close of this year if God spair me as the interest is bad to pay on account of Mrs Graham non payment of a part of A.

---

59 BPO: Will of Mary Hicks Hayes 1907.
60 *Post Office Directory of Northumberland and Durham* 1855.
61 TNA: HO107/2419 1851 Census Amble.
62 TNA: RG9/3877 1861 Census.

I can only say the Party may with all safety get their money on as what they are stopping at is what I have wanted of I hope will do shortly

I am sir your obedient servant

Isabella Sanderson.

The man to whom she wrote is probably William Dickson, a banker and the founder of the Alnwick & County Bank of Narrowgate and Fenkle Street in Alnwick, or his son, also called William. Both men were solicitors and had offices in Bailiffgate.[63] Any financial embarrassment in 1857 was temporary, as Table 29 indicates, and Isabella continued to be a significant investor in the family ships, holding most of her shares until 1876.

Table 29. Isabella Sanderson's shares

Ship	Shares: 64	Owned	MO
Aaron Eaton	11	June 1859–January 1863	
Agenoria	12 shared with Thos Leighton	November 1861–November 1868	Yes
Amble	12 increased to 30	April 1857–1878	Yes
Perseverance	24 increased to 48	August 1852–1876	Yes
Providence	8	April 1855–1862	

Source: R. E. Keys, *The Sailing Ships of Aln and Coquet* (Newcastle, 1993).

In the first three cases the motivation of Ann, Sarah and Jane can be attributed to a need to provide an income for their children. Yet only in the cases of Ann and Jane were there underage children at the time of their ship management responsibility, and, in Jane's case, she retained her role even when her son, Robert, came of age. Neither Mary nor Isabella had children of their own, but both seemed to have fulfilled a breadwinner role for other relations. In Isabella's case this is confirmed in her letter to Dickson.

Case Study 6: Mrs Susanna Anning, Exeter (two vessels)

In some cases the motivation for becoming a managing owner was a simple matter of needing to obtain control in order to dispose of a vessel. Susanna Anning inherited shares in two vessels on her husband's death in 1858. Her majority shareholding, forty shares, was in the *Susan*, a 182-ton schooner employed in trade between London and the West Indies, possibly in the fruit trade as the previous year she was also in the Mediterranean. The ship was surveyed to A1 status with Lloyd's and at just ten years old it would have been considered a good invest-

---

[63] Letter from Isabella Sanderson to William Dixon 16 June 1857, courtesy of Doug Ford, curator Jersey Museum; *Slater's Commercial Directory of Northumberland*, 1855.

ment.[64] The two other initial shareholders with John Anning were John South-wood of Starcross, gentleman, and Thomas Anning Bond of Stoketeignhead, master mariner. Both of these had died earlier, in 1855 and 1849 respectively. Two years after her widowhood, in March 1860 Susanna bought twelve shares from Southwood's legatees and twelve shares from Elizabeth Bond, widow of Thomas Bond. Susanna now owned the whole vessel and had complete control. The reason for this sudden buying activity is apparent when one month later the vessel was sold at public auction to Don Jose Senaz Herin, a Spanish merchant of Gijon on the north coast of Spain. The auction raised 29,000 reals.[65] Without knowing more details of the vessel it is impossible to say whether Susanna gained or lost from this sale, but as sole owner the risks and decisions were all hers. She also had inherited sixteen shares in the *Experiment*, a rather older vessel. It had been built in 1826 and was a 117-ton schooner employed in the coastal trade. Susanna retained her minority interest in this vessel for four years until it was lost in 1862.[66]

Summary

The role of the woman managing owner was not just the traditional role of the wife managing the books, but was a far more significant role for men and women than has been previously acknowledged. Lack of personal experience of command at sea does not appear to have been a hindrance. Many wives of master mariners, particularly the wives of those who wholly owned their vessels, were in effect the managing owner, but their presence was rarely recorded in official documents.

The effective woman managing owner needed to have a far greater range of skills than just a head for figures. In particular, she had to manage the key relationship with the master or masters. All of these were men who were not just accustomed to being in command, but who spent the majority of their lives in almost totally male company. The managing owner needed to know enough about the complexities of maritime law and insurance to know when and where to get advice. At any time any aspect relating to the voyage, the weather, the employ-ment of crew, the ship and its trade, might turn from advantage to disaster. These women also had to manage the officials in shipping, wives of crew members and last, but not least, their fellow owners. While family relationships undoubtedly helped some of these women to take on these roles, this was also true for many male managing owners. Finally it needs to be remembered that managing owners, especially those with a minority shareholding, were appointed by their fellow shareholders, most of whom who had a direct interest in appointing an effective, efficient and trustworthy manager.

Women continue to feature as managing owners throughout the nineteenth century, but by 1887 just 1 per cent of the listed ships in *Lloyd's Register of Ship-*

---

[64] A1 was the highest category of survey for a Lloyd's-registered ship.
[65] DRO: 3289s/10, 19/1848.
[66] DRO: 3289s/10, 15/1837.

ping were managed by women.[67] The 64th system of ownership was dying out as larger, more expensive company-owned ships appeared. The move to larger limited companies meant a wider geographic spread of owners rather than the close-knit community-based management group of the 64th owners. Shareowners in limited companies had no managerial or operational role by simply owning shares. Larger companies also meant professional managers and boards of directors and so the opportunities for women shareholders to become managing owners were reduced in these circumstances. However, for at least three-quarters of the nineteenth century, women were in control of sailing vessels of all sizes and engaged across a wide spectrum of trade.

[67] *Lloyd's Register of Shipping*, 1887.

7

Port Businesswomen

Ship management could be seen as a natural step from investment, but ports provided many other opportunities for business management. For every ship that was built there were the ancillary trades of sailmaking, ropemaking, block-making and victualling. Similarly, shipbrokers, insurance agents, and many other similar service occupations and middlemen became increasingly evident during the century. Women are found running almost every business, with the exception of professions such as customs officials, brokerage and insurance.

This chapter will examine the wide range of roles in which women appear. Here the maritime trades that supported both shipbuilding and shipowning are examined, while shipbuilding is covered in the next two chapters. Ancillary trades have received little attention from a business perspective, although there is one exception which sought to capture the unsung and forgotten craftsmen and their tools and trades; the workshops and business premises were situated in close proximity within the maritime community.[1] *The Merchant Schooners* gives a glimpse of the sailmaker and blockmaker and briefly mentions the surviving account book of John Popham, a north Devon sailmaker.[2] Overall, it is hard to find much published information on ship chandlers, small foundries, blockmakers or marine store dealers. The main sources are trade directories, but these give little information on the business, so this is supplemented by the rare survival of busi-ness documents, wills, census material and other relevant sources. Each trade will be briefly explained and then followed by some case studies of businesswomen.

Were these considered suitable roles for women and what were the partic-ular challenges for the businesswoman? The separate spheres model argues that women were increasingly confined to the domestic role.[3] Other research on women running businesses has extended this to show that women were mainly involved in roles that reflected their domestic skills, such as innkeeping, dressmaking and millinery.[4] So how does a woman blacksmith fit this pattern? The case studies presented in this chapter illustrate many of the circumstances faced by women,

---

[1]   John E. Horsley, *Tools of the Maritime Trades* (Newton Abbot: David & Charles, 1978), pp. 66–69.
[2]   Greenhill, *Merchant Schooners*, pp. 71–84.
[3]   Shoemaker, *Gender in English Society*.
[4]   Alison Kay, 'A Little Enterprise of Her Own: Lodging House Keeping and the Accommoda-tion Business in Nineteenth-Century London', *London Journal*, 28 (2003); Shoemaker, *Gender in English Society*.

from running a major business and managing a large workforce to dealing with demanding customers and chasing them for payment.

This chapter also considers the two major factors that affected the maritime industry in the nineteenth century: the technological changes that were brought about by the move from sail to steam, and the significant growth of trade. The former had an obvious impact on the shipbuilding industry and there was a significant regional impact as shipbuilding and investment moved north.[5] The growth of trade had an effect on the ports, particularly the facilities for loading and unloading, as well as transportation and distribution from and to the ports.[6] Ports had to create new facilities to attract trade, dig new docks, and build warehouses and railway links. These were expensive and caused much debate within the relevant port authorities who had to make the investment, and with those who had to pay the dues to repay such vast investments. While the overall impact of changes and the attitudes of authorities have been considered, the ancillary businesses and trades have had little attention to date in this context of the changing needs of the industry. A study of the businesses in Fowey over the nineteenth century saw the gradual rise of the service industry and the middleman.[7] Were all trades or businesses affected to the same degree or were there differences between occupational groups and between ports? What was the impact for the businesswoman?

The Ancillary Maritime Trades

These trades encompassed anything that could be carried on a ship or supplied to a ship and its occupants, together with services for shipowners, masters, mariners and passengers. Many were too small to leave much trace and the origin and role of some of the trades have become obscured. There were two main groups of supply, those that met the needs of local shipping in the port or area, and those that provided for the visiting vessels and the people aboard them.

The first group, local shipping, involved a variety of businesses in getting a ship to sea. When the contract was agreed between shipbuilder and owners, the building commenced. The items required to build and fit out the vessel included both skilled and unskilled labour, timber from the timber merchants and a variety of other items such as blocks, ropes, sails, ironwork and the internal fittings of the vessel. When all was done, the master and owners needed mariners, the cargo needed to be found and the victuals provided for the voyage. The shipping directories published by Clayton, Marwood and Turnbull show the range of businesses advertising in the ports, and chief among them are the sailmakers and ropemak-

---

5   Ville, ed., *Shipbuilding in the United Kingdom.*
6   Jackson, 'The Ports'. Gordon Jackson, 'Do Docks Make Trade?' in *Port and Harbour Engineering*, ed. Adrian Jarvis (Aldershot: Variorum, 1998); Jarvis, 'Port History'.
7   Doe, 'Blockmakers, Sailmakers, Ropemakers, Blacksmiths and Brokers'.

ers.[8] In the early part of the period the sails and ropes were a large proportion of the cost, but by the third quarter of the century, as the construction of the vessel became more complex, these ratios changed and a wider range of contractors was involved in fitting out a vessel.[9]

The second group includes the businesses meeting the maintenance and repair needs of vessels, and supplying victualling and chandlery. However, it also includes all the hospitality needs of passengers and mariners, such as inns, taverns and rented rooms. These hospitality occupations were much the same as those found in any town which was a transport hub and will not be considered here.

The ancillary maritime businesses can be grouped generally into retail, manufacturing, educational, publishing and merchants and bankers. Those that had a largely retail function were chandlers and marine store dealers. Manufacturers, including the small craft workshops, were the sailmakers, ropemakers, blacksmiths and foundries. Educational businesses included navigation schools and teachers of mathematics. Publishers provided guides for mariners, charts and nautical tables. Finally the merchants and the bankers provided freight and capital. In addition to these were the myriad of small operators who got by on leasing boats, finding labour and providing any service that was needed.

Ship's Chandler

The chandler supplied a wide range of necessities to ships. Anything that was needed on board, from food to rope to medical supplies, could be provided by the chandler. Over the nineteenth century, Burnyeats of Whitehaven became a national company supplying ships stores. Philip Burnyeat ran the White Lion Inn, in King Street, Whitehaven in the early nineteenth century. Innkeeping was a role that was often combined with victualling for ships. Burnyeats were also butchers, another business that supplied ships. With the growth of Whitehaven in the early years, from the development of the coal and iron industries, there were plenty of vessels needing supplies. John had married Elizabeth Dalzell, but he died in 1832. She continued the business until her eldest son, William Burnyeat, took over the business on 17 October 1840. There is a mention of the account book she kept which she handed to her son.[10] In the 1841 census William's age is given as twenty and his occupation is given as a butcher.[11] The main credit for building up the business into what became a major national company, eventually moving to Liverpool, is given to him, but this overlooks Elizabeth's eight years of steady management which left sufficient legacy on which to build his empire.

---

8   *Clayton's Register of Shipping, 1865; Marwood's Annual Directory, Shipping Register and Commercial Advertiser, 1854–5; Turnbull's Annual Maritime Advertiser Directory & Shipping Register,* 1854–5.

9   Doe, 'Blockmakers, Sailmakers, Ropemakers, Blacksmiths and Brokers'.

10 Rolt, *Mariners' Market*, p. 3.

11 TNA: PRO HO 107/178/6 1841 Census Whitehaven.

Aaron Ross was a ship chandler and blacksmith of Hull who died in 1852. In his will, made three years earlier, he left his estate to his trustees and friends, Thomas Booth and William Rowson. The usual bequest was made of household goods plus his property and stock in trade to his wife, Ann Ross, as long as she remained his widow. The will mentions both real and personal estate, stocks and shares, mortgages and government bonds. With regard to his business, his wish, presumably with her agreement, was clear:

> That my said wife shall continue and carry on the business of shipchandler and blacksmith and other business connected therewith in which I am engaged then it shall be lawful for her so to do during her widowhood and for that purpose I empower my said trustees in their discretion to employ in the said trade all the capital stock and effects which shall be employed in or ongoing in respect of my said business I direct that any gains and profits to arise during such time as she runs the business shall belong to my wife for her own use benefit absolutely for the bringing up and maintaining and educating my said children during their minority.[12]

Ann thus had a clear mandate to run the business, and she built up a very successful company. Like many other similar operations they dealt in almost anything. A trade directory of 1858 refers to Ann Ross of 1 Railway Street and 16 Castle Street, with an entry describing the business in much greater detail as

> Ship chandler, ship anchor and engine smith, paint manufacturer, tinner & brazier, marine store dealer, dealer in oils, tar, turpentine, pitch, rosin, brushes, ballast & well shovels, spades, scrapes, ships hearths, chain & iron blocks.[13]

Items for the whaling and fishing industry were also supplied.[14] The goods listed in the advertisement show many inflammable items, which is why ship chandlery was considered a high risk business from an insurance perspective. It was in the same hazardous category as brewers, bakers, and tallow chandlers.[15]

Ann had a large family, six daughters and two sons, and her eldest son, Francis, was only fourteen when his father died. Despite Francis coming of age in 1859, Ann did not relinquish the reins. This may have been choice or necessity as her youngest child was still only seven years of age.[16] The 1861 census shows that Mrs Ross had apprenticed her second son as a blacksmith and her occupation was now described as ship chandler and smith, employing fewer men – only seven but with the addition of nine boys. Boys, especially apprentices, were much cheaper but were also an important part of a chandler's business as they could deliver the goods or collect orders. The business still featured in the local directory as 'Ann

---

12   TNA: PRO Prob 11/2167 will of Aaron Ross, shipchandler, Hull.
13   *White's Directory Hull & District*, 1858.
14   Personal correspondence. Mr R. Pett, 6 May 2006.
15   Phillips, *Women in Business*, p. 149.
16   Ages derived from census details. TNA: PRO HO 107/2363/382 and RG9/3592/115.

Ross, Shipchandlers' in 1867.[17] By 1871, aged sixty, she had retired and was living with four of her daughters, aged from nineteen to twenty-six. Francis and Thomas had taken over the business (now aged thirty-three and twenty-eight). In 1881 she was described as an annuitant, with just one daughter, Fanny, aged twenty-nine, still at home, but now she had the luxury of a servant.[18] The business continued to thrive and it became one of the largest ironmongers in northern England.[19]

Ann also had a sideline in mortgage provision. She initially bought a new vessel, a sailing trawler, from the shipbuilders in 1861. The shipbuilders, Houghy's, provided Ann with finance for the ship in the form of a mortgage of £500 at 5 per cent. The vessel was lost in December 1862.[20] Her subsequent link with shipping was as a provider of mortgages, but not at the 5 per cent she had received herself from the shipbuilders. Ann charged her mortgages at 7 per cent. Like the financiers described in Chapter 5, she preferred the more certain return from interest payments. From 1866 to 1869 Ann received 7 per cent per annum for a loan of £250 secured on the *Lady*, and then from 1869 to 1879 she received 7 per cent per annum on £400 secured on the *Rising Sun*.[21] Ann's case shows how a woman could succeed despite having a large family to bring up over many years (she was forty-one when she had her last child). Servants do not feature in the census information for Mrs Ross at any stage until her retirement. She had an advantage in having so many daughters as it avoided the need for domestic support since they were able to act as carers for their siblings.

Chandlery was a retail trade, but it required premises close to the quays and close links with the masters of the ships, so was not something a widow could run out of her front room while caring for her children. In Ann's case she expanded to premises in Castle Street and at the dockside.[22] Chandlers were in competition with one another in supplying the visiting vessels and often employed men or boys to row out to the ships and get orders. John Keast could recall the sons of the proprietor of a local chandlery going aboard the larger vessels. They interviewed the master or mate seeking orders for such items as canvas, paint, oil and ropes, and also the chief steward for provisions.[23]

Marine Store Dealers

If the chandler's business was not one that could easily be run from a front room, some types of marine store dealers could do just that. Dickens's description of marine store dealers was as pawnbrokers or second-hand dealers who had a ready market in the sailors and their relations in ports around the coast.

---

[17] *White's Hull & District Directory*, 1867.
[18] TNA: PRO RG11/4780/52 1881 Census Hull.
[19] *Hull Times*, 14 January 1939, p. 17.
[20] Hull City Archives (HCA): DPC 1/16 Hull Shipping Registers *Trusty*.
[21] HCA: DPC 1/16 Hull Shipping Registers.
[22] *Jones Mercantile Directory of Hull, Great Grimsby and Goole*, 1863–4.
[23] John Keast, 'Ship Chandling Days Remembered', *Old Cornwall*, XI (1996), 478–85.

Look at a marine-store dealer's, in that reservoir of dirt, drunkenness, and drabs: thieves, oysters, baked potatoes, and pickled salmon – Ratcliff-highway. Here, the wearing apparel is all nautical. Rough blue jackets, with mother-of-pearl buttons, oil-skin hats, coarse checked shirts, and large canvas trousers that look as if they were made for a pair of bodies instead of a pair of legs, are the staple commodities. Then, there are large bunches of cotton pocket-handkerchiefs, in colour and pattern unlike any one ever saw before, with the exception of those on the backs of the three young ladies without bonnets who passed just now. The furniture is much the same as elsewhere, with the addition of one or two models of ships, and some old prints of naval engagements in still older frames. In the window, are a few compasses, a small tray containing silver watches in clumsy thick cases; and tobacco-boxes, the lid of each ornamented with a ship, or an anchor, or some such trophy. A sailor generally pawns or sells all he has before he has been long ashore, and if he does not, some favoured companion kindly saves him the trouble. In either case, it is an even chance that he afterwards unconsciously repurchases the same things at a higher price than he gave for them at first.[24]

Dickens described marine store shops again in *Bleak House* and in *David Copperfield*, usually in their context as pawnbrokers and second-hand shops. In the 1851 census 2,068 people gave their occupation as marine store dealer. Of these, 16 per cent were women; by 1861 the number of reported dealers had doubled and women made up 20 per cent.[25]

These dealers proliferated in ports such as Plymouth with its high turnover of seamen both naval and mercantile. In 1850 there were twenty dealers listed in the Plymouth directory, of whom four were women.[26] It was an occupation in which single women could engage. The 1851 census for Plymouth lists three young spinsters: Georgianna Ferguson, aged twenty-three, a marine store dealer, Charlotte Brimacombe, aged twenty-one, a workwoman in a marine store, and Mary Waterfield, aged thirty-three, a dealer living at home with her parents. A partnership with a male relative seems to have been useful in a business that handled a wide array of materials and items. Elizabeth Martain and her husband Samuel both gave their occupation as dealers, and Sarah Foster, aged sixty-nine, was head of a household and in partnership with her son-in-law. James Pasere was a marine store dealer whose wife, Elizabeth, is listed as 'works at the Business (wife)'.[27]

Jenns alludes to the role of the marine store dealers as illicit pawnbrokers and money-lenders.[28] Yet the range of these businesses was wider than this. Many marine stores not only dealt in items of seaman's wear and marine artefacts, but also played a part in the black market economy for government stores. These could range from pilfered stores to major rerouting of supplies destined for Her

---

[24] Charles Dickens, 'Brokers and Marine Store Shops', *Sketches by Boz* (first published 1836). http://www.litfix.co.uk/dickens/onlinetexts/boz/part28.html (accessed 27 June 2006).
[25] BPP 1853 LXXXVIII: Census of England and Wales 1851 Population Tables, 1851, Part II; BPP 1863 LIII: Census of England and Wales 1861: Population Tables Volume II.
[26] *White's Directory of Devon*, 1850.
[27] TNA: HO/107/1878 Census 1851 Plymouth.
[28] Jenns, 'Female Business Enterprise', pp. 285–6.

Majesty's Navy. Old metal, scrap metal, broken metal, or partly manufactured metal goods and defaced metal goods (where the government mark had been removed) were all items handled by some of these stores. The increasing investment in steam and iron increased the flow of valuable naval supplies and gave yet more opportunities for the illegal redirection of items into the private sector. There were concerns by mid-century about this dealing in naval stores, and bills to regulate this sector were put before Parliament. Regulation and licensing of marine store dealers was recommended in 1860, and again in 1864 a bill was put forward to protect the government's naval and victualling stores.[29] The women running such stores could have been involved in anything from minor money-lending and pawning to handling stolen goods. For those that handled smaller items it was a relatively easy business for a woman to set up and run, since it could be run from her home. Dealing in larger items such as ironmongery required sites and premises similar to those for chandlers, a role with which they overlapped. Marine store dealers are an under-researched business group; they provided a wide range of services both legal and illegal and deserve more attention than can be given in this overview.

Sailmakers

Sailmaking was not necessarily an ideal role for women. It seems domestically linked, with its image of sewing, but it was physically hard work as the materials had to be tough to survive the battering by wind and rain. The making of the sails was a highly skilled craft of hand and eye. Greenhill, in his *Merchant Schooners*, covers this point well.[30] The quality of fit was essential to the sailing craft. A poorly fitting sail reduced speed and efficiency and did not last long. For this reason, sailmakers were often ex-mariners and the apprenticeship was the usual seven years.

The sails were large and each business needed to have a suitable large covered space close to the shipbuilding yards and sometimes within the yards. Both the making of new sails and the repair of existing sails made up their business. If there was a choice of sailmakers in a port, the master mariner or shipowner had their preferred sailmaker with whom they ran an account. Each business was small and employed just a few men. Isabella Curry was aged forty-six in 1851 and was the widowed head of the household. She was described as a sailmaker mistress employing three men. It is not clear whether this was in addition to her twin sons aged sixteen, Alexander and George, who were apprentice sailmakers.

Mrs Ann Bowmaker was based in North Shields and she provided sails for two vessels belonging to Henley and Son of London, *Henley* and *Freedom*. Her name occurs for a brief time in correspondence with Henley's in 1798, discussing

---

[29] 1860, Bill for Regulating Business Dealers in Marine Stores; 1864, Bill, intituled, Act for the more effectual Protection of Her Majesty's Naval and Victualling Stores.
[30] Greenhill, *Merchant Schooners*.

the different types of canvas and the work involved. Henley's replied on 26 July and made it quite clear what they wanted.

> Your letter of 23rd duly received. You will get the canvas from Mr Walker on your account and we will pay you the price mentioned in your letter. We do expect the sail will be well made if we see you do what is right we may be future customers. Take care to have the best bolt rope. The Price is as high as at London we expect the work will be better done. Make the under mentioned sail for the under mentioned vessels.
>
> > *Freedom* Capt. Cummins Foresail (have this ready by the 8 August)
> > *Henley* Capt. Watson 1 topsail, 1 jibb
> > *Pitt* Capt. Bone 1 topsail, 1 jibb[31]

On 29 December 1798 Ann wrote to Henley's asking for payment of her bill for £57 2s for work on the *Freedom* and *Henley*. Henley's, being the careful businessmen they were, noted an apparent overcharge of £2 16s. However they did place work with her again and by 1802 her son Thomas was now writing to Henley's regarding other work done by Bowmaker's.[32]

Dealing with such demanding customers, who knew exactly what they wanted, was part of the management role and some men and women were happier to do this than others. Henley's were careful not to get the sailmaker to buy in the canvas as they did not want to pay any handling commission or mark up, thus paring the bill to the bone.[33] At least, however, the outstanding fees which were paid well in arrears were for the labour of making the sails and Bowmaker's did not have to handle the pressure for payment from canvas suppliers.

A role often combined with that of sailmaker was chandler. When supplying the sails most small businesses were also prepared to supply the rest of the master's requirements for his vessel. Another sailmaker was Sarah Starbuck who is listed in the 1851 census as aged fifty-four, but she appears in the trade directory as a chandler.[34] Living with her in Gravesend were her three sons, all in their twenties: John, a shopman (presumably linked to the chandlery business), Robert, a sailmaker, and Richard, a butcher. There was also her widowed mother, aged eighty-four, and one servant, aged twenty-two.[35]

The range of business interests was broad, from sailmaking to supplying goods and victualling. The Starbuck family were well based, beside the Thames, for the significant business available there. It seems to have been a whole family of sailmakers as Sarah's father-in-law and his sons Robert and Richard were also sailmakers.[36] Small businesses could not afford to be in too narrow a niche busi-

---

[31] National Maritime Museum (NMM): HNL/23/2 Henley and Son correspondence with Mrs Ann Bowmaker.

[32] NMM: HNL/23/2 Henley and Son correspondence with Mrs Ann Bowmaker.

[33] The price quoted by Bowmaker to Henley did not include the cost of the canvas

[34] *Kelly's Trade Directory*, 1846.

[35] TNA: PRO HO 107/1608 Gravesend 1851 census.

[36] TNA: PRO Prob 11/1788 Will of Robert Starbuck, 1831; 11/1836 Will of John Starbuck, 1864; 11/2131 Will of Richard Starbuck, 1851.

ness. So flexibility and, in the case of Mrs Bowmaker, the ability to deal with demanding customers were the keys to survival.

Blockmakers

Blockmakers made the wooden blocks to ensure that the running rigging moved smoothly and to assist with the lifting of sails and yards. They also made the deadeyes that provided tension on the ropes. Early in the century this was a job for a small businessman, often an ex-shipwright, who had a workshop with perhaps one or two others to produce blocks for local use. They were local carpenters or ex-mariners who had small workshops in the ports. A coasting smack might need just twenty blocks, a two-masted schooner perhaps fifty, while a more complex vessel needed 1,000.[37]

The evidence for women blockmakers is limited although more extensive research in directories would uncover others. Sarah Trevethick in 1851 was living with her husband, a master blockmaker, employing one man. There was a daughter, Elizabeth, aged twenty, and one son, Thomas, aged sixteen. Sarah shortly afterwards was widowed and took over the business. Blockmakers on the whole were micro-businesses with at most one or two men, so the loss of the chief blockmaker was highly significant and few widows could afford to also employ other skilled men. This may be the reason why so few women were involved, but it was also one of the first businesses to be challenged by mass-produced goods.

Ropemakers

Ropemakers, like sailmakers, needed a large space, but in this case it was a lengthy space, up to 300 yards or more. This was a very labour-intensive industry and the workforce consisted of young men and boys and sometimes women. This put a widow in a different situation from the blockmaker's widow.

Mary Lettis and Elizabeth Bramwell were both widows who continued the business after the death of their husband and had young families to bring up. In Elizabeth's case she employed four men and nine boys and her children were part of the family support network. Four of her five children gave their various occupations as housekeeper, dressmaker, bootbinder and twine spinner.[38] Clearly her business could not also support them, but Mary Lettis in Yarmouth provides a different picture. In 1851 Mary's husband had employed twenty men and they lived with their five children in a household with two servants. By 1861 Mary was widowed and listed as a ropemaker. Her eldest daughter had left home, but she remained with four children to support from the business, who were aged between

---

[37] Greenhill, *Merchant Schooners*, p. 83.
[38] TNA: HO 107 2267 1851 Census Preston; *Mannix Trade Directory*, 1851.

twenty-one and fourteen, and she still kept two servants. Just one of her children gave an occupation and that was her sixteen-year-old son, Thomas, who is listed as a medical student.[39]

Ropemaking ranged from the small local firm to national businesses and by mid-century many were based not in ports but inland. The larger concerns were often suppliers to the smaller ones as investments in machinery enabled greater savings. This type of expansion was not often available to the space-squeezed business in the smallest ports. Ann Wright was such a supplier based in Birmingham. She is an example of the problems a wife could face if her husband was incompetent or incapable of running the business. William Wright was accused by his wife of 'assaults and acts of ill treatment' in 1838 and he eventually came to an agreement with his wife regarding both separation and the management of the business. Ann remained in the family home and the premises 'to carry on the same trade and business on her own account and as if she were sole and unmarried'. This enabled her to maintain herself and her children. William moved out and was to be paid one guinea a week for the rest of his life. It seems that William was an alcoholic and Ann had, in effect, been running the business. She continued to run the business in her own name for twenty years until her death in June 1859. Two of her three sons took over the business, and the third, William, described as a gentleman of London, received an annuity of £100.[40]

Small port-based ropemakers were threatened by mass production and Ann's business was one that worked on the factory principle supplying their rope and wire around the country. Birmingham seems to have had a monopoly on the making of wire ropes.[41]

Blacksmiths and Foundries

Blacksmithing was highly skilled, heavy physical work. Long associated with horses the port blacksmith provided the essential iron items for ships, from anchors to chains.[42] In common with the other businesses blacksmiths needed to be sited close to their customers. Blacksmithing required a seven-year apprenticeship and the businesses ranged from the blacksmith in port providing the various metals for vessels, to massive foundries turning out large and complex ironwork.

Women occasionally appear as blacksmiths, but, unless they were large concerns, the woman suffered much the same problems of paying for extra skills. Hannah Whitford of Fowey advertised in *Pigot's Directory* in 1830.[43] By 1841, aged

39 TNA: HO 107 1806 1851 Census Yarmouth and RG 9 1194 1861 Census Yarmouth.
40 Jenns, 'Female Business Enterprise', pp. 187–92.
41 Samuel Timmins, ed., *The Resources, Products, and Industrial History of Birmingham and the Midland Hardware District: Reports, Collected by the Local Industries Committee* (London, 1886), p. 578.
42 Doe, 'Blockmakers, Sailmakers, Ropemakers, Blacksmiths and Brokers', p. 156.
43 *Pigot's Directory of Cornwall*, 1830.

seventy, she had abandoned the business and was a draper with four adult daughters at home. Her son James was a carpenter.[44]

Women did run large, heavily capitalised manufacturing concerns such as foundries. In the eighteenth century Philippa Walton ran a large gun foundry. She took over the business at the age of thirty-six after the death of her husband and ran a highly successful business in difficult times. She did not fully retire until she was sixty-five.[45]

Mrs Christiana Rose is a different example from the majority cited here as her inheritance was from her father not her husband. She inherited his foundry business in 1833, which had been left with an outstanding mortgage on it. Attempts by the trustees to sell the business were unsuccessful and so Mrs Rose took over the business herself. From August 1840 the insurances for the premises, stock and machinery were in her name, and she acquired the land in 1841.[46] According to the business history of the firm written in 1949 Christiana was married to John Rose, a 'local seafaring man of some repute', but he had died, leaving her with one daughter, Susan.[47] Christiana ran the business with the help of a manager until 1859 when she advertised for a new manager. James Downs was appointed. He had previously worked for James Hunter and Company, a shipbuilding firm in Worcester, and before that he had worked with Robert Napier, a shipbuilder in Glasgow.

By 1871 he had been taken into partnership and the firm was known as Rose and Downs. It was not, however, a smooth transition from manager to partner initially. There was lengthy correspondence between Downs and his employer, Mrs Rose, and her daughter, Susan Thompson. Susan had married John Thompson, a seed crusher in Hull, in 1850. The 1851 census shows Thompson, aged twenty-five, living at 7 Jarrett Street, Hull with his wife Susan, aged twenty-nine, and his mother-in-law, Christiana. The latter is described as a widow aged fifty-nine, 'Iron and brass founder employing 50 men'.[48] The foundry itself was half a mile to the north.

Just one year after his appointment Downs was asking for an increase in his salary of £150 and wanting to expand the business into a new building, spending £60. He pointed out that the business made a profit of £700 a year. This was firmly turned down by Mrs Rose and her reply indicated her concern over cost.

> This has been the worst Spring for getting money we have experienced and the alterations of the last two years have been very expensive. You will remember that we laid down when you entered with us that we wished to have the business conducted with as little outlay in machinery & on the premises as possible.[49]

44 TNA: PRO HO 107/145/1 Fowey Census 1841.
45 K. P. Fairclough, *Walton [née Bourchier], Philippa.* www.oxforddnb.com (accessed 9 June 2006).
46 HCA: DBR Article Laurie Whittle, *The Gentler Sex?*
47 HCA: DBR *At the Tail of Two Centuries*, Rosedowns News Bulletin, 1949.
48 TNA: PRO: RG 9 3584 Hull census 1851.
49 HCA: DBR 1146 Mrs Rose to Downs 30 April 1860.

One year later he was refuting criticism and threatening to resign and again asking for a salary increase. Christiana's daughter, Susan, now became the main correspondent and her concerns about the creditworthiness of customers were similar to her mother's.

> If you think that a good profit can be obtained in the London job it will be as well to see after it, but not without. I read it as amounting to two thousand pounds. Are they sound in circumstances and prompt payers?[50]

Downs pressed to meet with Mrs Thompson as he believed 'she did all the business'.[51] In his correspondence with Susan Thompson he offered to buy into the business and by 1868 at last terms were agreed, and by 1871 it was the partnership of Rose and Downs. In 1874 the name changed again when John Campbell Thompson, Susan's son, was of age.[52]

The relationship between Downs and Susan was not all problems. It might be tempting to think that Susan was advised by her husband as the firm did move into seed crushing, but the Thompson marriage was not a happy one. By 1861 Thompson had left Jarrett Street and Christiana, Susan and Susan's seven-year-old son were alone there.[53] The business had grown well, as Christiana, now nearly seventy, was head of the household and was described as an 'Ironfounder employing 88 men and 13 boys'.

They lived modestly with just one eighteen-year-old servant. The Thompsons had separated and in 1867 Thompson was trying to gain custody of his son. The company history says that Susan had taken her son to a secret address.[54] Mrs Rose and her daughter travelled extensively around Britain at this time, visiting most of the well known resorts and spa towns. James Downs not only corresponded with Susan regarding the business, but he also now acted as adviser on her matrimonial difficulties and as an intermediary with her husband.[55]

The business thrived and continued to expand. The foundry had originally cast cannon and other ship fittings, but with Downs's help it expanded into oil presses and seed crushers. The business diversified successfully as technology changed, and exported its goods across the world. An advertisement in a shipping directory in 1865 extols the benefits of the 'J. Downs patent pumps and stops, C. Rose only maker'. It lists C. Rose as 'engineer, millwright, boiler maker, iron and brass founder'.[56] Later generations of the firm were Downs's two sons and Susan's son Campbell who died unmarried in 1916. The firm continued into the twentieth century.

---

[50] HCA: DBR 1202 Mrs Thompson to Downs 30 May 1865.
[51] HCA: DBR 1136 Downs to Mrs Rose 26 June 1865.
[52] HCA: DBR *At the Tail of Two Centuries*.
[53] Hull census 1861.
[54] HCA: DBR *At the Tail of Two Centuries*.
[55] HCA: DBR 1257–1478 Correspondence.
[56] *Clayton's Register of Shipping*, 1865.

Mrs Rose is featured in the company histories as the main driver of the business, but her daughter, Susan, was the key individual from 1860. Her correspondence with Downs in 1865, when she and her mother decided to bring in an auditor, is revealing of their sense of total control over the business.[57] Mrs Rose and her daughter are a rare example of matrilineality.

Women in Education and Publishing

Teaching was deemed a suitable profession for women, especially teaching of infants, but it has been suggested that women were not considered appropriate for the teaching of boys for reasons of propriety and in view of women's intellectual limits.[58] Female teachers in maritime communities did not solely teach girls and were valued for their teaching of nautical arithmetic, as in the earlier example of Mrs Mitchell given in Chapter 2.

Mrs Janet Taylor was very definitely not in the usual mould of spinster or widowed schoolteacher of young children. The daughter of a North Country clergyman, Janet was taught navigation by her father.[59] When her father died in 1821 Janet and her seven siblings each received several thousand pounds. Thus she had the elusive capital proposed by Bessie Parkes in 1865 (see page 31). It is suggested that she needed to get married to pursue her chosen profession and that her solicitor brother ensured that her money remained her own under equity. But this is not such an odd arrangement. Taylor was a publican and a widower so perhaps not a great catch from the family point of view. However with the support of her husband she started her first nautical academy for 'merchant service officers' in London, and had success with her *Luni Solar and Horary Tables* in October 1833.[60]

Mrs Taylor was helped and supported in her career not just by her husband, but by some significant figures in the world of navigation. Captain, later Admiral, Beaufort, the Hydrographer to the Navy, was both a mentor and supporter. He gave her work, getting her to translate a French pilot book, and commended her work to others such as the Admiralty and Trinity House. Her work and her fame grew and her school expanded. In her advertisement for the school Janet used the female touch:

> Mrs Taylor's establishment offers superior advantages, she is able to place those pupils who have no relatives in town, under the care and superintendence of families, where they will receive every domestic comfort and attention, when not engaged in the Academy[61]

---

57 HCA: DBR 1201, 1202 Correspondence.
58 Kathryn Gleadle, *British Women in the Nineteenth Century* (Basingstoke: Palgrave, 2001), p. 54.
59 K. R. Alger, *Mrs Janet Taylor 'Authoress and Instructress in Navigation and Nautical Astronomy', 1804–1870*, Fawcett Library Papers No 6 (London, 1982).
60 Alger, *Mrs Janet Taylor*, pp. 7–8.
61 Alger, *Mrs Janet Taylor*, p. 14.

Family matters intruded into the business sphere. During an earlier troubled phase in her career she wrote to Captain Beaufort and referred to the future welfare of her 'infant family and all I hold dear' being dependent on his support.[62] Her work on the translation was delayed by the illness of her children and she was anxious to reassure Captain Beaufort of her hard work on his behalf.

> Sir
>
> Amidst the mighty and passing events of these times, it is hardly to be supposed you remember me or the work on which I am engaged, but, nevertheless I feel anxious to account for any apparent dilatoriness about Baron Rouisson's Brazil Pilots. My young family have been ill for some weeks past and during the last fortnight my Baby has not been expected to live from day to day. Unlike a lady you once named to me, who could by magnetism or other <u>ism</u>, communicate maternal care and attention to her children though <u>separated</u> from them, my mind and <u>personal</u> attendance have been accorded to them night and day, and I am thankful my cares have been rewarded by the restoration of health of my darlings, and now with freshened activity I shall return to my literary duties.
>
> In a week or two I hope to shew you I have not been idle[63]

However she was well able to defend herself from critics. Questions were asked about the sale through her shop of inferior, but more expensive charts as opposed to the Admiralty charts for which she was an agent. Her reply was robust, clear and logical (reproduced in full in Appendix IX).[64] One senior commentator, Rear Admiral Beechey, the Superintendent of the Marine Division of the Board of Trade, referred to Mrs Taylor as 'a very sensible person'.[65]

The support of her husband was important indeed as he ran the publishing part of the business, although all business continued to be conducted in her name. Mrs Taylor was based in the City of London and here until 1852 a married woman could trade as a *feme sole* merchant. This was the last remaining bastion of this borough custom, where a woman could trade in her own name, make contracts and be liable for her own debts. Phillips's view on examining many London cases is that it was less often used to support a woman's right to trade, but more often a useful family strategy used by both husband and wife. If a husband was bankrupt, his wife's business could be claimed as *feme sole* to avoid the clutches of the creditors. Or in the case of the wife's debts, *coverture* could be claimed and the husband could deny any responsibility for her contracts and refuse to pay.[66] Whether the Taylors took advantage of the *feme sole* custom in London or not, there were many married women trading in their own name in the City.

---

[62] UKHO: T 186 Captain Beaufort to Mrs Taylor, 27 June 1837; T 192 Mrs Taylor to Captain Beaufort 1835.

[63] The underlining is as in the original letter. UKHO: T 186 Mrs Taylor to Captain Beaufort 1837.

[64] UKHO: T 63 Mrs Taylor to Captain Beaufort 16 February 1848.

[65] Alger, *Mrs Janet Taylor*, p. 25.

[66] Phillips, *Women in Business*, pp. 48–68.

Mrs Taylor's husband died in 1853 and this loss was compounded by Beaufort's death two years later. However her business carried on for another thirteen years and included the tricky art of compass adjusting on iron ships. She did not get the same support from the new Hydrographer, but her reputation was already well established.[67] On retiring to Durham one of her last letters a few years before she died was to the Society for Improving the Conditions of Merchant Seamen. She made an impassioned plea for better care of seamen and for improved welfare and education, showing a considerable knowledge of their lives and circumstances.[68]

In Mrs Taylor's case the varied attitudes of the official world and the men with whom she was linked highlight the complexity of the women's world. Beaufort's successor at the Hydrographic Office was dismissive of her, yet her father, husband, Admiral Beaufort, the Astronomer Royal and the many men who were taught by her and who used her nautical instruments and tables thought highly of her ability.

Publishing seems to have been an area where women could gain acceptance, perhaps because it was aligned to their perceived drawing skills. There were many women in publishing. In the 1851 census there were 376 people in the category of map maker and publisher, of whom 195 were men and 181 women.[69] Mrs Steel was the widow of a map publisher and chart maker. Her late husband, David, published titles that 'represent the high water mark of English nautical publishing'. Among his publications were books on rigging, seamanship and naval architecture. He was also the producer of the *Navy List*.[70]

When Steel died in 1803 he left his business to his wife, if she wished, and there were none of the usual conditions on her remaining a widow. He had some concerns about the welfare of his children and the will included an unusual demand that their mother give her personal bond to 'bind herself to provide for them until they reached 21 years of age'.[71] Penelope did take on the business and did remarry, in 1806. Her second marriage may not have been a happy one; it was short and during this time her son fell out with her over his inheritance and left home in 1809. Perhaps the clause inserted by her first husband had a reason behind it. She married her third husband Goddard in 1818.[72]

In David Steel's obituary in the *Navy List*, placed there by his wife, there was a plea for sympathy and the support of her subscribers, referring to his 'four fatherless children'. Her business sense, however, ensured that she also gave full promotion to his published works which she committed to carry on. This she did and completed an important work of his that was due for publication before his death.

---

[67] Susanna Fisher, *Taylor [nee Ionn], Janet*. www.oxforddnb.com (accessed 2 August 2006).

[68] TNA: PRO MT 9/36. Report respecting seamen's health, accommodation, wages, pension and protection. 6 March 1867, letter from Janet Taylor.

[69] BPP 1853 LXXXVIII Census of England and Wales 1851 Table 53 Occupations of the People.

[70] Mario M. Witt, *A Bibliography of the Works Written and Published by David Steel and His Successors* (Greenwich: Anthony & Setitia Simmonds, 1991), p. 1.

[71] TNA: PRO 11/1387 will of David Steel 1803.

[72] Witt, *Works Written and Published by David Steel*, pp. 13–15.

She continued to publish charts and the *Navy List*, using her subsequent married names. She died in 1840 aged seventy-two, having outlived her third husband.[73]

Women were not averse to using the emotive family card when dealing with situations in order to elicit sympathy or to buy time. However, being a business-woman and a mother could take its toll on relationships. Penelope Steel fell out with her son, and Janet Taylor seems to have been distanced from her children in her later years, ending her days in her sister's home.

Merchants

Merchants were the essential individuals who provided the freight to be shipped. They also bought ships and invested heavily in shipping. Women could and did act as merchants and there are several examples in the shipping registers and trade directories. One woman shipowner in Norfolk owned four vessels, a snow and three schooners, between 1839 and 1845. Margaret Moore, a widow from Cley, described her occupation as merchant. She is not an isolated example.[74] Rebecca Martin was mentioned in a previous chapter in relation to her ship ownership. She was a china clay merchant in St Austell, one of the many merchants holding clay deposits on lease from landowners in mid-Cornwall. In 1848 Rebecca, now a widow, was one of a group of adventurers leasing from a local estate. Her hold-ings were significant: the output in tons from her holdings exceeded all the other annual production figures for the major works. This led her to be one of the leading figures in an attempt to regulate the prices of materials and to avoid bad debts. Her letter organising this and putting forward the proposals was signed by her and her eldest son, William, now aged twenty-three. She remained a major figure until her death in 1863.[75]

Not all women were content to take such a high-profile role as Rebecca and the other port businesswomen. In Poole earlier in the century lived Katherine Penney. Her husband George was a coal merchant, agent for shipments of clay and 'employed in the commission business'. When he died in April 1805 he left his business to his wife. She managed the business for just a few months until 24 June when she involved her son, George, who was also a coal merchant. What is not evident is why the business had not been left to her son. The period between June 1805 and November 1806 seems to have been a trial. It appears this way because after this period an agreement was drawn up giving George a half-share of the business in partnership with his mother. The business was valued (just on its assets and not including the premises which remained in Katherine's hands)

[73] Witt, *Works Written and Published by David Steel*, pp. 10–14.
[74] NRO: King's Lynn, Wells, Cley and Great Yarmouth 1825–1989 P/SH.
[75] Barton, *Cornish China Clay Industry*, pp. 86–90; TNA: PRO HO 107/1907 1851 census St Austell 1851.

at £3,700 and George raised £1,150 plus a loan of £700 from his mother to pay for his share.[76]

Katherine continued to own the estate, which comprised 'a Coal yard, counting house, stores, hereditaments & premises abutting the Quay in Poole. She to keep for the term of her natural life to be used for the joint trade and business.'[77] Whoever drew up the partnership agreement was well versed in both business and the perils of partnerships. The agreement between mother and son was very formal and contained the phrase

> In consideration of the mutual trust and confidence which the said parties hereto have & repose in each other and for the improvement of the several estates and for divers other good causes and considerations[78]

It allowed for (and limited) the partners' drawings, assumed they would reinvest to help the business and detailed how the employees would be paid by the partners. The accounts were to be audited (allowing for a £10 error) and the partners were only to be liable for their own debt. Both were to 'diligently employ themselves in and about the said business'. Katherine was therefore owner of all the premises, half-owner of the profits and was fully expected to play a full part in the business, with one exception. There was one clause that declared that Katherine was not to 'be obliged to take any active part in the management of the business'.[79] It is not obvious whether the emphasis was on the words 'obliged' or 'management'.

The case of Katherine Penney is instructive, not just because of the formal contract between mother and son, but because of the glimpse it gives of a woman who was quite clear in which aspects of the business she was prepared to work, and in this case a prominent front role was not her choice. Hers was the behind-the-scenes, but equally influential, role as a business partner.

Petty Businesses

The range of other roles of women in the shipping industry was extensive. Petty businesses provided anything and everything, from labour to load and unload goods, men to act as watchmen on moored vessels, to ferrying of passengers and goods from ship to shore, and the hire of small craft. Early in the century women appear as providers of hoys for the Navy Board. These were small sloops, usually single-masted, used as the main carriers for short-distance work along the coast or rivers. A number of women were in business supplying to the Ordnance Board,

---

[76] Dorset Record Office (DSRO): D/504/5 Articles of co–partnership between Katherine & George Penney of Poole.
[77] *Ibid.*
[78] *Ibid.*
[79] *Ibid.*

as in the case of Thomas Ady and Sarah Barrows who were paid the sum of £81 18s for hire of the hoy *Success* and three men.[80]

In small communities an individual made money in any way that they could and multiple occupations were the norm. The range of services provided by the smaller business was extensive and women like Grace Tadd were involved in almost anything that might earn income. Grace Tadd's husband, Peter, was a typical master mariner who held many shares in local ships. In 1851 they had two young children. Peter was fifteen years her senior and Grace had previously been his housekeeper. In her husband's absence at sea, Grace often had to deal with matters on his behalf. Peter had become the lessee of the Polruan passenger ferry, a rowing boat operating to and from Fowey. Unlicensed competition was a problem and she wrote[81] to the local land agent determined to protect her husband's (and her) interests.

> Polruan, 23rd November 1864
> Dear sir
> We are very sorry to trouble you again in reference to Tomy Hill who is getting more daring than ever in crossing the passage and has more custom than the Ferry Boat with the exception of the Children and those who go by the week. Its no use to say anything to him he is so impudent and abuseful . if a poor man had the Ferry that is to rent their would be fearful nowt(work) as he dares to take passengers before their face and claims the right to do so. He is as big a Rouge as would be found this side Newgate Gaol.
> Our man have not got more than his wages for 3 weeks past as then he has to be smart to get that. We sincerely hope you will be able to do something by him soon as its so perplexing to be keeped in such an agitated state with the bad Fellow every day Sunday as well. Peter is very unwilling to trouble you and would have suffered it if it had been at all possible but the old fellow goes to far and ought to be punished to the utermost
> > Trusting to hear from you shortly
> > I am yours most respectfully
> > > Grace Tadd   For Peter Tadd[82]

Tommy Hill's competition was eventually stopped. In 1868 Grace was widowed but she continued to manage the ferry. By September 1874 Grace was not managing her finances very well, as her share dealings showed in Chapter 4. In 1874 she had to sell her heavily mortgaged house. In another of her robust letters, regarding an incident involving a ferry passenger, she is clearly having money difficulties. The passenger in question was the well-known Cornish architect, Sylvanius Trevail.

---

[80] TNA: PRO WO 52/203. 30 June 1805. With thanks to Gareth Cole for the reference.
[81] Her spelling and punctuation are left unchanged.
[82] CRO: F/1/294–295 Fortescue Estate Papers.

Mr Pease

Sir

Mr Trevail's falling overboard was quite his own fault. The ferryman had in his oars giving change to another passenger and told him to wait until he got the boat into the rocks instead of waiting he jumped out and missed his footing hence his falling in the water It was said he is a land surveyor and wanted a job

The other accident he referred to had nothing to do with the ferry and that he knew

I am

     Yours most respectfully

Grace Tadd

P S I hope in the course of few days to be able to remit your £20 as I expect to receive cash next week.[83]

Grace's mixed fortune does not place her in the same league as many of the women already mentioned here. Her business, as such, was unlikely to have been worth advertising in the directory, but such petty businesswomen were to be found everywhere, frequently unnoticed by any official source.

A Suitable Job for a Woman?

The maritime businesswomen described here were heading apparently male businesses and dealing successfully in a male environment. These findings are at odds with conventional history. Ivy Pinchbeck was a pioneer in women's history and she argued that for the woman worker the industrial changes of the late eighteenth and nineteenth centuries brought greater benefits from the demands of home-based working, but mostly for single working women. The married woman became more dependent, and middle-class women were in an even worse position.[84] Victorian ideas of 'refinement' prescribed a life of idleness for women, unless stern necessity ruled otherwise. Even then they were limited to the genteel but overcrowded trades of dressmakers, milliners and governesses. Pinchbeck quotes Margarett Gregg writing in 1853 that a 'lady, to be such, must be a lady and nothing else'.[85] She contrasts the vigorous life of the eighteenth-century businesswoman with the 'sheltered existence of the Victorian woman, that they had lost all initiative and independence'.[86] These views are echoed by the description of the economic and domestic ghetto into which women were driven by 1850.[87] Yet women are found in the heavy metal trades in Birmingham, and other studies have shown women

83 *Ibid.*

84 Ivy Pinchbeck, *Women Workers and the Industrial Revolution, 1750–1850* (London: Virago Press, 1930, repr. 1981), pp. 306–14.

85 Pinchbeck, *Women Workers*, p. 315.

86 Pinchbeck, *Women Workers*, p. 316.

87 Davidoff and Hall, *Family Fortunes*.

in less 'suitable' occupations.[88] In the maritime world women ran a complete cross-section of businesses, from foundries to retail businesses such as chandlers.

What does seem to fit with the general view of women in business is the size of the enterprise. With the exception of shipbuilding, the majority of these ancillary trades in port communities tended to be small, in terms of both output and number of employees, and women are more often found running small businesses. This was true of Glasgow, London and Birmingham, and lack of access to capital has been given as a reason.[89] The problem with this, however, is that there is no way of knowing what the ratio of small, medium and large businesses was. What is certain is that the vast majority of businesses in the nineteenth century can be considered small businesses.[90] Self-made entrepreneurs were considered a risk, but the family firm had a certain market respectability.[91] The businesswoman gained from this positive view of the importance of the family firm since she was ensuring its continuity by stepping in to manage the enterprise. That she might have been closely involved before her husband's death or that she enjoyed the experience of being in charge were simply not relevant.

The Impact of Technology and Trade Changes

In the early part of the century, with the growth of the shipping industry, all trades had gained benefits. However the century also saw great changes in industrialisation and the impact on shipbuilding was the introduction of steam and the increased concentration of shipbuilding in the north. This had an inevitable impact on both the businesses and port activity. It is claimed that women were 'increasingly hampered by the growth in scale of manufacturing enterprises'.[92] This indeed was true, but not just for women. Businessmen also had problems of losing out to the larger concerns, and as work moved to other areas men did not always move with it.

Technological factors that affected these occupations were varied. Those running small workshops such as blockmakers came under threat as these products could be cheaply mass-produced. Brunel's blockmaking factory in Portsmouth was a very early example, but the impact of such new production methods was slow while the ports had the local workshop to rely on. A blockmaker had few assets to sell, but the skills of the men could be moved into shipcarpentry for a time. Ropemakers in many ports were also casualties impacted by factory production. However, the ropewalk itself, usually based near the sea, was a valuable site and

88 Jenns, 'Female Business Enterprise'; Guest and John, *Lady Charlotte*.
89 Gordon and Nair, 'The Economic Role of Middle-Class Women in Victorian Glasgow'; Jenns, 'Female Business Enterprise'; Kay, 'A Little Enterprise of Her Own'.
90 Stana Nenadic, 'The Small Family Firm in Victorian Britain', *Business History*, 35 (1993) 89–114 (pp. 89–91).
91 Nenadic, 'Small Family Firm', pp. 86–7.
92 Davidoff and Hall, *Family Fortunes*, p. 304.

could be sold for development. Sailmakers were less affected immediately, and the introduction of sewing machines was a boon, although taken up somewhat reluctantly.[93] For a small number of sailmakers, there was a limited substitute market in the increasing needs of the leisure sector for yachts. Blacksmiths could move more into supply, challenging the role of the chandlers, or move into engineering.[94] The first option offered a better role for the technically unskilled businesswoman. The foundries could expand, but as in the case of Rose Downs and Thompson, professional knowledge and skills had to be brought in if they were to survive. Diversification was the key to survival for most of these businesses.

The change in the occupational profile in ports is shown in Table 30, with a comparison across four ports. Here the number of occupations in each town is compared from mid-century to the beginning of the twentieth century. The trade directories as a source for this information are problematic. It is clear that they did not list all the businesses in Cornwall, either because Cornwall was too far away to get a really good coverage or because the businesses did not wish to spend limited incomes on advertising. In the table those trades known to have been in Fowey, but unlisted, are included in brackets. Neither is the coverage consistent as different directories had different rules on content. However, despite their limitations, directories can give an indication of the businesses that once existed even if it is not a total view.

The increasing tourist trade of Fowey and Whitby can be seen in Table 30. It shows the rise of holiday apartments, and the other ancillary trades drop in significance. In Whitby, two of the master mariners were also advertising apartments. The role that grew in significance was that of the broker, the middleman, matching ships and cargoes, owners and ships. Even if local shipbuilding ceased and there were fewer shipowners, the ports continued to be places of trade for other vessels. Whitehaven with its coal export and Fowey with its china clay were busy ports right through the century. The shipbrokers dealt with passengers or commodities. All that was needed was an extensive network of contacts and winning ways. It was, however, an occupation in which women were rarely found.

By the end of the century, the shipping industry in small ports had moved from manufacturing to service industries as cheaper mass-produced items were made elsewhere. What remained were brokers, insurance shipping, and tourism – hotels and apartments. There is no evidence of women as brokers and this more professional role had long been out of reach, perhaps due to a perceived lack of the education and training that were deemed necessary for the role. In view of the successful women seen in a variety of other port businesses, also requiring good knowledge and contacts, it seems an anomaly. Tourism, however, was a different story and Perry has shown how the changing nature of the industry brought opportunities for women. 'Women dominated the tourist sector; running 80 per cent of hotels and in St. Ives nearly all boarding house proprietors were women

---

93   Greenhill, *Merchant Schooners*, p. 80.
94   Doe, 'Blockmakers, Sailmakers, Ropemakers, Blacksmiths and Brokers', pp. 160–2.

Table 30. Port business in the nineteenth century

	Fowey		Lynn		Whitby		Whiteh'vn	
	1852	1914	1854	1912	1854	1913	1847	1901
Apartments		14				177		
Agents & ship brokers	2	5	2		4		5	13
Anchor & shipsmiths	(1)*		3				5	
Block & mast makers	(1)*		3	1			5	1
Boat builders		3			3	2	2	
Marine store dealers			6	1	4		4	3
Master mariners		13	53	7	158	29	94	7
Math. instrument maker							1	
Pilots		18	34	6	16			
Ropemakers	1		4		3		3	2
Sail cloth manufacturer							3	
Sailmakers	1	2	6	2	5	1	4	
Ship chandlers		3		1	7			6
Ship insurance assns					5			
Ship owners	1	5			166		62	6
Shipbuilders	4		2		4		4	
Stock & share brokers							3	
Timber merchants			8	3	5	3	4	1
Wharfingers			2					

Note: Known trades have been put in brackets for Fowey, but were not listed in the directory.
Source: Fowey details from *Slater's Directory*, 1852–3 and *Kelly's Directory*, 1914; Lynn details from *White's Directory*, 1854 and *Kelly's Directory*, 1912; Whitby details from *White's Directory*, 1854 and *Kelly's Directory*, 1913; Whitehaven details from *Mannix and Whellan's Directory*, 1847 and *Kelly's Directory*, 1901.

and the principal hotels were managed by women.'[95] In Fowey, Mrs Thomas, the ropemaker's wife, was advertising apartments, the ropewalk having now gone.[96] While Mary Hicks Hayes sensibly spotted the new trend and invested in the large and grand Fowey Hotel, built in 1870.[97]

Summary

Women were certainly active in business within the maritime industry throughout the period and their activity was not confined to the traditional domestic roles within the hospitality or millinery trades. Women were able to deal just as

[95] Ronald Perry, 'The Breadwinners: Gender, Locality and Diversity in Cornwall', *Cornish Studies*, 8 (2000), 115–26 (p. 121).
[96] Doe, 'Blockmakers, Sailmakers, Ropemakers, Blacksmiths and Brokers', p. 161; *Kelly's Directory*, 1902.
[97] BPO: Will of Mary Hicks Hayes 1907.

effectively as men with problems of bad debts, critical customers and a range of management crises. What they also had to deal with in many situations was the additional pressure of being a mother, but as was seen in the cases of both Mrs Steel and Mrs Taylor, there were times when this could be used to elicit sympathy or to bolster support. Some of the businesses were significant, and Mrs Rose and her daughter, Mrs Thompson, despite their physical absence from the business insisted on being fully informed and communicating their views to their manager. They were also prepared to make unpopular decisions such as bringing in auditors to ensure that their business was being properly run.

The changes that occurred within some of the smaller ports, as shipbuilding moved away and the visiting sailing vessels declined in favour of steam, affected everyone, not just businesswomen. These changes did not occur at the same time and in the same way in each port. If new shipbuilding ceased there was still a need for repair and maintenance of visiting vessels, and as some business opportunities disappeared others were created by the demands of the increasing tourist trade.

8

Warship Builders

The most prominent business in a maritime community was the shipbuilding yard. It was physically large, noisy and used a large amount of labour, and on its output rested many other businesses such as sailmakers, ropemakers and block-makers. The largest yards were major industrial concerns in their time directly employing hundreds of men. Women feature as the owners of shipbuilding yards throughout the nineteenth century and in this chapter one specialised area of shipbuilding will be considered. The building of warships was high value and high risk to the shipbuilder and the peak time for navy contracts with merchant yards was during the French Revolutionary and Napoleonic wars. What was it like to deal with such a large customer and how well was a woman accepted in this role? Unlike the community-based examples in the next chapter, where there might be an element of local support for a widow, warship builders could not expect any favours from the Navy Board and competition was both national and intense. The two examples discussed here are Mrs Frances Barnard of London, who owned her yard from 1796 until 1825, and Mrs Mary Ross, who owned her yard on the Medway from 1808 to 1815. Both examples will be considered in the overall context of the merchant yards of the time.

Building for the Navy

Mrs Frances Barnard's yard at Deptford was one of the largest yards in England and built ships for the East India trade and warships for the navy. Mrs Ross of Rochester also built warships and ships for the Hudson's Bay Company, but her operation was on a smaller scale than Barnard's. Both women, however, had to deal with the formidable Navy Board.

The navy had, for many years, depended on the merchant yards to supply the extra vessels needed in a time of war. In peace time the King's yards were able to provide the navy with its supply of both new and repaired ships, but war put additional strains on the dockyards with the extra requirements for the fast repair of damaged vessels, and the 'Royal Yards had neither the capacity nor the flexibility to comply with the demands made on them'. Keeping the building of the largest vessels, the first or second rates, with the King's yards, the Navy Board contracted with an ever widening number of merchant builders during the French Revolutionary and Napoleonic wars, as can be seen in Figure 6.[1]

---

[1]   John F. Barnard, *Building Britain's Wooden Walls: The Barnard Dynasty c.1697–1851* (Oswestry: Anthony Nelson, 1997), p. 5.

7. Mrs Mary Ross of Rochester, warship builder
Source: Copyright Rochester Museum

Figure 6. Naval shipbuilding tonnage from the merchant and the King's yards

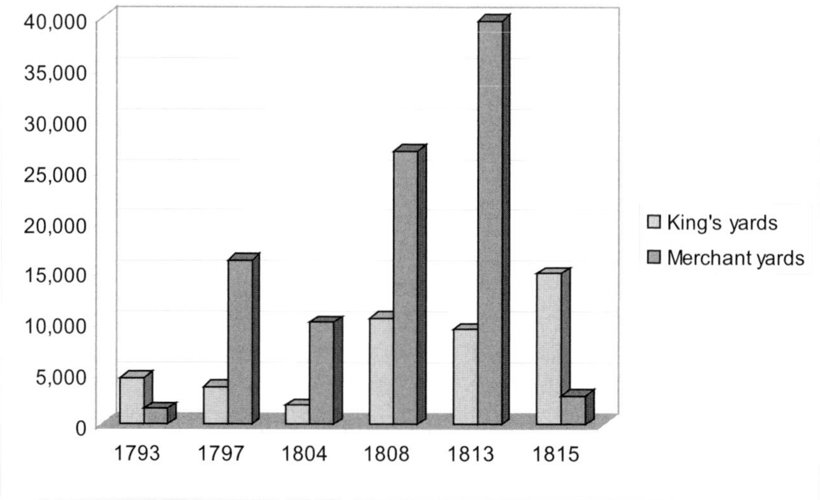

Source: Derived from data shown in R. Morriss, *The Royal Dockyards during the Revolutionary and Napoleonic Wars* (Leicester, 1983), p. 28.

Building under contract for the navy could be lucrative, but could alternatively bring financial ruin when prices were pared too close, material costs went up on fixed contracts or the size of the job was underestimated. Yet there was no shortage of merchant builders keen to build warships. Several of the yards were run by men who had previously served their time in the King's yards and had an inside knowledge of what was expected. Indeed due to the movement of shipwrights between merchant and King's yards there were few yards that did not have access to information if they were based anywhere near a royal dockyard.

Shipbuilders constantly lobbied for contracts and to ensure that the Navy Board knew of their existence. However the process normally began with a formal advertisement with an invitation to tender:

Navy Office 13th February 1813

The principal officers and commissioners of his Majesty's Navy do hereby give Notice that on Wednesday the 24th instant, at one o'clock, they will be ready to treat with such Persons as may be willing to contract for building Ten Sloops of War, of the burthen of about 444 tons each; to be launched in Twelve Months.

A Draught of the Sloops, and a Form of Tender, may be seen at this Office. No tender will be received after one o'clock on the day of Treaty; nor any noticed unless the Party, or an Agent, for him attends.

Every tender must be accompanied by a Letter addressed to the Navy Board, and signed by Two responsible Persons, engaging to become bound with the persons tendering in the sum of £800 for the due performance of the Contract for each Sloop.[2]

Table 31. Successful tenders to the Navy Board, 1809–1813

Year	Shipbuilder	Location
1809	Baker, Will	Sandgate
1809	King, J	Upnor
1809	Lowes, Jn	Sandgate
1810	List, D	Fishbourne, IOW
1810	Tyson & Blake	Bursledon
1811	Pelham, J	Frinsbury
1811	Taylor, W	Bideford
1812	Bussel & Son	Lyme Regis
1812	Chapman, Rich	Bideford
1812	Davy, Robt	Topsham
1812	Davy, Robt	Topsham
1812	Good, W	Bridport
1812	Good, W	Bridport
1812	Hills	Sandwich
1812	Hobbs, Benj	Redbridge
1812	Larkin, Edw	Lynn
1812	Richards & co	Heath, Nr Southampton
1812	Ross, Mary	Rochester
1812	Tyson & Blake	Bursledon
1812	Wigram & Green	Blackwall
1813	Adams, B	Bucklers Hard
1813	Adams, B	Bucklers Hard
1813	Adams, E	Bucklers Hard
1813	Bayley	Ipswich
1813	Brindley, J & T	Frinsbury
1813	Cortney, W	Chester
1813	King J	Upnor
1813	Wigram & Green	Blackwall
1813	Wigram & Green	Blackwall

Note: These are the tenders and could be for more than one vessel.
Source: BPP 1813–14 VIII: Minutes of the Evidence, pp. 650–7.

---

[2]   BPP 1813–14 VIII: Minutes of the Evidence on Petitions relating to East India Built Shipping, p. 561.

The Thames yards were at an advantage in being physically close to the Navy Board offices in Somerset House. They could visit in person more easily and did not have to rely on agents acting on their behalf. Relatively fast as the post was, there were nevertheless inevitable delays in news or requests for decisions for those yards based at a distance from London. The outports were additionally disadvantaged by the sheer numbers of the London yards and the information flow that came from the interchange between shipwrights working in those yards.

Competition was intense. A total of 140 tenders were received by the Navy Board between October 1809 and September 1813 and just 21 per cent were successful. Despite apparent advantages the Thames and Medway yards, which had high labour costs, began to lose their competitive edge. The Thames shipbuilders believed they were superior to yards elsewhere in the country, a view supported by William Fearnell, a surveyor of shipping to the Transport Board. But they won fewer contracts as superiority and reputation counted less than price (see Table 31). All the thirty tenders accepted in this period at the end of the wars were the lowest priced. The Thames builders were simply not bidding at the right price and the only bids won on the Thames in the later period were all won by Wigram (later Perry Wells).[3]

Occasionally the contracts included a requirement to use timber supplied by the navy, as in the case of an advertisement for fir frigates in November 1812. The shipbuilder bought the timber at whatever price they could negotiate with the King's yard and organised and paid for the transport of the timber to their own yard. The bond differed according to the contract size: for example, bomb vessels and brig sloops £600 and gun brigs £500.

Once the contractor was selected, a payment was made by the Navy Office on signing the contract to begin the work; subsequent payment stages were 'when the floors are all crossed and keelson bolted', 'when the frame bends are up', 'when the ship is timbered', 'when the lower deck beams are in', 'when the middle deck are in and kneed' and 'when the upper deck and roundhouse is laid'. The final payment was after the ship had been launched, surveyed by the King's yard and pronounced fit for purpose.[4]

Fulfilling the Contract

All of these stages required careful management of supplies and payments. The men's work on the ship had to be managed around other pressing matters, such as a non-government customer requiring urgent repairs. John Preston of Great Yarmouth frequently took his workmen off the building of the navy sloop *Racoon* to work on the repairs of merchant vessels, and this caused the *Racoon* to be sixteen months late in launching which incurred a £300 penalty in 1808. A vessel

<hr>

[3]   BPP 1813–14 VIII: Minutes of the Evidence on Petitions relating to East India Built Shipping, pp. 118, 650–7.

[4]   TNA: PRO ADM 106/1454 Attached to letter from Barnard & Co 17 Sept 1795.

might be prevented from being launched, as happened to Mr Cock in Dartmouth who explained that he had 'every expectation to complete the vessel in time and that the *Hesper* sloop stopping in the launch was the reason the *Partridge* was not launched in time"[5]

There were penalties for late launching and the shipbuilders were quick to give their reasons – for example, non-arrival of parts such as copper bolts supplied by the King's yards – and on the whole these reasons were accepted. Other reasons for delay included 'men and materials not arriving from Plymouth in time', as Bools and Good explained in 1808 when the ship was ten months late. Their penalty was reduced to £120 instead of £400. Dudman on the Thames explained that his workmen had stood out for more pay, hence he was one month late.[6] While in July 1810 Guillaume junior 'was disappointed of two companies of shipwrights', and the Thames yard of S. and D. Brent had problems with the tides and the 'chance of impediment from the ice' in 1812.

Letters from the overseers on occasion supported the shipbuilder's efforts, as in the case of Richard Chapman of Bideford where the vessel was nine months late: 'the loss of a quantity of timber and plank which was not insured and the want of cash by the contractor to be the real cause of delay in launching and that he believes Mr Chapman did exert himself as much as his circumstances would permit him'. The fine was reduced by £300.[7]

The overseer for Mr Parson explained he was obliged to move from Bursledon to Warsash and there had been a non-arrival of deals and the sawyers left the yard for higher wages. The overseer's letter in relation to Mr Graham's difficulties in completing the *Vengeur* explained that 'the people that would have been employed on this ship were ordered on board ships and transports bound to Copenhagen which demanded immediate attention'.[8]

The overseers could also contradict the builder's explanations. Richard Thorne gave his reason for a sloop being eight months late as the 'loss of a cargo of timber and the inclemency of the weather'. However Mr Stuart, the overseer, thought the cause was in letting 'the vessel to be built by the ton to men who failed in their assignment'. In the case of the *Acorn*, a sloop launched eleven months late, the overseer's report was caustic: 'Mr Crocker was in every respect unequal to the task of building a sloop, and that he had no idea of the difficulty attending the building of the *Acorn* or he would not have undertaken it.' The terms of the contract allowed for a penalty in such an event of £400 and yet, despite the overseer's comments, the penalty inflicted was only £150.[9]

---

5   TNA: PRO ADM 49/102.
6   *Ibid.*
7   *Ibid.*
8   *Ibid.*
9   *Ibid.*

A Question of Quality

Sea officers had an enduring faith in the superiority of dockyard construction compared to ships built in merchant yards and were concerned that the navy was too dependent, in their view, on ships of 'dubious quality'. There have been suggestions that speed of construction in the push for profitability and the lack of lengthy seasoning of timber in the merchant yards supported this view. However, large numbers of ships were built in merchant yards and many gave good service.[10] St Vincent, who was First Sea Lord between 1801 and 1804, was of the view that all contractors were venal if not incompetent. He prosecuted the builder of the *Ajax*, but it brought about a refusal of all merchant builders to sign future contracts unless exempted from such action.[11] St Vincent's distrust of merchant builders led to a gap in construction that had to be speedily filled by his successors.

The case of the *Ajax*, and the suing of its merchant builders, is often quoted in support of the poor quality of merchant-built ships,[12] but the details of the case suggest that the shipbuilders were not as incompetent as St Vincent believed. The case came before an arbitrator in 1807 with Sir Andrew Snape Hammond leading the plaintiffs, the Navy Board, who were suing John, Samuel and Daniel Brent for £40,000. Serious faults were cited in caulking, the knee of the head, knees, timber and planks, throating of the knees, dry rot, hair and tar between the scarphs, the flemishing and finally the ironwork. The case on all aspects was dismissed and the only breach found in the fulfilment of the contract related to the ironwork which was not of the 'best tough Swedish iron' as stipulated, but was of rolled iron. S. and D. Brent were fined just £450.[13] However the last ship they launched for the navy was the *Achates* in 1808 and they do not appear to have tendered for any other navy work.[14] Brent and Sons continued in business and are evident in the list of Thames shipbuilders in 1814 (see Table 32), and the number of men employed by them over the period was unaffected by any loss of work from the navy or damage to their reputation.[15] The sea officers, whose lives depended on their ships, were liable to be critical of any perceived shortcoming, and the royal dockyards were unlikely to heap praise on merchant builders.

---

[10] Roger Morriss, *The Royal Dockyards During the Revolutionary & Napoleonic Wars* (Leicester: Leicester University Press, 1983), pp. 27–9.

[11] Morris, *The Royal Dockyards*, p. 20, quoting TNA: PRO ADM 106/2234 22 May 1804.

[12] Roger Knight, 'Devil Bolts and Deception? Wartime Naval Shipbuilding in Private Shipyards, 1739–1815', *Journal for Maritime Research* (2003); Morriss, *The Royal Dockyards*, p. 29.

[13] BPP 1813–14 VIII: Minutes of the Evidence on Petitions relating to East India Built Shipping, pp. 470–3.

[14] TNA: PRO ADM 49/102.

[15] BPP 1813–14 VIII: Minutes of the Evidence on Petitions relating to East India Built Shipping, p. 414.

Table 32. Average number of shipwrights and other men employed
in the Thames yards

	1803	1804	1805	1806	1807	1808	1809	1810	1811	1812	1813
Wigram & Green	325	498	604	598	505	496	462	554	614	392	758
Francis Barnard & Sons*	225	317	343	168	290	278	274	285	306	350	172
Brent & Sons	248	401	418	364	289	403	528	452	483	452	134
Pitcher	126	173	247	153	211	150	171	130	248	178	157
Pitcher at Blackwell					122	169	150	193	121	141	117
Dudman & Sons	160	290	309	193	229	313	238	340	316	174	21
Mester	145	64	157	67	67	127	134	116	126	103	91
Thompson	41	21	48	39	33	40	39	61	52	29	33
Joshua Young	87	104	97	106	40	119	119	100	90	114	99
Hills	66	101	140	98	92	126	179	221	174	114	211
Curling & co	170	154	196	132	224	218	309	304	339	232	370
Dowson & co	67	91	63	60	70	117	103	121	71	68	120
Tebbet, Hichcock & co	35	60	55	59	51	95	64	94	47	74	83
Ayles & co	123	122	122	123	102	133	104	136	122	108	101
Longbottom & co	55	48	38	59	36	38	51	69	35	40	26
Beatson & co					48	58	52	59	86	87	87
Mews & co				33	23	34	27	35	43	29	32
Blackett & co										85	
Fletchers	113	108	100	122	88	108	102	108	109	85	101

* Note: Name as published.

Source: BPP 1813–14 VIII: Minutes of the Evidence on Petitions relating to East India Built Shipping, 414.

Financial Risks

Bankruptcy was a common problem in shipbuilding and was often the result of shipbuilders overreaching themselves and then being forced into bankruptcy by the timber merchants who were their largest creditors.[16] Dealing with the Admiralty was not easy. While the potential gains were large, so also was the bureaucracy, and the Navy Board had the power of a major customer and used it. Barnard's yard had severe problems in August 1784 when William Barnard, Frances's husband, gave notice that the two 74-gun ships, *Tremendous* and *Majestic* were ready for launching. The board wished to delay launching (and final payment) until 1785 so Barnard laid out the severe and expensive consequences of this. The fire insurance for the two vessels at a cost of £20,000 per ship was due to expire in November and December 1784. His contract to build two further vessels on the

---

[16] A. J. Holland, *Ships of British Oak: The Rise and Decline of Wooden Shipbuilding in Hampshire* (Newton Abbot: David & Charles, 1971), pp. 11–12.

same slipways would be severely delayed and his payments to his timber suppliers had to be met.[17] The ships were eventually launched many months later.[18]

Poor estimating or bad judgements on pricing had severe consequences. Benjamin Tanner in 1804 had the largest yard in the southwest at Dartmouth, with sixty-eight shipwrights and thirteen apprentices. But he went bankrupt in 1807 with debts of £12,066 10s over a problem with his contract, 'having contracted to build 6 sloops of war at a peace price only to find his labour & material costs escalating with unexpected resumption of war in 1803'.[19] In Fowey, Nickels overreached himself by attempting to build a brigantine, HMS *Primrose*, and also went bankrupt, the ship being finished by his trustees.[20]

Managing Work Flow

All shipyards had the challenge of managing constant work flow, but the stakes were higher and the competition more fierce for the Thames and Medway builders. Table 32 shows the change in the numbers of men employed over ten years as contracts came and went. It shows that the smaller Thames yards, such as Ayles and Company, had a more consistent number of men in their employ compared to the greater number range for the larger yards. Tables 33 and 34 show the range of work that two yards, Barnard's and Dudman's, had to win and manage.

Table 33. Barnard's yard workflow

Year	King's ships built	Private ships built	Ships repaired
1803	1	3	72
1804	2	5	81
1805	1	2	87
1806	1	1	66
1807	3	1	75
1808	4	1	79
1809	3	0	93
1810	2	1	77
1811	2	2	90
1812	2	1	69
1813	1	0	65
Total	22	17	854

Source: BPP 1813–14 VIII: Minutes of the Evidence on Petitions relating to East India Built Shipping, 449.

[17] TNA: PRO ADM 106/1454 Barnard to Navy Board.
[18] Barnard, *Building Britain's Wooden Walls*, pp. 52–3.
[19] David J. Starkey, 'Devon's Shipbuilding Industry, 1786–1970', in *A New Maritime History of Devon, Vol. II*, ed. M. Duffy *et al.* (London: Conway, 1994), pp. 78–90; David J. Starkey, 'Shipbuilding in the Southwest during the Napoleonic War', *Maritime Southwest*, 6 (1993), 7–11 (pp. 8–9).
[20] Doe, 'Politics, Property and Family Resources', p. 67.

Table 34. Dudman's yard workflow

Years	King's built	Merchant built	King's repair	Transport repair	Merchant repair
1803		2			38
1804	9	1	1	14	21
1805	1	2	3	9	10
1806		1		10	12
1807	1			3	13
1808	6			13	18
1809	6			3	11
1810		4		26	12
1811	1	2		16	11
1812	1	1		29	9
Total	25	13	4	123	155

Source: BPP 1813–14 VIII: Minutes of the Evidence on Petitions relating to East India Built Shipping, 443.

Together with managing work flow was the task of managing cash flow and, while this was a challenge for all shipbuilders, inevitably the larger yards had larger sums of money to balance. A small yard in Mevagissey, Cornwall had a turnover of £11,000 between 1799 and 1805.[21] For the large yards at the same time just one 1,000-ton East India ship was charged out at £31,000, and a 64-gun ship built for the navy earned Randall and Company £17,250 for the first seven stage payments in 1795.[22] Maintenance and repair work was essential in providing cash flow for the yards. The navy was reluctant to outsource maintenance and repair but was forced to do so on some occasions. Each East India ship that came back to the merchant yard for repair and maintenance was worth a considerable sum to the shipbuilder over its lifetime, as Tables 35 and 36 show.

Table 35. Cost of repair work on *Tigris* (500-ton, British-built), Barnard's yard

			£	s	d
1803	Mar 27	to shipwright's bill and stores	1243	16	8
1807	May 24		1357	6	11
1809	Jun 28		6915	16	7
1810	May 25		855	9	1
1814	April		1200		

Source: BPP 1813–14 VIII: Minutes of the Evidence on Petitions relating to East India Built Shipping, 133.

---

[21] Doe, 'The Business of Shipbuilding', pp. 197–8; BPP 1813–14 VIII: Minutes of the Evidence on Petitions relating to East India Built Shipping, p. 45.
[22] ADM 106/1454 Attached to letter from Barnard & Co 17 Sept 1795.

Table 36. Cost of repair work on *Sir William Pulteney*
(India-built ship), Barnard's yard

		£	s	d
1805	Feb 02	863	16	4
1807	Jun 06	1,174	10	2
1807	Feb 17	771	11	5
1810	Nov 12	1,851	10	3
1812	Nov 07	1,032	9	6

Source: BPP 1813–14 VIII: Minutes of the Evidence on Petitions relating to East India Built Shipping, 133.

Relationships with Other Yards

It was a wise contractor who remained on friendly terms with the nearest royal dockyard as there were some benefits in working on government contracts. One advantage was the willingness of the navy to provide expensive equipment such as bilgeways and cokeing machines, plus men and materials if it meant getting the ships when the navy wanted them.[23] But this nearness was also a disadvantage when men left to seek work in the royal yards.[24] Cooperation between the merchant yards also occurred on occasion, as in the case of their combined determination to hold out against undue pressure from either the navy or their own workmen.[25] Barnard's sold timber to Perry's of Blackwell in 1800/1801 when Barnard's were overstocked. Barnard's could not accommodate it at their yard so Perry's 'had it from the wharf where it laid for us at Ipswich'.[26] Competitive information also circulated between the yards; Mary Ross, Barnard and Nickels were all able to quote the terms of contracts of other suppliers when writing to the Navy Board. Some information of that type could also have come indirectly from the movement of men between yards.[27]

Navy and Merchant Shipbuilding Comparisons

While many of the management challenges of navy and merchant shipbuilding were similar, such as workflow management, sourcing of men and materials and financial control, there were advantages and disadvantages between the two types

[23] Cokeing machines were for fitting knees to beams, and bilge ways were large pieces of timber for use in launching.
[24] TNA: PRO ADM 49/102, PRO ADM 106/1612 27 Dec 1810.
[25] TNA: PRO ADM 106/1454, ADM 106/2234 22 May 1804.
[26] BPP 1813–14 VIII: Minutes of the Evidence on Petitions relating to East India Built Shipping, p. 130.
[27] TNA: PRO ADM 16/1587 24 Jan 1806, ADM 106/1454, ADM 106/1613 16 May 1813.

of customer. The relationship between the Navy Board and the contractor was more formal than that between the shipowner and the shipbuilder, especially for the latter in a small community. St Vincent's violent attack on what he saw as corrupt practices was just one extreme example of Parliament's concern over undue influence. Parliament had previously passed an act in 1782 to restrain its members from voting or sitting if they had any interest in government contracts.[28] Robert Wigram, father and son, of the major Thames shipbuilding firm, were Members of Parliament from 1802 to 1830. Robert Wigram senior made way for his son at Fowey in 1806.[29] In the smaller ports the relationship between the shipbuilder and the shipowner or owners was much closer in a tight-knit community, with kinship ties adding an extra dimension, as in the case of Slade's yard in Polruan where the shipowning families of Tadd and Hocken were linked with the Slades by marriage through Jane's son, Thomas, and her daughters, Susan and Elizabeth.[30]

The Navy Board had significant buying power and was able to use this when dealing with the shipbuilders. Private shipowners had less leverage in negotiations with shipbuilders in wartime conditions. Henley and Son of London had great difficulty in buying new vessels during the French wars as one after another of the shipbuilders approached replied they were too busy with orders.[31] This did not stop customers from attempting to get other quotes, but not always successfully. The Select Committee on East India Shipping were aware of a Mr Bonham, who had previously been a regular customer of Barnard's, who had also approached Wigram for an alternative quote for the EIC ship *Asia*. In the event he could not agree a suitable contract with Wigram and it was built by Barnard's.[32]

The navy ships were large contracts; individual ships could be up to 2,000 tons, although the majority of ships such as frigates and gun vessels were below 500 tons. East India ships were also large contracts – 800 to 1,400 tons. Most other ships were below this size and this includes the smaller ships built for the West Indies trades. The biggest difference was in repair. The navy repaired its own ships when it could, but the East India and other merchant ships were repaired in the yards in which they were built. Despite the difference in new build figures of 10,926 tons built for the Navy Board and 7,231 tons for the East India Company, Lordan, who worked for Dudman's yard, estimated the 'service was the same' as the East India ships came back for repair but not the King's ships.[33]

28 Bernard Pool, *Navy Board Contracts 1660–1832* (London: Longmans, 1966), pp. 111–12.
29 R. G. Thorne, *History of Parliament: House of Commons, 1790–1820, Vol. V* (London: Secker & Warburg, 1986), pp. 554–7.
30 Doe, *Jane Slade of Polruan*, p. 10.
31 Ville, *English Shipowning*, p. 45.
32 BPP 1813–14 VIII: Minutes of the Evidence on Petitions relating to East India Built Shipping, pp. 449, 457.
33 BPP 1813–14 VIII: Minutes of the Evidence on Petitions relating to East India Built Shipping, p. 445.

Mrs Frances Barnard of London

Barnard's were one of the largest yards and it was in the difficult conditions of war that Frances took over the management of the yard. Frances Clarke was married at the church of St Saviour, Southwark in 1760. Her husband William Barnard came from a shipbuilding family based in Harwich, Essex where his father and grandfather had been building naval vessels for some years. Two years later William and Frances moved to London where he set up a business in partnership with Henry Adams and William Dudman. The yard at Grove Street Yard was spacious, with two dry docks, one wet dock and three building slips. It was situated close to the navy dockyard at Deptford and amidst the many other merchant shipbuilding yards based in this part of the Thames. It was an ambitious move from the provincial town of Ipswich, and William continued to expand his business, taking out a lease on his own on a yard with one dry dock and two slips in Deptford Green in 1779. He subsequently added a third building slip and confidently renewed the lease for sixty-three years in 1786. Business matters in the other yard at Grove Street were not straightforward and a falling out between the partners led to a court case that was eventually settled out of court in 1794, when William was already a very ill man. He died in March 1795.[34]

Table 37. Tons built 1803–14 in selected yards

		King's ships		Merchant ships incl. EIC	
		No.	Tonnage	No.	Tonnage
Dudman	1803–12	25	10,926	13	7,231
Barnard	1804–13	23	19,529	33	19,189
Wells	1803–13	24	29,616	13	12,576
Ross	1805–14	11	9,100	n.k.	n.k.

Source: BPP 1813–14 VIII: Minutes of the Evidence on Petitions relating to East India Built Shipping, 443, 449 and 457; TNA: PRO ADM 49/102; D. Lyons, *Sailing Navy List.*

William left his complete estate to Frances and appointed her sole executrix; his eldest son William was aged nineteen and still an apprentice. This was a heavy responsibility – Barnard's was one of the foremost yards on the Thames – yet William did not consider setting up a trust with some experienced male trustees. His recent dispute with his former partner, Henry Adams, may have prejudiced him against such a move, no doubt against legal advice. Neither did he make any specific reference to his sons in relation to the business; the whole of William's estate was 'for her absolute use and benefit and disposal'.[35]

Immediate steps had to be taken to reassure customers that it was business as usual. The Navy Board was informed in a letter from William Barnard junior of

---

34 Barnard, *Building Britain's Wooden Walls*, pp. 37–8, 50–61.
35 TNA: PRO 11/1257 will of William Barnard 1795.

the death of his father. The letter made it clear that his mother was in charge and that when he and his brother had served their apprenticeships they would be 'in a situation to join her'. Further reassurance was given that she had the assistance of a 'very able foreman who served his time to my father and who has acted as a foreman under him upward of twenty years', thus satisfying any concerns there might be in the board about the changes. Careful though this letter was to allay any male prejudices, the business name was changed to Mrs Frances Barnard and Sons.[36] The lease of the yard at Deptford Green (which still had fifty-four years to run) was changed to the name of Frances Barnard and it remained in her name until her death in 1825.[37]

The published history of the Barnard business struggles with the concept of a woman running such a large business and believed that she became 'de facto senior partner', but doubted whether she played an active part in day-to-day affairs. The fact that Frances moved away from the yard in 1803 to a grand house and estate in Mitcham is used as proof of the latter. This disbelief in a woman's ability to run a business is expressed at least three times in the book, in one instance being used in reference to a previous Mrs Barnard who was left in a similar situation. This earlier Mrs Barnard, Mary, was grandmother to Frances's husband and she had run the yard in Ipswich from the death of her husband in 1716 to 1734. Mary was fifty when her husband left his whole estate including his yard to his wife outright. Her son was aged about twelve when her husband died and she continued to run the yard, including moving premises at some stage.[38]

When writing about Frances, John Barnard admits that living on the premises as she had for many years and having taken into her home her father-in-law (son of Mary Barnard) when he became bankrupt, she had an 'insight into the ship-building business'. As its owner, the author agrees, 'she controlled the purse-strings and as a result must have been party to all matters concerning finance, a matter of major concern to any merchant shipbuilding business'.[39] However, a business owner needs more than a passing knowledge and while Frances may have had a good foreman to run the technical aspects and buy materials and hire men, she alone had to make the key decisions. Her move to Mitcham did not occur until eight years after her husband's death, during which time, while Frances was living at the yard, Barnard's did extensive business by launching twelve ships for the navy and nine ships for the East India Company.[40] On her move away from the yard in 1803 she was aged sixty-four and her two sons had come of age in 1797 and 1799. The name of the firm remained Mrs Frances Barnard, Sons and Co. until 1801 when Thomas Roberts became another partner. Could he have been the foreman mentioned in William Barnard's letter of 1795? Whoever he was, Frances was able

---

[36] TNA: PRO 1454 1790–1797 Navy Board letters.
[37] Barnard, *Building Britain's Wooden Walls*, p. 61.
[38] Barnard, *Building Britain's Wooden Walls*, pp. 9–10, 63, 93.
[39] Barnard, *Building Britain's Wooden Walls*, p. 93.
[40] Barnard , *Building Britain's Wooden Walls*; David Lyon, *The Sailing Navy List: All the Ships of the Royal Navy – Built, Purchased and Captured, 1688–1860* (London: Conway, 1993).

to remove herself from the noise and bustle of the yard having seen the business through the potentially difficult times after the death of William senior and once she had a partner to share the load in addition to her two sons.

Managing the business had not been an easy task and an error over the costing of the work on the *York*, which was an East Indiaman that had been purchased on the stocks by the Navy Board and was converted into a warship, seems to have cost them £5,240 in 1795.[41] The project had been a very difficult one; the alteration had not been straightforward and delays had occurred due to problems with the sawyers who were making, in the company's words, 'exorbitant demands'.[42] They had survived this early difficulty and in 1798 Frances's two sons purchased a yard from the Wells family and established a mast yard at Rotherhithe. The named partners of this new business included Frances plus her brother-in-law, Thomas Barnard.[43]

Frances's son William died aged twenty-nine in 1805 and Edward George Barnard was now the third partner in the business which was renamed F & E G Barnard and Roberts. Barnard's continued to build navy and East India ships, but the last vessel for the navy was the *Pactolus* in 1813.[44] Frances died, aged eighty-eight, at her house in Mitcham on 17 July 1825 and was interred in the burial ground of the Meeting House, Butt Lane, Deptford. She bequeathed to her son Edward, 'all pictures, models, draughts of ships, drawings, instruments, moulds, cabinets of woods and such printed books as are anyway related to the art of shipbuilding'. It is worth noting that she had taken all of these with her in her move from the yard to Mitcham. She was a wealthy widow and left shares in East India ships, although the will does not itemise them.[45]

By the time of Frances's death, the great days of wooden shipbuilding on the Thames had gone. Peace brought the end of merchant warship-building and the East India Company lost its monopoly. Edward Barnard wrote that his two yards were 'virtually shut' as a result of business problems.[46] All of the Thames yards were struggling as work dried up and large numbers of shipwrights were out of work.[47] Where in 1803 to 1804 there had been 2,500 ships being built on the Thames, now in 1814 there were just 250. In 1813 there had been 4,000 men employed in the yards, one year later there were just 200.[48] The result was a great loss of business and only half the yards were to survive, with just eight yards eventually moving into steam. The yards limped on with the occasional repair

---

[41] TNA: PRO ADM 106/1454 17 September 1795 letter from Frances Barnard and Co.

[42] TNA: PRO ADM 106/1454 1, 30 December 1795 letter from Frances Barnard and Co.

[43] Barnard, *Building Britain's Wooden Walls*, p. 68.

[44] TNA: PRO ADM 49/102 An account of ships of war built in merchant yards since 1st Jan 1801.

[45] TNA: PRO Prob 11/1703 Will of Frances Barnard, 1825.

[46] Barnard, *Building Britain's Wooden Walls*, pp. 72–5.

[47] BPP 1813–14 VIII: Minutes of the Evidence on Petitions relating to East India Built Shipping, pp. 1–661.

[48] BPP 1813–14 VIII: Minutes of the Evidence on Petitions relating to East India Built Shipping, p. 414.

work on East India ships, and even this was not what it was as ships now were expected to do more voyages than previously.[49] For the committed businessman it was possible to survive such a recession, and ten Thames yards did survive including Barnard's biggest competitor, Wigrams.[50] However, Edward Barnard was not committed to the business. Still unmarried at the age of forty-seven, his mother's death seems to have given him a new purpose. At last in full control of the finances, that same year he purchased Gosfield Hall for £150,000 and then was married the following year in April. By 1832 he had entered politics as a Member of Parliament for Greenwich and, in the manner of Joseph Warner Henley of Henley and Sons, he left the business to manage itself while he lived the life of a country gentleman.[51] It is interesting to note that during his time as an MP his view towards women was liberal, voting 'with the minority in favour of admitting women into the visitors gallery of the House'. Frances would have approved of the motion, but not of the loss of the business. The yards were abandoned and on Edward's death it appears that he was insolvent, having taken out numerous mortgages including one for £25,000 in 1832 to fund his seat in Parliament.[52]

Mrs Mary Ross of Rochester

Acorn Wharf, at Rochester, is situated close to the bridge across the Medway between Rochester and Strood. Here Charles Ross had been in business since 1791, when he rebuilt the French frigate '*L'Aimable*', followed by the 365-ton *Albatross* launched in 1795.[53] After this there was a lengthy gap in his work for the Navy Board until the 14-gun brig *Martial*, ordered in 1804 and launched in April 1805, followed a few months later by the 38-gun frigate *Resistance*.[54] In 1806 he launched another gun brig *Spartan* and then also was given a contract for a 74-gun 3rd rate, a vessel he had offered to build as far back as 1795.[55]

The contract for *Vigo* was signed in October 1806 and the keel was laid in April 1807. His last letter to the Navy Board was in August 1807 when he wrote offering to build further gun ships and at the same time reassured the board of his reliance as a contractor:

8 Aug 1807
The Board lately having let several gun ships to be built by contract and as the frames of HMS *Vigo* will be in a very short time be complete humbly beg leave to tender my services to Your Honours to build another at the price and time granted.

49 *Ibid.*
50 Helen Doe, 'Thames Shipbuilders in the Napoleonic Wars', Conference Proceedings, 3rd *Thames Shipbuilders Conference*, Greenwich, August, 2006, pp. 10–21.
51 Ville, *English Shipowning*, pp 159–61.
52 Barnard, *Building Britain's Wooden Walls*, p. 96.
53 Medway Record Office (MRO): DE 567 Harris poster; Lyon, *The Sailing Navy List*.
54 TNA: PRO ADM 106/1613 letter from Roberts 17 April 1805; Lyon, *The Sailing Navy List*.
55 TNA: PRO ADM 106/1613, 25 Jan 1795.

I humbly hope from my past and present conduct in expending the work of HM ships in my charge that the Honourable Board will have no doubt in their minds as to my fulfilling the terms of my contract

I pray Your Honours to remember that I was the first person who devised the strong chain and took the 74 gun ships to build at present price and time.[56]

The note on the letter confirms his reputation as a government supplier when the writer ordered his clerk to 'Recommend to the Board that Mr Ross in our opinion is a person whom we can recommend to their Lordships as likely to fulfil his contract to our satisfaction.'[57]

Charles died in 1808 leaving Mary his widow and seven children, four sons and three daughters, ranging from Edward, aged sixteen, to the youngest, Thomas, aged six.[58] He left no will and Mary took control of the yard or, as her rapid ability to grasp the business essentials suggests, continued to run the yard. The building of *Vigo* could not be held up and with an eye to the continuing needs of the business she wrote on 28 November 1808:

Honourable sirs

Having a considerable quantity of small sized timber laying useless in my possession in consequence of building the two seventy fours I take the liberty of making this application to request that I may be permitted to build one of His Majesty's small gun boats of class of about 235 tons

Your answer will be esteemed a favour by

Your obedient servant

Mary Ross[59]

Her letters to the Navy Board are a contrast to those written by her husband or by Barnard's yard. She wrote briskly and to the point, and while they conformed to the written etiquette of the time, they were never overly flowery or humble.

The launch of the *Vigo* was delayed at the request of the board, a difficult situation as this delayed payment and left a slip occupied unnecessarily. This would have an impact on both cash flow and work flow and could cause severe problems for the delicate balancing of shipyard finances. The board then, after all, decided the ship should be launched. Good news as this was to Mrs Ross, she could not restrain herself from showing some irritation in her letter to the board and laying out quite clearly the implications of their dithering, underlining her words to emphasis her frustration:

Rochester Jan 25 1810

I received your letter of 22 informing me that it is now your intention that the *Vigo* shall be launched instead of being kept on the slip until April or May and you

---

[56] TNA: PRO ADM 106/1613 8 Aug 1807.

[57] *Ibid.*

[58] IGI website: www.familysearch.org/Eng/Search/igi/individual_record (accessed 2 May 2004).

[59] TNA: PRO ADM 106/1613 28 Nov 1808.

desire to know when she will be ready – in answer to which I beg leave to acquaint yr. Hon Board that after you had expressed a <u>wish</u> to have the ship remain on the slip, I fully signalled in my mind that such was your determination and in consequence I had some of the shipwrights & joiners discharged. She would otherwise have been finished <u>and long before this launched</u> but you are now pleased to alter from your first intent I beg to assure you that every exertion shall be used to have her launched as soon as possible which I hope will be the 20 or 21 February[60]

The attitude of the Navy Board towards Mrs Ross was pragmatic; as seen in the previous chapter, they were used to dealing with women suppliers. A note was made relating to *Stirling Castle* that 'the contract was made with Mr Charles Ross but on his death was transferred to Mrs Mary Ross in whose name the final bill was made out.'[61]

The *Vigo*, and final payment, continued to be a concern for Mrs Ross. Further delays led to a request from her on 4 February that the ship be surveyed on the slip and the certificate granted as she had 'several heavy payments to make about that time'. The board could not agree to that but did promise to 'endeavour to have her docked & surveyed as she is launched'.[62] This was not to be and Mrs Ross wrote again on 24 February to explain that Chatham could not dock the vessel and she asked if the ship could be surveyed afloat. The board graciously agreed:

27 Febry 1810

Direct Chatham Officer under the particular circumstances of the case and the probability that she will not be taken into dock for some time to survey her afloat & grant a certificate noting thereon the works deficit and how far their objections if any extend to grant the builder the final payment on the ships
Acquaint Mrs Ross with order given.[63]

Mary Ross kept the yard going and remained completely in charge, living in some style in Acorn House in the yard. The house had been built in the second half of the eighteenth century and the 'furnishings and fittings of the interior in its heyday were said to have been exquisite'.[64]

After launching eight vessels the final vessel to be launched for the navy was the bomb vessel *Fury* which moved off the slipway in April 1814.[65] Philip Banbury in his book on the Thames and Medway builders incorrectly assumed that at this point Mrs Ross died.[66] As previously described, the situation for the shipbuilders on the Thames and Medway had changed considerably for the worse with peace in

[60] TNA: PRO ADM 106/1613 25 Jan 1810. The underlining is as in the original.
[61] TNA: PRO ADM 49/102.
[62] TNA: PRO ADM 106/1613 1810–1813 Mrs Ross to Admiralty 4 Feb 1810.
[63] TNA: PRO ADM 106/1613 1810–1813 Note on letter from Mrs Ross to Admiralty 24 Feb 1810.
[64] B. Parle, *Rochester in Old Photographs* (Gloucester, 1989).
[65] TNA: PRO ADM 49/102; Lyon, *The Sailing Navy List*, p. 148.
[66] Philip Banbury, *Shipbuilders of the Thames and Medway* (Newton Abbot: David & Charles, 1971), p. 151.

1815.[67] There was to be no further shipbuilding in the yard; Mary may have been astute enough to realise that the future of shipbuilding was not looking bright or, judging by their later careers, her sons were not keen to take over the business.

Mary began to settle various affairs left from the administration of her husband's estate. Between 1815 and 1821 she assigned some of her estate between her seven children.[68] The family owned several pieces of farming land in Kent, and her eldest son, Edward, was a farmer, living in Rochester. Her second son, Charles, had been apprenticed to Edward Crump of Rochester, a shipbuilder, on 17 September 1808. Crump does not seem to have had a separate yard and seems to have been a relation, possibly an uncle, and may have been working with Ross.[69] Charles did not pursue the career of shipwright or shipbuilder and became a brewer in Stoke Newington. Her other two sons, Stephen and Thomas, were later described as gentlemen, one living in Essex and the other in Ipswich. Mary moved to Stoke Newington and the yard and premises were taken over by her daughter Rebecca and her husband, John Foord. Foord was a general builder and contractor and he continued to use the yard.

Mary Ross died in 1847 leaving her estate equally divided between her surviving children, Edward, Stephen Ross, Thomas Baldock, Sarah Hardy and Rebecca Foord, and the children of her late son Charles and late daughter Mary Christopherson. The land was retained by the family and administered by the Foord estate with the rental income split into sevenths until 1923. Then the Ross properties were sold and the final lump sum divided between the descendants of Mary's seven children.

Technical Knowledge

A consistent question asked by the 1813–14 Select Committee on Petitions relating to East India Built Shipping of the witnesses was to ascertain whether the shipbuilders, not just the shipwrights, had been 'bred to the work', and the answer in all cases was affirmative. Isaac Sparrow, a clerk from Barnard's yard, confirmed that 'Messrs Barnard and Roberts were regularly brought up to the business of shipwrights and reside on the premises and superint their own concerns'.[70] In this context of technical knowledge Sparrow referred only to the qualified shipwrights; of Mrs Frances Barnard there was no mention, although all the statistics presented to the committee bore her name.

Overseers were placed by the navy into the merchant yards to watch all aspects of the building of the contract vessels. These overseers had to sign a certificate

[67] BPP 1813–14 VIII: Minutes of the Evidence on Petitions relating to East India Built Shipping, p. 13.

[68] MRO: TI 117–121,132 Various Leases.

[69] MRO: RCA 02/20 Register of Apprentices 1806–63; TI 115 Lease on yard referring to Edward Crump.

[70] BPP 1813–14 VIII: Minutes of the Evidence on Petitions relating to East India Built Shipping, p. 133.

detailing the dimensions of the vessel by contract and as built, details of any materials supplied by the royal dockyards such as copper and iron that were chargeable to the contractor, and once she was safely launched confirm that 'she is built agreeably to contract'.[71] This was a heavy responsibility and one that might leave the individual open to pressure from less scrupulous contractors. The overseer was, in most cases, a man with experience of the navy's way of doing things; for example, Henry Adams, who served his apprenticeship in the royal dockyard in Deptford, was appointed overseer at Bucklers Hard in Hampshire where later he started his own building business.[72] In 1814 Mr Hillman, a surveyor of East India Company shipping, told a select committee that for navy ships 'A carpenter in addition to a surveyor is appointed early and he then sails with the ship.' 'To risk his life upon the workmanship which he superintends?' the committee asked. 'Yes' was the answer.[73]

This could support the claim that women, who were not taken on as shipwright apprentices (except in the case of Mary Lacy who disguised herself as a man and called herself William Chandler in 1760), could not be technically competent in shipbuilding[74] – except for the fact that the Navy Board did recognise the technical knowledge and competence of women when they appointed two women as overseers in 1783. These women were not only found in rural outports, but also working on the Thames. Similarly, they were not just supervising small contracts. In 1783 Mrs Peake was the appointed overseer for *Bellerophon* built by Greaves at Frindsbury, Rochester.[75] A 3rd rate 74-gun Arrogant class of 1,604 tons, it was ordered in 1782 and launched in 1786 and survived until 1816 when it was hulked.[76] The published history of the *Bellerophon* quotes the minutes of the Surveyor's office in 1786 which give Henry Peake as the overseer, perhaps her son.[77] Mrs Peake appears again on the 1783 list as the overseer on the 5th rate 32-gun *Meleager* built by Graves at Frindsbury; this was wrecked in 1801 in the Gulf of Mexico.[78] Mrs Guyer was the overseer for the *Woolwich*, built by Colhorn and Nowlan at Bursledon. This was a 5th rate 44-gun ship that was initially used as a troopship. It was wrecked in 1813.[79] It is reasonable to suppose that they may have had men working for them, or a young son, but it was still the signature of Mrs Peake or Mrs Guyer that would appear on the contract.

71 BPP 1813–14 VIII: Minutes of the Evidence on Petitions relating to East India Built Shipping, p. 473.
72 Barnard, *Building Britain's Wooden Walls*, p. 39.
73 BPP 1813–14 VIII: Minutes of the Evidence on Petitions relating to East India Built Shipping, p. 7.
74 Stark, *Female Tars*, p. 147.
75 BPP 1805 VIII: A List of persons who have been employed as Overseers since the 1st of January 1783, p. 52.
76 Lyon, *The Sailing Navy List*, p. 69.
77 David Cordingly, *Billy Ruffian: The Bellerophon and the Downfall of Napoleon* (London: Bloomsbury, 2003, repr. 2004), p. 329n.
78 Lyon, *The Sailing Navy List*, p. 150.
79 Lyon, *The Sailing Navy List*, p. 80.

Summary

It is a simple matter to brush aside or ignore one example of a woman apparently running a business, by assuming she had no 'day-to-day' involvement or merely held the 'purse-strings', but the evidence of Mrs Barnard and Mrs Ross suggests that their successful involvement in these complex, financially risky businesses was more than just chance.

In both cases, with their husband's death there was an immediate concern to reassure their biggest customer, the Navy Board, that the yard was in safe hands and that the contracts were safe. Such large vessels were major investments in time, money and risk. Whether the widow wished to or not, if the yard was in her name she had to complete the existing contracts and then pay off the debts to the timber merchants and other suppliers. Both women had lived in the yards since their marriage, although, aged sixty-four, Frances eventually moved out to a more suburban setting. By just being present in the yard, the day-to-day dealings and problems with suppliers, shipwrights and customers were familiar to them. Both Frances and Mary continued to seek further work for their yards. The competition for the navy contracts was fierce and they were successful in winning new business.

Merchant yards often had problems fulfilling the navy's exacting demands and many overstretched themselves, leading to delays that were contractually fined and, in the worst cases, bankruptcy. Both the Barnard and Ross yards had to manage the same problems of men, materials, cash flow, weather and customer requirements. Yet the ships launched from the yards of Mrs Barnard and Mrs Ross never gave cause for any penalty, the majority of them being launched within time. On their deaths they left sizeable estates for the next generation.

Wooden shipbuilding for the navy on such a large scale ended with peace in 1815, but Mrs Barnard and Mrs Ross were not the only women to run shipbuilding yards during the nineteenth century, as the following chapter will demonstrate.

9

Merchant Shipbuilders

The two warship builders, Mrs Barnard and Mrs Ross, were not wartime aberrations. Women had been managing shipyards for many years and continued to do so throughout the nineteenth century, albeit only in wooden shipbuilding. Building for the navy had its own challenges and wartime conditions brought problems of timber and labour supplies. However, building for merchants and shipowners was not without its problems and many of the same types of challenges had to be faced. Researching government suppliers is helped by the records that were kept, but this is not the case in the commercial world where few business accounts survive. The information on the merchant shipbuilders has therefore come from a wide variety of sources, from wills and ship registers to trade directories and government statistics. In this chapter the work of the merchant shipbuilder will be discussed and the challenges that men and women faced in running the business. Each woman had different circumstances to contend with both personally and professionally and so these are shown in a series of case studies.

The Women's 'Art and Business' of Shipbuilding

Cyprian May, shipbuilder of Plymouth, wrote his will in 1785 two years before his death. He left all of his 'yard buildings and fixtures' and half of his 'tool stock and materials relating and belonging to the art and business of a shipwright', not to his sons, but to his wife, Elizabeth.[1] Elizabeth May is not the only example of a wife who was considered by her husband to be capable of managing a shipbuilding business. Women shipbuilders described in this chapter had significant challenges to overcome in order to be successful, and for some shipbuilders, male or female, this simply meant avoiding bankruptcy. Business success was important, not because they were women, but because a good reputation and the trust of the customers were critical elements for a shipbuilding yard. The nature of these challenges in managing the business together with the importance of trust and reputation in attracting custom will be examined. There is also the question of why they ran these businesses. The cases identified are all widows, so were they merely acting as caretakers for underage sons or were there other motivations?

---

[1] TNA: PRO Prob 11/1154 Will of Cyprian May, Plymouth 1787.

8. The barquentine *Koh I Noor* (built by Mrs Jane Slade, managing owner Mrs Mary Hicks Hayes)
Source: Mrs Isabel Pickering

Every decade of the period from 1780 to 1880 had a woman in charge of a ship-building yard (see Table 38), even if some were in charge for the briefest of periods, such as Mrs Catherine Forster of South Shields who ran a yard between 1786 and 1791.[2] Margaret Reay is listed as a shipbuilder at Sun Hylton, North Township, Sunderland, Northumberland in *White's Directory* in 1847.[3] Margaret Wilson of Barrow-in-Furness is noted as the builder in 1868 of the *Mary Ann Mandel* and of the *Annie Brocklebank* launched in 1869.[4] These cases are not exclusive to Britain. Celestine Robicheau of Meteghan, Canada gave her occupation as shipbuilder when registering her thirty-two shares in the schooner *Friendly*, built in 1866.[5] The only woman shipbuilder in the *Oxford Dictionary of National Biography* is Isabella

[2] Amy M. Flagg, *Notes on the History of Shipbuilding in South Shields, 1746–1946* (South Tyneside, 1979), p. 5.
[3] *White's Directory of Northumberland 1847*.
[4] Tim Latham, *The Ashburner Schooners: The Story of the First Shipbuilders in Barrow-in-Furness* (Manchester: Ready Rhino Publications, 1991), p. 93.
[5] *Ships and Seamen of Atlantic Canada*, Memorial University of Newfoundland (1998), CD-Rom.

Elder of Govan who 'ran the business successfully for nine months' in 1869.[6] This is hardly a major achievement when compared with Ann Nicholls's twenty years and Elizabeth Evans's twenty-two years in charge.

Table 38. List of women shipbuilders

Name	Place	Known period of control*
Mrs Elizabeth May	Plymouth	1787
Mrs Catherine Forster	South Shields	1786–91
Mrs Frances Barnard	Thames	1795–1807
Mrs Elizabeth Gowan	Berwick	1802–4
Mrs Mary Ross	Rochester	1808–15
Mrs Ann Nicholls	Dartmouth	1829–49
Mrs Margaret Reay	Sunderland	1847
Mrs Rosanna Tucker	Bristol	1849–51
Mrs Margaret Salkeld	Blyth	1855
Mrs Ann Johnson	Bideford	1855–9
Mrs Margaret Wilson*	Barrow	1868
Mrs Isabella Elder	Govan	1869
Mrs Elizabeth Evans	Salcombe	1856–78
Mrs Elizabeth Luke	Charlestown	1873
Mrs Jane Slade	Polruan, Fowey	1870–83

* In some cases such as Mrs Wilson there is just one reference to her so the period of ownership is not known.

Sources: See text.

Among these women shipbuilders, seven case studies have been identified that represent the different phases in wooden shipbuilding during the nineteenth century, and the histories of these seven businesswomen show both differences and similarities in their approach to the challenges they faced. There are examples here from early to mid-century and then two further examples in the last days of wooden shipbuilding, which takes the evidence up to 1880.

The Business

In the days of the wooden sailing vessel, there were shipyards, or boatyards, in every maritime community.[7] The shipbuilder's yard was often the single largest employer of labour in that community and this was certainly the case in places

[6] Joan MacAlpine, 'Isabella Elder', Oxford Dictionary of National Biography. www.oxforddnb. com (accessed 18 June 2006).
[7] BPP 1805 VIII: An account showing the number of shipwrights and also of apprentices employed in the merchant yards of Great Britain according to the returns made to the Admiralty in April 1804, pp. 467–91.

such as Fowey, Polruan, Salcombe, Whitby and Mevagissey.[8] The shipyards were highly visible businesses, situated at the heart of the community, and the noise of the work served as a constant reminder of their presence. The launching of a ship was a major event with crowds of onlookers turning it into a festive occasion. Significant orders for new ships or major repairs were indeed matters for celebration for local tradesmen and women since the positive effect sent ripples well beyond the confines of the shipyard. In the majority of cases, the shipbuilder built the hull and main decks and fitted the masts and spars.[9] This provided work for shipwrights, caulkers, sawyers and apprentices, plus extra labour for non-skilled rough work. Suppliers of various materials, such as the wooden fastenings or treenails, the paint and ironwork, and the biggest single supplier, the timber merchant, all stood to gain. Once the basic vessel was built, it had to be rigged, and this involved the sailmakers, blockmakers, ropemakers and, in bigger towns, specialist mast and spar makers. To get the vessel ready for sea, depending on its role, further work had to be done to provide fixtures and fittings and this could involve a variety of additional workmen such as carpenters.[10] Finally the ship had to be crewed and victualled. For every ship built, the additional cost of the work was between 30 and 40 per cent of the first build cost (i.e. what the shipbuilder charged).[11]

The shipbuilder was a major contributor to the maritime economy and the women who ran the yards were significant figures. These businesses were not the small commercial trade businesses of the milliner, dressmaker or innkeeper which have been traditionally associated with women.[12] The sums of money and the business risks were of a different order, as will be seen.

The Merchant Yards in 1804

In 1804 the government, concerned with the urgent need to build up the nation's naval strength, commissioned a survey of the number of shipwrights in Britain and Ireland and this reveals a large number of shipyards around the coast. This is hardly surprising in a time when waterborne transport was an essential means of movement of goods and people. There were 510 merchant yards with an average of sixteen men to a yard.[13] Eighty per cent of the yards had a workforce of fewer than twenty men. The survey had required a separate category for caulkers, but the majority of shipwrights combined the two jobs, with the exception of the London-

8   CRO: PRO HO 107 1903, Lanteglos by Fowey Census 1851; PRO HO 107 1906, Mevagissey and Fowey Census 1851; Devon Local Studies Library (DLSL): RG 9 1424 Parish of Malborough Devon Census 1861; Whitby Library: HO 107/2374 1851 Whitby census.

9   Clive N. Ponsford, *Shipbuilding on the Exe: The Memoranda Book of Daniel Bishop Davy* (Exeter: Devon and Cornwall Record Society, 1988), p. 13.

10 Doe, 'Small Shipbuilding Businesses', p. 60.

11 Doe, 'Blockmakers, Sailmakers, Ropemakers, Blacksmiths and Brokers', p. 159.

12 Phillips, *Women in Business*.

13 BPP 1805 VIII: Account of the number of shipwrights, pp. 467–91.

based yards and those with strong London links such as Bucklers Hard, run by an ex-London shipwright, Adams.[14] Apprentices made up 42 per cent of the totals in the survey.[15] The twenty ports with the largest number of shipwrights and caulkers are shown in Table 39, and already by 1804 the northeast and Scotland are demonstrating the beginning of what was to become their dominance in shipbuilding.[16]

Table 39. Twenty largest ports for shipbuilding in Britain, 1804

		Shipwrights and caulkers			
	No. of yards	Above 50 yrs	Under 50 yrs	Apprentices	Total
Shields (North)	27	120	870	1089	2079
London	37	132	825	236	1193
Liverpool	17		327	160	487
Leith	4	19	135	208	362
Hull	8	34	171	129	334
Greenock	4	28	163	118	309
Whitby	8	38	89	138	265
Bristol	8	29	97	118	244
Yarmouth	14	6	96	135	237
Dartmouth	6	4	103	56	163
Scarborough	7	15	68	63	146
Dover	24	7	78	38	123
Guernsey	4		76	27	103
Chester	3	13	34	43	90
Falmouth	2	8	54	23	85
Bideford	6	8	13	63	84
Port Glasgow	3	4	24	50	78
Northfleet	1	3	57	18	78
Dundee	2	2	39	37	78
Poole	5	7	16	43	66

Source: BPP 1805 VIII: An account showing the number of shipwrights and also of apprentices employed in the merchant yards of Great Britain according to the returns made to the Admiralty in April 1804, 467 to 491.

The survey has limitations as there are omissions such as the Whitehaven shipbuilders, Brocklebank being one of them.[17] It must also be considered as just a snapshot of the numbers of men at a yard since the numbers of shipwrights and

---

[14] *Ibid.*; Barnard, *Building Britain's Wooden Walls*, p. 39.
[15] BPP 1805 VIII: Account of the number of shipwrights, p. 491.
[16] Ville, *Shipbuilding in the United Kingdom*.
[17] Michael K. Stammers, '"The High Character Obtained by Cumberland Ships": A Shipbuilding District in the Mid-Nineteenth Century', *International Journal of Maritime History*, 10 (1998), 121–50 (p. 129).

caulkers fluctuated considerably as work came and went.[18] Large numbers were unattached to yards for different reasons; in Greenock there were about 150 shipwrights 'out of employment for want of work' and at Liverpool there were between 500 and 600 working shipwrights unlinked to yards.[19]

The Site

For the majority of shipwrights/shipbuilders who set up in business the site of the yard was critical. While in the Westcountry, in particular, it has been common to talk of a single shipwright building a ship with some help from a few friends, the reality of business has been demonstrated from the records of the Mevagissey yard of Dunn and Henna. A shipbuilding business required a substantial site if large vessels were to be built and repaired. A site close to maritime activity was essential, unless like Dunn and Henna you and your customers had good reason to prefer a less noticeable site away from official eyes.[20] The site had to be spacious as timber took up a lot of room and space was needed for repair work alongside the building of new vessels, in order to provide an ongoing revenue stream.[21] It had to have ease of access to timber supplies and access to a source of manpower, although it has been suggested temporary accommodation for shipwrights could be provided by a hulk.[22] For small simple vessels a flat piece of beach above high water, or alongside a sufficiently deep river or inlet, was sufficient, but for the majority of yards this was inadequate. However, purpose-built docks were expensive and, in some cases, those built in the early nineteenth century in some of the smaller places were incapable of accommodating the later need for larger vessels.[23] Waterfront space was at a premium as the century continued, challenged by railways and later by new houses.[24] Shipyard sites rarely remained unoccupied; as soon as one shipbuilder vacated a site another swiftly moved in.[25]

Management

Shipwrighting was highly skilled and required a seven-year apprenticeship. Many of the shipyards were owned by men who had served their apprenticeship and then eventually set themselves up in business. The capital requirements for starting a

---

[18] Doe, 'Small Shipbuilding Businesses', pp. 53–4.
[19] BPP 1805 VIII: Account of the number of shipwrights, p. 475.
[20] Doe, 'Small Shipbuilding Businesses', pp. 21–4.
[21] See also, Stammers, '"The High Character Obtained by Cumberland Ships"', pp. 135–6.
[22] Holland, *Ships of British Oak*, p. 26.
[23] Doe, 'The Business of Shipbuilding', pp. 192–3; Michael Stammers, 'Slipways and Steamchests: The Archaeology of 18th–19th Century Wooden Merchant Shipyards in the United Kingdom', *International Journal of Nautical Archaeology*, 28 (1999), pp. 253–64.
[24] Doe, 'Blockmakers, Sailmakers, Ropemakers, Blacksmiths and Brokers', pp. 153–5; Stammers, '"The High Character Obtained by Cumberland Ships"', pp. 135–6.
[25] Doe, *Jane Slade of Polruan*, pp. 18, 43.

new business often meant that a business partner with access to funds was needed. The role of the shipbuilder was to provide the capital and the financial management, source supplies and get the orders. In this way, non-shipwrights owned and ran yards, such as Captain Dunn of Mevagissey and Robert Davy of Topsham.[26] The technical work needed fully qualified and experienced foremen, but the overall management required business knowledge and expertise which was not something that the shipwright apprenticeship necessarily provided. Shipbuilding was a lengthy business. A new vessel could take six months to two years or more to complete, depending on size and complexity.[27] Financial control was essential to maintain payments to suppliers and the workforce. Only the most financially secure builders could afford to build speculatively, paying out for men and timber before realising income from a sale.

Repair and New Build

The need for significant capital in shipbuilding meant that repair work was an essential revenue stream, but figures for new ships are more easily acquired than good information on repair work. In James Dunn's yard in Mevagissey 55 per cent of their revenue came from repair over the period from 1800 to 1815.[28] The view in the London yards at the same time was similar; Samuel Lordan, who worked for Dudman's yard, estimated that repair and building work were about equal.[29] The two types of work were, of course, tightly linked. A ship tended to return to its original yard for maintenance work and repairs, as the following evidence to the Select Committee of 1813–14 shows:

> Question: 'By seeing the ship when she comes in you know generally the sort of repairs she wants?' Answer: 'Paint may make ship look very fine, and when you come to look it may want everything.' Question: 'Before they begin to work upon her you have general idea what is the sort of repair she wants?' Answer: 'Certainly they always know the age and service she has done; her history tells us.'[30]

Managing Men

The shipbuilder had to be able to manage, usually with the help of the foreman, a supply of labour, both skilled and unskilled.[31] Men could be laid off when there

26 Doe, 'The Business of Shipbuilding', p. 192; Ponsford, *Shipbuilding on the Exe*, p. 70.
27 TNA: PRO C10/167 Main Ledger; Doe, *Jane Slade of Polruan*, p. 61; Stammers, '"The High Character Obtained by Cumberland Ships"', p. 125.
28 Doe, 'The Business of Shipbuilding', p. 198.
29 BPP 1813–14 VIII Minutes of the Evidence on Petitions relating to East India Built Shipping, p. 137.
30 *Ibid.*, Evidence of Larkin shipowner, p. 119.
31 Doe, 'The Business of Shipbuilding', pp. 204–9.

was no work, but hiring enough men when there was work to be done could be problematic.[32] In 1809 it was reported that William Row in Newcastle had 'great difficulty in procuring timber and workmen to carry on the work, the workmen having left the North of England to work in His Majesty's yards'.[33]

The men had to be prepared to work at the wages offered and, in a very small community with few competitive options for the shipwright, the arrangements could be settled easily between the foreman and the men he knew. John Hillman, a Thames surveyor, recalled shipwrights' strikes over pay in 1801 and 1802 in London, and wages rose as a result. Caulkers and sawyers had also gone on strike at various times.[34] This type of situation was less likely in the smaller communities, but here the loss of men to other yards was the bigger problem, which made the recruiting of apprentices even more important. The increase in the price per ton of ships on the Thames was put down to the increase in wages demanded by the shipwrights and the increased cost of materials.[35] These costs had to be managed and passed on, if possible, to the customer, a task that was not easy when the market was slack. The men worked in gangs under a foreman and on a large ship each gang was assigned part of the ship to work on. One ship of 1,200 tons might require twenty-four to thirty shipwrights plus other labour.[36] This was only the number of men working on the new building. Repair work was less predictable and new building was 'the kind of employ that affords the most steady and constant employ to shipwright and artificers'.[37] Much of the hiring and management of the men was the responsibility of the foreman, who was a senior shipwright.[38] Hillman, a surveyor, confirmed that only fully served shipwrights were employed in building, although there was also a lot of rough work done by unskilled men. The men came from different parts of the country, but were all skilled shipwrights.

Management Matters and Trust

As a later Victorian declared, talking of the days of the building of vast steel ships, 'A shipyard may be equipped with the most modern plant, may have a highly trained technical staff, and first class foremen', but he foresaw problems 'unless the commercial department is thoroughly efficient, and organised'.[39] In the same way,

---

[32] Holland, *Ships of British Oak*, p. 54.
[33] TNA: PRO ADM 49/102.
[34] BPP 1813–14 VIII: Minutes of the Evidence on Petitions relating to East India Built Shipping, pp. 14–15.
[35] BPP 1813–14 VIII: Minutes of the Evidence on Petitions relating to East India Built Shipping, p. 121.
[36] *Ibid.*
[37] BPP 1813–14 VIII: Minutes of the Evidence on Petitions relating to East India Built Shipping, p. 135.
[38] Doe, 'The Business of Shipbuilding', pp. 209–10.
[39] Gordon Boyce and Simon Ville, *The Development of Modern Business* (Basingstoke: Palgrave, 2002), p. 256.

his predecessors in the days of the wooden vessel also needed to be highly efficient in managing current contracts and bidding for future work, while retaining
customers.

Trust was a vital element in commercial success. The customers had to have
faith in the honesty and integrity of the shipbuilder, first because comparatively
large sums of money were involved, and second because the ship represented a
significant ongoing investment that could only be realised if it was well built, with
good sailing qualities. For the customer it was impossible to check the shipwright's
bill.

> The fact is when you put a ship into a builder's hands, a respectable man, you put
> her into his yard and you have every confidence in him, and he goes on with repairs;
> you have a surveyor to see the work is well done, but you have no check whatever
> on the number of men employed, or time, at all.[40]

Larkin was speaking as a London shipowner, but his words reflected the views
of most customers. He was pressed on this point by the Select Committee who
queried: 'You therefore must rely entirely on the person who contracts?' 'On the
honour and integrity of the person who contracts', replied Larkin.[41] As in all
complicated and technical projects, even with the most careful of checks or the
use of specialist surveyors, in the end the customer had to rely on his choice of
contractor and let him, or in this case her, get on with the job for which they were
paid. In the smaller communities where there was less competition, and sometimes just one shipyard, fraudulent or just incompetent practice by the shipbuilder
was a potentially greater betrayal of trust.

Reputation

The ship itself, its lines, soundness and reputation for sailing qualities, was the
testimonial to the shipbuilders. These matters were a regular topic of conversation among the masters and men and the word on the street (or in most cases in
the public houses in ports) was the advertisement for the shipbuilder. Newspaper
announcements of launches were additional advertisements with phrases such
as 'beautifully modelled schooner' or 'fine clipper schooner' or 'superior clipper
schooner'.[42] Almost every part of the country laid claim to the excellence of their
ships, with phrases such as 'Shipshape and Bristol fashion' reflecting the toughness

---

40 BPP 1813–14 VIII: Minutes of Evidence taken before Select Committee on East India shipping. Evidence of John Pascal Larkin, p. 128.
41 *Ibid.*
42 *Royal Cornwall Gazette*, 11 May 1872 launch of *Snowflake*, 7 May 1870 launch of *The Highland
Lass*; see also Doe, *Jane Slade of Polruan*, p. 37.

of the Bristol ships, and the recognition by Lloyd's of the well built Cumbrian ships.[43]

The men and women who ran shipbuilding yards had an important task to maintain the reputation of the yard and to keep the business going, an aim supported by those both within and outside the business who were dependent upon its success. The following case studies of eight women shipbuilders and their careers highlight some of the challenges.

Merchant Shipbuilding during the French Wars

The period of the French wars was a highly productive time for shipyards and not just for the building of war ships as seen in Chapter 8. The five-year period from 1800 to 1804 was the peak of merchant shipbuilding for the southwest during which time they produced 10 per cent of the national total. The region did not see such levels of activity again as shipbuilding moved increasingly northwards during the rest of the century.[44] Plymouth was dominated by the royal dockyard, but there were also merchant yards, one of which was owned by Cyprian May.

Mrs Elizabeth May of Plymouth

In contemplating the future in 1785, May was concerned to 'avoid controversies after my death'. He had three sons, Charles, Richard and John, and two daughters, one of whom was married. In his lengthy will he made his wife Elizabeth the executrix, and made bequests of £20 each and various properties, of which he seemed to own several, to his children. So far, this was unexceptional until it came to the matter of his disposal of his shipbuilding business. His wife Elizabeth was left the use of his yard, building and fixtures. After her death or remarriage it was to go to his son John and his son-in-law, Wendy Oxford.[45] He also left half of 'all my tool stock and materials relating and belonging to the art and business of a shipwright' to his wife and half to Wendy Oxford. He made the 'express condition that my said wife Elizabeth and Wendy Oxford shall and may jointly carry on the business of a shipwright'. Cyprian passed over his son, Charles, who may have been working in another occupation. Of his son, Richard, his view was that he 'may continue to be employed in my said yard as long as he behaves well'. He also requested that his son, John, and his daughter, Patient, were to be maintained 'in the same manner and form which I myself do now', which suggests they were underage and still at home. The will expresses his belief in the business abilities

---

[43] G. Farr, *Shipbuilding in the Port of Bristol* (Greenwich: National Maritime Museum, 1977); Stammers, "'The High Character Obtained by Cumberland Ships'", p. 147.

[44] D. Starkey, 'The Shipbuilding Industry of the Southwest', in Ville, *Shipbuilding in the United Kingdom*, p. 78.

[45] Wendy was a man's name in Devon and Cornwall in the eighteenth century.

of his wife, but with the safeguard of his experienced son-in-law Wendy Oxford at her side as the technical partner. Elizabeth was not merely caretaking the yard until her sons were of age as they could not inherit until her death or remarriage. Elizabeth and Wendy, whether they wanted it or not, were in partnership.[46]

Cyprian died in 1787 and in June the same year Elizabeth began the process of settling her business affairs by advertising to 'all persons having any claim of demand on the estate of Cyprian May'. With an eye to the importance of continuity in the business and to ensure potential customers were clear that the firm was still in business she additionally announced that 'The business of ship-building will be carried on ... under the firm of May & Co.'[47] Not, it is interesting to note, May and Oxford, since Elizabeth owned the premises and Wendy Oxford owned just half of the stock and tools.

There is no other information about the size of this yard and no identification of any vessels built. The early shipping registers did not note the name of the shipbuilder, so there is no reliable way of identifying vessels built by Cyprian or his successors, May and Co. In the event, the partnership between mother-in-law and son-in-law did not survive; 'a new brig now on stocks at Teat's hill ... length of keel 52 ft 6 ... 103 tons measurement – must be positively sold to close a partner-ship account between the builders'.[48] The partnership between Mrs Elizabeth May and Mr Wendy Oxford was dissolved in August 1790.[49] After this the information disappears and by 1844 in the local trade directory there is a John May who is a ship and commission agent and there is no mention of anyone by the name of Oxford.[50]

Mrs Elizabeth Gowan of Berwick

Less is known of the one woman who does appear in the 1804 list of shipbuilders. Mrs Gowan (or Gowans) of Berwick is listed in the parliamentary survey with a comparatively large yard with twenty-nine shipwrights and apprentices. Her father, Arthur Byram, established the business in 1751. Elizabeth married Robert Gowan, a ship carpenter, in 1781 and had six children, two sons and four daugh-ters. Her husband took over from her father and when Elizabeth was widowed, in 1802, she was aged forty-five and her eldest son only thirteen. Robert Gowan died intestate leaving a reasonable-sized estate assessed for duty between £1,000 and £2,000.[51] This compares well with the Henna and Dunn yard in 1806 which had an inventory value of £551. This inventory was mainly timber and some equipment

---

46   TNA: PRO Prob 11/1154 Will of Cyprian May, Plymouth 1787.
47   *Western Flying Post*, 4 June 1787.
48   *Western Flying Post*, 14 June 1790.
49   *Western Flying Post*, 2 August 1790.
50   1844 *Pigot's Directory*.
51   TNA: PRO IR/26/323 Administration of Robert Gowan of Berwick, 1802; Berwick Record Office, 'Gowans Shipyard' typescript (with thanks to Mr Derek Janes).

as the qualified shipwrights provided their own tools and the yard was rented at a rate of £20 per year. For most shipbuilding yards the needs were simple – space for building, repair and storage.[52] Mrs Gowan's yard is listed in an 1806 directory which refers to her yard building large vessels of 500 tons, and her stewardship kept the firm going. The business continued after her death; it was still very active in 1855, but went out of business in 1878.[53]

Mid-Century Shipyards

An 1833 parliamentary committee investigated the reasons for the prolonged depression that had impacted the country's industry as a whole. In particular it examined the plight of the shipping industry which was described as unprofitable with high levels of bankruptcy and declining shipowning and shipbuilding.[54] As Ville points out, shipping and shipbuilding can often appear to increase after the downturn in an economy because of the length of time taken to build ships, and he also suggests that the employment of apprentices encouraged shipbuilders to continue building even in the early part of a depression.[55] From the 1850s, however, production rose, but the southwest never again saw the scale of the tonnage output at its peak in 1800 as the yards in the north continued to grow their share of the market.[56] All the examples here are from the southwest. There was one woman shipbuilder in Blyth, Durham noted in *Slater's Directory* in 1855, but little else is known of her.[57]

Mrs Ann Nicholls of Dartmouth

Ann Nicholls was left the shipyard in Dartmouth in her husband's will in 1830. Ann and Ambrose had three sons – the two eldest were over twenty-one – and there seems to have been some doubt whether the sons wished to carry on the business. Ambrose Nicholls bequeathed the shipyard to his wife outright, but after her death it was to be offered to his first son, William Henry, for £500. If he refused to take it then the second son, Henry, was to have the chance to buy it, and the same for the third son, Ambrose, should Henry refuse. Ambrose senior died on 12 December 1829.[58] The yard was run by Ann until her death twenty years later and in 1841, seven years before her death, she had drawn up plans

52 Doe, 'Small Shipbuilding Businesses', p. 22.
53 *Clayton's Directory*; *Good's Directory*, 1806; Berwick Record Office, 'Gowans Shipyard' typescript.
54 Simon Ville, 'Shipping in the Port of Sunderland 1815–45: A Counter-Cyclical Trend', *Business History*, 32 (1990), 32–51 (p. 32).
55 Ville, 'Shipping in the Port of Sunderland 1815–45: A Counter-Cyclical Trend', p. 33.
56 Starkey, 'Devon's Shipbuilding Industry, 1786–1970', p. 78.
57 *Slater's Commercial Directory of Durham, Northumberland and Yorkshire*, 1855.
58 DRO: Will of Ambrose Nicholls 1830.

to extend the yard. William Henry had predeceased his mother in 1844, Henry refused the yard (he was already running a yard in Kingswear) and Ambrose junior also refused (he subsequently emigrated). The yard was put up for auction and sold on 30 September 1849 to Henry Nicholls who purchased it for £300.[59] Here again is an example of a woman running a yard in her own right, but little further information on Ann is available.

Mrs Rosanna Tucker of Bristol

John Whitfield Tucker senior was a shipbuilder in Appledore, north Devon and moved to Bristol in 1818. By 1843 he was in partnership with his son of the same name.[60] Tucker senior died in 1844 and his will divided the estate, including his share of the yard, equally between his four children. In recognition of his existing share in the yard, John Whitfield Tucker junior received £100 less than his siblings. He was, however, given the chance to buy his father's share of the business and was given a period of time in which to pay for this should it become necessary. Cash was needed and so John junior together with his brother-in-law, a co-executor, began to sell his father's shares in ships.[61] John senior had invested in ships other than his own such as the Ilfracombe-built *Venus* and the Cape Breton-built *Champion*.[62] The 43-ton *Mary*, built by Tucker senior, was wholly owned and was sold to the master, not outright but on a two-year mortgage.[63] So John junior became the sole owner of a cash-strapped business and in the short time remaining to him did not invest in any other ships. He built two ships, 79-ton *Idea* and 185-ton *Ann*, and died five years after his father, leaving no will.[64]

Rosanna Tucker thus became a Bristol shipbuilder in late 1849. In the 1851 census her occupation, however, is given as needlewoman and she has three children under the age of five, but there is no doubt that she was active in the shipbuilding business. There was a half-finished ship on the slipway and when the *Leonore Devas* was launched in November 1849 for the Llanelli owners, Rosanna signed the certificate as the executor to her late husband.[65] The next vessel from the yard was the 46-ton sloop *Elizabeth* which was launched in 1851, and the shipping register confirms that the builder's certificate was signed by Rosanna on 11 November.[66] The ship was owned by Henry Cawser, a master mariner, but he had difficulty raising the full amount so Rosanna provided a mortgage for twenty-four shares. From this arrangement she had the benefit of small sums of interest on the

59 Ivor Smart, 'Dartmouth – the Hardness Shipyards from Zion Slip to King's Quay', *Maritime Southwest*, 10 (1997), 99–136 (pp. 122–3).
60 Farr, *Shipbuilding in the Port of Bristol*, p. 6.
61 Bristol Record Office (BRO): 37908/1/7 1/1846, 22/1846, 11/1847.
62 BRO: 37908/1/7 46/1843.
63 BRO: 37908/1/7 27/1846.
64 BRO: 37908/1/7 29/1847, 21/1849.
65 TNA: PRO BT/107/323 Llanelli register 2/1849.
66 BRO: 37908/1/7 62/1851.

outstanding balance when she might instead have had a share in any proceeds from the trade of the vessel. This has the appearance of a struggling yard, yet Rosanna had confidence in the continuity of the yard when she signed up an apprentice in February 1855. William Robertson was apprenticed to Rosanna Tucker, widow of John Whitfield Tucker, shipbuilder, for seven years.[67] Apprentices were also a source of labour and brought in a small income.

In 1858 Rosanna finally obtained the administration of her husband's estate, but just one year later she also died young.[68] Her will left no specific information relating to the yard, her main concern being for the upkeep and maintenance of her children. The business appears to survive, as the name J W Tucker reappears as a builder on a different site in Bristol in 1858, launching a barque called *Aid*.[69] Overall, from 1819, Farr identifies eighteen vessels built by the Tuckers, one of which was the schooner *Magic* built in 1833. Most of the vessels were schooners and were an average of 93 tons, showing that Tucker's yard was small in comparison with the dominant Bristol shipbuilder, Hilhouse, and his output.[70] This probably explains the constant cash problems that beset the shipyard.

Mrs Ann Johnson of Bideford

Rosanna's contemporary was Mrs Ann Johnson who in 1851 was aged fifty-two and living in Barnstaple Street, Bideford, in a shipyard at East-The-Water close to the bridge. Her husband Robert was a shipbuilder employing twenty-four men and they had one son aged seventeen, John, and two daughters, Emma and Mary, all still at home. In the same road lived another son, William Johnson, aged twenty-nine, described as a shipyard labourer. Three of the Johnson children were born in Monmouthshire from where they had returned to Robert's home town of Bideford about nine years before.[71]

Robert died in 1855 and in his will he did not envisage his wife having any involvement in his business, leaving her the contents of his house except 'my account books papers and all articles of trade relating to my business of a shipbuilder'. The rest of his property was put in trust and his trustees were Richard Martin, harbourmaster, and John Toms, accountant. The business was to be offered to his son John if at the time of death he was working with his father, and the terms were generous. He only needed to pay for one-quarter of the business and no consideration for goodwill or trade. If he bought on a loan then he could, with suitable security, pay for it over time. If he refused to buy, then the trustees, after completing the building of any vessels on contract, could sell the business.

[67] BRO: 39449/1: City of Bristol Apprentice indenture.
[68] BRO: 08025(59) Administration of estate of John Whitfield Tucker granted to Rosina Tucker, widow June 11th 1858.
[69] Farr, *Shipbuilding in the Port of Bristol*, p. 6.
[70] Farr, *Shipbuilding in the Port of Bristol*, pp. 37–46.
[71] TNA: PRO Census HO/107/1895.

Ann was to receive the interest of the estate during her lifetime and after her death or remarriage the property was to be divided into eight parts with one part each to his sons William, Robert, Charles and John and two parts each to his two daughters. The executor was named as John Toms.[72]

It does seem that John Johnson took over from his father as a shipbuilder although the attribution of the shipbuilder's name on the subsequent vessels is somewhat confusing. However, Ann, far from fading into the background as the grieving widow, is said to have taken an 'active part for the following four years or so, even signing builder's certificates. The son, John, carried on from 1858, at first using the title Robert Johnson and son.'[73] The ships built during Ann's steward-ship are shown in Table 40.

Table 40. Ships built by Johnson's, Bideford, 1855–1858

Year	Ship name	Tons
1855	*Alma*	121
	Coronation	42
1856	*Louisa Braginton*	280
	Renown	64
1857	*Criteria*	126
	Sanspariel	132
	Sarah Smith	192
	Try Again	104
	Circe	128
	William S Green	92

Source: G. Farr, *Shipbuilding in North Devon*, National Maritime Museum Monograph no. 22 (Greenwich, 1976), pp. 39–40.

Ann's involvement may lie in the clause in her husband's will that gave John the opportunity to buy the business over time. Providing financial security or working with the trustees, Ann could help him run the business until 1858 when, with the proceeds of the sale of ships, he could fully own it. The yard built a range of ships from small smacks to barques and, thanks to Ann's help, in the first few years after the death of Robert, the yard continued successfully until 1877.[74]

The Last Years of Wooden Shipbuilding

In the mid-nineteenth century, despite the inroads made into some of their tradi-tional routes by steam, wooden sailing ships still had a future. Steam was not yet as efficient and sail was still the predominant class in the registers. Steam, while

---

[72]   TNA: PRO Prob: 11/2208 Will of Robert Johnson, Bideford 1855.
[73]   G. Farr, *Shipbuilding in North Devon* (Greenwich: National Maritime Museum, 1976), p. 10.
[74]   Farr, *Shipbuilding in North Devon*.

useful for taking ships in and out of harbours, had yet to make its presence felt in trade. However, by 1871, with the invention of the compound engine and increased bunkering sites around the world, steam was beginning to encroach on traditional sailing routes.[75] Shipowners needed to look at niche markets where sail, which was cheaper to build and maintain, could still compete effectively with steam for freight. The transatlantic fruit trade provided such an opportunity.

The main vessel being built in the yards was the topsail schooner. Shipowners had been trading for some time in the salt fish trade from Newfoundland and the fruit trade from the Azores, West Indies and Mediterranean. The fruit schooners were purpose-built, designed for speed, with a cargo-carrying capacity that ensured the delicate fruit was not damaged on the voyage and was carried in small quantities to maintain good prices in the market. Salcombe vessels were particularly well known for this trade which had the ships racing back from the West Indies in the winter to get to the markets in London and Bristol.[76]

Mrs Elizabeth Evans of Salcombe

In the 1861 census Elizabeth Evans is shown as a widow aged fifty-four and her occupation is given, and accepted by the enumerator, as a shipbuilder employing twenty-three men and boys. Her son Joseph, then aged twenty-one, was a ship carpenter as was her fourteen-year-old son, William.[77]

Elizabeth had inherited the yard from her husband John who died in 1856. At this time their eldest son, Joseph, was just fourteen, the age at which apprentices might start their seven years of training. John had made a simple will leaving his estate to his 'dear wife Elizabeth Evans formerly Trinnick'.[78] Unlike Ann Johnson or Elizabeth May, Mrs Evans had clear title to the whole business from the beginning of her widowhood and there was no stipulation about the yard in the event of her potential remarriage.

The Evans shipyard was well established and had been in business since 1815.[79] On the stocks at the time of her husband's death was the *Eugenie*, a 136-ton brigantine, and the ship was duly launched.[80] In 1858 the 171-ton *Clara* was launched and the newspaper report speaks of the launch of the 'clipper' from Mr Evans's shipyard.[81] Shares in the *Clara* were owned by a wide range of local names including Henry Grant who was also the main owner of the *Eugenie*. Elizabeth is listed as an

[75] Mercantile Navy List 1872, xxii–xxvi; see also Graham S. Graham, 'The Ascendancy of the Sailing Ship, 1850–85', *Economic History Review*, 9 (1956), pp. 74–88.

[76] Starkey, 'The Ports, Seaborne Trade and Shipping Industry', p. 46.

[77] DLSL: RG9 1424 Census Malborough 1861.

[78] DRO: Will of John Evans shipbuilder ref 399.

[79] Muriel Murch, David Murch and Len Fairweather, *Salcombe Harbour Remembered* (Plymouth: P.D.S. Printers ,1982), p. 13.

[80] Pers. corr. Roger Barrett, 2 October 2005.

[81] *Kingsbridge Gazette*, 3 July 1858.

investor with two shares and her occupation is given as widow.[82] The news report on the *Clara* has an unusual additional piece of information mentioning that the vessel was built 'under the superintendence of Mr Bunker'.[83] The reporter intended to give further confidence in the yard by naming the male supervisor.

Whether the Salcombe shipowners were concerned about a woman running a yard or not, the ships continued to be launched: the *Mary Ann* in 1860 for Balkwill, the *Mary Helen* in 1861 and the *Avon* in 1863.[84] Elizabeth Evans owned shares in the last two vessels, with four shares in the 140-ton schooner *Mary Helen*, built for Sladen, a well known shipowner.[85] The *Ringleader* in 1864 was the 'largest schooner built in Salcombe' and was followed by the *Argyra* and *Phantom*.[86] By 1870, when Mrs Evans was aged sixty-three, despite the persistence of the news reports that the ships were launched from the yard of Mr Evans, Elizabeth is listed as a shipbuilder in the trade directory and her son Joseph is also a shipbuilder, but based at the Shipwrights Arms. The third named shipbuilder in Salcombe at this time is Mr James Vivian.[87]

Two years later the *Sophie* was launched and among the many shareowners is Joseph with four shares; however he is listed not as a shipbuilder, but as a shipowner. The shipbuilder's name, which in the ship register transcripts was not stated for the previous ships, is now given in full: 'Mrs Elizabeth Evans of Salcombe'.[88] At the age of sixty-five she was still running the yard. Elizabeth died in 1876 and her headstone simply notes her as the wife of John Evans, shipbuilder.[89] After her death there was just one final ship launched from the yard, *Creole*, in 1878, which was quite likely to have been started before 1876. Mrs Evans was one of the most successful women shipbuilders; during her time at least twelve ships were built in her yard, many of them destined for the fruit trade (see Table 41).

Mrs Jane Slade of Polruan

Also a yard with a reputation for fine schooners in the fruit trade was Slade's yard at Polruan where Jane Slade became the head of the firm in 1870. Jane was born and brought up in the Cornish village of Polruan across the harbour from Fowey. Her father, William Salt, was a master mariner and the harbourmaster for Fowey harbour. Polruan still is today a small tight-knit community and was even more so in the nineteenth century. The biggest employers were the shipyards, and Jane, like Elizabeth Evans, grew up with the sights and the sounds of ships being built. Jane

82 TNA: PRO BT 108/54.
83 *Kingsbridge Gazette*, 3 July 1858.
84 TNA: PRO BT 108/69, 79.
85 *Ibid.*
86 *Kingsbridge Gazette*, 14 November 1864, TNA: PRO BT 108/97, 102.
87 *Malborough and Salcombe Commercial Directory*, 1870.
88 TNA: PRO BT 108/127.
89 Cookworthy Museum Notes by L. Collin's: Monumental inscriptions.

Table 41. Ships built in Evans's yard, Salcombe, 1856–1878

Year	Ship name	Tons
1856	*Eugenie*	136
1858	*Clara*	171
1860	*Mary Ann*	144
1861	*Mary Helen*	140
1863	*Avon*	184
1864	*Ringleader*	203
1866	*Argyra*	229
1867	*Phantom*	249
1869	*Leader*	112
1870	*Endymion*	252
1872	*Sophie*	106
1878	*Creole*	289

Note: Three further ships are also said to have been built: *Aurora* (1860), *Vesper* (1874) and *Lady Mary* (1875) (personal correspondence, Mr Brian Harding, descendant of Mrs Evans, 3 March 2005).

Source: TNA: PRO BT 108/54, 69, 79, 87, 97, 102, 112, 117, 127 Shipping Register transcripts.

married Christopher Slade, a shipwright, in 1830. The couple started their married life in the new Russell Inn, owned by William Salt. William and his son-in-law went into business together in ship repair and shipbuilding – William who owned considerable property providing the site for a new shipyard. While Christopher ran the yard, Jane brought up her family of nine children and ran the Russell Inn, helped by various nieces who lived in. As the ship size increased, Christopher expanded his sites and by 1870 he owned or leased four of the five shipbuilding sites in Polruan. Polruan was by now the main shipbuilding location in the port of Fowey. Slade's yard and Butson's yard were the biggest shipbuilders and both firms built ships for local owners, many of which were in the fruit trade.[90]

Christopher died in February 1870, at which time his eldest son William, aged thirty-five, worked in the yard alongside his brothers, John, aged thirty-one, and Philip, aged twenty-one. Another son, Christopher, had trained as a shipwright, but was now a customs officer in Fowey. Christopher senior had drawn up his will in 1860 and left his whole estate including his stock in trade as a shipbuilder and innkeeper in trust for his children. Jane as sole executrix was to have the full use of the trust during her widowhood. He had neither assumed nor demanded that his sons carry on the business; it was to be their decision.[91]

It was not his sons who took over the business. While they continued to work in the yard providing the technical knowledge and supervision, the firm's name was changed to Mrs Jane Slade and Sons. Christopher had died in February and in June of that year the *Jane Slade* was launched in Polruan and the largest

90 Doe, *Jane Slade of Polruan*, pp. 53–7.
91 Doe, *Jane Slade of Polruan*, p. 35.

shareholder with thirty-six shares was Jane Slade, shipbuilder. The schooner's first master was Jane's eldest son, Thomas, and the crew agreement in 1871 gives Jane as the managing owner. Jane continued to run the Russell Inn and also had an interest in the local coal business. In 1871 when her father William Salt died, she inherited his shipyard (which he had purchased in order to set up Christopher in business) and the Russell Inn. Perhaps the most telling evidence of his view of Jane's business abilities was that he left her all his business papers, the contents of his desk, and appointed her, rather than her brother, as the executrix of his will.

Throughout the rest of her life the yard was known as Mrs Jane Slade and Sons and she was listed as shipbuilder in the local directory, although the press, as with Mrs Evans, continued to refer to Messrs Slade and Sons. Her yard turned out four more vessels (see Table 42) and the last was the *E S Hocken*, which was billed as the largest vessel built in the Port of Fowey.[92]

Table 42. Ships built in Slade's yard, Polruan, 1870–1879

Year	Ship name	Tons
1870	*Jane Slade*	159
1872	*Snowflake*	157
1874	*Silver Spray*	176
1877	*Koh I Noor*	243
1879	*E S Hocken*	296

Source: Cornwall Record Office: MSR FOW/5–6. Shipping Registers.

A list of shares shows that Jane traded widely in shares in ships, buying and selling shares in many non-Slade-built vessels (see Table 43). The evidence of these shares may also suggest these were ships repaired or maintained by her business. In 1881 she had given her occupation as ship's accountant. While having retired from day-to-day work in the yards and inn, she was still keeping a close eye on financial matters and remained as head of the firm until her death in 1883. She left no will, possibly assuming that Christopher's will was sufficient. The business survived remarkably well to become one of the last ship repair yards on the south coast of Cornwall, eventually being finally sold out of the Slade family in 1943.[93]

Unfit for Purpose? The Businessman's Wife

Bessie Rayner Parkes called for a change of culture and railed against a system that gave middle-class women few occupations other than governess. She pointed out that the lower classes of women who were housemaids, cooks and nurses

---

92 Ward-Jackson, *Ships and Shipbuilders*, p. 60.
93 Doe, *Jane Slade of Polruan*, pp. 115–16, 103.

Table 43. List of shares owned by Jane Slade

Year	Ship	Built	Occupation	No.	Source	
1871	Concord	PEI	Widow	4	Buys	
1870	Jane Slade	Slade, Polruan	Shipbuilder	26	Buys*	
1870	Alert	Butson, Polruan	Widow	46	Inherits	Sells 1870
1873	Alexandrina	Banff	Innkeeper	2	Buys	
1872	Calenick	Llanelly	Widow	4	Buys	
1870	Isabella	Dartmouth	Widow	2	Inherits	
1871	Kingaloch	Nova Scotia	Widow	4	Buys	
1877	Koh I Noor	Slade, Polruan	Shipbuilder	2	Buys*	
1876	Louise Charlotte	Germany	Shipbuilder	4	Buys	
1874	Silver Spray	Slade, Polruan	Widow	17	Buys	Sells in 1874
1872	Sir Robert Hodgson	PEI	Widow	2	Buys	
1872	Snowflake	Slade, Polruan	Shipbuilder	6	Buys*	Sells 1 in 1872
1865	Jane & Ann	Fife	Widow	2	Inherits	
1870	Wild Wave	PEI	Widow	2	Inherits	
1870	Mary Helen	Ramsgate	Widow	2	Inherits	
1872	Ocean Traveller	Appledore	Widow	1	Buys	
1877	Adelaide	Padstow	Widow	3	Buys	
1873	Lady Ernestine	Cremyll	Widow	2	Buys	

* Original investor on launch.

Source: Cornwall Record Office: MSR FOW/5–7. Shipping Registers.

> are all women working on their own account and away from their own home,
> yet we do not find that tradesmen consider them unlikely to make good wives.
> Again all dressmakers, shopkeepers, charwomen etc earn an independent liveli-
> hood before marriage and in many cases continue to do so afterwards, yet we
> never hear a word about the unfitness of their purpose. The real truth is that very
> nearly three fourths of the adult women of this country, above the age of 20 are
> independent factors.

She was quoting from the census figures of 1851 and 1861.[94] Her call was
directed mainly at the lack of real opportunities for single women since there
was an assumption that a married middle-class woman had no such need as her
husband would provide for her. Yet not all husbands were able to provide for their
wives. 'An absent, ailing or incompetent husband still brought many women into
business because of the need to support a family.'[95] Nor were all wives content to
take a back seat in family enterprises.

When considering the occupations of wives and widows in the 1851 census, the
Registrar General wrote that 'the duties of a wife, a mother and a mistress of a
family can only be efficiently performed by unremitting attention', although he did
concede that 'women in certain branches of business at home render important
services; such as the wives of farmers, of small shopkeepers, innkeepers, shoe-

---

94 Parkes, *Essays on Woman's Work*, p. 146.
95 Kwolek-Folland, *Incorporating Women*, p. 59.

makers, butchers'.[96] Both he and Bessie Parkes might have been surprised by the numbers of businesswomen in this book.

Women have been rightly described as the hidden investment and the extent of the wife's influence on the business cannot be determined. The rare cases such as Mrs Janet Taylor, who ran her navigation school and business fully in her own name and not her husband's, hint at a breed of woman who was not content to be just the power behind the throne. There are just a few other examples, such as Lady Wigram. Sir Robert Wigram was a very powerful man. Self-made, he had come from being a ship's surgeon to become one of the wealthiest men in London. He was a significant shipowner, particularly of East India ships, a promoter of the East India docks, an MP and a shipbuilder. He married twice and his second wife, Eleanor, was a very active philanthropist. Wigram said of his wife, 'I never did undertake any businesses of moment without consultation with my wife, and can truly say it has much promoted my fortune.'[97] He was not the only man who saw his wife as an important figure in his business deliberations. Lady Charlotte Guest worked alongside her husband in his foundry in Wales and, although it is a non-British example, so did Sophia Henschel whose husband ran the largest locomotive manufacturing company in Germany.[98] Such visibly companionate marriages and supportive partnerships are known, and another example is that of Mrs Beeton.[99] Isabella became an active partner in her husband's publishing business, working as a journalist and editor and accompanying him to work on the commuter train into London and on business trips to Paris.[100] These situations were not unusual, just hard to uncover.

Parkes believed that the two great obstacles facing the woman who wished to be independent in business were the 'want of courage to face social opinion in a new path, and the want of a little Money to start with'.[101] A disregard for convention or the support of a husband could help with the first and an inheritance could help with the second.

The majority of women who ran maritime businesses are discovered when they become widows as they step out from behind the veil of coverture. It was a significant challenge for a woman to manage both home and business. While a married man was able to leave the family considerations and social concerns to his wife, many of these businesswomen had young children or grandchildren to care for. The businesses they ran were not necessarily easy or simple concerns, many were

---

[96] BPP 1853 LXXXVIII Census of England and Wales 1851 Population Tables, 1851.
[97] Henry Green and Robert Wigram, *The Chronicles of Blackwall Yard, Part 1* (London, 1881), p. 54.
[98] Guest and John, *Lady Charlotte*; Robert Beachy, 'Profit and Propriety: Sophie Henschel and Gender Management in the German Locomotive Industry', in *Women, Business and Finance in Nineteenth-Century Europe: Rethinking Separate Spheres*, ed. Robert Beachy, Beatrice Craig and Alistair Owens (Oxford: Berg, 2006), pp. 67–80.
[99] Vickery, 'Golden Age to Separate Spheres?', p. 300.
[100] Kathryn Hughes, *The Short Life and Long Times of Mrs Beeton* (London: Fourth Estate, 2005), pp. 266–7.
[101] Parkes, *Essays on Woman's Work*, p. 142.

significant industrial businesses with large contracts. It is necessary to understand what these challenges were for both men and women to see how successful they were in meeting them. In some cases it is evident that a smooth transition of a business from a husband to a wife is reasonable indication of her prior and active involvement or at least more than a passing knowledge of the business.

Women ran shipbuilding yards throughout the nineteenth century, from the great Thames yard of Mrs Barnard to the small shipbuilding yards elsewhere.

Summary

Women tend to appear most in connection with small businesses, yet these shipbuilding yards were large industrial concerns producing large ocean-going vessels. Frances Barnard ran one of the largest industrial concerns on the Thames. Even a shipbuilding yard in a smaller port with just twenty shipwrights was a large industrial concern within its locality. To classify such women merely as caretakers is to undervalue their considerable energy and ability in keeping these businesses going. They were significant businesses and they supported not just themselves, but the many men and their families who relied on the jobs created, plus the other local businesses that also relied on the work generated. Thriving communities and thriving businesses were mutually supportive and success bred success.

The women business owners faced many of the same challenges as businessmen, but also had the limitations of their sex: family ties, geographic limits, often a lack of formal education and difficulty in gaining access to significant capital. Yet these women took over the businesses, kept them going and employed men. They were accepted in this role by customers and business contacts. Many businesses, especially shipbuilders, whether managed by men or by women were subject to the same problems of incompetence, harsh economic conditions or loss of reputation and trust. But these businesswomen were not trained or brought up to run businesses. Some of them may have had some mathematical teaching perhaps, but they were not in the same position as the young men who were placed in business to learn the trade and who had greater freedom to travel and make connections.

In what is often seen as a very paternalistic nineteenth-century world where men were very protective of their wives and daughters and preferred them to remain within the safe domestic sphere, the wills of Cyprian May, John Barnard, John Evans, Ambrose Nicholls, Christopher Slade and William Salt show otherwise. In each case the wife was left the management of the business. It almost becomes an assumption that these widows are caretakers, temporary guardians of a family business empire and thrust by fate not choice into doing a man's job; and that they must have been wholly dependent on male advisers and their expertise. Yet the cases described do not bear this out. Apart from the case of Mrs Johnson who clearly was helping her son, the other widows either had sons already of age, some of whom did not wish to take over the yard, or they did not relinquish control even when their sons were of age. This compares interestingly with Mrs Sophie Henschel in Germany who ran Henschel and Sons from 1894. She had been very involved during her husband's lifetime. The business was left to her despite her son Carl being aged twenty-one. Sophie ran the business until 1911 when, aged seventy, she at last relinquished control to her son, but not without insisting that he sent regular reports to her.[102] The fate of the business after the death of the widow is at times as significant as the years before.

A critical starting point was the full and unencumbered inheritance of a business that already had a good reputation so that the widow had full access to the property, and was not sharing it with another or burdened by debt. However, the continued success was still dependent on the ability and the will of the woman concerned. Because the businesses they ran were high profile, with existing contracts to complete, it was essential to keep the yard running, but the reputation of the yard was also critical for future orders and it seems not to have occurred to the shipowners or the Navy Board to be concerned when dealing with a woman shipbuilder. These highly capitalised, complex ventures were at risk from cash flow problems, interruption of material supplies, lack of availability of skilled workmen and dealing with occasionally capricious and powerful customers. Further business came from having a reputation for excellent workmanship and working to contracts and the development of trust in the relationship between builder and customer. Not all of them were successful. Mrs Forster, one of the early examples mentioned, went bankrupt in 1791. But then neither were all their male counterparts successful.[103]

The number of shipyards found to be run by women is a very small percentage of the shipyards in operation during the time of wooden shipbuilding. Because of coverture, these women can only be revealed when they become widows. The examples shown here, in the context of the businesses they ran, raise the question of their prior and active involvement. The cases of Mary Ross, Elizabeth Evans and Jane Slade suggest a thorough working knowledge and this brings into focus the many other firms where the wife's presence may have been more significant than has hitherto been assumed. How many other yards had, as the invisible partner, an active, financially aware and technically competent wife?

[102]   Beachy, 'Profit and Propriety: Sophie Henschel and Gender Management in the German Locomotive Industry', pp. 67–80.
[103]   Flagg, *Notes on the History of Shipbuilding in South Shields*, p. 5.

10

Conclusion: 'A Respectable and Desirable Thing'

In 1865 Bessie Parkes wanted women to be able to practise a profession or run a business and for this to become 'a respectable and desirable thing'.[1] The locally owned wooden sailing vessel gave women that opportunity. This was the heyday of the merchant sailing vessel and since most were owned under the 64th system, this was also the time of the fractional shipowner. In 1871 the number of sailing vessels registered in England and Wales was 17,606 and the number of steamships was just 2,557. The gap between London and Liverpool, with a total of 2,829 vessels and 2,499 vessels respectively, and the next largest port, Rochester, with 807 vessels, was significant. Sixty-nine per cent (fifty-eight out of eighty-four) of the ports had up to 200 vessels on their register and 70 per cent of ports had less than 20,000 tons registered.[2] In these ports around England, women were shipowners; they managed men, dealt with customers, handled the logistics of complex businesses and were not limited to 'feminine' trades.

A new view of the nineteenth-century middle-class woman is beginning to emerge. Historians have been challenging the separate spheres theory in studies of businesswomen in Birmingham and London.[3] Most recently the investments of the nineteenth-century woman have been scrutinised in a series of articles, all of which are developing themes of independent activity.[4] It is clear that despite the apparent limitations of law and society's strictures, women have been running businesses throughout the centuries and the historian's main problem has been to uncover their activity. The aim has not been merely to show that women were in business in the maritime sector, but that they acted as independent economic agents and businesswomen in roles that have traditionally been seen as male. Each of the chapters has considered a different aspect relating to maritime businesswomen.

The national background from a legal, financial and cultural perspective is an important one, but does not seem to have had such a major impact on women's

---

[1] Parkes, *Essays on Woman's Work*, p. 163.
[2] BPP 1871 LXI.1 Return of Number of Sailing and Steam Vessels registered at each Port of Great Britain and Ireland, 1870.
[3] Jenns, 'Female Business Enterprise'; Kay, 'A Little Enterprise of Her Own'; Phillips, *Women in Business*.
[4] Green, 'Independent Women, Wealth and Wills'; Green and Owens, 'Gentlewomanly Capitalism?'; Maltby and Rutterford, 'She Possessed Her Own Fortune'; Rutterford and Maltby, 'The Widow, the Clergyman and the Reckless'.

lives as might be supposed. The legal constraints for women were a major insult to the dedicated feminists who campaigned for the Married Women's Property Act, yet before 1870 women and men had been using different legal devices to ensure that women retained their property. The complexity of the different legal systems, equity, common law and *feme sole* trading, were no barrier to those who wished to circumvent them. The cases cited of married women using trusts and men making gifts[5] are just those that were formally notified and many other situations were under a less formal arrangement. Trusts were not only employed by the wealthy,[6] but by a wide range of men and women who wished to ensure that their legacies were protected.

Maritime law has been seen as specialised and somewhat narrow and yet everyone doing business within the shipping sector had to have an appreciation of its main differences from other commercial law. This applied equally to the businesswomen, whether they were shipowners, managing owners or shipbuilders. All of them, in their regular dealings, came across situations of insurance or trade that required a good understanding of the very different circumstances when dealing with assets that were physically removed from those who had an interest in them. What seemed a strange and archaic system to the outsider was everyday business to those who had been brought up within a maritime community.

The financial opportunities grew in the nineteenth century with the advent of a wide range of joint stock companies and increasing advice to potential investors, yet throughout the century, and well before any new legislation, women had been investing in ships. The women shipowners provide a continuity of female investment across the century.

Women in maritime communities had to be independent. Indeed they had little choice as marrying a mariner meant separation for long periods and a constant concern over their fate. In a community where many women were also alone, there would have been less sympathy for those who felt unequal to the role. The structure of a maritime community with its high percentages of married women as heads of household provided an entrepreneurial and independent environment. This is a picture that seems to be in contradiction to their North American counterparts in Nantucket and to some extent in Salem.[7] It is hard to believe that the many businesswomen found in seaports in the eighteenth century simply disappeared in the nineteenth.

Ports in which these men and women lived were thriving places and for mariners' families this also meant opportunity. Upward mobility within the local community was available for the hard working and the entrepreneurial through the system of fractional shareholding. In this they were supported and encouraged by communities to whom this was a traditional way of life and an essential part of the local economy. The majority of women shipowners were far from the passive inheritors of their husband's wealth. Fifty-one per cent were active investors or

---

5 See Chapter 1: The Legal, Financial and Cultural Environment.
6 Morris, 'The Reform of the Married Women's Property Act 1870', p. 186.
7 Norling, *Captain Ahab Had a Wife*; Vickers, *Young Men and the Sea*.

providers of finance, and even divesting shares or selling ships took some effort. In this regard they were akin to the middle-class women of Victorian Glasgow who were 'by no means without money, control of money or the power that goes with it'.[8] When both the aggregate numbers and the individual cases are considered, the female investors in ships were not timid in their investments. Fifty per cent of the sample actively bought and sold shares.[9] They did not rely on safe, but dull annuities, but risked their capital on fragile and vulnerable ships, although maritime law gave some limited protection. Additionally there was some protection for those owners who took out insurance, although this did not cover their full investment.[10] In many cases women took their inheritance and expanded it. In this way they were supporting not just their family members, but the whole community whose livelihoods depended on the locally owned ships. It is this family and community aspect that holds the key to the behaviour of these investors. The close-knit nature of the family and business contacts in these mid-sized ports encouraged the retention of the women's capital. Local knowledge was a key component of decision making on investment in shipping and family knowledge enabled the decisions to be made on a less speculative basis for those within the community.[11]

The figures mainly reflect the activities of spinsters and widows. A key question that comes from the activity of the widows who bought and sold shares is to wonder whether they were influential in driving share investment during the lifetime of their husbands. Just to what extent were they indeed the aptly named 'hidden investment'?[12] The higher numbers of maritime widows reflect the importance of the transfer of shares by inheritance within the community. Ship shares were kept within the local network. Wives do appear as shipping investors and constitute 10 per cent of the shareholders in the data. This is a topic that deserves further investigation since this level of activity is in sharp contrast to the lack of wives found investing in railways, canals and government stock.[13] The drop in activity relating to wives in the years before the 1870 Married Women's Property Act also deserves further investigation.

The differences in the levels of female activity between the ports reflect the smaller amounts of capital available in Cornwall for investment compared with elsewhere.[14] The investors in Cornwall cannot be compared to the relatively wealthy 'gentlewomanly' examples holding government stock. While Bank of England holdings were suggested as being suitable for female dependants, suit-

---

8   Gordon and Nair, *Public Lives*, p. 197.
9   See Chapter 5: Active and Passive Female Shipowners.
10   Platt, 'Straws in the Winds of Change'.
11   Milne, *Trade and Traders*; Graeme J. Milne, 'Knowledge, Communications and the Information Order in Nineteenth-Century Liverpool', *International Journal of Maritime History*, 14 (2002), 209–24 (pp. 223–4).
12   Davidoff and Hall, *Family Fortunes*, pp. 272–315.
13   Davidoff and Hall, *Family Fortunes*; Hudson, 'Attitudes to Investment Risk'.
14   See Chapter 3: Five Investor Ports.

ability does not seem to have been a concern for the men who left shares in ships to their female dependants.[15]

The expansion of limited company shares and their lower prices did offer greater opportunities for women from the late nineteenth century.[16] Yet in these shipping communities from the very beginning of the century women shareholders owned in excess of 10 per cent of the available shares and in some ports an even higher percentage. They gained their knowledge through the local connections and business networks. These women from 1780 to 1880 were active managers of their funds.

It has also been suggested that women preferred the security of government stock and indeed that holdings in the Bank of England were a substitute masculine provider, while men invested in new ventures that 'fitted more masculine notions of risk and property ownership'.[17] Women in the shipping communities did not feel constrained by such notions and were able to use their local knowledge to invest or disinvest in the risky world of shipping. The vast majority of these women could justify their actions, if they needed to, as support for their families and the business communities within which they operated. The expanding shipping sector needed capital and whether the origins of that capital were male or female mattered little. These women who, alongside their male counterparts, waited for their ships to come in, reflect an even greater blurring of the divisions suggested by separate spheres and notions of what was a proper occupation for a woman.

The managing owner's role was a more complex one than it might appear. The women who took on this responsibility needed to be familiar with maritime law and insurance. This was not just a book-keeping job as managing owners needed good contacts and an ability to work with a wide range of people. The knowledge needed was not something the inexperienced could speedily acquire. The other shipowners, many of whom were experienced mariners, had to be able to trust the good management and accounting skills of the managing owner. A good background, either from seafaring experience or in the women's case being part of a family of shipowners and mariners, was essential. The absence of women in brokerage, which required many of these qualities, may be partly explained by the wide range of contacts needed. While a woman could manage a vessel or two, these were often family- or friend-linked. Close connections within the immediate local community could also be supportive of a women taking over a local business. The role of a broker required not just local connections, but strong business connections in other ports in the United Kingdom and abroad, and this provided a very much greater barrier for the more locally based woman.

The businesswomen can be found in a wide range of trades and businesses of all sizes, from petty business to major industrial concerns. The changing impact of technology and the economics of the shipping industry affected trades in different

[15] Hudson, 'Attitudes to Investment Risk', p. 529.
[16] Maltby and Rutterford, 'She Possessed Her Own Fortune', p. 222.
[17] Green and Owens, 'Gentlewomanly Capitalism?', p. 530.

ways, and some were more able to diversify than others. This affected men and women, but women had the added disadvantage of not being able to move so easily to another part of the country and were less able to access capital to fund new ventures. As with the industrial change across all the sectors, the effects of technological changes were not consistent and did not happen in the same way, at the same time, or to the same extent everywhere. Some ports were more affected than others, depending on their geographic limitations or advantages. Here again, the woman was more limited and constrained by family needs so was more likely to remain *in situ*.

The women's personal circumstances feature heavily in the various examples. The businesswoman could never escape her domestic and familial responsibilities. She had no 'wife' to delegate to, but daughters and nieces became a critical part of the support network. Essentially these women took on two roles and had to balance sometimes conflicting demands, as the cases of Janet Taylor and Susan Thompson demonstrate.[18] The family tie was also an advantage since the positive view of the family firm allowed a woman to be seen to be acting as caretaker even if in reality she was acting on her own behalf.

Women were willing to be managers of large industrial concerns, such as the foundry business in Hull and as demonstrated in the chapters on the shipbuilders in war and peace. Women shipbuilders overcame a series of business challenges to ensure the continuity of the business they inherited. In these roles they challenge several images of women in the nineteenth century. There is the paternalistic view that they were just widows caretaking for their sons and this is contradicted most clearly in the cases of Mary Ross, Jane Slade and Elizabeth Evans, and quite possibly Frances Barnard, all of whom continued to be in charge of the business despite having adult sons.[19] The caretaker argument also assumes there were sons who wished to take over, and Mary Ross's sons and Frances Barnard's son show that this is not always the case. Proving that these women were actually in charge rather than figureheads is a more difficult matter, but in several cases (again in the three cited above) there is good evidence to show that they were fully aware of the business needs in the actions they took and the investments they made in ships. Whether they were making these decisions without any other advice is impossible to state, as indeed is the case for any male shipbuilders. The evidence of the navy's appointment of women overseers proves that they were accepted as being technically competent.

The women themselves may not have seen anything out of the ordinary in what they did, neither is it likely that they considered themselves in the same way as the ardent feminists like Bessie Parkes, arguing for women's rights. As widows they had full control and, if they had to defend the appropriateness of what they were doing, they could always use the ideal reason that they were acting out of a sense of duty to their family and their late husband. The family tie and the

18 See Chapter 7: Port Businesswomen.
19 See Chapter 8: Warship Builders, and Chapter 9: Merchant Shipbuilders.

legacy of a dead husband were not always the hindrances they might seem. The family could be a reason, an excuse or a shield in different circumstances and was always a resource. Just as men and women have been shown to be highly flexible in using the most effective system of law to suit their means, businesswomen were not averse to using family or widowhood as a way of achieving the desired result. This tactic was a way of eliciting a more sympathetic response, usually from men.

These women were running large, highly visible businesses and providing continuity of the business, not just for their successors, but for the other businesses and workers who relied upon them. It has been a consistent argument of this research that the achievements of these women cannot be fully appreciated unless there is a good understanding of their business, its role within the industry and the critical decisions that had to be made. This has meant that previously under-researched aspects of maritime history needed to be explored, highlighting the role that both men and women played, such as marine store dealers and managing owners. Businesswomen had to face the challenges of their time and their industry and, as in the case of Mrs Ross, show their determination to deal fearlessly with large and very powerful customers.[20] Those that succeeded in managing these complex businesses did so when others around them failed. Whether male or female the critical success factors were strong customer relationships, management ability, financial control and willingness to take risks.

The evidence of women's continued involvement as economic agents has appeared throughout this research. Maritime women do not appear to have been severely disadvantaged by the limitations on women during much of the nineteenth century, but as steam and iron gradually replaced sail and wood their local investment opportunities and close networks were eroded. Nor does their economic activity suddenly improve in the late nineteenth century after the changes in law on joint stock companies and married women's property. The evidence from the maritime perspective is that women's activity was part of a continuation of female involvement in many aspects of maritime business life. Continuity is also seen in the role of women as shipowners and maritime business managers. There is evidence of women in these roles from the sixteenth century, but in support of Phillips's view on complexity, what helped or hindered the woman's position had more to do with the changing technology and the fortunes of the communities in which they were based.[21]

Not all women took the opportunities available in the maritime sector and some were no more or less successful than their male counterparts in business. Women were involved when they wished to be and the community ethos of support, combined with a strong family culture, provided the reason or in some cases the excuse for female intervention. Was the maritime sector so different from other industry sectors? While the culture brought about by the absence of men at sea might seem to provide an answer, it is not the only one. It is highly likely

---

[20] See Chapter 8: Warship Builders.
[21] Cook, "'A True, Faire and Just Account'"; Dyer, 'A Woman Shipowner'; Holland, *Ships of British Oak*.

that there were other women acting as independently in other parts of British industry at this time and not just in the feminine trades. The excellence of the shipping registers as a source for the maritime women should not overstate the case. However maritime women had the opportunity and acted on it.

Measuring the success of businesswomen is not always easy as many businesses were very small and few records survive. Because of this it has been suggested that the type of measurements that depend on longevity and growth exclude many women's businesses.[22] Many of the businesses here were small in some respects, but so were many of the businesses in England.[23] The history of the small business whether run by men or women is an important part of the overall picture and success of nineteenth-century Britain, where the small workshops and businesses supplied the larger businesses at a cheaper cost with their low overheads. There is no clear definition of a small or medium-sized business at this time. The shipbuilders with their twenty or so shipwrights were supporting a much wider range of other occupations and businesses than a mere headcount might suggest. Just as the smaller ports supported the larger ports such as Liverpool and London, in the same way, the role of the smaller business must be appreciated.[24] Without such businesses these large concerns could not have managed, as they all relied in some way on small suppliers.

Longevity is a real problem in discussing businesswomen as it raises the vexed question of the hidden contribution of wives who supported their husbands. Who is to say which of the partners was the most active? To just measure longevity by the date at which a woman takes over an enterprise is to undervalue what may have been occurring for some time. A total absence from the concerns of the business hardly led to a successful transition in widowhood. Most of the widows had a clear vote in their favour from their husbands who decided that theirs were the most capable hands in which to leave the family business, in some cases despite the existence of adult sons. Out of seventeen of the cases where the information was known only four women, Gowan, Mary Ross, Tucker and Luke, inherited because their husband left no will, and the rest were chosen as the preferred safe pair of hands by their husband, or in one case their father. These decisions were made in the full knowledge of the difficulty of many of the business sectors, where bankruptcy was a regular feature. The existence of adult sons on inheritance, or the evidence of those women who continued to run the business when their sons came of age, indicates a degree of choice by the women. These were not women forced by circumstance to take on an unwelcome job. Mary Ross, Ann Ross, Jane Slade, Frances Barnard, Elizabeth May, Elizabeth Evans, Christiana Rose, Rebecca Martin and Janet Taylor all chose their careers. Power once grasped proved hard to relinquish. The maritime world that accepted women as independent actors supported women in running their husbands' businesses, and the fractional system of 64ths enabled more women with smaller amounts of capital to participate as

---

22 Kwolek-Folland, *Incorporating Women*, p. 5.
23 Nenadic, 'The Small Family Firm', pp. 89–91.
24 Jackson, 'The Significance of Unimportant Ports'.

active shipowners. These women played a significant role, alongside their male counterparts, in keeping Britain's ships at sea and trade moving. In the maritime environment there were, in effect, few real blockages to the determined woman who wished to invest in shipping or run a business. It was indeed both respectable and desirable for a woman to act in this way.

APPENDIX I

Relevant Statutes (with brief notes on their significance)

1786 An Act for the Further Increase and Encouragement of Shipping (26 Geo III, c.60)

The act required the customs officials to keep registers of all the ships registered in their home port. The act was titled 'An Act for the further Increase and Encouragement of Shipping and Navigation'. The vessel might have been built in the port or elsewhere. It did not need to be trading out of the port and, indeed, it might rarely be seen in its home port in some circumstances.

The shipping registers were required to include the following:

Details of the ship
No. (allocated within the year of registration)
Where and when registered
Ship or vessel's name
Of what place
Master's name
When and where built (occasionally the name of the builder was also given but was not a requirement)
Full description of the vessel, such as rig, decks, dimensions, tonnage, figurehead, etc.

Ownership
In the pre-printed registration books the owner information was headed as

> OWNERS, with their Residence and Occupation; distinguishing Subscribers from Non Subscribers.

Subscribers in the context of shipping were those owners who personally attended the Customs House and swore the necessary oath on registering the vessel. Non-subscribers were simply those owners who could not be personally present to swear the oath due to living at a distance or who were too ill to attend.

1825 Act for the Registering of British Vessels (6 Geo 4, c.110)

Established the proportion of owners who were subscribers and who had to be sworn in.
Maximum of sixty-four shares and a maximum of thirty-two owners with provisos for equitable title of heirs, joint stock companies, etc.
A mortgagee was not deemed an owner.

1854 Merchant Shipping Act (17 & 18 Victoria c.104)

An Act to amend and consolidate the Acts relating to Merchant shipping
All British ships to be registered except:

1. Ships already registered
2. Ships under 15 tons employed solely on navigation on the rivers and coasts of United Kingdom or British Possessions in which the Managing Owners are resident
3. Ships not exceeding 30 tons burthen and not having a whole or fixed deck and employed solely in fishing or trading coastwise, Newfoundland, St Lawrence New Brunswick

Section 37 confirmed:

1. Property in 64 shares
2. Not more than 32 owners, see below
3. No person shall be entitled to be registered as owner of any fractional part in a share in a ship, but any number of persons not exceeding five may be registered as joint owners of a ship or a share or shares within
4. Joint owners shall be considered as constituting one person only
5. A body corporate may be registered as owner by its corporate name

Section 58. Transmission of shares by death, bankruptcy or marriage, etc.

1. If property becomes transmitted in consequence of the death or bankruptcy or insolvency of any registered owner or in consequence of the marriage of any female registered owner

Proof of marriage certificate or Form H

Statement

I declare that on the -- day of --- I intermarried with and am now the husband of -- the Person appearing on the Register Book to be the owner of -- shares in the said ship, and I declare that on such marriage the interests of the said -- became by law vested in me, and that I am entitled to be registered as Owner of the said shares in place of the said --

2. Sale of ship out of country or colony confirmed requirement for a certificate for the person noting who is to exercise the power to sell, minimum price of sale, place and time.

1857 Matrimonial Causes Act (20 & 21 Vict., c 85)

XXV In case of judicial separation the wife to be considered as *femme sole* with respect to Property she <u>may</u> acquire or which may come to be devolved on her
XVI Also for purposes of contracting or signing

1861 Admiralty Court Act (24 & 25 Vict., c 10)

Ship's husband not necessarily the owner

1862 Merchant Shipping Amendment (25 & 26 Vict., c 63)

Definition of owner of ships

1870 Married Women's Property Act, 1870 (33 & 34 Vict., c 93)[1]

1876 Merchant Shipping Act (39 & 40 Vict., c 80)
    Sec. 4 Sub. Sec. 4 of Act
    The owner of every British ship shall from time to time register at the custom-house of the port in the UK at which such ship is registered the name of the managing owner of such ships, &, if there be no managing owner, then of the person to whom the management of the ship is entrusted by and on behalf of the owner.

    The name and address of the managing owner for the time being of every British ship registered at any port shall be registered at the Customs House of the ship's port of entry
    When this is not the MO then shall be so registered the name of the ships husband or other person to whom the management of the ships is entrusted by or on behalf of the owner.

1882 Married Women's Property Act , 1882 (45 & 46 Vict., c 75)[2]

---

[1]   For details see Holcombe, *Wives and Property,* pp. 243–46.
[2]   Holcombe, *Wives and Property,* pp. 247–52.

APPENDIX II

Maritime Occupations from Trade Directories

Number of women listed in brackets

Agents

Emigration agent

General East India passage agent

Marine insurance agent

Ship agent

Steam packet agent

Custom house agent

Lloyds agent

Brokers

Agent & passage broker

Broker colonial

Broker ship insurance

Ship & insurance broker

Ship insurance broker

Ship and boat builders

Boat & barge builder

Boat barge & ship builder (3)

Master shipwright

Master Shipwright of Dock yard

Ship builder

Shipwright

Sloop builder

Yacht builder

Associated trades: steam engines

Steam boiler & saltpan manufacturer

Steam engine & boiler manufacturer

Steam engine boiler Gasometer iron boat &
tank manufacturer

Steam engine boiler maker

Steam engine builder

Steam engine manufacturer

Yacht upholsterer

Rope makers

Flat & round rope manufacturer

Master rope maker

Master Rope maker of Dock yard

Rope & nail bagging maker

Rope & sacking maker

Rope & sheep net maker

Rope & twine dealer

Rope & twine maker (13)

Rope maker (2)

Rope spinner

Sailmakers

Canvass & sail cloth dealer

Sail canvas factor

Sail cloth manufacturer (2)

Sail maker (5)

Waterproof sail manufacturer

sailmaker, ship chandler & slop seller

Cooper (18)

Ships colour maker

Ship rigger

Raff merchant

Tar merchant & dealer in navigation canvas

Marine cooper

Oar manufacturer

Timber & raff merchant (6)

Bonded store merchant

Bonded warehouse

Purveyor of sea stock

Wharfinger (6)

Slop warehouse

Slopseller (6)

Ship & ornamental carver
Ship carver

Supplies
Chandler (1)
Chandlers shop
Ship chandler (1)
Ship bread baker
Ships biscuit baker
Marine store dealer (43)
Ship stores furnisher
Ships store merchant

Block and Mast makers
Block & mast maker (1)
Block maker
Block turner
Mast block & pump maker

Customs, Excise and Coastguard
Assistant Inspector of Gaugers Custom House
Assistant Port Surveyor Excise office
Assistant Registrar of tide waiters
Ass Supt of Quarantine Custom House
Boat gauger
Boatman of Customs
Chief boatman coastguard
Chief boatman Preventative station
Chief clerk at Customs house
Chief coast guard officer
Chief officer Preventative station
Coast guard
Coast officer of customs
Coast waiter of customs
Collector Custom house
Collector of excise
Comptroller of Customs
Customs officer
Excise officer
Exciseman
Landing surveyor Customs
Landing waiter Customs house

Sailors palm maker
Sailors hat maker

Smiths
Ship & anchor smith
Ship smith (3)
Anchor & shipsmith
Anchor ship smith & chain cable manuf
Anchor manufacturer
shipsmith & chain maker (2)

Instruments, maps etc
Instrument maker
Mathematical Instrument Maker
Nautical Instrument Maker
Optical & mathematical instr Maker
Watch & clock maker (chronometer)
Map & chart seller

Port Officials
Collector of merchant seamans dues
Collector of Navigation dues
Collector of Pier
Collector of tonnage duty
Deputy Harbour master
Deputy pier master
Grants passports to persons visiting France
Harbour inspector
Harbour master
Licensed shipping master
Pier master
Pier warden
Port & harbour commissioner
Port officer
Receiver of Port dues customs
Ship inspector
Superintendent of harbour works
Receiver of Droits of Admiralty

Pilots and Trinity House
Haven master Trinity House

Lieutenant of Coast guard station
Long room clerk of Customs
Port gauger & searcher Custom house
Preventive officer
Preventive station
Principal Coast officer of customs
Principal officer of customs
Ride officer excise
Searcher & clerk Customs
Searcher of Customs
Supervisor of excise
Tide surveyor customs
Tide waiter
Weighing porter of customs

Dock & Harbour Officials
Baggage clerk of the Docks
Boatswain of Dock yard
Chief converter in dock yard
Dock master

Dock master Dock office
Stevedore
Store Receiver of Dock yard
Assistant Harbour master
Ballast master
Ballast officer
Barmaster
Captain of the landing stage
Captain Superintendent of victualling yard
Collector of Ferry boat
Collector of Harbour dues

Seamen's Support
Collector Seamans Friend Society & Bethel Union
Naval & Military Bible Soc committee member
Sailors missionary
Seamans fund
Shipping Master Sailors Home Registry & Savings Bank
Shipping Officer Sailors Home Registry & Savings Bank

Dock master Trinity House
Elder brethren Trinity House
Buoy master Trinity House
Collector of Trinity lights
Collector Pilots Office
Commodore Pilots office
Crewman Pilot boat
Lighthouse keeper
Pilot
Pilot master
Receiver of light dues customs
Sub Commissioner of Pilots

Surveyor
Surveyor (export)
Surveyor for Lloyd's
Surveyor of ships
Surveyor of ships & cargoes
Surveyor to Port & harbour commissioners
Lloyd's surveyor of shipping

Owners
Pleasure boat proprietor

Ship owner (46)
Ship owner & master
Ship owner & underwriter
Smack owner (1)

Smack owner & master

Office for Merchant Seamen's fund

Mariners
Boat steerer
Boatswain rigger
Captain of Steam Packet
Lighterman
Mariner
Master mariner
Master of Private steam packet
Master Pilot boat
Ship captain
Ship carpenter
Ship master
Sloop master
Waterman
Ferryman

Steam boat owner
Steam packet proprietor
Barge & smack owner
Barge owner
Bargemaster
Boat owner
Coasting vessel owner

Teachers
Nautical teacher
Naval instructor
Professor & teacher of navigation

Note: The number of women listed is in brackets. The understatement of women running maritime businesses shows the limitations of trade directories as a reliable source for data on women. The number of titles is a reflection of how individuals described themselves rather than the number of different occupations.

Source: Data kindly supplied by David Foster from his database created for: David Foster, 'Albion's Sisters: A Study of Trade Directories and Female Economic Participation in the mid 19th Century' (unpublished doctoral thesis, University of Exeter, 2002).

Statistics on Businesswomen across England

Maritime counties in bold

County	Records	People	Women	% women	Total
Westmoreland	**2324**	**2319**	**443**	**19.10**	**397162**
Cumberland	**6756**	**6743**	**1284**	**19.04**	**40549**
Gloucestershire	20462	20258	3511	17.33	107950
Devon	16735	16589	2811	16.94	67332
Sussex	9104	8932	1506	16.86	366630
Middlesex	7858	7779	**1294**	**16.63**	250961
Hampshire	**13282**	**13154**	**2081**	**15.82**	**121104**
Herefordshire	3564	3485	546	15.67	124589
Surrey	**8800**	**8643**	**1323**	**15.31**	**357698**
Northumberland	**21234**	**21035**	**3155**	**15.00**	**280769**
Somerset	**10940**	**10813**	**1531**	**14.16**	**320834**
Monmouthshire	**4329**	**4245**	**598**	**14.09**	**255206**
Berkshire	4641	4594	647	14.08	7271
Durham	**6612**	**6514**	**908**	**13.94**	**77699**
Worcestershire	11151	10921	1505	13.78	413011
Shropshire	7656	7514	1028	13.68	310021
Lancashire	**75646**	**75151**	**10162**	**13.52**	**221223**
Cheshire	**15184**	**14891**	**1997**	**13.41**	**30085**
Nottinghamshire	157393	155678	21531	13.83	406639
Huntingdonshire	1528	1500	191	12.73	130376
Yorkshire	**59481**	**59090**	**7400**	**12.52**	**472101**
Leicestershire	8167	8111	989	12.19	229334
Kent	**15933**	**15696**	**1905**	**12.14**	**146072**
Essex	**10091**	**9993**	**1203**	**12.04**	**87692**
Bedford	2703	2677	319	11.92	2677
Oxfordshire	4718	4633	550	11.87	301894
Dorset	**3923**	**3853**	**453**	**11.76**	**71185**
Lincolnshire	**13914**	**13848**	**1621**	**11.71**	**243182**
Norfolk	**8919**	**8804**	**1017**	**11.55**	**289573**
Suffolk	**6680**	**6542**	**738**	**11.28**	**349055**
Hertfordshire	4411	4287	483	11.27	128876
Derbyshire	10714	10194	1143	11.21	50743
Warwickshire	28351	28213	3154	11.18	394843
Buckinghamshire	2664	2630	275	10.46	9901

Northamptonshire	4542	4528	472	10.42	259734
Staffordshire	21800	21679	2244	10.35	342513
Wiltshire	4998	4928	503	10.21	402090
Rutland data	618	613	62	10.11	302507
Cambridgeshire	5397	5293	519	9.81	15194
Cornwall	**3790**	**3721**	**323**	**8.68**	**33806**

Source: Data kindly supplied by David Foster from his database created for: David Foster, 'Albion's Sisters: A Study of Trade Directories and Female Economic Participation in the mid 19th Century' (unpublished doctoral thesis, University of Exeter, 2002).

Registered Shipping in England and Wales, 1871

Showing the change in total tonnage since 1870

Port	Sailing no.	tons	Steam no.	tons	Total no.	tons	1871 Change	% port Tonnage
London	2114	734820	715	341845	2829	1076665	62943	6%
Liverpool	2023	1087331	476	326941	2499	1414272	3244	0%
Rochester	798	35670	9	322	807	35992	373	1%
Sunderland	645	181101	111	40466	756	221567	1116	1%
Hull	492	35877	181	122795	673	158672	25132	16%
Yarmouth	653	32684	12	620	665	33304	301	1%
Shields (Nth)	427	138964	193	27402	620	166366	-3215	-2%
Newcastle	319	98993	184	52159	503	151152	-5361	-4%
Caernarvon	455	41402	3	131	458	41533	-1921	-5%
Goole	409	25784	21	3066	430	28850	-989	-3%
Grimsby	351	19783	27	6641	378	26424	3289	12%
Plymouth	354	42053	11	455	365	42508	-1389	-3%
Faversham	341	31299	2	22	343	31321	-990	-3%
Aberystwyth	332	38873	4	315	336	39188	296	1%
Lowestoft	326	13670	3	69	329	13739	317	2%
Colchester	313	15754	2	98	315	15852	-644	-4%
Bristol	252	51285	51	6495	303	57780	-1737	-3%
Whitby	283	55804	10	4119	293	59923	-3552	-6%
Portsmouth	277	18591	13	608	290	19199	233	1%
Shields (Sth)	216	83790	47	263	263	84053	-3734	-4%
Southampton	202	14223	59	18033	261	32256	-335	-1%
Beaumaris	252	16054	1	8	253	16062	-910	-6%
Gloucester	234	10580	6	293	240	10873	-41	0%
Cowes	225	10673	9	491	234	11164	401	4%
Swansea	202	46570	31	2766	233	49336	716	1%
Dartmouth	195	17333	8	280	203	17613	-286	-2%
Scarborough	197	25291	2	66	199	25357	-1412	-6%
Ramsgate	176	6875	2	19	178	6894	-216	-3%
Shoreham	171	35540	1	15	172	35555	931	3%
Fowey	169	15542	1	19	170	15561	-201	-1%
Ipswich	154	13508	10	661	164	14169	-440	-3%
Whitehaven	158	21838	4	368	162	22206	103	0%
Maldon	161	10912			161	10912	-221	-2%

Lancaster	152	19128	5	106	157	19234	-4416	-23%
Brixham	145	15516			145	15516	968	6%
Bridgwater	138	8503	7	440	145	8943	13	0%
Cardiff	82	21758	54	6604	136	28362	3580	13%
Falmouth	125	16291	7	195	132	16486	485	3%
Padstow	131	10623			131	10623	-264	-2%
Chester	115	7445	10	2375	125	9820	233	2%
Harwich	117	8937	7	3381	124	12318	-87	-1%
Fleetwood	115	13642	7	1571	122	15213	991	7%
Bideford	122	10364			122	10364	38	0%
Cardigan	118	7423	1	65	119	7488	186	2%
Runcorn	115	6384	3	44	118	6428	299	5%
Preston	102	6951	12	624	114	7575	142	2%
Maryport	108	19302	4	99	112	19401	-585	-3%
Lynn	**109**	**10088**	**1**	**121**	**110**	**10209**	**-680**	**-7%**
Hartlepool W	48	10500	60	27533	108	38033	12753	34%
Milford	102	7701	5	934	107	8635	-96	-1%
Middlesboro	52	7328	53	7274	105	14602	-157	-1%
Wells	103	8406	2	20	105	8426	-359	-4%
Penzance	103	8050	2	94	105	8144	-224	-3%
St Ives	103	6371			103	6371	-166	-3%
Newport	91	17545	9	966	100	18511	263	1%
Boston	95	5162	3	101	98	5263	-218	-4%
Exeter	**93**	**10395**	**3**	**1607**	**96**	**12002**	**-73**	**-1%**
Llanelly	87	12243	6	302	93	12545	361	3%
Rye	89	6579			89	6579	305	5%
Barnstaple	78	3573	2	39	80	3612	-100	-3%
Hartlepool	70	17053	8	4790	78	21843	1249	6%
Workington	71	17949	1	17	72	17966	298	2%
Poole	69	7717	3	140	72	7857	-714	-9%
Littlehampton	63	7541			63	7541	694	9%
Salcombe	62	12231			62	12231	586	5%
Weymouth	52	4209	6	599	58	4808	-196	-4%
Dover	53	4181	4	268	57	4449	-100	-2%
Woodbridge	55	2831			55	2831	-230	-8%
Truro	49	4428	1	29	50	4457	-227	-5%
Teignmouth	48	5656	1	23	49	5679	-107	-2%
Newhaven	31	3543	8	1287	39	4830	-198	-4%
Wisbech	26	3068	11	5515	37	8583	0	0%
Folkestone	37	3582			37	3582	-167	-5%
Scilly	35	5097	1	67	36	5164	-1645	-32%
Hayle	27	3579	4	731	31	4310	-46	-1%
Stockton	15	2685	15	1528	30	4213	-71	-2%

Barrow	22	2400	7	1489	29	3889	212	5%
Berwick	25	2640	2	176	27	2816	165	6%
Chepstow	26	1040			26	1040	20	2%
Carlisle	21	2372	4	691	25	3063	-53	-2%
Gainsborough	12	539	9	465	21	1004	59	6%
Bridport	8	1425			8	1425	0	0%
Lyme	8	592			8	592	-35	-6%
Deal	7	682			7	682	0	0%
Total (England & Wales)	17606	3431715	2557	1030161	20163	4461876	86358	2%

Source: Mercantile Navy List 1872, xxii–xxvi.

APPENDIX V

The Investor Database[1]

Sources

Shipping Registers
Cornwall Record Office (CRO): MSR/FOW/ 3–9 Fowey Shipping Registers
North Yorkshire Record Office (NYRO): NG/RS/WH/2, 9 & 10 Whitby Registers
Whitehaven Record Office (WRO) YTSR 1/9–12 and YTSR 16–21 Register of shipping
Devon Record Office (DRO) 3289s/3–17, 10 Exeter shipping registers
Norfolk Record Office (NRO): P/SH Shipping Registers: King's Lynn, Wells, Cley and Great Yarmouth 1825–1892

Additional Sources
Census returns, Lloyd's Register

Coverage

The shipping registers date from 1786 and are now held in the relevant county record offices. Not all the early registers have survived, but most ports have coverage from 1825.

The dates of the registers in the archives are the dates when the registers were in use, that is the years in which the ships were registered, but they could contain transactions relating to earlier or later periods. For example, a vessel registered in 1830 might well have been registered previously in the port, but under the *de novo* system any major changes meant it was reregistered in a new year and the shareholders could have held their shares from that earlier date. If the earlier registers are not available there is no method of checking this. Conversely, when the system of transaction registers was introduced from 1855 a ship originally registered in 1860 might have details of transactions relating to 1890. As the database was designed to examine transactions the earliest and latest dates of noted transactions are listed below.

Exeter	1824–82
Fowey	1834–99
Lynn	1836–92
Whitby	1848–92
Whitehaven	1840–92

[1] This database has been deposited with the UK Data Archive and can be accessed via: www.data-archive.ac.uk and search for SN6142

Method

All data relating to female investors from each set of registers were entered into an Access database and duplications due to *de novo* registration of the ship or marriage and name change of the shareholder were deleted.

Criteria for Classification

The database was designed to examine the level of independent dealing by women. As the registers do not reveal what was paid for the shares on initial purchase or later sale it is not possible to use this source to consider speculative behaviour. What can be measured is to what extent women were active purchasers of shares or were passive holders of shares that had been acquired through inheritance.

Passive

Women were described as passive holders of shares in all cases where no share dealing is noted after inheritance. This will over-report where transaction registers could not be accessed, e.g. Whitehaven.

Divestors

These were the women who sold their shares within one year of inheritance. The registers in most cases showed the date of the shareholder's death, the date of probate and the name of the executors. If there was a willing buyer, shares could be sold within weeks of probate being cleared. Cases of larger or more complex estates could mean that liquidising the assets might take longer.

Active

The active category is of women who appear to take independent action in buying shares. This excludes all cases of inheritance unless the women subsequently went on to buy and sell in their own name. It includes all cases where a women is noted as buying shares from another shareholder or where the woman was listed as an initial shareholder in a newly built vessel. The early system of *de novo* registration can cause some problems here as the trail of share transfer can be interrupted. For example, if a male shareholder had died and his widow now held the shares, in some cases the death may not have been noted but the new registration gives the widow as the new owner.

Financiers

This category covers where a woman is noted as providing a mortgage. This only includes situations where a formal mortgage was registered and will not include the many informal loans.

Subscribers

Subscribers were those owners who personally registered the vessel at the Customs House and who therefore signed their names to the registration document and swore the necessary oath. Non-subscribers were those who for reasons of infirmity or distance did not personally attend. Both groups were shareholders in the same way in the vessel. By 1855 this difference had gradually disappeared and all owners of vessels were generally noted as subscribers. In the database, where it may be unclear just how the woman obtained her shares, but she is shown as a subscriber of a reregistered vessel, then her method of acquisition is noted as unknown. If, however, she is shown as an initial subscriber of a new vessel or one transferred to the port from elsewhere then the method of acquisition is noted as a purchase.

Until separate transaction registers were introduced mid-century, vessels were reregistered *de novo* if the ownership substantially changed. Therefore details are sometimes missing of how the new owners acquired their shares. Women subscribers were only classified as active investors if they were subscribers at the time of the ship's registration when newly built or purchased from another port. This results in an under-reporting of active investors such as those who bought shares rather than inherited or who purchased shares in a vessel coming from another port.

Tonnage Measurement

Tonnage measurement changed several times during this period so comparisons are not always accurate. Tonnage is given as noted in the registers.

64th System

Ships could have multiple owners and part owners were tenants-in-common under maritime law, so that shares could be passed on by sale or through a will without consultation with the other shareholders. Conventionally ships were owned in fractions of sixty-four shares although this was not enshrined in law until 1825. When joint stock companies owned ships the shipping registers merely noted that the company owned all sixty-four shares. Details of the investors in the company were not shown. Under the 64th system shareowners could own shares in multiple vessels, could buy further shares in one vessel and sell their shares in different amounts at different times. Vessels could have more than one woman shareholder.

Design

See figure below:

Figure 7. Relationship Table

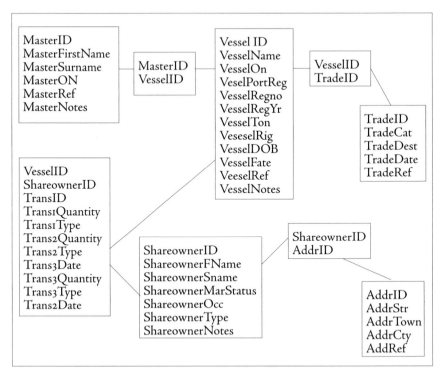

The most significant tables for analysis are the Transactions, Vessels, and Shareholders. These tables contain the full details collected from the shipping registers. The tables for Masters and for Trades are less complete as data were not available for all vessels. Additional information was collected from selected years of Lloyd's Register but this did not contain matching data for all the relevant vessels.

Managing Owners with Multiple Vessels in 1865

Name	Port	Vessel	Ton.	Year built	Trade (1866)
Jane B. Avery	N. Shields	Blair Atholl	409	1864	India
	N. Shields	British Lion	656	1856	
	N. Shields	Eddystone	400	1860	Med
	N. Shields	George Avery	468	1862	Singapore
	N. Shields	Hesse Darmstadt	333	1863	Med
Joanna Barnard	Whitby	Emerald	217	1836	
	Whitby	Gratitude	198	1840	
Mary Ann Bell	Newcastle	Amity	206	1811	
	S. Shields	Thetis	195	1826	
Harriet Booth	Goole	Blessing	42	1832	
	Goole	H.M & R	50	1857	
Miss Butchart	Arbroath	Symmetry*	235	1858	
	Dundee	Symmetry*	235	1857	Natal
Jean Crawford	Greenock	Jason	1022	1857	India
	Greenock	Ulysses	934	1854	India
	Greenock	Vittoria	837	1856	
Mrs Edgar	Whitehaven	Cumberland	76	1856	
	Whitehaven	Maria Lowther	97	1840	
Jane Gray	Newcastle	Annie Comrie	339	1861	Plymouth
	Newcastle	Express	324	1857	W. Indies
Mary Josey	Middlesboro	Jane & Ann	216	1839	
	Middlesboro	Pacific	184	1832	
Mrs Mary Melmore	Maryport	Hazard	112	1823	
	Maryport	Margaret	118	1845	
	Maryport	Salus	89	1838	
	Maryport	Sealby	85	1840	
	Maryport	Woods	84	1793	
Mary Mollard	Hayle	London	114	1825	Coastal
	Hayle	Orwell	92	1826	
Ann A Morton	Exeter	Devon	79	1823	
	Exeter	Fame	81	1824	
	Exeter	Grocer	81	1822	
	Exeter	Thames	95	1826	
Sarah Nesfield	Whitby	Jane	200	1839	
	Whitby	Star of Hope	238	1854	
	Whitby	Ubla	341	1841	
Miss Isabella Sanderson	N. Shields	Agenoria	175	1861	
	N. Shields	Amble	142	1857	
	N. Shields	Perseverance	271	1852	Baltic
Hannah Wood	Whitby	George	142	1836	
	Whitby	Hector	244	1801	

* These look suspiciously like the same vessel but they are listed under separate ports.

Source: Clayton's Directory of Shipping, 1865 (Liverpool: Merseyside Maritime Museum, n.d.); *Lloyd's Register of Shipping*, 1866.

APPENDIX VII

Port Businesswomen

Source	Year	Surname	Name	Town	Occupation
White	1850	Cox	Charlotte	Harwich	Banker
Pigot	1830	Whitford	Hannah	Fowey	Blacksmith
Slater	1848	Wray	Maria	York	Boat builder
Slater	1850	Hipwood	Frances	Glos	Boat builder
Slater	1851	Morris	Sarah	Manchester	Boat builder
Kellys	1846	Corner	Mrs	Lewes	Chandler
HCA		Ross	Ann	Hull	Chandler
Witt		Steel	Penelope	London	Chart maker
Note 1		Martin	Rebecca	St Austell	China clay merchant
Mannix	1847	Gilkerson	Ann	Carlisle	Cooper
Whites	1850	Skews	My	Plymouth	Cooper
CRO	1864	Tadd	Grace	Polruan	Ferry lessee
Mannix	1847	Borbridge	Margt	Whitehaven	Fishing tackle maker
HCA		Rose	Christiana	Hull	Foundry owner/engineer
Note 2		Desforges	Phoebe	Birmingham	Marine store dealer
Williams	1850	Podmore	My	Redruth	Marine store dealer
Williams	1850	Mason	Eliz	Redruth	Marine store dealer
Mannix	1847	Stubbs	Sarah	Whitehaven	Marine store dealer
Whites	1850	Forest	Eliz	Plymouth	Marine store dealer
Whites	1850	Pedlar	My	Plymouth	Marine store dealer
Whites	1850	Sladen	My	Plymouth	Marine store dealer
Whites	1850	Waterfield	My	Plymouth	Marine store dealer
Whites	1850	Wingett	My	Plymouth	Marine store dealer
Whites	1850	Dunn	Hannah	Exeter	Marine store dealer
Census	1851	Brimacombe	Charlotte	Plymouth	Workwoman in marine store
Census	1851	Ferguson	Georgianna	Plymouth	Dealer in marine stores
Census	1851	Foster	Sarah	Plymouth	Dealer in marine stores
Census	1851	Harvey	Jane	Plymouth	Dealer in marine stores
Census	1851	Honey	Ellen	Plymouth	Dealer in marine stores
Census	1851	Martain	Elizabeth	Plymouth	Dealer in marine stores
Census	1851	Pasere	Elizabeth	Plymouth	Dealer in marine stores
Census	1851	Waterfield	Mary	Plymouth	Dealer in marine stores
Whites	1856	Trevethick	Sarah	Gainsborough	Mast block and pump maker
Note 3		Taylor	Janet	London	Navig teacher/instrument maker
Note 4		Mitchell	Mrs	Polruan	Navigation teacher

Slater	1848	Strickland	Ellen	Wigan	Rope & twine maker (dealer)
Slater	1847	Elliot	Eliz	Cockermouth	Rope & twine manufacturer
Mannix	1851	Bramwell	Eliz	Preston	Rope and twine makers
Slater	1848	Hodgson	Ellen	York	Rope and twine makers
Slater	1848	Walker	Ann	York	Rope and twine makers
Slater	1848	Young	Sarah	Hull	Rope and twine makers
Slater	1848	Kellett	Ellen	Bolton	Rope twine & cotton banding
Slater	1848	Lloyd	Sarah	Bolton	Rope twine & cotton banding
Slater	1848	Richardson	Eliz	York	Rope twine and mattress maker
Slater	1848	Hitchin	My	Chester	Ropemaker
Slater	1848	Williams	Ann	Chester	Ropemaker
White	1856	Howe	My	Bourn	Ropemaker
Note 2		Wright	Ann	Birmingham	Ropemaker
Census	1861	Lettis	Mary	Yarmouth	Ropemaker
White	1847	Reed	My	Sunderland	Sailcloth manufacturer
Slater	1850	Baker	Joanna	Yeovil	Sailcloth manufacturer
Slater	1848	Speakman	Ann	Runcorn	Sailmaker
White	1847	Curry	Isabella	Hartlepool	Sailmaker
White	1848	Forge	Mary	Barking	Sailmaker
Kellys	1846	Hubbard	Hannah	Margate	Sailmaker
Slater	1848	Kelso	Eliz	North Shields	Sailmaker
Note 5		Bowmaker	Ann	North Shields	Sailmaker
Kellys	1846	Starbuck	Sarah	Gravesend	Sailmaker, chandler & slop seller
Slater	1848	Kelso	Eliz	North Shields	Shipowner
Slater	1848	Bird	Catherine	Blyth	Shipowner
Slater	1848	Stradon	Sarah	Hull	Shipowner lighter
White	1847	Dewar	Eliz	Newcastle	Shipsmith
Slater	1848	Livingston	Martha	Hull	Shipsmith & bell hanger
White	1847	Lumsdon	My	Sunderland	Shipsmith & chain maker
Slater	1848	Wood	My	York	Timber & raff merchant
Slater	1848	Birch	My	York	Timber dealer
Slater	1851	Bailey	Fanny	Portsea	Timber dealer
Slater	1850	Lock	Ann	Cirencester	Timber merchant & dealer & hellier
Slater	1850	Oakley	Sarah	Glos	Wharfinger
Slater	1850	Oakley	Sarah	Bristol	Wharfinger

Note 1: Barton, *A History of the Cornish China Clay Industry*, pp. 86–8.
Note 2: Jenns, 'Female Business Enterprise', pp. 285–6 & 187–92.
Note 3: Alger, *Mrs Janet Taylor*.
Note 4: Pickering, *Some Goings on!*, p. 28.
Note 5: NMM: HNL/23/2: Henley and Son correspondence with Mrs Ann Bowmaker.

Source: Trade Directories; D. Foster database; TNA: HO 107 2267, RG 9 1194, HO 107 1878 Census returns.

Rose Downs Thompson Correspondence

Selected letters to Mr Downs from Christiana Rose and Susan Thompson

DBR 1146 Monday 30th April 1860

Dear Sir

The consideration on Friday led us to examine our accts, for the purpose of ascertaining what the outlay of the present year had been. We find that Mr Neville has drawn cheques since 19th Feb 1860 £830 … of bills paid away – we now hold J Clarks bills £500 amount we consider at lost in bills having been returned so frequently late, we shall be a good deal later when others that we hold are cashed under these circumstances we have fully decided to incur no further expenditure with the exception of the new arrangements of the smiths fires & the smith for some it might be made at a lesser expense than what you named or doing as much as possible ourselves

This has been the worst Spring for getting money we have experienced and the alterations of the last two years have been very expensive. You will remember that we laid down when you entered with us that we wished to have the business conducted with as little outlay in machinery & on the premises as possible.

The reply to your query concerning account of salary we intended it as stated income When Mr Akester [?] first managed the works up to within 2½ years of his death he had no more than £2 in a week wages, he was then advanced to £150 with which sum he was fully satisfied. We cannot in our present position increase our salaries as the returns of the business will not allow of it. Should times become more prosperous it will be in our power to make some advance. The Glasgow order appears a reliable one but previous to doing anything on it you will make enquiries of his references at the Clydesdale banking co & also have the agreement made out fully satisfactory. I have enclosed all the papers and remain
Yours respectfully
C Rose.

DBR 1201 Sat morning, Feb 25 1865

Dear Sir

I have written to Mr Thwaite requesting him to look out all the books & papers belonging to the Foundry since 1848, will you assist him in doing so. The reason they are wanted to day is that the gentleman who is going to audit them is now at liberty and looking to start at once. We had intended having them done sooner, but never met with an efficient person until lately. It is I fear an awkward day for you both but that is unavoidable, as he would not do them anywhere but in his own office. You will take the books in a cab. The addressee is
Mr Gamble
22 Parliament Street

my assistance he may need I hope you will give Mr Neville etc ... what I said about how it looks for temporary use then you will settle between yourselves
I remain
Most respectfully

S Thompson

DBR1202 26th May 1865

Dear Sir
If you think that a good profit can be obtained in the London job it will be as well to see after it, but not without, I read it as amounting to two thousand pounds. Are they sound in circumstances and prompt payers? In reference to the rest of your letter we cannot imagine what has caused you to take such a view of Mr Gamble's statements, there as our auditor should not have properly fulfilled his commission, had he not laid before us an unbiased and full report of all transactions connected with business. Of course this department came in among the rest every facility has been given to you to trace to the source of his information, & now we wait for you to do something towards handling the matter. I know in an equitable for ... should you like Mr. Jackson opinion for it all ... it is perfectly fair & I am sure you will see that it is your duty to pay a full percentage of £30 for every £100 free of the extra expenditure as laid before. Let a proper figure be drawn out by both parties, then the future transactions will be on a proper basis.

Yours respectfully
S Thompson

Source: Hull City Archives: DBR Rose Downs Archive.

APPENDIX IX

Selected Correspondence, Mrs Taylor

27 June 1837

Mrs Taylor

Captain Beaufort presents his compliments to Mrs Taylor and is really much rejoiced to learn that the improving health of her children has enabled her to resume her usual industrious pursuits and he will be glad to see the result of her labours – and the more so because he would be glad to learn in conversation which is a much briefer method than by writing what her views are on this office with respect to her present work.

Source: United Kingdom Hydrographic Office, Taunton (UKHO) T 186 Captain Beaufort to Mrs Taylor.

Feb 14 1848

Mrs Taylor
Madam
A bill of yours to Capt Rawlinson of the Tribune (dated Nov 7th 1846) has been submitted to the Board of the Admiralty and is now before me, which is headed 'Under the patronage of the Admiralty' and in which you style yourself 'Agent for the sale of Admiralty Charts' By the same bill however you appear to have sold to Capt Rawlinson a Chart of the English Channel (Nories I believe) for 13 shillings when the Admiralty Chart of the Channel might have been supplied to him for two or three shillings. This inconsistency has naturally excited some surprise here and Admiral Beaufort would therefore thank you for some explanation on the subject.

Source: UKHO 1848 Letter book no 15 page 128 Captain Miles to Mrs Taylor.

1 Hammond Street
16 Feb 1848
Sir
I think it best to give the 'explanation' required in Captain Miles letter to you direct which I will do briefly. In the first place I regret that Captain Rawlinson was not asked why <u>he</u> selected Nories Chart at 13/- in preference to that published by the Admiralty at 3/- because you could then have heard the painful truth Which the gentlemen in my establishment receive in 99 cases out if 100 from Captains who have the advantage here of selecting their charts from the best and most recent publications viz. 'that the Admiralty Channel Chart is on so small a scale and consequently so confused with soundings that it is of no use' – I have been an Agent for Admiralty charts ever since I came to reside in the city, and I think a reference to Mr Bates' Books prior to and

since that period, will shew that the publicity I gave to them in the Merchant services where they were not known or scarcely so, will prove that I have been a more efficient agent than the Admiralty have ever had and it is with regret I should frequently see their charts returned to our shelves, and charts of less merit selected. It is not the lower price of a chart that will induce a man to take that which he considers of use, in preference to one of double the price. Neither, I beg you to believe, is it the paltry extra profit I might desire that would induce <u>me</u> to supply one that I knew to be incorrect. I have had the Admiralty Channel Charts coloured framed and mounted in my window ever since it was published, … copies of it in my portfolio which are exhibited on all necessary occasions. I have regularly supplied all the Captains trading between here and the Irish coast with Admiralty charts of that coast, and since they were published with the Irish Channel, but there is not one of them <u>will</u> take the Admiralty Channel Charts. I cannot see how I am accountable for Capt Rawlinson's acts, neither can I see in what way his having made the selection he did nearly 10 months ago, can have had anything to do with the loss of the 'Tribune'.

I remain sir

Yours respectfully

Janet Taylor

Source: UKHO: T 63 16 Feb 1848 Mrs Taylor to Captain Beaufort.

APPENDIX X

Penney Agreement

Edited Articles of co-partnership between Katherine & George Penney of Poole in family coal & clay shipping business, 1806; inventory of ships and stock 1805[1]

Dated: 5th November 1806

Parties: Between Katherine Penney, widow, and her son, George Penney, coal merchant.

Assets: George Penney died 15 April 1805. 'He had carried on the trade of coal merchant and was an agent for shipments of clay and employed in the commission business'. At time of death he was sole owner of Brig *Mary*, ketch *Betsey* and the hull of a new sloop or vessel called the *Perseverance*, also a moiety of the ship *Hope* 'and of a considerable stock & other effects.'

Will: He left all his personal property & effects to Katherine. She carried on the trade of a coal merchant and the shipping concern and the agency & commission business until the 24 June 1805 after his death.

Agreement: 'Whereas the said Katherine Penney has agreed to admit the said George Penney party hereto as co partner in the said coal trade and shipping concern and the agency in shipping clay and the commission business'
Trades & businesses to be carried on by them in their joint account of profits and loss.
George junior executed a bond of £1,150 in part of the moiety of the valuation plus interest at £5 per year.
Katherine gave George for his own use the sum of £700 in order that he could make the balance of the moiety.
Katherine Penney was seized of the Coal yard, counting house, stores, hereditaments & premises abutting the quay in Poole. She was to keep these for the term of her natural life to be used for the joint trade and business.

Terms: In consideration of the 'mutual trust and confidence which the said parties hereto have & repose in each other and for the improvement of the several estates and for divers other good causes and considerations.

Period: 14 years from date of document

Subject to: 1. Name of business to be George Penney & Company.
2. Proceeds to be split 50/50

---

[1]   DSRO: D/504/5 Penney Agreement.

3. Future money invested by either party in the business at the rate of £5 per 100 per annum.

4. Drawings from stock and increase and profits not to exceed £800 annually.

5. Partners individually not to draw more than £400 each.

6. Katherine to be paid £40 per annum for the use of the premises which she will keep in good repair.

7. George Penney to 'manage the business' but receive no pay for this.

8. Each partner on proportion to their share to advance the wages & salaries & expenses of the captains, clerks, servants, porters and apprentices.

9. Not to engage in any other business or trade which may injure the business without the agreement of each other.

10. Both to diligently employ themselves in and about the said business 'except that Katherine Penney shall not be obliged to take any active part in the management of the business'.

11. Any debts incurred by either to be their debts

12. 'Partners will be just true & faithful to each other in all and every transaction, receipts & accts relating to or concerning the partnership.

13. Each to enter into books the details of all money disbursed and received

14. Each partner free access to the books at all times. Neither shall make any obliteration or alteration to the accounts

15. Accounts to be agreed annually

16. Both parties to sign agreement and no accounts 'so signed shall be afterwards disputed'. Allowing for an error of £10

17. 12 months notice in writing of leaving partnership

18. Any dispute at end of partnership to go to arbitration

19. Finally they bound themselves in the penal sum of £500 each

Inventory:	Coal £359 deduct for inferior £4	£354
Stone coals		£247 10s 6d
Coals/*Mary's* cargo		£347 8s
Blubber		£66 9s 11d
Grindstone		£24 7s 6d
Tyne iron		£67 8s 7d
Bar iron		£24 0s 11d
Stock at Creekmore farm		£101 12s
Brig *Mary*		£1,100
Ketch *Betsey*		£700
Ship *Hope* (half)		£1,300
Hull of *Perseverance*		£502 16s 9d
Nails		£4 10s 14d
4 June 1806 *Mary* captured		-£1100
		Final Sum £3,700

Parties agreed to valuation plus

As it had been agreed that George should have £100 for his management of the trade in the first year from 24 June 1805 to 24 June 1806 it is agreed that he shall be accountable to his mother for as much of his moiety of the profits of that year as it exceeds £100

Bibliography

Primary Sources

National Archives, PRO, Kew
ADM 2 Letters from Admiralty to Navy Board
ADM 49/106 An account of ships of war built in merchant yards since 1st Jan 1801
ADM 106/1454–1614 Letters to Navy Board
IR/26/323 Administration of Robert Gowan of Berwick, 1802
Prerogative Court of Canterbury (PCC) Wills: 1787–1855
BT/31 Board of Trade Dissolved Companies
BT 107 and 108 Board of Trade Shipping Register Returns
BT 162/19 Shipping Register Transcripts 31 Dec 1850
HO 107 1851 Census Whitehaven, Plymouth, Preston, Yarmouth
WO 52 Ordnance Office: Bill books (series III) 1794–1806
MT 9/36 Society for improving Conditions of Merchant seamen. Report respecting seamen's health accommodation, wages, pension and protection

Bodmin Probate Office, Cornwall
Wills 1868–1907

Bristol Record Office
39449/1 City of Bristol Apprentice indenture
0825(59) Administration of estate of John Whitfield Tucker
37908/1/7&8 Register of Ships 1845–1854

Bristol Reference Library
Bristol Presentments or Bills of Entry, 1 January 1874

Cornwall Record Office
PRO HO 107, Lanteglos by Fowey, Pelynt, Mevagissey, Fowey Census 1851
F/1/294–295 Correspondence relating to Polruan ferry
B/Los 295 List of harbour dues of Corporation of Lostwithiel 1799–1800
R/5088 Notice of public meeting 1830 (Poster) Cornwall Record Office
MSR/FOW Fowey Customs House Ship Registers
MSR/PENZ/ Penzance Ship Registers

Cumbria Record Office, Whitehaven
D/BH/24/22/43 Records of *Warlock*, barque
YTSR 1/9–21 Registers of shipping

Devon Local Studies Library
RG 9 Exeter & Marlborough 1861 Census

Devon Record Office
MF 37–45 Parish Register for St Mary Steps Exeter
Crew Lists *Devon, Ataxerxes, Thames*
MRC 44 Bideford, Exeter Ships Registers
Inland Revenue Wills 1830–1856

Dorset Record Office
D 504/5 Articles of co-partnership between Katherine and George Penney of Poole
in family coal and china clay shipping business, 1806, inventory of ships and stock
1805

Exeter Probate Office
Will of Peter Palmer, 1863

Hull City Archives
DBR Rose Downs Archive
DPC 1 Hull Shipping Registers

Medway Record Office, Strood
TI 109 Deed 23 April 1804: Charles Ross lease of land from Samuel Baker
VFI 920/FOO Transcript 'The Foords of Rochester' by W Coles Finch 1917
RCA 02/20 Register of Apprentices 1806–1863
7E/N2, 7E/N3 Ross Foord Rental ledgers

Merseyside Maritime Museum, Liverpool
C/EX/L/7/5 Liverpool Register of shipping Transactions 1853

National Maritime Museum, Greenwich
HNL/23/2: Henley and Son correspondence with Mrs Ann Bowmaker

Norfolk Record Office
P/SH Shipping Registers: King's Lynn, Wells, Cley and Great Yarmouth 1825–1989
Bradfer-Lawrence (Bagge) collection
BLXIIk/45 Accounts of Ship *Elizabeth*
BL Xc/2 Accts of ship *Brilliant*
BL II e/18 Ships accounts
MF 1313 203: Will of Stephen Lee February 1872
MC 352 Shipmaster's protests 1787–1808

North Yorkshire Record Office, Northallerton
NG/RS/WH/ Registers of Whitby ships
NG/RS/SC/6 Scarborough Shipping Registers

United Kingdom Hydrographic Office, Taunton
Taylor/Beaufort correspondence

Whitby Library
HO 107/2374 1851 Whitby census

Whitby Literary and Philosophical Society

0099/1 Shareholders Register, Robin Hood's Bay Steamship Company Ltd, 1868–71
0101/7 Register of Members
Whitby Mutual Marine Iron Steamship Co & Whitby Iron Steamship Insurance Co
0102/2 List of ships insured 1851–52
0115/1 Protest Book 1844
0040/259 Marriage settlement Emma Forrest Usherwood and the Rev John Bolton 1856
0040/309 Bill of Sale *Oswin* 21 Sep 1890

Private collections

Bill of sale of shares in *Kate & Anne* 1860
Bill of sale of shares in *Princess Alexandra* 1867
Deeds of Holly House, Polruan
Ledger of *E. S. Hocken*, sailmaker
Notice from Whitby Standard Insurance Association, 10 September 1866
Account books of *E S Hocken* and *Ocean Ranger*

Parliamentary Papers

BPP 1805 VIII: An account showing the number of shipwrights and also of apprentices employed in the merchant yards of Great Britain according to the returns made to the Admiralty in April 1804, 467 to 491.
BPP 1805 VIII: A List of persons who have been employed as Overseers since the 1st of January 1783, 52–3.
BPP 1813–14 VIII: Minutes of the Evidence on Petitions relating to East India Built Shipping, 1–661.
BPP 1852 XLIX.1: Return of Number of Sailing and Steam Vessels registered at each Port of Great Britain and Ireland, 1851.
BPP 1860 XXIX: Twenty-first Annual Report of the Registrar General of Births, Deaths and Marriages in England and Wales, 543.
BPP 1853 LXXXVIII: Census of England and Wales 1851 Population Tables, 1851, Part II. Ages and Occupations. Volume I. Report, England and Wales, I.–VI., Appendix.
1860 Bill for regulating Business of Dealers in Marine Stores.
1864 Bill, intituled, Act for the more effectual Protection of Her Majesty's Naval and Victualling Stores.
BPP 1871 LXI.1: Return of Number of Sailing and Steam Vessels registered at each Port of Great Britain and Ireland, 1870.

Census Transcripts

Barker, Rosalin, Extract of Statistics from Census Enumerators' Books from Whitby, 1851.
Carter, David, Transcript and Index for Census Enumerators' Books Appledore, Devon 1851.
Cumbria Family History Society, Transcript and Index for Census Enumerators' Books Whitehaven, Cumbria 1851.

Printed Primary Sources

Published Directories

Shipping Directories

Lloyd's Register of Shipping 1866/7
Mercantile Navy List 1872
Turnbull's Annual Maritime Advertiser Directory & Shipping Register Vol 1854–55
Turnbull's Shipping Register, British and Foreign, 1881
A List of Cumberland Shipping: Corrected to February 1840, William Sawyer

Trade Directories

Kelly's Directory of Norfolk, 1858
Kelly's Directory of Yorkshire 1913
Mannix & Whellan Whitehaven Directory 1847
Pigot & Co Directory of Kent 1832
Pigot's Directory of Cornwall, 1830
Pigots Directory of Yorkshire 1834
Post Office Directory of Cornwall 1873
Slater's Directory of Cornwall 1852–3
Slater's Directory of Cornwall 1852–3
Slaters Directory of Whitby 1849
Slater's Directory of Durham, Northumberland and Yorkshire, 1855
White's Directory Hull & District 1858
White's Directory of Norfolk, 1854
White's Directory of Northumberland 1847
White's Directory of Yorkshire 1851
Williams' Directory of Rochester 1849

Secondary Sources

Theses and dissertations

Foster, David, 'Albion's Sisters: A Study of Trade Directories and Female Economic Participation in the mid 19th Century' (unpublished doctoral thesis, University of Exeter, 2002).

Hagmark, Hanna, 'Women in Maritime Communities: A Socio-historical Study of Continuity and Change in the Domestic Lives of Seafarers' Wives in the Aland Islands, from 1930 into the New Millennium' (unpublished doctoral thesis, University of Hull, 2003).

Hudson, Sarah J., 'Attitudes to Investment Risk amongst West Midland Canal and Railway Company Investors, 1700–1850' (unpublished doctoral thesis, University of Warwick, 2001).

Jenns, Katherine R. P., 'Female Business Enterprise in and around Birmingham' (unpublished doctoral thesis, University of Birmingham, 1997).

Jones, Stephanie A., 'Maritime History of the Port of Whitby, 1700–1914' (unpublished doctoral thesis, University of London, 1982).

Books and Articles

A Banker's Daughter, 'Guide to the Unprotected in Everyday Matters Relating to Property and Income' (1864) www:indiana.edu/~letrs/vwwp/anon/unprotected. html (accessed 26/05/2004).

Abrams, Lynn, 'The Best Men in Shetland: Women, Gender and Place in Peripheral Communities', in *Cornish Studies*, ed. Philip Payton (Exeter: Exeter University Press, 2000), pp. 97–114.

Aldcroft, D. H. and P. L. Cottrell, *Shipping, Trade and Commerce: Essays in Memory of Ralph Davies* (Leicester: Leicester University Press, 1981).

Alger, K. R., *Mrs Janet Taylor 'Authoress and Instructress in Navigation and Nautical Astronomy', 1804–1870*, Fawcett Library Papers No 6 (London, 1982).

Aspinall's Report of Maritime Cases 1870–1941 (London: Butterworth, 1961).

Banbury, Philip, *Shipbuilders of the Thames and Medway* (Newton Abbot: David & Charles, 1971).

Barker, Hannah, *The Business of Women: Female Enterprise and Urban Development in Northern England 1760–1830* (Oxford: Oxford University Press, 2006).

Barker, Hannah and Karen Harvey, 'Women Entrepreneurs and Urban Expansion: Manchester 1760–1820', in *Women and Urban Life in Eighteenth Century England*, ed. Rosemary Sweet and Penelope Lane (Aldershot: Ashgate, 2003), pp. 111–29.

Barnard, John E., *Building Britain's Wooden Walls: The Barnard Dynasty c.1697–1851* (Oswestry: Anthony Nelson, 1997).

Barney, J. M, 'Shipping in the Port of King's Lynn, 1702–1800', *Journal of Transport History*, 20 (1999), 126–40.

Barton, R. M., *A History of the Cornish China Clay Industry* (Truro: Bradford Barton, 1966).

Beachy, Robert, 'Profit and Propriety: Sophie Henschel and Gender Management in the German Locomotive Industry', in *Women, Business and Finance in Nineteenth-Century Europe: Rethinking Separate Spheres*, ed. Robert Beachy, Beatrice Craig and Alistair Owens (Oxford: Berg, 2006), pp. 67–80.

Berg, Maxine, 'Women's Work; Mechanisation and the Early Phases of Industrialisation in England', in *The Historical Meanings of Work*, ed. Patrick Joyce (Cambridge: Cambridge University Press, 1987), pp. 64–98.

—— 'Women's Property and the Industrial Revolution', *Journal of Interdisciplinary History*, XXIV (1993), 233–50

Berggreen, Brit, 'Dealing with Anomalies? Approaching Maritime Women', in *The North Sea: Twelve Essays on Social History of Maritime Labour*, ed. Lewis R. Fisher, Harald Hamre, Poul Holm and Jaap R. Bruijn (Stavanger: Stavanger Maritime Museum, 1992), pp. 111–25.

Best, Geoff, *Mid-Victorian Britain, 1851–75* (London: Fontana Press, 1975).

Bowen, H. V., 'Investment and Empire in the Later Eighteenth Century: East India Stockholding 1756–1791', *Economic History Review*, 42 (1989), 186–206.

Boyce, Gordon, '64thers, Syndicates and Stock Promotions: Information Flows and Fund Raising Techniques of British Shipowners before 1914', *Journal of Economic History*, 52 (1992), 181–205.

—— *Information, Mediation and Institutional Development: The Rise of Large-Scale Enterprise in British Shipping, 1870–1919* (Manchester: Manchester University Press, 1995).

—— 'Network Knowledge and Network Routines: Negotiating Activities between Shipowners and Shipbuilders', *Business History*, 45 (2003), 25–59.

Boyns, Trevor and John Richard Edwards, 'Cost and Management Accounting in Early Victorian Britain: A Chandleresque Analysis?', *Management Accounting Research*, 8 (1997), 19–46.

Branca, Patricia, *Silent Sisterhood: Middle-Class Women in the Victorian Home* (Pittsburg: Carnegie-Mellon University Press, 1975).

Broeze, Frank, 'Information and Decision Making', in *Financing the Maritime Sector: Proceedings from the Fifth North Sea History Conference*, ed. Leo M. Akveld, Frits R. Loomeijer and Morten Hahn-Pedersen (Esbjerg: Fiskeri-og Sofartsmuseet, 2002), pp. 63–70.

Burt, Roger, *The British Lead Mining Industry* (Redruth: Dyllansow Truran, 1984).

——'Freemasonry and Business Networking During the Victorian Period', *Economic History Review*, 56 (2003), 657–88.

Burt, Roger and Norikazu Kudo, 'The Adaptability of the Cornish Cost Book System', *Business History*, 25 (1983), 30–41.

Clark, E. A. G., 'The Ports of the Exe Estuary, 1701–1972', in *The New Maritime History of Devon, Vol. 2*, ed. M. Duffy *et al.* (London: Conway, 1994).

Combs, Mary Beth, 'Wives and Household Wealth: The Impact of the 1870 British Married Women's Property Act on Wealth-Holding and Share of Household Resources', *Continuity and Change*, 19 (2004), 141–63.

Cook, Bronwen, '"A True, Faire and Just Account": Charles Huggett and the Content of Maldon in the English Shipping Trade, 1679–1684', *Journal of Transport History*, 26 (2005), 1–18.

Cordingly, David, *Billy Ruffian: The Bellerophon and the Downfall of Napoleon* (London: Bloomsbury, 2003, repr. 2004).

Cottrell, P. L., 'Britannia's Sovereign: Banks in the Finance of British Shipbuilding and Shipping, c. 1830–1894', in *Financing the Maritime Sector: Proceedings from the Fifth North Sea History Conference*, ed. Leo M. Akveld, Frits R. Loomeijer and Morten Hahn-Pedersen (Esbjerg: Fiskeri-og Sofartsmuseet, 2002), pp. 191–254.

Craig, Robin, *British Tramp Shipping: 1750–1914* (Newfoundland, 2003).

——'Millionaires and Enterprising Nobodies', *International Journal of Maritime History*, 16 (2004), 1–15.

Craig, R. and R. C. Jarvis, *Liverpool Registry of Merchant Ships* (Manchester, 1967).

Craig, R., B. Greenhill, J. H. Porter and W. J. Slade, 'Some Aspects of the Business of Devon Shipping in the Nineteenth Century', in *A New Maritime History of Devon, Vol. II: From the Late Eighteenth Century to the Present Day*, ed. M. Duffy *et al.* (London, 1994), pp. 99–107.

Crane, Elaine Forman, *Ebb Tide in New England: Women Seaports and Social Change 1630–1800* (Boston: Northeastern University Press, 1998).

Creighton, Margaret S. and Lisa Norling, eds, *Iron Men, Wooden Women: Gender and Seafaring in the Atlantic World, 1700–1920* (London: Johns Hopkins University Press, 1996).

Davidoff, Leonore and Catherine Hall, *Family Fortunes: Men and Women of the English Middle Class, 1780–1850* (London: Hutchinson, 1987).

Davis, Ralph, *The Rise of the English Shipping Industry in 17th and 18th Centuries* (Newton Abbot: David & Charles, 1962).

Deacon, Bernard and Moira Donald, 'In Search of Community History', *Family & Community History*, 7 (2004), 13–18.

Dixon, Conrad, 'Pound and Pint: Diet in the Merchant Service, 1750–1980', in *Charted and Uncharted Waters*, ed. Sarah Palmer and Glyndwr Williams (London: National Maritime Museum, 1981), pp. 164–80.

Doe, Helen, 'Politics, Property and Family Resources', *Family & Community History*, 4 (2001), 59–72.

—— *Jane Slade of Polruan* (Truro: Truran, 2002).

—— 'Blockmakers, Sailmakers, Ropemakers, Blacksmiths and Brokers in the Port of Fowey', *Journal of the South West Maritime History Society*, 16 (2003), 148–71.

—— 'Positions, Patronage and Preference: Political Influence in Fowey before 1832', in *Cornish Studies 12*, ed. P. Payton (Exeter: Exeter Press, 2004), pp. 249–67.

—— 'Challenging Images: Mrs Mary Ross of Rochester, Nineteenth Century Businesswoman and Warship Builder', *Journal for Maritime Research* (2006).

—— 'Thames Shipbuilders in the Napoleonic Wars', Conference Proceedings, *3rd Thames Shipbuilders Conference*, Greenwich, August, 2006, pp. 10–21.

—— 'The Business of Shipbuilding: Dunn and Henna of Mevagissey, 1799–1806', *International Journal of Maritime History*, 18 (December 2006), 187–217.

—— 'Government Sources and Private Business: Shipbuilding in Merchant Yards during the Napoleonic Wars', *Business Archives Sources and History*, 94 (November 2007), 1–15.

Druett, Joan, *Hen Frigates: Wives of Merchant Captains under Sail* (New York: Simon & Schuster, 1998).

Duffy, Michael, Stephen Fisher, Basil Greenhill, David J. Starkey and Joyce Youings, *A New Maritime History of Devon, Vol. II: From the Late Eighteenth Century to the Present Day* (London: Conway, 1994).

Dyer, Florence E., 'A Woman Shipowner', *Mariner's Mirror*, 36 (1950), 134–8.

Eames, Aled, *Ventures in Sail* (Denbigh, 1987).

Erickson, Amy Louise, 'Common Law Versus Common Practise: The Use of Marriage Settlements in Early Modern England', *Economic History Review*, 43 (1990), 21–39.

Farr, G., *Chepstow Ships* (Chepstow, 1954).

—— *Shipbuilding in North Devon* (Greenwich: National Maritime Museum, 1976).

—— *Shipbuilding in the Port of Bristol* (Greenwich: National Maritime Museum, 1977).

Farr, Graham E., *Records of Bristol Ships, 1800–1838: Vessels over 150 Tons* (Bristol: Bristol Records Society, 1950).

Fingard, Judith, *Jack in Port: Sailortowns of Eastern Canada* (Toronto: University of Toronto, 1982).

Finn, Margot, 'Women, Consumption and Coverture in England, c. 1760–1860', *Historical Journal*, 39 (1996), 703–22.

Fischer, Lewis R., 'Information Flows and Decision-Making Structures around the North Sea: The Case of Fearnley and Eger, Shipbrokers, 1869–1914', in *Financing the Maritime Sector: Proceedings from the Fifth North Sea History Conference*, ed. Leo M. Akveld, Frits R. Loomeijer and Morten Hahn-Pedersen (Esbjerg; Fiskeri-og Sofartsmuseet, 2002), pp. 11–22.

Fischer, Lewis R. and Helge W. Nordvik, 'Economic Theory, Information and Management in Shipbroking: Fearnley and Eger as a Case Study, 1869–1972', *Research in Maritime History*, 6 (1994), 1–29.

Flagg, Amy M., *Notes on the History of Shipbuilding in South Shields, 1746–1946* (South Tyneside, 1979).

Gamber, Wendy, 'A Gendered Enterprise: Placing Nineteenth-Century Businesswomen in History', *Business History Review*, 72 (1998), 188–217.

Gerstenberger, Heidi, 'Old Forms of Capital and New Forms of Shipping', in *Financing* the Maritime Sector: Proceedings from the Fifth North Sea History Conference, ed. Leo M. Akveld, Frits R. Loomeijer and Morten Hahn-Pedersen (Esbjerg: Fiskeri-og Sofortsmuseet, 2002), pp. 115–30.

Gleadle, Kathryn, *The Early Feminists: Radical Unitarians and the Emergence of the Women's Rights Movement, 1831–51* (Basingstoke: Palgrave, 1995).

—— *British Women in the Nineteenth Century* (Basingstoke: Palgrave, 2001).

Godley, A. and D. M. Ross, 'Banks, Networks and Small-Firm Finance', *Business History*, 38 (1996), 1–10.

Gordon, Eleanor and Gwyneth Nair, 'The Economic Role of Middle-Class Women in Victorian Glasgow', *Women's History Review*, 9 (2000), 791–814.

—— *Public Lives: Women, Family, and Society in Victorian Britain* (New Haven and London: Yale University Press, 2004).

Gourvish, T. R., 'Railways 1830–70: The Formative Years', in *Transport in Victorian Britain*, ed. Michael J. Freeman and Derek H. Aldcroft (Manchester: Manchester University Press, 1988), pp. 57–91.

Graham, Graham S., 'The Ascendancy of the Sailing Ship, 1850–85', *Economic History Review*, 9 (1956), 74–88.

Grannum, Karen and Nigel Taylor, *Wills and Other Probate Records* (London: National Archives, 2004).

Green, David R., 'Independent Women, Wealth and Wills in Nineteenth-Century London', in *Urban Fortunes: Property and Inheritance in the Town, 1700–1900*, ed. Jon Stobart and Alastair Owens (Aldershot: Ashgate Press, 2000), pp. 195–222.

Green, David R. and Alastair Owens, 'Gentlewomanly Capitalism? Spinsters, Widows, and Wealth Holding in England and Wales, c. 1800–1860', *Economic History Review*, 56 (2003), 510–36.

Green, Henry and Robert Wigram, *The Chronicles of Blackwall Yard, Part 1* (London, 1881).

Greenhill, Basil, *The Merchant Schooners* (London: Conway, 1988).

Guest, Revel and Angela V. John, *Lady Charlotte: A Biography of the Nineteenth Century* (London: Weidenfeld & Nicolson, 1989).

Hall, Catherine, *White, Male and Middle-Class: Explorations in Feminism and History* (Cambridge: Polity, 1992).

Harley, Charles K., 'British Shipbuilding and Merchant Shipping: 1850–1890', *Journal of Economic History*, 30 (1970), 262–6.

Harris, E., 'The Riverside', *Old Rochester*, 27 (n.d.).

Hay, Daniel, *Whitehaven, an Illustrated History* (Whitehaven, 1979).

Henderson, A. and S. Palmer, 'The Early Nineteenth Century Port of London: Management and Labour in Three Dock Companies', *Research in Maritime History*, 6 (1994), 31–50.

Higgs, Edward, 'Occupational Censuses and the Agricultural Workforce in Victorian England and Wales', *Economic History Review*, 48 (1995), 700–16.

Hill, Bridget, *Women, Work, and Sexual Politics in Eighteenth-Century England* (New York: Blackwell, 1989).

—— 'Women's History: A Study in Change, Continuity or Standing Still?' *Women's History Review*, 2 (1993), 5–22.

—— 'Women, Work and the Census: A Problem for Historians of Women', *History Workshop Journal*, 35 (1993), 78–94

—— *Women Alone: Spinsters in England, 1660–1850* (New Haven and London: Yale University Press, 2001).

Hill, J., *Shipshape and Bristol Fashion* (Liverpool, n.d.).

Hillen, H., *History of the Borough of King's Lynn* (Norwich, 1907).

Holcombe, Lee, *Victorian Ladies at Work: Middle-Class Working Women in England and Wales, 1850–1914* (Newton Abbot: David & Charles, 1973).

—— *Wives and Property: Reform of the Married Women's Property Law in Nineteenth Century England* (Toronto: University of Toronto Press, 1983).

Holland, A. J., *Ships of British Oak: The Rise and Decline of Wooden Shipbuilding in Hampshire* (Newton Abbot: David & Charles, 1971).

Holman, H., *A Handy Book for Shipowners and Masters* (London: Maisey, 1915).

Hope, Ronald, *A New History of British Shipping* (London: John Murray, 1990).

Hopkins, Manley, *The Port of Refuge: Advice and Instruction to the Master Mariner in Situations of Doubt, Difficulty and Danger* (London, 1873).

Horsley, John E., *Tools of the Maritime Trades* (Newton Abbot: David & Charles, 1978)

Hudson, P., 'A New Introduction to Trade and Business: Very Useful for the Youth of Both Sexes' (London: Johnson, 1786).

Hudson, Pat, 'Financing Firms, 1700–1859', in *Business Enterprise in Modern Britain from 18th to 20th Century*, ed. Maurice W. Kirby and Mary B. Rose (London, 1994), pp. 88–113.

Hudson, Pat and W. R. Lee, eds, *Women's Work and the Family Economy in Historical Perspective* (Manchester: Manchester University Press, 1990).

Hughes, Kathryn, *The Short Life and Long Times of Mrs Beeton* (London: Fourth Estate, 2005).

Hunt, Margaret R., *The Middling Sort: Commerce, Gender, and the Family in England, 1680–1780* (Berkeley: University of California Press, 1996).

Jackson, Gordon, *The History and Archaeology of Ports* (Tadworth: World's Work, 1983).

—— 'The Ports', in *Transport in Victorian Britain*, ed. Michael J. Freeman and Derek H. Aldcroft (Manchester: Manchester University Press, 1988), pp. 218–52.

—— 'Do Docks Make Trade?' in *Port and Harbour Engineering*, ed. Adrian Jarvis (Aldershot: Variorum, 1998).

—— 'The Significance of Unimportant Ports', *International Journal of Maritime History*, 13 (2001).

Jarvis, Adrian, 'Port History', in *Harbours and Havens*, ed. Lewis R. Fischer and Adrian Jarvis (St John's, Newfoundland: International Maritime Economic History Association, 1999), pp. 13–34.

Jarvis, R. C., 'British Ship Registry: The Quantification of Source Material', in *Ports and Shipping in the South West*, ed. H. E. S. Fisher (Exeter: University of Exeter, 1971).

Jarvis, Rupert, 'Fractional Shareholding in British Merchant Ships with Special Reference to the 64ths', *Mariner's Mirror*, 45 (1959), 301–19.

—— 'Ship Registry – to 1707', *Maritime History*, 1 (1971), 29–45.

—— 'Ship Registry – 1786', *Maritime History*, 4 (1974), 12–30.

Jeula, Henry, 'The Present Aspect of Statistical Inquiry in Relation to Shipping Casualties', *Journal of Statistical Society of London*, 31 (1868), 418–25.

Johnsen, Berit Eide, 'From Integration to Segregation; Ship Ownership in Agder, Southern Norway, c. 1860–1930', in *Financing the Maritime Sector: Proceedings from the Fifth North Sea History Conference*, ed. Leo M. Akveld, Frits R. Loomeijer and Morten Hahn-Pedersen (Esbjerg: Fiskeri-og Sofartsmuseet, 2002), pp. 71–114.

Jones, Geoffrey and Mary B. Rose, 'Family Capitalism', *Business History*, 35 (1993), 1–16.

Jones, Stephanie, 'The Builders of Captain Cook's Ships', *Mariner's Mirror*, 70 (1984), 299–302.

—— 'Merchant Shipbuilding in the North East and South West of England, 1870–1913', in *British Shipping and Seamen, 1630–1960*, ed. Stephen Fisher (Exeter: University of Exeter, 1984), pp. 68–85.

Kaukiainen, Yrjö, 'Owners and Masters: Management and Managerial Skills in the Finnish Ocean-Going Merchant Fleet, c.1840–1889', *Research in Maritime History*, 6 (1994), 51–66.

Kay, Alison C., 'A Little Enterprise of Her Own: Lodging House Keeping and the Accommodation Business in Nineteenth-Century London', *The London Journal*, 28 (2003).

Keast, John, *The King of Mid Cornwall: The Life of Joseph Thomas Treffry, 1782–1850* (Truro: Dyllansow Truran, 1982).

——, 'Ship Chandling Days Remembered', *Old Cornwall*, XI (1996), 478–85.

Kennerley, Alston, 'Navigation Schools and Training Ships: Educational Provision in Plymouth for the Mercantile Marine in the Nineteenth Century', in *West Country Maritime and Social History: Some Essays*, ed. Stephen Fisher (Exeter: Exeter University 1980), pp. 53–78.

Kent, David A., 'Small Businessmen and Their Credit Transactions in Early Nineteenth-Century Britain', *Business History*, 36 (1994), 47–64.

Keys, Richard E., *The Sailing Ships of Aln and Coquet* (Newcastle: Author, 1993).

—— *Dictionary of Tyne Sailing Ships: A Record of Sailing Ships Owned, Registered and Built in the Port of Tyne from 1830–1930* (Newcastle: Author, 1998).

Killick, John, 'An Early 19th Century Shipping Line: The Cope Line of Philadelphia and Liverpool Packets, 1822–1872', *International Journal of Maritime History*, 12 (2000), 61–87.

Kirby, Maurice, 'Quakerism, Entrepreneurship and the Family Firm in North-East England', in *Entrepreneurship, Networks and Modern Business*, ed. J. Brown and M. B. Rose (Manchester: Manchester University Press, 1993), pp. 76–105.

Kirby, Maurice W. and Mary B. Rose, eds, *Business Enterprise in Modern Britain from 18th to 20th Century* (London: Routledge, 1994).

Knight, Roger, 'Devil Bolts and Deception? Wartime Naval Shipbuilding in Private Shipyards, 1739–1815', *Journal for Maritime Research* (2003).

Kwolek-Folland, Angel, *Incorporating Women: A History of Women and Business in the United States* (New York: Palgrave, 1998).

Latham, Tim, *The Ashburner Schooners: The Story of the First Shipbuilders in Barrow-in-Furness* (Manchester: Ready Rhino Publications, 1991).

Lavery, Brian, *Building the Wooden Walls: The Design and Construction of the 74-Gun Ship Valiant* (Chatham: Conway, 1991).

Lee, Charles, *The Widow Woman: A Cornish Tale* (London: Dent & Sons, 1896).

'Lloyds Statistics of Marine Casualties for the Year 1878', *Journal of Statistical Society of London*, 42 (1879), 505–21.

Long, Anne and Russell Long, *A Shipping Venture: Turnbull Scott and Company, 1872–1972* (London: Hutchinson Benham, 1974).

Lyon, David, *The Sailing Navy List: All the Ships of the Royal Navy – Built, Purchased and Captured, 1688–1860* (London: Conway, 1993).

Macmurray, C. D. and M. Cree, *Shipping and Shipbroking: A Guide to All Branches of Shipbroking and Ship Management* (London: Pitman, 1934).

Maltby, Josephine and Janette Rutterford, 'Editorial: Women, Accounting and Investment', *Accounting, Business and Financial History*, 16 (2006), 133–42.

—— 'She Possessed Her Own Fortune: Women Investors from the Late Nineteenth Century to the Early Twentieth Century', *Business History*, 48 (2006), 220–53.

Marshall, M. A. N., 'Records of Norfolk Ships', *Mariner's Mirror*, 49 (1963).

McAlpine, Joan, *The Lady of Claremont House: Isabella Elder, Pioneer and Philanthropist* (Argyll: Argyll Publishing, 1997).

Mills, Dennis, 'Defining Community: A Critical View of Community', *Family & Community History*, 7 (2004), 5–12.

Mills, Dennis and Kevin Schurer, eds, *Local Communities in the Victorian Census Enumerators' Books* (Oxford: Leopard's Head Press, 1996).

Milne, Graeme, *Trade and Traders in Mid-Victorian Liverpool: Mercantile Business and the Making of a World Port* (Liverpool: Liverpool University Press, 2000).

—— 'Knowledge, Communications and the Information Order in Nineteenth-Century Liverpool', *International Journal of Maritime History*, 14 (2002), 209–24.

—— *North East England, 1850–1914: The Dynamics of a Maritime-Industrial Region* (Woodbridge: Boydell Press, 2006).

Mitchell, W., ed., *Maritime Notes and Queries* (London, 1881).

Moring, B., 'Nordic Coastal Communities in Historical Perspective: The Interaction of Economic Activity and the Household', *International Journal of Maritime History*, 14 (2002), 145–65.

Morris, R. J., 'Men, Women and Property: The Reform of the Married Women's Property Act 1870', in *Landowners, Capitalists, and Entrepreneurs: Essays for Sir John Habakkuk*, ed. F. M. L. Thompson (Oxford: Clarendon Press, 1994), pp. 171–91.

—— *Men, Women and Property in England, 1780–1870* (Cambridge: Cambridge University Press, 2005).

Morriss, Roger, *The Royal Dockyards During the Revolutionary and Napoleonic Wars* (Leicester: Leicester University Press, 1983).

—— 'St Vincent and Reform, 1801–04', *Mariner's Mirror*, 69 (1983), 269–90.

Murch, D. F., 'Trading Vessels of Salcombe Haven 1820–1890', in *Ports and Shipping in the South West*, ed. H. E. S. Fisher (Exeter: University of Exeter, 1971).

Murch, Muriel, David Murch and Len Fairweather, *Salcombe Harbour Remembered* (Plymouth: P.D.S. Printers, 1982).

Nadel-Klein, Jane and Dona Lee Davis, eds, *To Work and to Weep: Women in Fishing Economies* (St Johns, Newfoundland, 1988).

Nenadic, Stana, 'The Small Family Firm in Victorian Britain', *Business History*, 35 (1993), 89–114.

Norling, Lisa, '"How Frought with Sorrow and Heartpangs": Mariners' Wives and the Ideology of Domesticity in New England, 1790–1880', *New England Quarterly*, 65 (1992), 442–6.

—— *Captain Ahab Had a Wife: New England Women and the Whale Fishery, 1720–1870* (Chapel Hill: University of North Carolina Press, 2000).

Norton, Jane E., *Guide to the National and Provincial Directories of England and Wales, Excluding London, Published before 1856* (London: Royal Historical Society, 1950).

Owens, Alastair, 'Inheritance and the Life-Cycle of Firms in the Early Industrial Revolution', *Business History*, 44 (2002), 21–46.

—— '"Making Some Provision for the Contingencies to Which Their Sex Is Particularly Liable": Women and Investment in Early Nineteenth Century England', in *Women, Business and Finance in Nineteenth-Century Europe: Rethinking Separate*

Spheres, ed. Robert Beachy, Beatrice Craig and Alastair Owens (Oxford: Berg, 2006).

Palmer, S. R., 'Investors in London Shipping', *Maritime History*, 2 (1972), 46–68.

Palmer, Sarah, 'John Long: A London Shipowner', *Mariner's Mirror*, 72 (1968), 43–61.

—— 'Port Economics in an Historical Context: The Nineteenth Century Port of London', *International Journal of Maritime History*, 15 (2003), 27–67.

Parkes, Bessie R., *Essays on Woman's Work* (London, 1865).

Parle, B., *Rochester in Old Photographs* (Gloucester, 1989).

Paul, R. B., *Shipping Simplified, a Book for the Shipping Clerk* (Liverpool, 1918).

Pearson, Robin and David Richardson, 'Business Networking in the Industrial Revolution', *Economic History Review*, 54 (2001), 657–79.

Perry, Ronald, 'The Breadwinners: Gender, Locality and Diversity in Cornwall', *Cornish Studies*, 8 (2000), 115–26.

Petersson, Tom, 'The Silent Partners: Women, Capital and the Development of the Financial System in Nineteenth Century Sweden', in *Women, Business and Finance in Nineteenth Century Europe: Rethinking Separate Spheres*, ed. Robert Beachy, Beatrice Craig and Alastair Owens (Oxford: Berg, 2006), pp. 36–51.

Phillips, Nicola, *Women in Business, 1700–1850* (Woodbridge: Boydell & Brewer, 2006).

Pickering, Isobel, *Some Goings On! A Selection of Newspaper Articles About Fowey, Polruan and Lanteglos Districts from 1800–1899* (Fowey: Author, 1985).

—— *Pictures of a Parish* (Fowey: Author, 1993).

Pinchbeck, Ivy, *Women Workers and the Industrial Revolution, 1750–1850* (London: Virago Press, 1930, repr. 1981).

Platt, Alan, 'Straws in the Winds of Change: A Business Study of Two Barques in the Earlier Years of Sail's Decline', *Mariner's Mirror*, 92 (2006), 148–67.

Pollard, S., 'The Decline of Shipbuilding on the Thames', *Economic History Review*, 3 (1950), 72–89.

Pollard, Sydney and Paul Robertson, *The British Shipbuilding Industry, 1870–1914* (Cambridge, MA: Harvard University Press, 1979).

Ponsford, Clive N., *Shipbuilding on the Exe: The Memoranda Book of Daniel Bishop Davy* (Exeter: Devon and Cornwall Record Society, 1988).

Pool, Bernard, *Navy Board Contracts 1660–1832* (London: Longmans, 1966).

Poovey, Mary, ed., *The Financial System in Nineteenth Century Britain* (Oxford: Oxford University Press, 2003).

Pugh, Martin, *The Tories and the People 1880 to 1935* (Oxford: Blackwell, 1985).

Rendell, Jane, *Women in an Industrializing Society: England 1750–1880* (Oxford: Basil Blackwell, 1993).

Richards, Paul, *History of King's Lynn* (Chichester: Phillimore, 1990).

Rideout, Adelaide, *The Treffry Family* (Chichester: Phillimore, 1984).

Robinson, R., 'Investment, Ownership and Society: The Yorkshire Fishing Industry 1780–1890', in *Financing the Maritime Sector: Proceedings from the Fifth North Sea History Conference*, ed. L. M. Akveld, F. R. Loomeijer and M. Hahn-Pedersen (Esbjerg, 2002), pp. 331–58.

Rodger, N. A. M., *The Command of the Oceans: A Naval History of Britain, 1649–1815* (London: Allen Lane, 2004).

—— 'Roundtable Discussion of Daniel Vickers and Vince Walsh "Young Men and the Sea"', *International Journal of Maritime History*, 17 (2005), 336–41.

Rolt, L. T. C., *Mariners' Market: Burnyeat Limited, Growth over a Century* (Liverpool: Newman Neame, 1961).

Rose, Mary B., 'The Family Firm in British Business, 1780–1914', in *Business Enterprise in Modern Britain*, ed. Maurice W. Kirby and Mary B. Rose (London: Routledge, 1994), pp. 61–87.

Rutterford, Janette and Josephine Maltby, '"The Widow, the Clergyman and the Reckless": Women Investors in England, 1830–1914', *Feminist Economics*, 12 (2006), 111–38.

Senior, William, 'The History of Maritime Law', *Mariner's Mirror*, 38 (1952), 260–75.

Shanley, Mary Lyndon, *Feminism, Marriage and the Law in Victorian England, 1850–1895* (London: Princeton University Press, 1989).

Sharpe, Pamela, 'Continuity and Change: Women's History and Economic History in Britain', *Economic History Review*, 48 (1995), 353–69.

—— ed., *Women's Work: The English Experience 1650–1914* (London: Arnold, 1998).

Shoemaker, Robert B., *Gender in English Society 1650–1850: The Emergence of Separate Spheres?* (Essex: Longman, 1998).

Smart, Ivor, 'Dartmouth – the Hardness Shipyards from Zion Slip to King's Quay', *Maritime Southwest*, 10 (1997), 99–136.

Stammers, M., 'Liverpool's Last Blockmaking Company', *Industrial Archaeology*, 10 (1973), 148–51.

—— 'Shipowners in Rural British Ports in the 19th Century: A Study of North Norfolk Ports' (n.d.).

Stammers, Michael, 'Slipways and Steamchests: The Archaeology of 18th–19th Century Wooden Merchant Shipyards in the United Kingdom', *International Journal of Nautical Archaeology*, 28 (1999), 253–64.

Stammers, Michael K., '"The High Character Obtained by Cumberland Ships": A Shipbuilding District in the Mid-Nineteenth Century', *International Journal of Maritime History*, 10 (1998), 121–50.

Stanley, Jo, ed., *Bold in Her Breeches: Women Pirates across the Ages* (London: Harper-Collins, 1995).

—— 'And after the Cross Dressed Cabin Boys and Whaling Wives? Possible Futures for Women's Maritime Historiography', *Journal of Transport History*, 23 (2002), 9–22.

Stark, Suzanne J., *Female Tars: Women Aboard Ship in the Age of Sail* (London: Pimlico, 1996).

Starkey, David J., 'Ownership Structures in the British Shipping Industry', *Economic History Review*, 46 (1993), 702–22.

—— 'The Shipbuilding Industry of Southwest England', in Simon Ville, ed., *Shipbuilding in the United Kingdom* (St John's, Newfoundland, 1993) pp. 75–110.

—— 'Devon's Shipbuilding Industry, 1786–1970', in *A New Maritime History of Devon, Vol. II*, ed. M. Duffy *et al.* (London: Conway, 1994), pp. 78–90.

—— 'The Ports, Seaborne Trade and Shipping Industry of South Devon, 1786–1914', in *A New Maritime History of Devon*, ed. M. Duffy *et al.* (London: Conway, 1994), pp. 32–47.

—— 'Ownership Structures in the British Shipping Industry: The Case of Hull, 1820–1916', *International Journal of Maritime History*, 8 (1996), 71–95.

—— 'Growth and Transition in Britain's Maritime Economy, 1870–1914: The Case of South-West England', in *Exploiting the Sea*, ed. David J. Starkey and Alan G. Jamieson (Exeter: University of Exeter Press, 1998), pp. 7–36.

—— 'Concentration and Dependency? The Distribution of Britain's Maritime Industries 1870–1914', in *Financing the Maritime Sector: Proceedings from the Fifth North*

Sea History Conference, ed. L. M. Akveld, F. R. Loomeijer and M. Hahn-Pedersen (Esbjerg, 2002), pp. 261–84.

Steckley, G. F., 'Bottomry Bonds in the Seventeenth-Century Admiralty Court', *American Journal of Legal History*, 45 (2001), 256–77.

Stevens, *Elements of Mercantile Law*, 5th edn (London, 1911).

Stevens, E. F., *Shipping Practice with a Consideration of the Law Relating Thereto* (London, 1935).

Sutton, Jean, *Lords of the East: The East India Company and Its Ships, 1600–1874* (London: Conway, 2000).

Taylor, E. G. R., *Mathematical Practitioners of Hanoverian England, 1714–1840* (Cambridge: Cambridge University Press, 1966).

Thompson, Paul, 'Women in Fishing: The Roots of Power between the Sexes', *Comparative Studies in Society and History*, 27 (1985), 3–32.

Thorne, R. G., *History of Parliament: House of Commons, 1790–1820, Vol. V* (London: Secker & Warburg, 1986).

Timmins, Samuel, ed., *The Resources, Products, and Industrial History of Birmingham and the Midland Hardware District: Reports, Collected by the Local Industries Committee* (London, 1886).

van Voss, L. H., 'Trade and Formation of the North Sea Culture', in *Northern Seas Yearbook*, ed. Poul Holm, Olaf Janzen and Jon Thor (1996), pp. 7–20.

Vickers, Daniel, *Young Men and the Sea: Yankee Seafarers in the Age of Sail* (New Haven and London: Yale University Press, 2005).

Vickery, Amanda, 'Golden Age to Separate Spheres? A Review of the Categories and Chronology of English Women's History', *The Historical Journal*, 36 (1993), 383–414.

Ville, Simon, 'James Kirton, Shipping Agent', *Mariner's Mirror*, 67 (1981), 149–62.

—— 'The Deployment of English Merchant Shipping: Michael and Joseph Henley of Wapping, Ship Owners, 1775–1830', *Journal of Transport History*, 5 (1984), 16–33.

—— 'Shipping in the Port of Sunderland 1815–45: A Counter-Cyclical Trend', *Business History*, 32 (1990), 32–51.

—— 'The Growth of Specialisation in English Shipowning, 1750–1850', *Economic History Review*, 46 (1993), 702–22.

—— ed., *Shipbuilding in the United Kingdom in the 19th Century: A Regional Approach, Research in Maritime History No. 4* (Newfoundland: International Maritime Economic History Association, 1993).

Ville, Simon and David M. Williams, eds, *Management, Finance and Industrial Relations in Maritime Industries: Essays in International Maritime Business History, Research in Maritime History No. 6.* (St John's, Newfoundland: International Maritime Economic History Association, 1994).

Ville, Simon P., *English Shipowning During the Industrial Revolution: Michael Henley and Son, London Shipowners, 1770–1830* (Manchester: Manchester University Press, 1987).

Walsh, Margaret, 'Gendering Transport History: Retrospect and Prospect', *Journal of Transport History*, 23 (2002), 1–8.

Walton, John K., 'Fishing Communities, 1850–1950', in *England's Sea Fisheries: The Commercial Fisheries of England and Wales since 1300*, ed. David J. Starkey, Chris Reid and Neil Ashcroft (London: Chatham Publishing, 2000), pp. 127–37.

Ward, J. R., *The Finance of Canal Building in Eighteenth Century England* (London, 1974).

Ward-Jackson, C. H., *Stephens of Fowey: A Portrait of a Cornish Merchant Fleet 1867–1939* (Greenwich: National Maritime Museum, 1980).

—— *Ships and Shipbuilders of a Westcountry Seaport: Fowey 1786–1939* (Truro: Twelveheads Press, 1986).

Weatherell, R., *The Ancient Port of Whitby & Its Shipping* (Whitby, 1908).

Williams, David M., 'Introduction', in *The World of Shipping*, ed. David M. Williams (Aldershot: Ashgate, 1997), pp. ix–xxvi.

Wilson, John F and Andrew Popp, 'Business Networking in the Industrial Revolution: Some Comments', *Economic History Review*, 56 (2003), 355–61.

Wiskin, Christine, 'Women, Business and Credit: Sources for the Historian', *Business Archives*, 74 (1997), 31–44.

—— 'Urban Businesswomen in Eighteenth-Century England', in *Women and Urban Life in Eighteenth Century England*, ed. Rosemary Sweet and Penelope Lane (Aldershot: Ashgate, 2003), pp. 87–109.

Wiswall jnr, F. L., *The Development of Admiralty Jurisdiction and Practice since 1800* (Cambridge: Cambridge University Press, 1970).

Witt, Mario M., *A Bibliography of the Works Written and Published by David Steel and His Successors* (Greenwich: Anthony & Setitia Simmonds, 1991).

Index

Note: Page references in italics indicate figures or tables. References in bold indicate illustrations.

Index